Adolescent Dysfunctional Behavior

Issues in Children's and Families' Lives

AN ANNUAL BOOK SERIES

Senior Series Editor

Thomas P. Gullotta, *Child and Family Agency of Southeastern Connecticut*

Editors

Gerald R. Adams, *University of Guelph, Ontario, Canada*

Bruce A. Ryan, *University of Guelph, Ontario, Canada*

Robert L. Hampton, *University of Maryland, College Park*

Roger P. Weissberg, *University of Illinois at Chicago, Illinois*

Drawing upon the resources of Child and Family Agency of Southeastern Connecticut, one of this nation's leading family service agencies, **Issues in Children's and Families' Lives** is designed to focus attention on the pressing social problems facing children and their families today. Each volume in this series will analyze, integrate, and critique the clinical and research literature on children and their families as it relates to a particular theme. Believing that integrated multidisciplinary approaches offer greater opportunities for program success, volume contributors will reflect the research and clinical knowledge base of the many different disciplines that are committed to enhancing the physical, social, and emotional health of children and their families. Intended for graduate and professional audiences, chapters will be written by scholars and practitioners who will encourage readers to apply their practice skills and intellect to reducing the suffering of children and their families in the society in which those families live and work.

Volume 1: **Family Violence: Prevention and Treatment**
LEAD EDITOR: Robert L. Hampton
CONSULTANTS: Vincent Senatore, *Child and Family Agency, Connecticut*; Ann Quinn, *Connecticut Department of Children, Youth, and Family Services, Connecticut*

Volume 2: **The Family-School Connection**
EDITORS: Bruce A. Ryan and Gerald R. Adams

Volume 3: **Adolescent Dysfunctional Behavior**
EDITORS: Gary M. Blau and Thomas P. Gullotta

Volume 4: **Preventing Violence in America**
EDITORS: Robert L. Hampton, Pamela Jenkins, and Thomas P. Gullotta

Volume 5: **Primary Prevention Practices**
AUTHOR: Martin Bloom

Volume 6: **Primary Prevention Works**
EDITORS: George W. Albee and Thomas P. Gullotta

Volume 7: **Children and Youth: Interdisciplinary Perspectives**
EDITORS: Herbert J. Walberg, Olga Reyes, and Roger P. Weissberg

Volume 8: **Healthy Children 2010: Enhancing Children's Wellness**
EDITORS: Roger P. Weissberg, Thomas P. Gullotta, Robert L. Hampton, Bruce A. Ryan, and Gerald R. Adams

Volume 9: **Healthy Children 2010: Establishing Preventive Services**
EDITORS: Roger P. Weissberg, Thomas P. Gullotta, Robert L. Hampton, Bruce A. Ryan, and Gerald R. Adams

Adolescent Dysfunctional Behavior

Causes, Interventions, and Prevention

Editors
Gary M. Blau
Thomas P. Gullotta

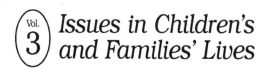

Vol. 3 *Issues in Children's and Families' Lives*

SAGE Publications
International Educational and Professional Publisher
Thousand Oaks   London   New Delhi

For information address:

SAGE Publications, Inc.
2455 Teller Road
Thousand Oaks, California 91320
E-mail: order@sagepub.com

SAGE Publications Ltd.
6 Bonhill Street
London EC2A 4PU
United Kingdom

SAGE Publications India Pvt. Ltd.
M-32 Market
Greater Kailash I
New Delhi 110 048 India

Printed in the United States of America

Library of Congress Cataloging-in-Publication Data

Main entry under title:

Adolescent dysfunctional behavior: Causes, interventions, and
   prevention / edited by Gary M. Blau, Thomas P. Gullotta.
      p.   cm.—(Issues in children's and families' lives; v. 3)
   Includes bibliographical references and index.
   ISBN 0-8039-5372-0 (cloth: alk. paper).—ISBN 0-8039-5373-9
(pbk.: alk. paper)
   1. Adolescent psychopathology. 2. Teenagers—Mental health
services. 3. Problem youth. I. Blau, Gary M. II. Gullotta,
Thomas, 1948-   . III. Series.
RJ503.A3144   1995
616.89'022—dc20   95-35479

This book is printed on acid-free paper.

      98 99 10 9 8 7 6 5 4 3

Sage Production Editor: Tricia K. Bennett
Sage Typesetter: Andrea D. Swanson

Contents

Preface   vii
THOMAS P. GULLOTTA

Acknowledgments   x

Part I - A Framework of Understanding

1. Dysfunctional Behavior: A Cautionary
   Statement   3
   THOMAS P. GULLOTTA

2. Selected Theoretical Frameworks of Individual
   and Group Behavior for Intervention and
   Prevention   11
   THOMAS P. GULLOTTA

Part II - Behaviors of Concern

3. Attention-Deficit/Hyperactivity Disorder   37
   H. ANN BROCHIN and JOSEPH A. HORVATH

4. Oppositional Defiant Disorder   61
   BURTON I. BLAU

5. Anxiety Disorders   83
   HARRY L. MILLS

6. Adolescent Drug Abuse: Contemporary
   Perspectives on Etiology and Treatment   114
   *RUTH BAUGHER PALMER and
   HOWARD A. LIDDLE*

7. Problem Sexual Behaviors in Adolescence   139
   LISA TERRE and BARRY R. BURKHART

8. Eating Disorders   167
   ROBERT J. WEINSTEIN

9. Adolescent Suicide and Depression   187
   GARY M. BLAU

10. The Neurobiology of Schizophrenia   206
    DEEPAK CYRIL D'SOUZA and
    JOHN HARRISON KRYSTAL

Part III - Directions for Future Practice

11. New Directions for Service Delivery:
    Home-Based Services   247
    WILLIAM EYBERSE, JAMES MAFFUID, and
    GARY M. BLAU

12. School-Based Health and Social Service Centers   267
    THOMAS P. GULLOTTA, LYNN NOYES, and
    GARY M. BLAU

13. Comments on Adolescent Behavior Problems:
    Developing Coordinated Systems of Care   284
    GARY M. BLAU and DAVID A. BRUMER

    Index   293

    About the Editors   298

    About the Contributors   300

Preface

Adolescents have always had the uncommon ability to excite substantial unease in the older generation. Based on personal observations, I can emphatically state that parents seem to age rapidly with the entry of offspring into puberty. School officials develop frown lines. Patrolman Friendly "morphs" into Officer Krupke, and religious leaders find ample evidence to support the coming apocalypse. This third volume in the Child and Family Agency book series **Issues in Children's and Families' Lives** is devoted to the topics that excite these concerned reactions. The images of youth presented in this volume are offered in a manner that places adolescent dysfunctional behavior in a theoretically based, intervention-focused context.

Thus, Thomas Gullotta in Chapter 1 offers a cautionary statement about dysfunctional behavior in adolescence. In Chapter 2, he provides an overview of theoretical understandings of human behavior, giving special attention to primary prevention.

The next eight chapters focus on specific issues of concern. Each chapter is rich in the attention it provides to theory, current research, and family influences. In Chapter 3, H. Ann Brochin and Joseph Horvath offer an insightful analysis of attention-deficit/hyperactivity disorder. Next, Burton Blau focuses needed attention on a subject given less consideration—oppositional defiant behavior. Harry Mills examines anxiety disorders in Chapter 5. The subject of substance abuse is deftly treated in Chapter 6 by Ruth Palmer and Howard Liddle. Lisa Terre and Barry Burkhart in Chapter 7 focus their attention on problematic adolescent sexual issues, such as victimization, sexually transmitted diseases, and unplanned pregnancies. In the next chapter, Robert Weinstein discusses eating disorders, and Gary Blau in Chapter 9 reviews the existing knowledge regarding suicidal behavior. The final chapter in Part II by Deepak D'Souza and John Krystal provides an insightful review of the development of schizophrenia.

Completing the volume, William Eyberse, James Maffuid, and Gary Blau in Chapter 11 examine one of two promising new programmatic approaches for working with youth and families in difficulty. The recent emergence of home-based family preservation services gives a long overdue professional acknowledgment to the reality that therapeutic change will most likely happen when interventions occur in the client's natural environment. The home is clearly just such a setting. In Chapter 12, Thomas Gullotta, Lynn Noyes, and Gary Blau consider the need for establishing school-based health and social services. In these authors' opinion, the development of school-based services by independent community agencies offers another vital ecological opportunity to make meaningful and significant change in the lives of young people. The volume concludes with observations by Gary Blau and David Brumer on the need for developing coordinated systems of care for youth.

After reading the chapters from the many fine authors who contributed to this volume, I take some comfort in intellectually recognizing that each of the behaviors discussed did not originate in the present time. Descriptions of each dysfunctional behavior can be found in the writings of historians and Western novelists. To illustrate this point, consider this fictional early adolescent case history I have assembled from the writings of an American author from the previous century.

The boy in question has a grim, violent drunkard for a father who has left him to his own devices on numerous occasions. The whereabouts of the boy's mother is unknown. The boy is ill-fed. His clothes are little better than rags attached loosely to his body. He is more accustomed to the closeness of animal fur against his body for warmth than to clean sheets and blankets. He has no use for school, and school no use for him. He is known to smoke, use foul language, mistreat cats, and participate in serious acts of property theft. He will lie; he will hide; and he will run away when pressures become too great.

He is Huckleberry Finn and apparently suitable for the diagnostic label of oppositional defiant disorder. Or is he?

For those readers who would acknowledge the relativity of some diagnostic categories but would cite the rise in anorexia nervosa as unique to our times, I would refer them to Bell's (1985) seminal historical examination of this dysfunctional behavior in *Holy Anorexia*. For those readers who would decry the current sexual victimization of youth, I would agree, but point out that in 1875, in proper Victorian England, girls were officially allowed to engage in prostitution at the age of 13 (Adams, Gullotta, & Markstrom-Adams, 1994).

Despite these observations, I am troubled by the times in which we live. My intellectual understanding does not adequately insulate me against the bitter reality that some 9 million youth in the United States each year will demonstrate dysfunctional behaviors. Many of these youth will find themselves on a judicial rapid transit system out of their communities and into settings in which a negative identity will be forever fused to their souls. Unlike my fictional companion, Huckleberry, who found acceptance and forgiveness from the Widow Douglas and the other residents of the village in which he resided, these youth are likely to be treated differently.

They are not romantic fictional characters. They are not handsome youth. They will make no epic journey. They will be given no opportunity for greatness. They will not have a sympathetic author searching for their redeeming features.

When I come to learn of them, their actions will be described as hideous, repulsive, or violent. These acts evidently will occur without provocation and may be directed against those they do not even know. I and others will be struck by how little we know about them, how little we grasp their understanding, and how much we hold them in fear.

It is my hope that this volume will cast some light on our collective ignorance. It is my hope that scholars, researchers, practitioners, and graduate students will draw from the materials in this book lessons that can be applied to intervene for good in the lives of these young people.

—Thomas P. Gullotta

References

Adams, G. R., Gullotta, T. P., & Markstrom-Adams, C. (1994). *Adolescent life experiences*. Pacific Grove, CA: Brooks/Cole.

Bell, R. M. (1985). *Holy anorexia*. Chicago: University of Chicago Press.

Acknowledgments

We gratefully acknowledge the love and support of our families. Without them, none of this would mean anything. We are also thankful for the help of two guest reviewers, Gary Minetti and Robert Gossart.

PART I

A Framework of Understanding

• CHAPTER 1 •

Dysfunctional Behavior:
A Cautionary Statement

THOMAS P. GULLOTTA

When an orchestra gathers to perform, each instrument has a particular part to play. An edited book is like an orchestration in several respects. Its editors can be seen as both the book's composers, conceiving its outline and flow, and its conductors, recruiting talented professionals and refining their performance for presentation. Similarly, each chapter author can be imagined to be both a lyricist bringing her own words to the concept and a soloist presenting his own unique interpretation to the topic under investigation. If successful, the edited volume should examine the topic with a similar structural style while respecting the individual creative perspective of the contributors.

The intention of this first chapter is to provide a quiet rhythm to the discussion about to unfold. Like the drummer in the orchestra, I would hope that the images to be shared in this chapter will linger in the background uniting the individual performances to follow. Not that the statements to be made in this first chapter will not sound a discord or two, as they certainly will, but that the author of this chapter is forgiving of adolescents and their frequently disturbing behavior. And it is that forgiveness, that tolerance, and that increasingly missing compassion that I wish to be heard by those who read this book.

Dysfunctional Behavior

Dysfunctional behavior may be understood to mean observable conduct that violates the established rules of an existing group. The relativity of this statement is immediately evident. Given the group, almost any imaginable behavior can be seen as dysfunctional. For example, consider this statement by Anna Freud (1958, cited in Bloom, 1990): "The adolescent manifestations of growth come close to the symptom formation of the neurotic, psychotic, or dissocial order and merge almost imperceptibly into borderline states, or fully fledged forms of almost all the illnesses" (p. 18). Next, study the observations of Eric Erikson (1968):

> Young patients can be violent or depressed, delinquent or withdrawn, but theirs is an acute and possibly passing crisis rather than a break-down of the kind which tends to commit a patient to all the malignant implications of a fatalistic diagnosis. (p. 17)

Finally, reflect on Kai Erikson's (1966) understanding that deviant behavior is ascribed and not inherent to any particular action:

> [Deviance represents] conduct which the people of a group consider so dangerous or embarrassing or irritating that they bring special sanctions to bear against the persons who exhibit it. Deviance is not a property inherent in any particular kind of behavior; it is a property conferred upon that behavior by the people who come into direct or indirect contact with it. (p. 6)

Against this backdrop, now examine the behavior of the following youth. The boy in question has a grim, violent drunkard for a father who has left him to his own devices on numerous occasions. No record exists as to the presence of the boy's mother. He is ill-fed. His clothes are little better than rags attached loosely to his body by means of a single button where two are needed. He is more accustomed to the contact of barnyard animals against his body for nightly warmth than to laundered sheets and woven blankets. He has no use for school, and school no use for him. He is known to smoke, use foul language, mistreat cats (I suspect), and participate in serious acts of property theft. He will lie; he will hide; and he will run away when pressures become too great. He is Huckleberry Finn and apparently suitable for the diagnostic label of oppositional defiant disorder. Or is he? Are there other mitigating circumstances that would have us understand this youth differently? For those who are familiar with Clemens's masterpiece, the answer is yes. Huckleberry's actions gain our support and alter the labeling process when placed in the context of the environment in which he lives. His escape from a cruel parent when the courts would rather keep father and son together is not only understandable but justifiable, as the following passage demonstrates:

[That night pap had consumed, as usual, enough whiskey] for two drunks and one delirium tremens [and takes after Huck] . . . [pap] jumped up on his feet . . . and went for me. He chased me . . . with a clasp-knife, calling me the Angel of Death and saying he would kill me. . . . I begged, and told him I was Huck, but he laughed . . . and kept on chasing me up. . . . Pretty soon he was all tired out . . . and said he would rest a minute and then kill me. He put his knife under him, and said he would sleep and get strong, and then he would see who was who.

So he dozed off, pretty soon. By-and-by I got the old split-bottom chair and clumb up, as easy as I could, not to make any noise, and got down the gun. I slipped the ramrod down it to make sure it was loaded, and then I laid it across the turnip barrel, pointing towards pap, and set down behind it to wait for him to stir. And how slow and still the time did drag along. (Clemens, 1884/1962, p. 52)

His journey down the Mississippi after running away from his father assumes a surrealistic quality as he encounters the Granger-fords and Shepherdsons. In this instance, Huck conceals his identity—much like a modern-day journalist would visiting a war-torn foreign land in which the cause for killing has long since been lost to retribution:

[Buck Grangerford—with Huck in tow—has attempted to kill Harney Shepherdson as he was horseback riding.]
"Did you want to kill him, Buck?"
"Him? He never did nothing to me."
"Well, then, what did you want to kill him for?"
"Why nothing—only it's on account of the feud."
"What's a feud? . . ."
"Well," says Buck, "a feud is this way. A man has a quarrel with another man, and kills him; then that other man's brother kills *him*;

then the other brothers, on both sides, goes for one another; then the cousins chip in—and by-and-by everybody's killed off, and there ain't no more feud. But it's kind of slow, and takes a long time."

"Has this one been going on long, Buck?"

"Well I should *reckon!* It started thirty year ago, or som'ers along there.

There was trouble 'bout something and then a lawsuit to settle it; and the suit went agin one of the men, and so he up and shot the man that won the suit.—"

"What was the trouble about, Buck?—land?"

"I reckon maybe—I don't know."

"Well, who done the shooting?—was it a Grangerford or a Shepherdson?"

"Laws, how do *I* know? It was so long ago."

"Don't anybody know?"

"Oh, yes, pa knows, I reckon, and some of the other old folks; but they don't know, now, what the row was about in the first place." (Clemens, 1884/1962, pp. 146-147)

His decision to conceal the runaway slave, Jim, from those who would capture and return Jim to slavery earns our respect and understanding in spite of the reality that Huckleberry's behavior violates every behavioral norm of southern society. Indeed, so severe is Huck's transgression that its discovery would result in his and Jim's death:

Why, *me* . . . I warn't to blame, because I didn't run Jim off from his rightful owner; but it warn't no use, conscience up and says, every time, "But you knowed he was running for his freedom. . . . What had poor Miss Watson done to you, that you could see her nigger go off right under your eyes and never say one single word. . . . I got to feeling so mean and so miserable I most wished I was dead. . . . [Huck leaves the raft with the intention of turning Jim in when he is confronted on the river by two men searching for runaway slaves. They ask:] Is your man white or black? [At that moment, Huck cannot find the words to betray Jim and chooses instead to protect him by lying. Afterward, he reflects on his actions:] They went off, and I got aboard the raft, feeling bad and low, because I knowed very well I had done wrong. . . . Then I thought a minute, and says to myself, hold on,—s'pose you'd a done right and give Jim up; would you felt better than what you do now? No, says I, I'd feel bad. . . . Well, then, says I, what's the use you learning to do right, when it's troublesome

to do right and ain't no trouble to do wrong, and the wages is just
the same? I was struck. I couldn't answer that. So I reckoned I
wouldn't bother no more about it, but after this always do whichever
come handiest at the time. (Clemens, 1884/1962, pp. 123, 127-128)

The situational context of decision making that Huck decides is
"handiest" is understandable when the rules of the society no longer
make sense. Clemens makes it clear that it is not Huck who is
dysfunctional but Huckleberry's surroundings. In this environment, other values like loyalty emerge to take the place of society's
rules. Thus, when Jim is betrayed and imprisoned, Huck grapples
again with notifying Miss Watson that Jim has been found or taking
some other action:

> [Huck tries to write Miss Watson that Jim has been caught and can
> be found below Pikesville. He attempts to pray but finds the words
> do not come.] I knowed very well why they wouldn't come. It was
> because my heart warn't right; it was because I warn't square; it was
> because I was playing double. I was letting *on* to give up sin, but away
> inside of me I was holding on to the biggest one of all. I was trying
> to make my mouth say I would do the right thing and the clean thing,
> and go write to that nigger's owner and tell where he was; but deep
> down in me I knowed it was a lie—and He knowed it . . .
>   [After deciding not to betray Jim and write the letter and accepting
> that, "I'll go to hell,"] I shoved the whole thing out of my head; and
> said I would take up wickedness again, which was in my line, being
> brung up to it, and others warn't. And for a starter, I would go to
> work and steal Jim out of slavery again; and if I could think up
> anything worse, I would do that, too; because as long as I was in, and
> in for good, I might as well go the whole hog. (Clemens, 1884/1962,
> pp. 270, 272)

Notice how Clemens conveys Huckleberry's thoughts. In his
words, we see the struggle between good and evil and a decision
that if Huck cannot maintain his membership in good society, then
he may as well raise hell. But Huck's raising hell in established
society fulfills the unarticulated expectations of the alternative
society that Huck and Jim have created for each other on the river:

> [I] got to thinking over the trip down the river; and I see Jim before me,
> all the time, in the day, and in the nighttime, sometimes moonlight,

sometimes storms, and we a floating along, talking, and singing, and laughing. But somehow I couldn't seem to strike no places to harden me against him, but only the other kind. I'd see him standing my watch on top of his'n, stead of calling me, so I could go on sleeping; and see him how glad he was when I come back out of the fog; and when I come to him again in the swamp, up there where the feud was; and such-like times; and would always call me honey, and pet me, and do everything he could of for me, and how good he always was . . . and said I was the best friend old Jim ever had in the world, and the *only* one he's got now. (Clemens, 1884/1962, p. 271)

The concepts of good and evil that Huck so clearly sees and his acceptance of his damnation through his rejection of the principles of that society grow confusing to readers as their knowledge of Huck increases. In place of Huckleberry's deviance, we see his loyalty. Instead of dishonesty, we see his trustworthiness emerging from a caring relationship between two societal outcasts. Other companion traits associated with social competency, such as friendship, kindness, bravery, helpfulness, humor, and reverence—even if Huck can't pray—are evident in his behavior (Gullotta, 1990). Huck fulfills his promise to himself, with the dubious aid of Tom Sawyer, to free Jim, and Jim keeps good the unspoken covenant they have developed when he sacrifices his freedom to ensure the safety of his two young friends. Unlike life, in literature, all problems can be resolved satisfactorily and are in *Huckleberry Finn*. But, at the end of this adventure and with all the innocence of a Forrest Gump, Huck's construction of the world makes it plain that the decision to light out for the territories is correct. The civilization found in *The Adventures of Huckleberry Finn* surely would destroy Huckleberry Finn: "But I reckon I got to light out for the Territory ahead of the rest, because Aunt Sally she's going to adopt me and sivilize me and I can't stand it. I been there before" (Clemens, 1884/1962, p. 366).

This construct of the person-in-the-environment and its relationship to dysfunctional behavior can be illustrated again with an advertisement currently being aired on television. In this second example, the Partnership for a Drug Free America has produced a powerful public service announcement that portrays a young inner-city black youth darting across back alleys and litter-strewn yards to avoid street-hardened, assumedly drug-selling and gang-connected, youth. From the perspective of the middle-class audience whom this commercial was designed to reach, the dysfunctional behavior belongs to the drug-selling youth.

The public service announcement conveys this image in several ways. First, the young lad using the back alleys to reach the safety of his home is smaller and younger than those he seeks to avoid. He is alone in his journey. He is physically clean. His hair is cut short, and he is appropriately dressed (by middle-class standards). On his back is a school sack. In contrast, the group he seeks to avoid is viewed by the camera as leaning idly against cars attired in loose-fitting grunge clothing. Although no conversation is heard, body gestures suggest that the youth controlling the streets are ill-intentioned. The narrator of the public service announcement commends the bravery of the lone child seeking to remain connected with the society viewing the commercial and states this youth is not to be forgotten.

How are these two fictional story images similar? First, they involve youth—whether Huckleberry or the street gang—who do not subscribe to the societal script. Next, they are young people who will and do break established norms. How are they dissimilar? Where Clemens shares Huckleberry's circumstances, the Partnership for a Drug Free America does not share the circumstances of the street youth. The perspective of the story is not that of the youth on the street but that of the lone child. One can only wonder, if Clemens had taken the perspective of Tom Sawyer's younger half-brother Sid, whether Huckleberry's complexity would have emerged, or whether he and Tom would have been seen merely as delinquents deserving of the switch and destined to repeat the sins of Huck's father. Where Clemens repeatedly confronts the reader with the illogic of Huckleberry's world, no similar statement emerges from the Partnership.

For example, Clemens uses biting sarcasm to examine the court's refusal to remove Huckleberry from his drunken father, but no narrator in the Partnership announcement points out the incongruities in the lives of these young men. We know not of their homes, their families, or their schools. We can infer from their setting that economic opportunity does not exist, and we can only wonder whether, if deprived of access to legitimate economic opportunity, these young people developed alternative economic markets in commodities that, although disfavored by legitimate society, are, nevertheless, principally consumed by that society.

For those readers who would complain that my comparison of a
366-page novel with a 30-second public service announcement is
unfair, it is, and it is intended to be. It is just as unfair as the
15-second sound bites the Speaker of the House, Mr. Limbaugh,
and others are wont to make about youth. Rapid visual and audio
images create caricatures that, when repeated with enough frequency, establish the stereotypes we apply to those different from
ourselves. Who knows but in another 366 pages or 30 minutes, we
might find reasons to understand the street gang's behavior and,
while not approve of their actions, see opportunities to, as Huck
phrased it, "sivilize" them. The remaining chapters in this volume
are an attempt at understanding youth in more than 15-second
sound bites with the intention of bridging the differences that
increasingly are pushing some youth away from us.

References

Bloom, M. (1990). The psychosocial constructs of social competency. In T. P.
    Gullotta, G. R. Adams, & R. Montemayor (Eds.), *Developing social competency
    in adolescence* (pp. 11-27). Newbury Park, CA: Sage.
Clemens, S. (1962). *The adventures of Huckleberry Finn.* San Francisco: Chandler.
    (Original work published 1884)
Erikson, E. H. (1968). *Identity: Youth and crisis.* New York: Norton.
Erikson, K. (1966). *Wayward Puritans.* New York: John Wiley.
Gullotta, T. P. (1990). Preface. In T. P. Gullotta, G. R. Adams, & R. Montemayor
    (Eds.), *Developing social competency in adolescence* (pp. 7-8). Newbury Park,
    CA: Sage.

CHAPTER 2

Selected Theoretical Frameworks of Individual and Group Behavior for Intervention and Prevention

THOMAS P. GULLOTTA

The year is 1915. Albert Einstein pushes back his chair and stands. He has just put the finishing touches on his theory of relativity. But instead of smiling, he appears disturbed. He mumbles to himself. "This cannot be correct." Einstein has predicted that the world exists in a universe that is ever changing. Such a notion is, unquestionably, pure poppycock. Since the time of Aristotle, the idea that the heavens are stationary has been accepted as truth by all. And so Einstein dutifully reworks his theory to correspond with accepted knowledge. For 12 years, his original version lies untouched, until the astronomer Edwin Hubble shakes the world with his observation that the universe is expanding. Einstein had been right after all (Lightman, 1983).

Einstein was the victim of something I refer to as "constituent validity," which means simply that an idea may be defined as true by a group of people whether it is true or not. History is littered with similar mistakes made by greater and lesser figures alike. This fact illustrates well a uniquely paradoxical human situation. Humans have a great need to understand, to fashion models of how things work, and to comprehend why they work the way they do. These understandings lead to explanations that are called theories. *Theories* seek to predict how something might respond in a given circumstance. For a theory to be useful, it must be applicable over many varying circumstances.

And yet, despite all this theoretical inquisitiveness, humans have a consistent track record of narrow-mindedness rooted in their present construction of truth. Consider Galileo's experiences with the Inquisition. His scientific curiosity led him to the observation that the earth was not the center of the universe, that the earth revolved around the sun. Galileo's proclamation was greeted with scorn and disapproval, and eventually he was tried by the church as a heretic and banished. Einstein's and Galileo's experiences illustrate the one certain truth contained in this chapter, which is that we should hold no explanation sacred. Theory, like truth, evolves. Its shape changes as curious human beings question and explore further how the world behaves. Remember also that these new explanations are always grounded in the defined reality of the time and, therefore, are subject to further revision as current understandings change.

To illustrate, contrast your early childhood classroom learning experiences of the discoverer Columbus with more recent memories of the 500th anniversary of his arrival to American shores. Unlike those lessons, this anniversary was tempered by discussions and demonstrations that not all people were joyous about this event. Native American Indians reminded us that the genocide of native populations was one prominent outcome of the arrival of Western Europeans.

This chapter will examine several explanations of how individuals and families behave. It is from these core theoretical foundations that the multitude of psychotherapies have emerged. Furthermore, it explores how theory can be used to construct a model for preventing individual and family dysfunctional behavior and for promoting their health. Such an understanding will serve as a foundation for comprehending much of the material in the remaining chapters.

Understanding Behavior:
Four Theoretical Frameworks

The sheer number of theories that have been offered to explain human behavior is (to use the vernacular) "truly awesome." Some of these focus on the individual and view behavior as emerging from within a person. These explanations are called *psychological theories.* Other explanations focus on the interaction between the individual and his or her environment. These explanations are called *social-psychological theories*. Still others examine the influence of social structure and society on behavior. These are called *sociocultural theories*. Finally, some theories explain human behavior in biological terms. For the purposes of convenience, I will use individual pronouns for psychological and biological theories and the word *family*, or a version thereof, for social-psychological and sociocultural theories.

Psychological Theories

Psychological explanations of behavior involve an understanding of the internal drives and motivations that influence behavior. Two of the most widely used person-driven explanations are psychoanalytic and social-learning theories.

Psychoanalytic Theory. This theory attempts to explain social development from infancy to adulthood. Early childhood experiences are regarded as leaving a lasting impression on the child's developing personality. As young children move from one psychosexual stage to another, they come to grips with two instinctual urges, the sexual and aggressive drives. Both these urges are thought to create a constant state of tension in which the body seeks pleasure and satisfaction. Psychoanalytic theory conceptualizes this tension as resulting from the interaction of three forces—the id, the ego, and the superego.

The *id* can be imagined as unbridled passion reflecting a desire to satisfy instinctual behavior. The *ego* evolves to satisfy the id's instinctual gratification but in ways that avoid punishment. The ego's major function is to attempt to satisfy the demands of the id while observing the dictates of the third component of personality, the superego. The *superego* is the judge of all behavior. It is our internalized moral code. It is thought to develop through a child's interactions with parents, who communicate standards of acceptable and unacceptable behavior (Freud, 1947).

The family is viewed as the societal force that creates and models a set of desirable characteristics that are internalized by the child and are called the *ego ideal*. The parents also facilitate sex role identification through a psychodynamic process. Thus, the family is thought to provide the societal conditions that encourage self-regulation through superego mechanisms, ideals of conduct, and sex role identification.

Early psychoanalytic theory places a heavy emphasis on a child's first several years of life. Behavior occurring in late adolescence or adult life is traced, in this model, back to an earlier childhood psychosexual stage and unresolved issues related to that stage. Therapeutic interventions using this theoretical framework attempt to assist the individual in uncovering and understanding events much earlier in the individual's life. It is assumed that this new knowledge will affect attitudes and change behavior.

Social-Learning Theory. Learning theory views human development as the cumulative effect of a multitude of learning experiences that are integrated to form a personality. This happens in a social-learning model in two ways.

The first way is through *reinforcement,* which is any event that occurs after a response and affects the chances that the response will occur again. In *positive reinforcement,* a desirable stimulus follows the response, increasing the chances that the response will recur. In *negative reinforcement,* an unwanted stimulus is removed following the response, also increasing the chances that the response will recur. In *punishment,* an undesirable stimulus (e.g., pain) is presented after the response, or a desirable stimulus is removed, decreasing the chances that the response will recur. The second way that learning occurs is through *modeling.* In modeling, people imitate the behavior of others whom they admire or respect (Bandura, 1969).

Those who subscribe to social-learning theory emphasize the rewards, negative sanctions, and punishments we have received over our lives that shape our behavioral responses to external events. Furthermore, learning theorists are interested in the role models whom individuals select to emulate. Although social-learning theory acknowledges that learning (and, therefore, personal growth) occurs over the life span, it focuses on an individual's reaction to some discrete event. In recent years, this concept of growth over the life span has been enriched by an understanding of the interrelatedness among behavior, cognition, and human development. The role of expectations and the meaning those expectations attach to an event are called *cognitive behaviorism.*

Social-Psychological Theories

Social-psychological theories of behavior examine the relationship of individuals to their social environment. These explanations of behavior are broader than psychological theories in that they extend beyond internal factors to include other individuals, groups, and organizations. Representatives of this type of theory are symbolic interaction and social exchange theories. Both are widely used to explain family functioning.

Symbolic Interaction Theory. A useful way to understand the remaining theories to be described in this chapter is to dissect the label attached to the explanation and examine its components. For example, symbolic interaction theory proposes that families *interact* through *symbols*. These interacting family members together develop roles (such as worker, parent, friend, father, husband, son, mother, wife, and daughter) and assign those roles to individuals in the family and society, who then "play" the assigned role (Hill & Hansen, 1960).

This model relies heavily on one's sensory experiences and perception of the environment. Self-concept is of major importance to symbolic interactionists. It involves processes of how we are seen by others, how we imagine ourselves to be seen, and how we feel (pleased or displeased) about those outsiders' views of us (Ritzer, 1983). Cooley (1964) has termed this the "looking-glass self." This self is a conscious process that Mead (1962) describes as having two parts. The first part, "me," is the one we are aware of. It is similar to the superego in that it reflects society's standards of social order, control, and conformity. The second part, the "I," is the part of which we are unaware until some act has been completed.

The symbolic interactionist sees human beings as capable of thought, which is shaped by social interaction. Social interaction permits people to learn symbols and their meanings. The symbols permit human beings to carry out human behavior. Moreover, individuals have the ability to change the meanings attached to symbols or to vary the meanings of symbols for different places, people, and times (Ritzer, 1983). Readers no doubt can think of symbols that hold special meaning for themselves and others. Gestures or statements may exist for yourself and friends that may mean something entirely different to others (Burr, Leigh, Day, & Constantine, 1979).

Symbolic interaction holds that people do not merely react to their environment but act on it as well. Life is in a constant state of flux in which individuals interpret what is happening and apply a meaning to it. Events that challenge the role an individual plays or suggest a loss of role may bring emotional suffering if so defined by the individual (Burr et al., 1979; Dager, 1964; Stryker, 1964).

To illustrate, a young person's entrance into college can create several changes in individual and family roles. The student begins to think of him- or herself in a new way: independent and adult. But the student's parents may not agree. One or both may be unwilling to assign an adult role to the child. What happens? When the student returns home from school, students and parents may find themselves arguing about curfews and other issues. And when parents end a fight with the statement, "As long as you live under this roof, young man (lady), you'll abide by my rules," they are really saying, "You're still a child in my eyes."

Social Exchange Theory. The word *social* in the name of this theory implies the interaction of the individual and the group. *Exchange* is commonly understood to mean the giving of one thing for something else of about equal value. People who subscribe to social exchange theory believe that individuals trade, as in the marketplace, emotions in exchange for other emotions. The business of exchange is transacted between individuals and others in society.

The rate and nature of exchange depend on four elements. The first is *rewards*—the satisfactions, pleasures, or attainments collected during exchanges. For example, suppose an individual were to approach another person and whisper in his or her ear, "I love you." If the other person should respond with a smile, a hug, or a kiss, the individual would have received a reward (Nye, 1979).

The second element involves the concept of alternatives and is often called "weighing costs." *Costs* are actions, feelings, or interactions that (a) are unpleasant or (b) are rewards lost. For example, if you are an adolescent seriously emotionally involved with someone, falling in love with someone else will result in costs to you in the form of painful experiences. Similar costs will befall the third party in this relationship, as well as the former significant other, who may experience feelings of depression and anger. The second kind of cost, lost rewards, can be understood in terms of the idea that *choice entails loss*. Let's imagine that the price of a meal includes one dessert, either pudding or ice cream. To choose the pudding "costs" the consumer ice cream. Becoming involved with another costs you the first relationship (Nye, 1979). It would appear that everything in life costs something. Nothing is free. Some things cost less, however, and on some emotional or social investments, a *profit* can be made—that is, one can maximize gain and limit loss. For example, two high school students I know passed up the opportunity to attend their junior prom because the invitations had come from rather unattractive individuals. By choosing not to attend the prom, these students had incurred a cost, but felt that they had profited by not losing stature in the eyes of their peers. Thus, they had minimized their loss. Had they accepted, their dates would have gained in prestige at their expense, or at least they so believed.

The fourth element involved in determining the rate and nature of exchange is the *norm of reciprocity*, the principle that receiving should approximate equal giving. Another way of saying this is that "people should help those who help them, and people should not injure those who have helped them" (Nye, 1979, p. 4).

In short, social exchange theory suggests that "humans avoid costly behavior and seek rewarding statuses, relationships, interaction, and feeling states to the end that their profits are maximized, or losses minimized" (Nye, 1979, p. 2). In this theory, humans are rational; they are actors as well as reactors; all behavior costs something, and people will usually choose the least costly behavioral option. One might also view this process of choice as striving for equity—that is, seeking appropriate rewards for equal costs.

Sociocultural Theories

Sociocultural theories focus on social structures or systems to explain behavior. Theories in this group tend to view individuals and families as they react to such societal influences as culture and social institutions. Two such theories in this tradition are structural-functionalism and general systems theory.

Structural-Functional Theory. The word *structural* suggests that something is arranged in a definite pattern, or organization, and that this arrangement is related to other parts of the structure and is dominated by the general character of the whole. The word *functional* means that each element in a group contributes to the development or maintenance of the whole. Structural-functionalism suggests that society is made up of a number of *structures,* each serving a useful *function* that maintains and/or further develops the whole. How might we understand this last, somewhat tautological statement? Think of a steel girder. Alone, it is nothing more than one building part. When it is assembled with other girders, however, it creates a structure and serves the function of supporting the walls or roof of a building. To the structural-functionalist, the individual is a component of the girder. Together with other components (mother, father, sister, brother, and so on), the individuals form a girder called family, and with other girders, such as schools and churches, they function to construct society.

The structural-functionalist position is that the social system is the basic unit for study, rather than either the family, as social-psychological theory would suggest, or the individual, as strict psychological theory would argue. Maintaining this position means that family members are not actors but reactors (Hill & Hansen, 1960; Pitts, 1964).

To illustrate, let's look again at our earlier example of a college student whose parents disapproved of his or her activities. The symbolic interactionist would argue that this incident occurred because of shifting roles and the meaning each player attached to those roles. The college student wanted to be treated as an adult, with the privilege of setting his or her own standard of behavior. The parents disagreed and wished to maintain this person's role as a child. The parents' motivations for opposing this role change may have ranged from disapproval of the student's behavior and peer group to reluctance to surrender their parenting roles.

Structural-functionalists would view this situation differently. They would argue that society needs to have people grow up, separate from their parents, and establish their own lives. The structures of college and the peer group in this example serve the function of helping this happen. Away from home and in the company of peers, students are separated from their parents and are engaged in the process of establishing their own lives. These school experiences and peer relationships contribute to the development of a new possible structure (i.e., the college student is able to leave the family and form a new family) that helps maintain the whole (i.e., the continuation of society). Notice that nowhere in this explanation did I include ideas that humans determine their own destiny or that their interactions or exchanges matter very much. The structural-functionalist position ignores these variables.

Note also that, although our example of the college student continuing society is structured to accentuate the positive, the converse is equally as possible. It has been offered that the growth of inner-city male youth gangs may be a (structural) response to the female-headed households that predominate in inner-city families. In this construction, gangs provide males with the necessary peer support to free them from home, to demonstrate their masculinity, and to establish new social units (see Huff, 1990).

Structural-functionalist theory, in proposing that structures serve the function of maintaining and developing society, suggests that the whole—that is, society—strives to maintain a level of homeostasis. It is logical that this theory would express the view that society needs to maintain a balance of functions through a state of equilibrium, so as not to be torn apart (Hill & Hansen, 1960). One part of maintaining equilibrium is the need for deviance, which is the glue that binds healthy societies together, establishing, as it does, good people like our slightly troublesome (likely middle-class) college student and his or her (significantly poorer and minority) gang-participating member (see Erikson, 1966). Notice here that the standard of good and bad is defined by the predominant group and is relative in both time and place.

General Systems Theory. What can we learn from examining the words *general* and *systems*? Well, the word *general* is commonly understood to mean "applicable to every member of a group." A *system* is defined as a group of interrelated parts forming a collective unit. General systems theory suggests that society is composed of many interrelated working parts.

Rather than an object like a girder that cannot act, imagine in this case a chip within a personal computer. This chip can perform certain functions with no input at all. It can perform other functions if a program is inserted. It can do still more if it is linked to other chips within other computers. It can act or react, depending on what it is called on to do. The chip alone does not make a usable computer system. Other elements, such as a keyboard, monitor, disk drive, and printer, are needed to have a system. The chip, in our example, is analogous to an individual or family, and the computer components to society.

The world is filled with systems. Each can operate independently. For example, it can rain or not. Food crops can grow or not. Trading between humans can occur or not. But if we are to have a society, these parts (systems) must come together. Without rain, there is a desert, and in a desert food cannot be grown. Without food, humans cannot survive. Fortunately, humans have usually established themselves where it is possible to at least eke out an existence. Whether an individual or family behaves as successfully as a system depends on several factors.

Systems theorists use several terms when speaking of families. One of these is *boundaries*, which define a system by establishing what elements belong to it. An *open boundary* suggests that the family has much interaction with the outside world—friends, clubs, and organizations, church activities. A *closed boundary* implies that the family keeps to itself, with a minimal amount of outside interaction—few if any friends, little if any involvement in civic or community affairs.

The chip in our earlier example, despite its small size, is not one part but many. So too, all individuals belong to families. A family is not one part but is made of two or more units. A unit, in systems language, is a component system. Unlike computer chips, families can grow in parts (by adding children or other family members) and shrink in parts (by losing family members) over their life span.

A family is a system, made up of units, that has established a more or less open or closed boundary with other systems. But how do families interact with other systems? Systems theorists suggest that an incoming stimulus, or *input*, is mediated within the family and a response, or *output,* returned. This process of mediation is called *transformation.* The process of transformation involves interrupting the input and either *amplifying* or *dampening* the significance of the input. Imagine the sudden loss of an adolescent friend as the input. A family might amplify this loss and become very despondent and unable to function, or it might dampen this loss by rationalization and, though saddened, go on with its normal activities. Transformation also involves what systems theorists call *cybernetic control*, which means that the response a family makes to some given input is measured against family rules. If the family does not have a satisfactory response for some input, it will engage in morphogenesis—a family's search for and/or creation of new responses to that input. These changes may be minor, leaving intact basic family rules, or they may be major, changing the family and its values dramatically (Broderick & Smith, 1979).

Developmental Theory: An Attempt at Integration

Is it possible to integrate the theories presented so far in this chapter? Can one perspective encompass the variations among these theoretical camps? Developmental theory has tried to bridge these different schools of thought to create a unified explanation of individual and family behavior.

The developmental approach is an attempt to create a comprehensive model capable of explaining behavior across the life cycle. From a developmentalist's perspective, a life cycle begins with birth and progresses through a series of tasks that need to be accomplished for the individual to progress to the next stage. This overall process is referred to as an individual's lifetime history or career (Aldous, 1978; Erikson, 1963; Hill & Hansen, 1960).

Evolution is an important concept within this framework. The individual evolves over the years, facing and accomplishing a number of challenges that mark off each stage in the life cycle of the individual that begins with birth and ends in death (Erikson, 1963; Hill & Rodgers, 1964). Furthermore, it is assumed that the life cycle stages happen for everyone at approximately the same time. Thus, an individual can be "on time" or "off time" in regard to the life cycle. The Broadway comedy *Never Too Late* helps to illustrate this last point. This show was about a late-middle-aged couple with a grown, married daughter who discover they are to become parents again. The story line of this entertaining comedy deals with the "off time" nature of the parents having a child in their later life and society's reaction to that event.

Developmentalists, like symbolic interactionists, view individuals and families as consisting of a group of interacting actors filling assigned roles. Like the structural-functionalist, the developmentalist believes that individuals and families have several vitally important functions to serve in society, including meeting needs for food, clothing, and shelter, biological reproduction, socialization, and maintaining social order (Rodgers, 1964).

From general systems theory, developmentalists borrow the concept of boundaries and propose that individuals and families are neither totally open nor totally closed but respond to the demands placed on them by family members and society (Rodgers, 1973).

Behavioral Genetics

Behavioral genetics refers to the influence of genes on behavior. Genes are composed of DNA, the building blocks of life. Vast multitudes of these building blocks collect to form chromosomes. Research has determined that humans have 23 pairs of chromosomes. These rod-shaped bodies separate during division in a process called mitosis to replicate the genes that convey the hereditary characteristics of the chromosome.

It is assumed by behavioral geneticists that most behavior can be explained by genes. This assumption has been tested most often by collecting data on twins living together with and apart from their biological families. By examining the life histories of identical twins who share the same 23 pairs of chromosomes, it is assumed that similar patterns of behavior may be genetic in origin. These assumptions are even more forcefully expressed when the same pattern of behavior emerges when those identical twins are reared apart. Findings from these studies point to the possibility of intelligence having strong biological origins (in some instances explaining two thirds of the variance). There is also agreement that the genes individuals inherit at conception from their parents provide strong explanations for height, eye color, and weight. There is significantly less agreement that genes explain an individual's personality and behavior (Plomin, 1990a, 1990b).

In biological studies examining dysfunctional behaviors, such as delinquency, substance abuse, and violent behavior, the evidence for genetic causality is, in my opinion, weak. It may be that biology exposes certain individuals to a higher risk of certain dysfunctional behaviors, but it is society that can either mitigate that risk or precipitate its appearance. For example, although many twin studies have reported a higher incidence of alcoholism among children with an alcoholic parent (Bohman, 1978; Cotton, 1979), the increased genetic weighting explains but a fraction of the variance. Repeatedly, the unaccounted variance is the soup of the environment that either nourished or famished the individual's psychic strength. As Holden (1991) reports: "Scientists are beginning to suspect that there may be no genes for alcoholism per se, but rather for a general susceptibility to compulsive behaviors whose specific expression is shaped by environmental and temperamental factors" (p. 163). It is those "environmental and temperamental factors" that prevention seeks to address.

Understanding the Principles of Primary Prevention

Primary Prevention: An Overview

Although the concept of prevention is not new, the idea of prevention as an attainable goal has emerged only recently as the result of the failure of the treatment model to reduce the ever-growing number of seriously emotionally ill individuals in our society (Albee, 1980, 1990, 1992). Prevention has evolved since the early 1960s, when Gerald Caplan (1961, 1964, 1974) introduced a model suggesting that emotional illness could be prevented. That three-tier model of primary, secondary, and tertiary prevention, similar to the prevention model found in public health, has been refined. Secondary prevention activities—which attempt to reduce the length of time an individual or family experiences an emotionally distressful situation—are now called "treatment activities." Tertiary prevention activities—which attempt to prevent the recurrence of a debilitating problem and to restore as high as possible a level of individual and family reorganization—are now called "rehabilitation activities." Prevention has emerged in a hybrid form called "primary prevention."

The goal of primary prevention remains basically unaltered from Caplan's (1974) original intention of reducing "the incidence of new cases of mental disorder in the population by combating harmful forces which operate in the community and by strengthening the capacity of people to withstand stress" (pp. 189-190). Parameters for this goal have now been established. Primary prevention focuses on groups and the specific problems those groups experience (Klein & Goldston, 1977). It is proactive; that is, prevention builds new coping resources and adaptation skills and thus promotes emotionally healthy people (Albee & Gullotta, 1986).

Finally, prevention activities are planned interventions that can be observed, recorded, and evaluated for effectiveness (Cowen, 1982b; Klein & Goldston, 1977).

From this understanding, different strategies emerge. They involve each of us as an active participant in preventing illness and promoting health. Preventionists reject the belief "that major [emotional] illness is probably in large part genetically determined and is probably, therefore, not preventable, at most modifiable" (Lamb & Zusman, 1979, p. 1349). Rather, prevention takes the position, as Albee has so eloquently expressed, that emotional problems are not diseases that can be traced to some microorganism or DNA thread. Rather, they are "problems in living, problems often created by blows of fate, by damaging forces of a racist, sexist, ageist society" (Albee, 1980, p. 70). Prevention views dysfunctional behavior, whether individual or family, as an outgrowth of multiple factors interacting to place groups of individuals at risk. Albee (1982) has expressed this prevention equation as follows:

$$\frac{\text{Incidence of}}{\text{dysfunctional behavior}} = \frac{\text{organic factors} + \text{stress}}{\text{coping skills} + \text{self-esteem} + \text{support groups}}$$

In the following sections, Albee's prevention equation will be examined further.

Stress Theory:
A Theoretical Paradigm for Preventive Interventions

One part of the numerator of Albee's equation is stress. As stress accumulates, the potential for dysfunctional behavior grows. If one understands stress to mean any change in life, then Rodgers's (1973) statement that stress theory is "a special case of general developmental theory" (p. 218) is essentially correct. The life events that mark off the life cycle carry with them positive stress (eustress) and negative stress (distress). Life can be filled with boredom and a lack of challenge (hypostress), or it can be filled with excessive demands on time, labor, and energy. These stressful situations mark transition points that, if coped with successfully, facilitate a healthier individual and family environment.

An initial understanding of how stress affects organisms must be credited to Cannon (1939) and Selye (1974). Selye's laboratory work with animals found that stress-producing agents (called stressors) create a reaction that Selye called the general adaptation syndrome. When stress exceeds some threshold, Seyle found, laboratory animals enter into a stage of alarm. During this stage, the organism is on alert, calling on its defensive systems to combat the stressor. The period during which the body fights the noxious stressor is called the stage of resistance. If the body cannot defeat the noxious stressor, it enters the stage of exhaustion. Unable to overcome the damaging virus, bacterium, or other adverse stimulus, the body surrenders to the stressor and expires.

The ABCX Model

Although there are a number of models that have drawn on the pioneering research of Cannon and Selye, one of the most useful and elegant models of these is Hill's (1949, 1958) ABCX paradigm. Intended to explain the behavior of families, it is just as applicable, in my opinion, to explaining individual behavior. The letter A represents some event that brings discomfort, such as the death of a family member, a job promotion, relocation, or unemployment. B stands for the internal and external resources the family can use to fight the discomfort—wealth, friends, level of self-esteem, internal locus of control, coping abilities, and so on. C is the meaning the family attaches to the event. X is the crisis. Together, A, B, and C result in X. That is, the magnitude of the crisis, its duration, and the individual's or family's level of reorganization after the crisis are determined by the sum of A (the event) + C (its meaning) − B (the available resources).

The second part of Hill's model predicts how most families will react in a crisis. The crisis (X) trips the family into a period of disorganization in which the family marshals its resources—those already existing and those created in response to the event—to meet the crisis. The angle of recovery reflects the time necessary for the family to find a solution to its distress; the level of reorganization reflects the family's success in returning to a precrisis state.

Now let's take a closer look at the ABCX model by examining its components individually.

A: The Stressor. A, the event that causes discomfort, can also be called the "stressor." Stressors are events "of sufficient magnitude to bring about change in the family system" (McCubbin et al., 1980, p. 857). In line with our earlier definition of stress as any change in life, a stressor may be either a good or a bad event.

Life is filled with stressors. Some of these are sudden changes, such as an unexpected loss of rental housing or loss of employment. Others can be more insidious, slowly sapping a family's energy over a period of years, such as poverty, alcoholism, or chronic physical or emotional illness. Still others mark the flow of life. These include the addition of family members, entry into school, adolescence, dissatisfaction over a marriage, possibly divorce and remarriage, and the loss of family members.

B: Resources. The B in Hill's ABCX equation stands for the strengths that the family calls on in time of need. Those B factors, as McCubbin et al. (1980) describe them, include personal resources, a family system's internal resources, social support, and coping. Personal resources include financial resources, high self-esteem, and an internal locus of control.

A family system's internal resources are its integrative abilities. The term *family integration* means the degree of unity existing in the family. Where there are common family interests, a common family agenda for the future, and affection for one another, there is a high degree of family integration. Social support involves people outside the family who, in time of need, lend their strength to the family. This is accomplished by helping the family to feel loved, cared for, valued, and worthy, and by communicating to the family that it belongs.

The last factor, coping, involves the adaptive ways families use their B resources to handle a crisis. A family's adaptive capability is judged by its ability to mobilize its resources to confront a challenge and adjust to overcome that challenge.

C: The Meaning. C in Hill's model represents the meaning the individual or family attaches to the event. Events are not stressors unless the individual or family perceives them to be, and the degree of positive or negative disruption is again determined by the individual or family. Suppose a job transfer has been offered to a family member. At first glance, this would seem to be a positive event for the family, but it may not be. It may mean the family member's extended absence from the home, or it may mean a move to a new community. A promotion may then become a negative event in this family's life and acquire the status of crisis (Gullotta & Donohue, 1981).

X: The Crisis. The X in Hill's model represents the state of disorganization after a crisis-producing event. There are two types of crisis events. The first are called developmental or normative crises and are considered a normal part of living life. The birth of a child, a child's entry into school, and the death of an aged family member are illustrations of normative crises. These events confront the family with developmental tasks that, if coped with successfully, move the family on to another life stage.

The second type of crisis is called situational or catastrophic. These are events that affect only some families and are considered tragic, sometimes ruinous. For example, whereas the death of an aged parent after several months' illness could be considered a normative crisis, the drive-by shooting death of an adolescent in a gang-related incident would most likely be considered a catastrophic crisis. The surviving family members probably expected the aged parent to die first. Although the death of the aged parent causes the family pain, the loss was expected; the developmentalist would say it was "on time." The sudden loss of the adolescent, however, was not expected. The death was "off time." No one in the family expected that this child would die before his or her parents. The suffering associated with this loss would be predicted to be intense and long lasting.

Many situational, or catastrophic, crises, such as natural disasters, are sudden and unexpected, but some are not. Problems such as alcoholism, family violence, racism, and chronic unemployment are also ruinous in their impact on family life and are considered nonnormative events in a family's lifetime history.

Functional and Dysfunctional Responses to Crisis

Some adaptations in response to a crisis are dysfunctional. For example, overuse of alcohol or other drugs may numb the pain associated with uncaring and nonnuturing parents, but most of society would find unacceptable this means of coping with loss. Most of us would judge it destructive to the individual and the society at large.

Other adaptations can be considered functional. For example, if the adolescent turned to friends and other positive adult role models like teachers or the clergy for emotional support and found that support so that the relationship among these individuals was strengthened, most of us would judge this coping process leading to adaptation as constructive—that is, beneficial to the health of the individual and the greater society. Such constructive, or functional, methods of coping and adaptation in mental health are called "primary prevention" or, in lay terms, "wellness."

Prevention's Technology

In the rest of this chapter, we'll look at the technology of the primary prevention movement and the important role each of us has in enhancing our own emotional health and that of others in society (Gullotta, 1987, 1994). We will see that prevention's technology consists of four tools or interventions that correspond with the elements of Albee's formula. Those tools are education, community organization/systems intervention, competency promotion, and natural caregiving. Notice how this technology closely parallels Albee's incidence formula.

Education. Of all of prevention's tools, education is the most widely used. The premise is that by increasing our knowledge, we can change attitudes and ultimately the behavior that harms ourselves or others. Education can be used to ease the passage from one life event to another; information can be given to individuals to enhance their well-being. It can be presented as the spoken word, a visual image, and/or printed material. This information can take three forms.

The first of these forms is public information. This information stirs, warns, and opens us to circumstances that can adversely affect our lives. For example, public service announcements about excessive alcohol consumption are attempts to enlighten the public and to promote healthier behavior in regard to this powerful drug. Education also includes written material, like this volume, that encourages individuals to take responsibility for their own lives while sharing with them the findings the social sciences can offer about individuals, relationships, and the family. Here, the intention is to inform the reader not only of potential health hazards but of health-promoting activities as well. Public information can include videos, role-plays, and group learning experiences that provide the learner with new or improved skills for managing life. Research is very clear on the point that humans want some warning about an event before it happens (see Elliot & Eisdorfer, 1982). The time between the warning and the actual occurrence permits us to gather emotional resources (Hill's "B" factor) to handle the event. Preventionists call the educational technique that builds these resources *anticipatory guidance*, which may take as simple a form as printed material that explains an upcoming life event, such as the booklet *Caring About Kids* by the National Institute of Mental Health (NIMH) (1981), which explains divorce to young children. Or it may involve a mixture of print, film, and lecture material, like that used by health organizations teaching expectant teenage parents about childbirth and the infant.

Some educational approaches use behavioral techniques to promote increased self-awareness. This category includes such approaches as biofeedback, progressive relaxation, and Eastern meditation philosophies. These techniques provide informational feedback that permits individuals to acquire the skills to cope with life.

Finally, readers clearly should understand that, although education is the most widely used of all of prevention's tools, it is also the most ineffective. Studies have repeatedly shown that educational approaches increase knowledge, occasionally alter attitudes, but rarely change behavior (Meyer, 1995). It is when education is combined with each of the following instruments that its effectiveness as an intervention increases. The importance of this last statement cannot be more strongly emphasized. Together, prevention's technology can reduce the incidence of dysfunctional behavior. The effectiveness of this technology is dramatically reduced as elements are used separately.

Community Organization/Systems Intervention. The ability to live life effectively is sometimes impeded by forces beyond one's personal abilities. Such forces impede or limit fair access to life options and opportunities. The second tool of prevention is used to redress these inequities. The promise is not equality of condition. Rather, it is a fulfilling of this nation's covenant with its citizens for equality of opportunity. Obstructions can be removed in any of three ways.

Where obstructions exist because of the institutional practices or policies of an organization, individuals can work to modify or remove institutional barriers. One example that has shown some success is the pressure exerted by parents on local school boards to have a more direct role in the governing of the schools their children attend.

A second area for community organization/systems intervention (CO/SI) behavior is community resource development. Even in prosperous times, unemployment among minority youth is at least twice the rate of that found with middle-class white youth. Unable to legitimately earn living wages, the lure of the underground, illicit street economy is sometimes too enticing to resist, in spite of the risks associated with it. In CO/SI, the activity is focused on achieving a more equitable distribution of power to improve the standard of living of a group of people within a community. Neighborhood associations and community-owned, community-directed operations to establish minority business enterprises are two examples of CO/SI activities.

The third activity within the area of CO/SI activity is legislative or judicial action. This is the most controversial of the three approaches because it involves a change in the balance of political power in the direction of politically enfranchising the weak or correcting legislative injustice against them. If one of the keys to explaining dysfunction is a lack of power, then organizing and mobilizing a group for the purposes of acquiring power in a free society is a necessary and legitimate function of prevention activity. Such initiatives have been undertaken by the American Civil Liberties Union, Mothers Against Drunk Drivers, Mothers of Murdered Sons, and the National Association for the Advancement of Colored People, among others. These organizations are attempting through legislative and judicial means to put teeth into the phrase *equality of opportunity.* Court and legislative activities such as the equalization of per pupil school expenditures, the increased regulation of the sale of handguns, and the economic integration of housing in suburban communities illustrate possible activities in this area.

Competency Promotion. Competency promotion activities promote a feeling of being a part of, rather that apart from, society. They encourage feelings of worth, care for others, and belief in oneself. Encouraging such "pride" promotes increased self-esteem, an internal locus of control, and community interest rather than self-interest. Activities such as affective education and assertiveness training are both education and competency promotion tools. They are also examples of passive approaches to competency promotion. Passive approaches involve group activities of a classroom nature. They differ from the activities typically undertaken by wilderness schools, scouting, 4-H, and arts programs. These programs teach skills like climbing, canoeing, or stage-set construction and acting but emphasize, first and more important, interpersonal and community relationships. Because these activities involve action and are usually directed toward accomplishment of some task, they are called active approaches.

Social Support. On almost every issue, adults and youth turn not to professionals but to friends or others (coaches, teachers, youth leaders, the parents of friends, the clergy, and so on) for advice and guidance. Natural caregiving recognizes the ability within each of us to help a fellow human being. Natural caregiving extends beyond activities like those of helping another in similar straits (mutual self-help groups) to acknowledge the responsibility each of us has to fellow human beings (Cowen, 1982a). Natural caregiving involves behavior such as the sharing of knowledge, the sharing of experiences, compassionate understanding, companionship, and, when necessary, confrontation. Such caregiving is a reference point for people to acknowledge that they are an important part of an emotional network (system) that extends beyond family members and friends to all people.

Some of us may choose professions in which we become trained indigenous caregivers, such as teachers and the clergy. Others of us will sometime in our lives join a mutual self-help group to give and receive help from others who find themselves in similar straits—for example, Alateen. Regardless of the circumstance, it is vital to remember that each of us is an indigenous caregiver with a responsibility to assist his or her fellow human beings.

Summary

This chapter has reviewed several common theories that have contributed to the growing number of psychotherapeutic techniques currently in use in the Americas. This chapter also provided the reader with an overview of primary prevention. In a society in which an estimated 15% are "mentally ill," the importance of prevention cannot be underestimated. If this epidemiological estimate is correct, then more than 38 million individuals could benefit from professional help each year in the United States (Albee, 1990). Given that this far exceeds the current capacity of the mental health disciplines and the nation's financial means to pay for such services, the importance of reducing the incidence of new cases by even a modest 10% or 3.8 million cases makes eminent sense (Gullotta, 1994).

References

Albee, G. W. (1980). A competency model must replace the defect model. In L. A. Bond & J. C. Rosen (Eds.), *Competence and coping during adulthood* (pp. 75-104). Hanover, NH: University of New England Press.

Albee, G. W. (1982). Preventing psychopathology and promoting human potential. *American Psychologist, 37,* 1043-1050.

Albee, G. W. (1990). The answer is prevention. In P. Chance & T. G. Harris (Eds.), *The best of psychology today* (pp. 197-201). New York: McGraw-Hill.

Albee, G. W. (1992). Genes don't hurt people: People hurt people. *Contemporary Psychology, 37,* 16-17.

Albee, G. W., & Gullotta, T. P. (1986). Facts and fallacies about primary prevention. *Journal of Primary Prevention, 6,* 207-218.

Aldous, J. (1978). *Family careers: Developmental changes in families.* New York: Wiley.

Bandura, A. (1969). *Principles of behavior modification.* New York: Holt, Rinehart & Winston.

Bohman, M. (1978). Some genetic aspects of alcoholism and criminality: A population of adopters. *Archives of General Psychiatry, 35,* 269-276.

Broderick, C. B., & Smith, J. (1979). The general systems approach to the family. In W. R. Burr, R. Hill, F. I. Nye, & I. L. Reiss (Eds.), *Contemporary theories about the family* (pp. 112-129). New York: Free Press.

Burr, W. R., Leigh, G. K., Day, R. D., & Constantine, J. (1979). Symbolic interaction and the family. In W. R. Burr, R. Hill, F. I. Nye, & I. L. Reiss (Eds.), *Contemporary theories about the family* (pp. 42-111). New York: Free Press.

Cannon, W. B. (1939). *The wisdom of the body.* New York: Norton.

Caplan, G. (1961). *Prevention of mental disorders in children: Initial explorations.* New York: Basic Books.

Caplan, G. (1964). *Principles of preventive psychiatry.* New York: Basic Books.

Caplan, G. (1974). *Support systems and community mental health.* New York: Behavioral Publications.

Cooley, C. H. (1964). *Human nature and the social order.* New York: Scribner.

Cotton, N. S. (1979). The familial incidence of alcoholism. *Journal of Studies on Alcohol, 40,* 89-116.

Cowen, E. L. (1982a). Help is where you find it: Four informal helping groups. *American Psychologist, 37,* 385-395.

Cowen, E. L. (1982b). Primary prevention research: Barriers, needs, and opportunities. *Journal of Primary Prevention, 2,* 131-137.

Dager, E. Z. (1964). Socialization and personality development in the child. In H. T. Christensen (Ed.), *Handbook of marriage and the family* (pp. 230-245). Chicago: Rand McNally.

Elliot, G. R., & Eisdorfer, C. (Eds.). (1982). *Stress and human health: Analysis and implications of research.* New York: Springer.

Erikson, E. H. (1963). *Childhood and society* (2nd ed.). New York: Norton.

Erikson, K. (1966). *Wayward Puritans.* New York: John Wiley.

Freud, S. (1947). *The ego and the id.* London: Hogarth.

Gullotta, T. P. (1987). Prevention's technology. *Journal of Primary Prevention, 7,* 176-196.

Gullotta, T. P. (1994). The what, who, why, where, when, and how of primary prevention. *Journal of Primary Prevention, 15,* 5-14.

Gullotta, T. P., & Donohue, K. (1981). The corporate family: Theory and treatment. *Journal of Marriage and Family Therapy, 7,* 151-158.

Hill, R. (1949). *Families under stress.* New York: Harper & Row.

Hill, R. (1958). Social stresses on the family. *Social Casework, 34,* 139-150.

Hill, R., & Hansen, D. A. (1960). The identification of conceptual frameworks utilized in family study. *Marriage and Family Living, 22,* 299-311.

Hill, R., & Rodgers, R. H. (1964). The developmental approach. In H. T. Christensen (Ed.), *Handbook of marriage and the family* (pp. 280-322). Chicago: Rand McNally.

Holden, C. (1991). Depression: The news isn't depressing. *Science, 254,* 1450-1452.

Huff, C. R. (1990). *Gangs in America.* Newbury Park, CA: Sage.

Klein, D. C., & Goldston, S. E. (Eds.). (1977). *Primary prevention: An idea whose time has come.* Washington, DC: Government Printing Office.

Lamb, R., & Zusman, J. (1979). Drs. Lamb and Zusman reply. *American Journal of Psychiatry, 136,* 1349.

Lightman, A. (1983, May). Nothing but the truth. *Science, 83,* 24-26.

McCubbin, H. I., Joy, C. B., Cauble, A. E., Comeau, J. K., Patterson, J. M., & Needle, R. H. (1980). Family stress and coping: A decade review. *Journal of Marriage and the Family, 42,* 855-871.

Mead, G. H. (1962). *Mind, self and society: From the standpoint of a social behaviorist.* Chicago: University of Chicago Press.

Meyer, A. (1995). Minimization of substance abuse: What can be said at this point? In T. P. Gullotta, G. R. Adams, & R. Montemayor (Eds.), *Adolescent substance misuse* (pp. 201-232). Thousand Oaks, CA: Sage.

National Institute of Mental Health. (1981). *Caring about kids: When parents divorce.* Washington, DC: Government Printing Office.

Nye, I. F. (1979). Choice, exchange, and the family. In W. R. Burr, R. Hill, F. I. Nye, & I. L. Reiss (Eds.), *Contemporary theories about the family* (pp. 1-41). New York: Free Press.

Pitts, J. R. (1964). The structural functional approach. In H. T. Christensen (Ed.), *Handbook of marriage and the family* (pp. 30-53). Chicago: Rand McNally.

Plomin, R. (1990a). *Nature and nurture.* Pacific Grove, CA: Brooks/Cole.

Plomin, R. (1990b). The role of inheritance in behavior. *Science, 248,* 183-188.

Ritzer, G. (1983). *Sociological theory.* New York: Knopf.

Rodgers, R. H. (1964). Toward a theory of family development. *Journal of Marriage and the Family, 26,* 262-270.

Rodgers, R. H. (1973). *Family interaction and transaction.* Englewood Cliffs, NJ: Prentice Hall.

Selye, H. (1974). *Stress without distress.* Philadelphia: Lippincott.

Stryker, S. (1964). The interactional and situational approaches. In H. T. Christensen (Ed.), *Handbook of marriage and the family* (pp. 54-80). Chicago: Rand McNally.

PART II

Behaviors of Concern

CHAPTER 3

Attention-Deficit/
Hyperactivity Disorder

H. ANN BROCHIN

JOSEPH A. HORVATH

T he disorder known as attention-deficit/hyperactivity disorder (ADHD) is estimated to affect between 3% and 5% of children (Hynd, Hern, Voeller, & Marshall, 1991). ADHD is often misdiagnosed, however, so actual population values are a subject of dispute (Barkley, 1981, 1989; DuPaul, Barkley, & McMurray, 1991). Beyond dispute is the fact that individuals with ADHD experience profound difficulties in academic, social, and emotional functioning. Contrary to popular conceptions of the "hyperactive" child, the difficulties experienced by individuals with ADHD go far beyond mere trouble in sitting still or paying attention. ADHD manifests itself in varying forms across individuals, each of whom presents with a different sampling from among a cluster of symptoms. It is this complex and varying character that makes ADHD both frustrating and fascinating for clinicians and researchers.

According to current diagnostic criteria (American Psychiatric Association, 1994), a diagnosis of ADHD requires evidence of persistent problems of inattention and/or hyperactivity and impulsivity that are not due to mental retardation, pervasive developmental disorder, or other psychiatric disorders. These problems must also be evident before the age of 7 (American Psychiatric Association, 1994). *DSM-IV* distinguishes three types of ADHD based on identification of symptoms of inattention and hyperactivity-impulsivity.

ADHD, Combined Type, is diagnosed when symptoms of inattention and hyperactivity-impulsivity are present. ADHD, Predominantly Inattentive Type, is diagnosed when symptoms of inattention are present but symptoms of hyperactivity-impulsivity are not. ADHD, Predominantly Hyperactive-Impulsive Type, is diagnosed when symptoms of hyperactivity-impulsivity are present but symptoms of inattention are not. *DSM-IV* also allows for a diagnosis of Attention-Deficit/Hyperactivity Disorder Not Otherwise Specified when there are significant symptoms of inattention or hyperactivity-impulsivity but the formal diagnostic criteria are not met (American Psychiatric Association, 1994).

In addition to the core symptoms described above, individuals with ADHD often present with a variety of secondary or related problems. These problems include (but are not limited to) academic underachievement, low self-esteem, oppositionality, antisocial behavior, peer rejection, disordered family relations, specific cognitive and metacognitive deficits, specific sensorimotor deficits, and sleep problems. As this list suggests, a major focus of research on ADHD has been distinguishing putative causal factors (e.g., impulsivity) from the effects of those factors on personality and behavior (e.g., oppositionality).

ADHD is a chronic disorder, often continuing through adolescence and into adulthood (Barkley, Fischer, Edelbrock, & Smallish, 1990; Fischer, Barkley, Fletcher, & Smallish, 1993; Ratey, 1991; Shekim, 1990). Because ADHD is so prevalent, and because it affects nearly every aspect of a person's functioning, a basic understanding of the disorder is essential for those who provide psychological and psychiatric treatment to adolescents. In this chapter, we provide a general overview of theory and research on ADHD. We begin with a brief history, intended to show how our understanding of the disorder has evolved. We review the primary or core symptoms of ADHD (inattention, impulsivity, and hyperactivity) along with four important classes of secondary or related problems (school failure, peer rejection, family problems, and comorbid or accompanying psychiatric problems). We briefly describe current theories of the biological basis of ADHD. We describe five approaches to the prevention and treatment of ADHD—medication, family intervention, school-based intervention, peer relationship intervention, and psychotherapy. We conclude with a chapter summary and some useful maxims for parents and practitioners.

History

Prior to the 1960s, symptoms of inattention, impulsivity, and hyperactivity (along with associated problems) were commonly attributed to brain injury. What we now know as ADHD was referred to as "minimal brain damage" to distinguish these children from those with more comprehensive mental deficits. Minimal brain damage was thought to result from birth trauma, prenatal infection, or environmental toxins. Beginning in the 1960s, the focus of research and theory shifted to the behavioral manifestations of the disorder and away from supposed organic damage. The most salient behavioral manifestation was, of course, hyperkinetic motor behavior, and this symptom became central to theories of the disease. Chess (1960, cited in Barkley, 1990) defined the syndrome as an abnormally high rate of activity, and the then-current diagnostic criteria (American Psychiatric Association, 1968) labeled the disorder as "hyperkinetic reaction of childhood." Note that symptoms of inattention and impulsivity were viewed as secondary to, and perhaps caused by, a tendency toward hyperactive motor behavior (i.e., Betsy can't pay attention because she can't sit still long enough).

The hyperactivity model dominated through the early 1970s when the focus again shifted, this time to attentional components of the disorder. Evidence had accumulated suggesting that affected children differ widely in the degree of hyperactivity and that hyperactivity was situationally dependent. Furthermore, an influential study (Douglas, 1972) showed that "hyperkinetic" children showed consistent deficits in sustained attention or vigilance tasks. Gradually, hyperactivity came to be seen as a consequence, and not a cause, of inattention; motor activity was seen as functioning to shift attention (i.e., Betsy can't sit still because she cannot sustain attention). Reflecting this change in conceptualization, *DSM-III* (American Psychiatric Association, 1980) renamed the disorder "attention deficit disorder," giving a central role to deficits in sustained attention.

The 1980s brought yet another core symptom into focus—impulsivity. Researchers found that, under conditions of precise experimental control, ADHD children do not consistently show deficits in sustained attention (Douglas & Peters, 1979). These and related findings led to speculation that ADHD might be a disorder of behavioral control or volition rather than a disorder of attention. This idea was consistent with observations that children with ADHD can sustain attention for long periods of time if they are doing what they want to be doing. There are currently several versions of this volitional hypothesis. Zentall (1985), for example, theorized that individuals with ADHD have higher-than-normal thresholds of arousal. That is, they need more arousing stimuli to stay motivated or interested. Quay (1988) suggested that individuals with ADHD have deficits in behavioral inhibition—the capacity not to act. According to this theory, people with ADHD show patterns of inattention, hyperactivity, and impulsivity because they lack the capacity to effectively inhibit their own responding. Similarly, Barkley (1993) suggests that individuals with ADHD suffer from a comparative inability to delay responding. This inability, Barkley suggests, diminishes a person's capacity to mentally represent, and thus to be governed by, rules of behavior.

In summary, the scientific conceptualization of ADHD has evolved over the past 40 years, with each of the core symptoms enjoying an era of dominance. The era of emphasis on hyperactivity gave way to an era of emphasis on attention deficit, which now gives way to an era of emphasis on behavioral disinhibition. In what follows, we consider each of these symptoms individually.

Core Symptoms

Inattention

As most people expect, children with ADHD have difficulty with attention. Yet the precise mechanisms that account for these difficulties are still unclear. Some investigators consider distractibility the key attentional problem (Wender, 1987), in that the child's attention does not stay focused on the appropriate information or task (Landau, Lorch, & Milich, 1992). According to Wender (1987), distractibility is one reason ADHD children have trouble completing tasks or following the instructions necessary to complete tasks; the ADHD child is distracted by a competing event, which then becomes the focus of attention. Other researchers emphasize the difficulty the child with ADHD has sustaining attention over time.

This difference, between distractibility and difficulty with sustained attention, depends on whether or not there is an environmental stimulus that captures the child's attention. For example, if, while reading this chapter, a clown walked into the room and you stopped reading to look at the clown, you would be distracted. If, while reading this chapter, you found that after 10 minutes you just could not continue reading (perhaps not so unlikely), you would be having difficulty sustaining attention.

Landau et al. (1992) investigated whether distractibility or difficulty sustaining attention was involved in ADHD by showing both ADHD boys and non-ADHD boys, aged 6 to 12, a segment of a television show. The boys watched the segment twice, once with toys in the room and once without toys in the room. Following the show, the boys were given free and cued-recall tests. The boys were also videotaped, and time spent visually attending to the show was measured. The control group attended more than the ADHD group when toys were present in the room, suggesting that the problem for the ADHD boys was one of distraction. The two groups did not differ in the amount of information recalled, though the authors suggested that the information may not have been difficult enough to elicit differences in recall on this task.

As described in a previous section, many researchers now believe that the attentional problems shown by those with ADHD are secondary to a more fundamental deficit in behavioral inhibition. In general, deficits in impulse control have been more consistently demonstrated than have deficits in sustained attention (Barkley, 1990). Furthermore, as will be discussed later, evidence concerning the neurobiological basis for ADHD seems now to favor a volitional rather than an attentional model. Regardless of the nature or primacy of attentional deficits, they do appear to be situation specific and are not manifested in all circumstances (Frick & Lahey, 1991; Wender, 1987). In general, variability across episodes and settings in the manifestation of attentional and other ADHD symptoms is an important and complicating feature of the disorder.

Hyperactivity

Hyperactive motor behavior is probably one of the first symptoms noticed in the ADHD child, usually during the preschool years (Fowler, 1992). Parents and teachers describe these children as "overactive," "hyper," "overly curious," and acting "as if driven by a motor." Hyperactivity, like other symptoms of this disorder, is not always salient and depends on the degree of structure in a given situation (Frick & Lahey, 1991). According to a volitional account of ADHD, of course, the term *hyperactivity* is a misnomer. It is not exactly that ADHD children are overactive but that they are unable to regulate or inhibit their motor activity in accordance with social requirements (Braswell & Bloomquist, 1991). As a result, sudden transitions in the amount of motor activity that is socially acceptable are very difficult for these children. Commonly discussed examples are the transition from free play, or recess, back to the classroom and changing classes as in the case of high school students. These transitions require that essentially unharnessed motor activity be suddenly ceased—a near impossibility for individuals with untreated ADHD.

In many cases, hyperactivity diminishes somewhat at adolescence (Barkley, 1991), but there are cases where this symptom persists into adulthood. In those cases, the hyperactivity may manifest itself differently than in childhood and adolescence; the ADHD adult may fidget, squirm, appear restless, and may still have difficulty staying in his or her seat for sustained periods of time (Braswell & Bloomquist, 1991; Wender, 1987).

Impulsivity

Like inattention, impulsivity varies across individuals and situations. As described earlier, Wender (1987) and Barkley (1993) believe that impulse control, or its absence, is central to understanding the disorder. Thus, according to Barkley (1993), the ADHD child's problem with impulsivity is not failing to think before he or she acts but, instead, acting "before permitting time to think" (p. 4). Impulsivity also implies that the behavior of the ADHD child is not as responsive to contingencies and consequences as is the behavior of children without the disorder. Barkley (1990) refers to an "inability to adequately regulate behavior by rules and consequences" (p. 23) that characterizes the ADHD child. Apparently, contingencies that are strong enough to motivate the behavior of non-ADHD children, adolescents, and adults are often not strong enough to motivate the behavior of ADHD children, adolescents, and adults.

Deficits in rule-governed behavior explain why ADHD children need and respond better to consequences that are more immediate and salient (Braswell & Bloomquist, 1991). According to Barkley (1990), the developmental process by which rules are gradually internalized does not occur in ADHD children. As a consequence, rule-governed behavior is not acquired in an age-appropriate fashion. The use of verbally mediated rules to govern behavior is, of course, critical to the development of self-control, problem-solving ability, and compliant behavior in adolescence and adulthood (Barkley, 1981).

Related Problems

Academic Failure

Academic underachievement and accompanying low self-esteem are commonly observed difficulties with ADHD children and adolescents (Greene, 1993; Rief, 1993). Although the symptoms of ADHD mean that these children do not come to a learning situation well prepared to learn, Fowler (1992) describes elements of the typical learning environment that exacerbate the difficulties that ADHD children experience at school. According to Fowler (1992), as children with ADHD get further along in school, the demands for increased autonomy, longer assignments, more writing, and the lecture presentation format serve to make academic success more difficult to attain. Furthermore, children and adolescents with ADHD are at risk for a self-perpetuating cycle in which academic failure leads to perceptions of low self-efficacy (with accompanying negative affect) and this, in turn, leads to avoidance behavior and further academic failure. Early detection and intervention is critical to disrupt this destructive cycle before it becomes fully established in the life of the ADHD child or adolescent.

Peer Rejection

It has been consistently demonstrated that ADHD children are more likely to be rejected by their peers than are non-ADHD children (Henker & Whalen, 1989). The importance of successful peer relationships to the mental health of children, adolescents, and adults cannot be overstated. Research has shown a strong relationship between social status and later adjustment (Cowen, Pederson, Babigian, Izzo, & Trost, 1973). In adolescence, the quality of peer relationships has been found to influence everything from adolescents' appearance and values to self-esteem (O'Brien & Bierman, 1988). In his book on psychotherapy with adolescents, Meeks (1986) considers peer relationships so important that he lists an increase in peer relationships as a signal to consider discontinuing therapy. In spite of the clear importance of peer relationships, it is not yet clear why ADHD children are more likely to be rejected by their peers.

Certainly, with rejected children in general, deficits in social cognition may affect social status (Brochin & Wasik, 1992; Hartup, 1983; Rubin & Daniels-Beirness, 1983). Research with ADHD children, however, does not provide consistent evidence of social-cognitive deficits (Henker & Whalen, 1989). Landau and Moore (1991) point out that ADHD children may not suffer from a particular deficit in ability or skill when it comes to social situations but, instead, from a deficit in putting what they do know into practice. These authors cite research that shows that ADHD children possess nearly all of the attributes that have been correlated with peer rejection in the population of peer-rejected children at large. For example, Landau and Moore (1991) discuss studies that found aggression, off-task behavior, disruptive behavior, and learning disabilities to be correlated with higher incidences of rejection by peers. All of these factors are overrepresented in the ADHD population.

Nonetheless, some investigators find support for the hypothesis of specific skill deficits in ADHD children. For example, ADHD children who are rejected by their peers have been found to remember fewer social cues in a tape-recorded "testimonial" of a peer describing his behavior. This may point to possible deficits in encoding social cues (Moore, Hughes, & Robinson, 1992). Studies like this one highlight the need to continue investigating social skills deficits in children with ADHD to successfully develop prevention and treatment efforts.

Family Problems

The major family contribution to ADHD is genetic; ADHD is considered a heritable disorder. There is no evidence that parenting practices per se cause ADHD, although parents of ADHD children report considerable stress, particularly when the child has concomitant aggressive and oppositional behavior (Anastopoulos, Guevremont, Shelton, & DuPaul, 1992; Barkley, Anastopoulos, Guevremont, & Fletcher, 1992). Although it cannot be said for certain that ADHD children cause parenting stress, research on the bidirectional relationship between parent and child interaction supports the notion that an ADHD child's behavior affects his or her parent's behavior, which, in turn, affects the child's behavior. Patterson (1975) describes mutual influences between parent and child, which appear to operate below the level of awareness for participants, and Barkley, Guevremont, Anastopoulos, and Fletcher (1992) report similar findings. In the latter study, mothers of ADHD adolescents reported more negative communication with their children than did mothers of non-ADHD adolescents. They also reported more intense anger when conflicts occurred. In this study, the adolescents with ADHD and a comorbid oppositional defiant disorder had negative interactions with their mothers, even during an ostensibly neutral discussion. Of particular interest, the mothers of adolescents with ADHD and a comorbid oppositional defiant disorder were more likely to use "put-downs" and commands. They also provided fewer alternatives for problem solving. Thus, the patterns of interaction between ADHD children and their parents may make effective communication and conflict resolution more difficult.

Because ADHD is strongly heritable, the parents of ADHD children may themselves have ADHD. As a consequence, these parents may have all the deficits and comorbid conditions that their ADHD children have, and this should, of course, affect their interaction with their ADHD adolescents as well as their ability to carry out effective behavior-management plans. This is an important area of research and one that seems to have been neglected. Anastopoulos (personal communication, December 7, 1993) reports that, clinically, he often sees the parents of ADHD children having a difficult time with parent training programs. He believes that this may be related to the increased incidence of ADHD among these parents, but he reports that, at the current time, there are insufficient data to support this hypothesis.

Comorbid Disorders

ADHD children have a higher incidence of several psychiatric disorders and learning disabilities than does the general population. These comorbid conditions generally exacerbate the difficulties that the ADHD child and adolescent experience. Chief among the psychiatric disorders likely to co-occur in ADHD children are conduct disorder and oppositional defiant disorder (see Chapter 4 in this volume). According to Fowler (1992), between 40% and 60% of ADHD elementary school-aged children have oppositional defiant disorder, and between 20% and 30% have conduct disorder. Approximately 25% of these children have accompanying learning disabilities.

ADHD adolescents are also more likely to engage in antisocial behavior than are non-ADHD adolescents (Hinshaw, Heller, & McHale, 1992), but outcomes for ADHD adolescents with comorbid conduct disorder are often substantially worse than for those ADHD children and adolescents without conduct disorder. For example, in a longitudinal study that followed ADHD children for 8 years, Barkley et al. (1990) found that ADHD adolescents with comorbid conduct disorder were more likely to use cigarettes, illegal drugs, and alcohol. ADHD adolescents without comorbid conduct disorder did not show higher incidences of use than did non-ADHD peers. Similarly, an accompanying conduct disorder was associated with an elevated risk of school suspension. This risk is already elevated in ADHD children, relative to the general population, although ADHD adolescents do not show higher rates of being expelled from school or dropping out completely.

Finally, recent research suggests that there is an increased incidence of internalizing disorders among adolescents with ADHD (Fischer et al., 1993). Internalizing disorders include anxiety and depressive disorders. In a recent study, ADHD boys received significantly higher scores on the Children's Depression Inventory (CDI) when compared with a control group. When items addressing school, peer, or behavioral problems were removed, the authors found no difference in CDI scores between the ADHD group and the control group (Hoza, Pelham, Milich, Pillow, & McBride, 1993). The authors suggest that ADHD children are not more depressed in general but that ADHD children may be more depressed about their academic, social, and behavioral problems. This seems logical, given the pervasive and severe nature of their difficulties in these areas. Clearly, we are just beginning to get an adequate picture of the way in which ADHD affects adolescents and adults.

Biological Factors

There is broad consensus among investigators that ADHD is heritable and, therefore, neurologically based. The evidence for heritability is strong. In a study of monozygotic and dizygotic twins, the monozygotic twins were found to have significantly higher concordance rates of ADHD than were dizygotic twins, even when the contributions of IQ and reading achievement were taken into account (Gillis, Gilger, Pennington, & DeFries, 1992). In general, ADHD children are four times more likely than normal children to show a positive family history of ADHD (Cantwell, 1972).

A great deal of research has been directed toward identifying the neurobiological mechanisms responsible for ADHD. Although a detailed discussion is beyond the scope of this chapter, current thinking on the subject can be summarized fairly simply. The dominant account of the neurological basis for ADHD targets structures in the subcortex (thought to be involved in arousal and motor regulation) and structures in the frontal cortex (thought to be involved in behavioral inhibition). There are extensive connections between these two brain areas, and the neurons that make up these connections are primarily dopaminergic (i.e., they communicate via the neurotransmitter dopamine). It has been suggested that anomalies in the ADHD brain cause inhibitory circuits formed by these two brain structures to malfunction, leading to generalized deficits in response inhibition. A general deficit in response inhibition is thought by many researchers to account for the impulsivity, hyperactivity, and inattention that characterize ADHD (Barkley, 1993; Quay, 1988).

This cortico-frontal hypothesis is consistent with evidence obtained from studies of cerebral blood flow. These studies show subcortical areas, with projections to the frontal cortex, to be metabolically underactive in ADHD sufferers (Lou, Henriksen, & Bruhn, 1984; Lou, Henriksen, Bruhn, Borner, & Nielsen, 1989). This hypothesis is also supported by evidence of abnormal frontal-lobe morphology in ADHD sufferers (Hynd et al., 1991), although findings on this point have been inconsistent (Barkley, 1990). Finally, the cortico-frontal hypothesis is consistent with the demonstrated therapeutic effect of stimulant medication. Stimulant drugs such as methylphenidate (MPH) are found to alleviate core symptoms of the disorder. Because these drugs are thought to act on catecholaminergic cells (Barkley, 1990) of the sort found in the projections between the subcortex and frontal cortex, their therapeutic effect supports the cortico-frontal hypothesis. That is, it is consistent with the explanation that stimulant drugs work by improving the functioning of neural circuits thought to underlie behavioral inhibition.

Lest we present too tidy a picture, however, we should note that there is disagreement about the particulars of this very general model (e.g., Hechtman, 1993). In addition, some researchers question the validity of any unified model of ADHD when the behavioral manifestations of the disorder are so variable. For example, Hunt, Harralson, Hoehn, and Turner (1993) offer a three-part model of neurobiological subtypes. In this model, separate neurofunctional systems (cognitive, arousal, and behavioral inhibition) correspond to the three hallmark symptoms of impaired attention, hyperkinesis, and impulsivity. These systems are hypothesized to involve different brain structures and different neurotransmitter systems. Suffice it to say that biological explanations for ADHD persist in a variety of forms, and these hypotheses enjoy considerable support.

Treatment

Medication

There is no cure for ADHD. Rather, the disorder is managed through a carefully choreographed system of interventions—which must address every aspect of the child's, adolescent's, or adult's life. Medication is probably one of the most important interventions. Stimulants are the most prescribed medication for ADHD (Barkley, 1990), and the efficacy of these drugs is widely studied. At one time, it was believed that the stimulants had a "paradoxical" effect on children, meaning that, while the arousal and activity level of adults was increased by stimulants, the opposite effect was obtained when children took these drugs. Thus, it was believed that children responded to stimulants in a paradoxical fashion—by becoming less aroused and more calm. We now know this theory to be incorrect— stimulants increase arousal in the central nervous systems of both children and adults (DuPaul et al., 1991).

Stimulants increase arousal by sustaining the action of catecholamines (such as dopamine) at the neuronal synapse (Hynd et al., 1991). Among the stimulants, methylphenidate (MPH), distributed under the trade name Ritalin, is the most widely prescribed and the most widely studied. Other stimulants include dextroamphetamine (distributed as Dexedrine) and pemoline (distributed as Cylert). Pemoline is the longest acting of the three stimulant drugs, lasting up to 8 hours after administration (DuPaul et al., 1991). Other medications have also been used to treat ADHD. For example, tricyclic antidepressants, MAO inhibitors, and clonodine have been effective with some patients. Still, most researchers consider the stimulants a better alternative (DuPaul et al., 1991; Pelham, 1993).

One reason that stimulants are preferred is that they have been shown to have wide-ranging effects on behavior. Everything from behavior in a summer day treatment program (Pelham et al., 1992) to attention during a baseball game (Pelham et al., 1990) has been shown to improve with MPH. For example, aggressive, disruptive, and noncompliant behaviors have been rated as less problematic when male children and adolescents with ADHD are given MPH (Granger, Whalen, & Henker, 1993).

Similarly, a study by Hinshaw et al. (1992) found decreased antisocial behavior in boys given MPH. In this study, desirable objects were placed in a laboratory along with an answer sheet corresponding to a worksheet the boys were working on. Boys who were not on medication stole more items from the room and engaged in more property destruction than boys given MPH. Surprisingly, there was an increase in cheating on the worksheet (with the answer key) among the boys on medication. Hinshaw et al. (1992) posit that the boys on medication were more interested in their performance compared with the boys not on medication.

With respect to academic performance, MPH has been shown to improve classroom success over the short term (Carlson & Bunner, 1993; DuPaul et al., 1991; Pelham, 1993), and children with

ADHD are often aware of these effects. Boys in one study predicted better behavior and higher math scores when told they were taking medication as opposed to a placebo (Whalen, Henker, Hinshaw, Heller, & Huber-Dressler, 1991).

Before concluding that MPH is a panacea, however, a review of its drawbacks is in order. MPH enters and leaves the body quickly (DuPaul et al., 1991), requiring that adults carefully monitor its timing and administration. Schoolchildren who take MPH commonly go to the school nurse's office at lunchtime to receive their midafternoon administration of the drug. Problems of stigmatization of these children by their peers are not uncommon. There is a sustained-release version of the drug, which obviates the need for administration while at school, but some have questioned its efficacy, and there has been a lack of research.

There are several side effects associated with MPH. First, it is contraindicated in cases where the child has tics or neurological disorders, like Tourette's syndrome, because MPH has a propensity to exacerbate these problems (DuPaul et al., 1991). Other possible side effects include headaches, stomachaches, reduced appetite, and insomnia (Barkley et al., 1990). A child's height and weight gain can also be temporarily reduced by stimulant therapy, but this reduction has been found to be temporary (DuPaul et al., 1991). Finally, DuPaul et al. (1991) note "behavioral rebound" as a side effect. Behavioral rebound is the exhibition of symptoms that are more severe than when the child or adolescent is not on medication. This effect commonly occurs after the midday administration of medication has worn off (i.e., in the late afternoon).

There is no evidence of long-term benefit from taking MPH; all of the research to date demonstrates only short-term gains (Carlson & Bunner, 1993; DuPaul et al., 1991). Furthermore, there have been very few studies of the effects of MPH conducted on adolescents (Pelham, 1993), although it has been found to be effective with adults (Murphy, 1992; Wender, 1987).

Which children and adolescents with ADHD should be taking medication? Wender (1987) believes that all ADHD children should receive a trial administration of medication. Factors that should be assessed include the severity of the disorder, whether other interventions may be successful, whether or not there is a comorbid internalizing disorder, the parent and child's attitude toward medication, and the ability of parents to follow through on the administration of medication (DuPaul et al., 1991).

Family Intervention

Interventions with the family are critical when treating children and adolescents with ADHD. As mentioned, the ADHD child and adolescent typically experience difficulty in many settings. Parents often report difficulty managing the behavior of these children. Parent training programs are often used to help increase compliance (Newby, Fischer, & Roman, 1991). Barkley (1987) has developed such a program. The program not only addresses compliance but also helps families change those behaviors that maintain noncompliance in their children.

Barkley's program involves teaching parents what variables cause and/or exacerbate misbehavior in children, how to interact with their children positively around play, how to attend to and reinforce positive behaviors, how to use time-out, how to manage children's behavior in public, and how to use a token economy. For example, when trained to use time-out, parents are taught what to say to a child when putting him or her in time-out, where to put a time-out chair, how long to leave a child in time-out, and what to do if a child leaves a time-out chair prematurely. There is empirical support for the program's efficacy. Anastopoulos, Shelton, DuPaul, and Guevremont (1993) found that parents of ADHD children, 6 to 11 years old, who participated in Barkley's parent training program reported decreased severity of ADHD symptoms in their children, increased esteem, and decreased reported stress. Furthermore, these gains were maintained at a 2-month follow-up. Barkley (1987) notes, however, that the program is not effective with every parent or every child, nor is it recommended for adolescents.

Robin (1990) developed a program for intervention with the parents of adolescents with ADHD. The program includes education about ADHD, addressing issues related to medication (though Robin is clear that he does not force adolescents to take medication), helping the parents to work as a team in setting firm limits and rules with the adolescent, addressing the parent's role in academic tasks (including homework), teaching the family how to engage in problem solving, and challenging some of the distorted beliefs held by parents and adolescents that may interfere with successful problem solving (Robin, 1990). Robin reports that his program takes into account the developmental tasks associated with adolescence. In addition, he believes that a problem-solving intervention is nonauthoritarian and, therefore, more likely to be more palatable to the adolescent.

Recently, Barkley, Guevremont, et al. (1992) found that behavior-management training (a modification of Barkley's program), problem-solving and communication training (Robin's program), and structural family therapy all produced some improvements in families who have a 12- to 18-year-old child with ADHD. This improvement consisted of decreases in reported depression in mothers of these children, number of conflicts, intensity of anger during the conflicts, and school adjustment problems. Improvements were not clinically significant, however, meaning that when individual progress was assessed, the percentage of subjects who made significant improvement was small (between 5% and 30%).

Finally, support groups have been found to be beneficial for families of ADHD children. The largest, CH.A.D.D. (Children and Adults with Attention Deficit Disorders) has 23,000 members and 530 chapters across the country. CH.A.D.D. offers monthly meetings at which participants can obtain information about ADHD as well as support from other parents. CH.A.D.D. also offers regional conferences and lending libraries. Joanne Evans, president of CH.A.D.D., reports that meeting other parents is often helpful in "learning how to meet the challenges of working with these [ADHD] kids" (personal communication, December 13, 1993). She notes that these groups help parents realize that they are not to blame for their child's disorder and that they are not alone. (The headquarters for CH.A.D.D. is located at 499 Northwest 70th Ave., Suite 109, Plantation, FL 33317.)

School-Based Intervention

The accompanying problems of academic failure, peer rejection, cognitive deficits, and conduct disorders all require that a strong system of intervention be established in the classroom if the child or adolescent with ADHD is to experience success (Pfiffner & Barkley, 1990). In the *CH.A.D.D. Educators Manual,* Fowler (1992) offers a comprehensive list of interventions for the classroom. For example, she suggests using a reward menu that includes activity rewards, tangible rewards, and group-activity rewards. Pfiffner and Barkley (1990) also cite empirical support for reward menus and token economy systems, and they recommend that students participate in choosing their own rewards. Response cost, or the "loss of a reinforcer contingent on inappropriate behavior" (Pfiffner & Barkley, 1990, p. 513), is also considered an important component of a behavior-management program for this population.

Fowler (1992) describes several classroom modifications that can be used to maximize productivity in the classroom. These include frequent breaks, scheduling academic subjects in the morning hours, preferential seating in the classroom near positive peers but close to the teacher, and cues for the child when he or she is off task. Finally, Fowler (1992) discusses the need for modifications in the student's curriculum. For example, she suggests using high-interest activities and computers. She also suggests reducing the quantity of work, thus allowing more time to complete tasks. Grade retention has not been found to be a successful intervention for these children, nor has sending unfinished schoolwork home to be completed in the evening. It should be noted that most studies that assess the effects of educational interventions use elementary school children, and this limits the ability to infer what would be effective with older children (Fiore, Becker, & Nero, 1993).

Peer Relationship Interventions

As mentioned earlier, there is still some debate about whether children with ADHD have particular social skill deficits or more general cognitive-behavioral deficits that account for their difficulties with peers. At this point, the same interventions that are applied to the general population of rejected children are often applied to children with ADHD as well. For example, social problem-solving training is often used to address the interpersonal and social problems of children with ADHD. Oden and Asher (1977) coached unpopular children in "getting started" in a peer interaction. The importance of peer-entry skills has been demonstrated in studies that distinguish children who are rejected from those who are accepted by their peers (Putallaz & Gottman, 1981). In a now classic study, Allen, Hart, Buell, Harris, and Wolf (1964) used reinforcement and extinction to increase the interaction of an isolated nursery school child. Results suggested that behavioral approaches may increase appropriate peer interaction.

Recent research suggests that we need to consider which types of situations are particularly problematic for rejected children when we design intervention programs (Feldman & Dodge, 1987). Brochin and Wasik (1992) found that unpopular kindergarten children had more difficulty generating appropriate alternative strategies for problems that involved conflict but not for problems involving initiation of interaction with a peer or the maintenance of a social interaction. Many interventions that have been studied in the at-large population of rejected children have not been studied in ADHD children. Peer relationship researchers note the need for continued research to help address when and how interventions can be most successful (Mize & Ladd, 1990).

Therapy

There is at this point a large body of research looking at the effects of cognitive-behavioral therapy with ADHD children. Cognitive-behavioral therapy involves applying cognitive processes like problem solving, relaxation techniques, and other strategies to help modify behavior. This therapy is based on behavior therapy but adds the tenet that what people believe about their behavior is also important (Reber, 1985). When working with ADHD children, cognitive-behavioral therapy can involve interventions such as problem-solving training, anger management, social-skills training, and/or relaxation training (Braswell & Bloomquist, 1991). Problem-solving training is frequently used as a cognitive-behavioral therapy with this population. Braswell and Bloomquist (1991) suggest that it addresses some of the deficits ADHD children exhibit (e.g., acting before they think). The most in-depth study of problem-solving training has been undertaken by Spivack, Shure, and Platt (Shure & Spivack, 1972, 1979; Spivack, Platt, & Shure, 1976). They have identified five interpersonal cognitive problem-solving skills necessary for adjustment (Spivack et al., 1976). These skills are the ability to be sensitive to problems, the ability to generate alternative solutions, the ability to state the means used to achieve solutions to problems, the ability to consider consequences, and the ability to understand causes of behavior. Braswell and Bloomquist's (1991) program, and most others, focus on teaching these skills.

In general, the success of cognitive-behavioral therapy has been limited and disappointing (Abramowitz & O'Leary, 1991). A major criticism of cognitive-behavioral interventions, and one that may shed light on their lack of demonstrated efficacy, is that children and adolescents with ADHD have performance deficits rather than skill deficits, and thus teaching skills will have limited effectiveness (Barkley, 1991). According to Barkley (1991), ADHD "is not a deficit in knowing what to do, but in doing what you know" (p. ix). Braswell and Bloomquist (1991) recognize these limitations and recommend changes that need to be made in the classroom and in the training of school personnel to help children generalize what is learned in therapy to the classroom.

Depending on what, if any, comorbid conditions are involved, other individual interventions may be needed for the ADHD child. For example, a child with ADHD who has a history of trauma may also benefit from more traditional therapy (Braswell & Bloomquist, 1991). Individual psychotherapy may also be indicated to treat accompanying depression or anxiety (Robin, 1990). We know of no empirical evidence, however, to support the proposition that individual psychotherapy, in itself, is an effective treatment for ADHD. It cannot be emphasized enough, therefore, that multiple treatment approaches are indicated when treating children and adolescents with ADHD (Braswell & Bloomquist, 1991).

In some cases, where the behavior of ADHD children cannot be managed in the regular education or home setting, residential schools can provide the comprehensive and multiple treatments that these children need. Generally, the goal of these programs is to provide interventions by educational, residential, and therapeutic staff who are knowledgeable and skilled in the treatment of ADHD. Families are encouraged to participate in this type of program to learn strategies for managing their children at home. Finally, in very severe cases, or in times of crisis, the ADHD child may need to be hospitalized. Inpatient hospitalization may be warranted to treat severe depression, severe anxiety, or, in particular, suicidality. In general, hospitalization represents a stopgap measure and usually does not address ADHD or its symptoms.

Conclusion

To summarize, we have said that ADHD is a pervasive and severe disorder, emerging in early childhood, that is characterized by inattention, impulsivity, and hyperactivity. Children and adolescents with this disorder are at increased risk for school failure, peer rejection, family problems, and comorbid conduct and internalizing disorders. ADHD is heritable, with a neurobiological basis that probably involves catecholaminergic pathways in the frontal and subcortex. ADHD is a multiplex disorder with different patients displaying different patterns of symptoms. Current conceptualizations of ADHD emphasize deficits in behavioral inhibition as primary in its etiology. Children and adolescents appear to benefit from multiple treatment approaches, including stimulant medication, family and school-based interventions, peer-related interventions, and psychotherapy.

Based on the clinical experience of the first author, we conclude with two take-home lessons for the parent, teacher, or clinician charged with the care of a child or adolescent with ADHD. The first of these concerns the necessity of early detection and accurate differential diagnosis. Undiagnosed ADHD creates a risk for persistent failure in the academic and social realms, with the attendant cost to self-esteem and psychological adjustment. Children in whom the disorder is detected and treated early can be spared a great deal of suffering and, in general, can expect better adult outcomes. Yet ADHD presents itself in a bewildering variety of forms and is apparently quite easy to misdiagnose. For example, clinicians sometimes rule out a diagnosis of ADHD as soon as they see evidence of a child's capacity for sustained attention to television or play—a serious mistake. As mentioned, the new diagnostic manual provides for diagnosis based on symptoms of either inattention or hyperactivity-impulsivity. Further research is needed to determine the differences among the subtypes identified by the new diagnostic criteria. Open and frequent communication between parents, teachers, and mental health professionals is also critical to arriving at an accurate picture of the pattern of difficulties that a child experiences across settings.

A second important lesson concerns the tendency for interventions with ADHD children and adolescents to lose their effectiveness over time and the corresponding need for flexibility and persistence on the part of the parent, teacher, or clinician. Children and adolescents with ADHD seem to habituate to rewards, and to punishments, much more quickly than other children. Similarly, children and adolescents with ADHD have a great deal of difficulty sticking with programs of treatment—they miss appointments, forget needed materials, and generally lose interest. As a consequence of this tendency for effects to fade, those charged with the care of children and adolescents with ADHD must arm themselves with variety and persistence. Single rewards must be replaced with menus of rewards, programs of treatment must be varied or rotated, and a great deal of patience must be exercised. At all costs, the frustrating inability of the ADHD child or adolescent to sustain effort and interest must be treated as a symptom of the disorder, and not as a sign of bad intentions or resistance. It seems to be in the strange, volitional character of this disorder that most individuals suffering with ADHD want very much to try but, in a real sense, need help in trying.

References

Abramowitz, A. J., & O'Leary, S. G. (1991). Behavioral interventions for the classroom: Implications for students with ADHD. *School Psychology Review, 20,* 220-234.

Allen, K. E., Hart, B., Buell, J., Harris, F. R., & Wolf, M. M. (1964). Effects of social reinforcement on isolate behavior of a nursery school child. *Child Development, 35,* 511-518.

American Psychiatric Association. (1968). *Diagnostic and statistical manual of mental disorders* (2nd ed.). Washington, DC: Author.

American Psychiatric Association. (1980). *Diagnostic and statistical manual of mental disorders* (3rd ed.). Washington, DC: Author.

American Psychiatric Association. (1994). *Diagnostic and statistical manual of mental disorders* (4th ed.). Washington, DC: Author.

Anastopoulos, A. D., Guevremont, D. C., Shelton, T. L., & DuPaul, G. J. (1992). Parenting stress among families of children with attention deficit hyperactivity disorder. *Journal of Abnormal Child Psychology, 20,* 503-520.

Anastopoulos, A. D., Shelton, T. L., DuPaul, G. J., & Guevremont, D. C. (1993). Parent training for attention-deficit hyperactivity disorder: Its impact on parent functioning. *Journal of Abnormal Child Psychology, 21,* 581-596.

Barkley, R. A. (1981). *Hyperactive children.* New York: Guilford.

Barkley, R. A. (1987). *Defiant children.* New York: Guilford.

Barkley, R. A. (1989). Attention deficit hyperactivity disorder. In E. M. Mash & R. A. Barkley (Eds.), *Treatment of childhood disorders* (pp. 39-72). New York: Guilford.

Barkley, R. A. (1990). *Attention deficit hyperactivity disorder.* New York: Guilford.

Barkley, R. A. (1991). Foreword. In L. Braswell & M. L. Bloomquist, *Cognitive-behavioral therapy with ADHD children* (pp. vii-xi). New York: Guilford.

Barkley, R. A. (1993). A new theory of ADHD. *ADHD Report, 1,* 1-4.

Barkley, R. A., Anastopoulos, A. D., Guevremont, D. C., & Fletcher, K. E. (1992). Adolescents with attention deficit hyperactivity disorder: Mother-adolescent interactions, family beliefs and conflicts, and maternal psychopathology. *Journal of Abnormal Child Psychology, 20,* 263-288.

Barkley, R. A., Fischer, M., Edelbrock, C. S., & Smallish, L. (1990). The adolescent outcome of hyperactive children diagnosed by research criteria: An 8-year prospective follow-up study. *Journal of American Academy of Child and Adolescent Psychiatry, 29,* 546-557.

Barkley, R. A., Guevremont, D. C., Anastopoulos, A. D., & Fletcher, K. E. (1992). A comparison of three family therapy programs for treating family conflicts in adolescents with attention-deficit hyperactivity disorder. *Journal of Consulting and Clinical Psychology, 60,* 450-462.

Braswell, L., & Bloomquist, M. L. (1991). *Cognitive-behavioral therapy with ADHD children.* New York: Guilford.

Brochin, H. A., & Wasik, B. H. (1992). Social problem solving among popular and unpopular children. *Journal of Abnormal Child Psychology, 20,* 377-391.

Cantwell, D. P. (1972). Psychiatric illness in the families of hyperactive children. *Archives of General Psychiatry, 27,* 414-427.

Carlson, L. L., & Bunner, M. R. (1993). Effects of methylphenidate on the academic performance of children with attention-deficit hyperactivity disorder and learning disabilities. *School Psychology Review, 22,* 184-198.

Chess, S. (1960). Diagnosis and treatment of the hyperactive child. *New York State Journal of Medicine, 60,* 2379-2385.

Cowen, E. L., Pederson, A., Babigian, H., Izzo, L. D., & Trost, M. A. (1973). Long-term follow-up of early detected vulnerable children. *Journal of Consulting and Clinical Psychology, 41,* 438-446.

Douglas, V. I. (1972). Stop, look, and listen: The problem of sustained attention and impulse control in hyperactive and normal children. *Canadian Journal of Behavioral Science, 4,* 259-282.

Douglas, V. I., & Peters, K. G. (1979). Toward a clearer definition of the attentional deficits of hyperactive children. In G. Hale & M. Lewis (Eds.), *Attention and the development of cognitive skills* (pp. 173-248). New York: Plenum.

DuPaul, G. J., Barkley, R. A., & McMurray, M. B. (1991). Therapeutic effects of medication on ADHD: Implications for school psychologists. *School Psychology Review, 20,* 203-219.

Feldman, E., & Dodge, K. A. (1987). Social information processing and sociometric status: Sex, age, and situational effects. *Journal of Abnormal Child Psychology, 15,* 211-227.

Fiore, T. A., Becker, E. A., & Nero, R. C. (1993). Educational interventions for students with attention deficit disorder. *Exceptional Children, 60,* 163-173.

Fischer, M., Barkley, R. A., Fletcher, K. E., & Smallish, L. (1993). The stability of dimensions of behavior in ADHD and normal children over an 8-year follow-up. *Journal of Abnormal Child Psychology, 21,* 315-337.

Fowler, M. (1992). *CH.A.D.D. educators manual.* Plantation, FL: CH.A.D.D.

Frick, P. J., & Lahey, B. B. (1991). Nature and characteristics of attention-deficit hyperactivity disorder. *School Psychology Review, 20,* 163-173.

Gillis, J. J., Gilger, J. W., Pennington, B. F., & DeFries, J. C. (1992). Attention deficit disorder in reading-disabled twins: Evidence for a genetic etiology. *Journal of Abnormal Child Psychology, 20,* 303-315.

Granger, D. A., Whalen, C. K., & Henker, B. (1993). Perception of methylphenidate effects on hyperactive children's peer interactions. *Journal of Abnormal Child Psychology, 21,* 535-549.

Greene, R. (1993). Hidden factors affecting the educational success of ADHD students. *ADHD Report, 1,* 8-9.

Hartup, W. W. (1983). Peer relations. In P. H. Mussen (Ed.), *Handbook of child psychology* (pp. 103-106). New York: John Wiley.

Hechtman, L. (1993). Neuroimaging findings in ADHD. *ADHD Report, 1,* 6-7.

Henker, B., & Whalen, C. K. (1989). Hyperactivity and attention deficits. *American Psychologist, 44,* 216-223.

Hinshaw, S. P., Heller, T., & McHale, J. P. (1992). Covert antisocial behavior in boys with attention deficit hyperactivity disorder: External validation and effects of methylphenidate. *Journal of Consulting and Clinical Psychology, 60,* 274-281.

Hoza, B., Pelham, W. E., Milich, R., Pillow, D., & McBride, K. (1993). The self-perceptions and attributions of attention deficit hyperactivity disordered and nonreferred boys. *Journal of Abnormal Child Psychology, 21,* 271-286.

Hunt, R. D., Harralson, P., Hoehn, R., & Turner, T. (1993). Neurobiological subtypes of ADHD. *CH.A.D.D.E.R., 7,* 7-10.

Hynd, G. W., Hern, K. L., Voeller, K. K., & Marshall, R. M. (1991). Neurobiological basis of attention-deficit hyperactivity disorder (ADHD). *School Psychology Review, 20,* 174-186.

Landau, S., Lorch, E. P., & Milich, R. (1992). Visual attention to and comprehension of television in attention-deficit hyperactivity disordered and normal boys. *Child Development, 63,* 928-937.

Landau, S., & Moore, L. A. (1991). Social skill deficits in children with attention-deficit hyperactivity disorder. *School Psychology Review, 20,* 235-251.

Lou, H. C., Henriksen, L., & Bruhn, P. (1984). Focal cerebral hypoperfusion in children with dysphasia and/or attention deficit disorder. *Archives of Neurology, 41,* 825-829.

Lou, H. C., Henriksen, L., Bruhn, P., Borner, H., & Nielsen, J. B. (1989). Stiatal dysfunction in attention deficit and hyperkinetic disorder. *Archives of Neurology, 46,* 48-52.

Meeks, J. E. (1986). *The fragile alliance* (3rd ed.). Malabar: Robert E. Krieger.

Mize, J., & Ladd, G. W. (1990). Toward the development of successful social skills training for preschool children. In S. D. Asher & J. D. Coie (Eds.), *Peer rejection in childhood* (pp. 338-361). New York: Cambridge University Press.

Moore, L. A., Hughes, J. N., & Robinson, M. (1992). A comparison of the social information-processing abilities of rejected and accepted hyperactive children. *Journal of Clinical Child Psychology, 21,* 123-131.

Murphy, K. R. (1992). Coping strategies for ADHD adults. *CH.A.D.D.E.R., 6,* 10.

Newby, R. F., Fischer, M., & Roman, M. A. (1991). Parent training for families of children with ADHD. *School Psychology Review, 20,* 252-265.

O'Brien, S. F., & Bierman, K. L. (1988). Conceptions and perceived influence of peer groups: Interviews with preadolescents and adolescents. *Child Development, 59,* 1360-1365.

Oden, S., & Asher, S. R. (1977). Coaching children in social skills for friendship making. *Child Development, 48,* 495-506.

Patterson, G. R. (1975). *Families.* Champaign, IL: Research Press.

Pelham, W. E. (1993). Pharmacotherapy of children with attention-deficit hyperactivity disorder. *School Psychology Review, 22,* 199-227.

Pelham, W. E., McBurnett, K., Harper, G., Milich, R., Murphy, D., Clinton, J., & Thiele, C. (1990). Methylphenidate and baseball playing in ADHD children: Who's on first? *Journal of Consulting and Clinical Psychology, 58,* 130-133.

Pelham, W. E., Murphy, D. A., Vannatta, K., Milich, R., Licht, B. G., Gnagy, E. M., Greenslade, K. E., Greiner, A. R., & Vodde-Hamilton, M. (1992). Methylphenidate and attributions in boys with attention-deficit hyperactivity disorder. *Journal of Consulting and Clinical Psychology, 60,* 282-292.

Pfiffner, L. J., & Barkley, R. A. (1990). Educational placement and classroom management. In R. A. Barkley (Ed.), *Attention deficit hyperactivity disorder* (pp. 498-539). New York: Guilford.

Putallaz, M., & Gottman, J. M. (1981). An interactional model of children's entry into peer groups. *Child Development, 52,* 986-994.

Quay, H. C. (1988). Attention deficit disorder and the behavioral inhibition system: The relevance of the neuropsychological theory of Jeffrey A. Gray. In L. Bloomingdale & J. Sergeant (Eds.), *Attention deficit disorder: Criteria, cognition, and intervention* (pp. 117-126). New York: Pergamon.

Ratey, J. J. (1991). Paying attention to attention in adults. *CH.A.D.D.E.R., 5,* 13.

Reber, A. S. (1985). *Dictionary of psychology.* New York: Penguin.

Rief, S. F. (1993). *How to reach and teach ADD/ADHD children.* West Nyack, NY: Center for Applied Research in Education.

Robin, A. (1990). Training families with ADHD adolescents. In R. A. Barkley (Ed.), *Attention deficit hyperactivity disorder* (pp. 462-497). New York: Guilford.

Rubin, K. H., & Daniels-Beirness, T. (1983). Concurrent and predictive correlates of sociometric status in kindergarten and grade one children. *Merrill-Palmer Quarterly, 29,* 337-351.

Shekim, W. O. (1990). Adult attention deficit hyperactivity disorder, residual state (ADHD, RS). *CH.A.D.D.E.R., 4,* 16.

Shure, M. B., & Spivack, G. (1972). Means-ends thinking, adjustment, and social class among elementary school-aged children. *Journal of Consulting and Clinical Psychology, 38,* 348-353.

Shure, M. B., & Spivack, G. (1979). Interpersonal cognitive problem-solving and primary prevention: Programming for preschool and kindergarten children. *Journal of Clinical Child Psychology, 2,* 89-94.

Spivack, G., Platt, J. J., & Shure, M. B. (1976). *The problem-solving approach to adjustment.* San Francisco: Jossey-Bass.

Wender, P. H. (1987). *The hyperactive child, adolescent, and adult.* New York: Oxford University Press.

Whalen, C. K., Henker, B., Hinshaw, S. P., Heller, T., & Huber-Dressler, A. (1991). Messages of medication: Effects of actual vs. informed medication status on hyperactive boys' expectancies and self-evaluations. *Journal of Consulting and Clinical Psychology, 59,* 602-606.

Zentall, S. S. (1985). A context for hyperactivity. In K. D. Gadow & I. Bialer (Eds.), *Advances in learning and behavioral disabilities* (Vol. 4, pp. 273-343). Greenwich, CT: JAI.

• CHAPTER 4 •

Oppositional Defiant Disorder

BURTON I. BLAU

Overview

The *DSM-IV* (APA, 1994) includes attention-deficit/hyperactivity disorder, conduct disorder, and oppositional defiant disorder under the broad heading of "Attention-Deficit and Disruptive Behavior Disorders." Although several attempts have been made to differentiate among these disorders, they have not proven totally successful because the disorders share similar behaviors and the relationships among them are very complex. There has been a great deal written about attention-deficit/hyperactivity disorder (ADHD) and considerable attention given to conduct disorders, but there is a paucity of information about oppositional defiant disorder (ODD). As a case in point, Kazdin (1993) refers to most clinical dysfunctions and the at-risk behaviors that emerge, but does not identify ODD specifically. There is the observation that "adolescents are dependent on living conditions of their parents . . . and are vulnerable to the impact of conditions well beyond their control" (p. 129). ODD is the most recently reformulated disorder among the three mentioned above and has begun to take on an identity of its own. A very brief review of some of the differences and similarities of these three disorders follows, with the intent to discover why oppositional defiant disorder receives its own recognition in the *DSM-IV* (APA, 1994).

AUTHOR'S NOTE: The able assistance of Michelle Mattingly in the preparation of this chapter is gratefully acknowledged and appreciated.

ADHD concentrates on hyperactivity, attention problems, and impulsivity found in children as early as 4 years old but usually not recognized until the child attends school. Rapoport and Ismond (1990) report that the course of the disorder typically follows one of these patterns: (a) All symptoms continue into adulthood with possible development of antisocial personality disorder; (b) symptoms dissipate or disappear in adolescence; or (c) hyperactivity disappears but inattention, impulsivity, and social immaturity persist into adolescence and adulthood.

In school, difficulties exist in completing work and following or listening to directions and intensify when the situation demands sustained attention in a group setting where distracting stimuli are always present (Rapoport & Ismond, 1990). Age is a factor in behavior or symptom emphasis. Younger children usually display more gross motor overactivity, whereas older children generally exhibit excessive fidgeting, restlessness, or impulsive behaviors. The *DSM-IV* (APA, 1994) lists a total of 18 symptoms or behaviors of which 6 must be met for a diagnosis of having one of the two types of ADHD. For example, the inattentive type includes behaviors consistent with problems organizing tasks and activities, being easily distracted by extraneous stimuli, and shifting from one uncompleted activity to another. The hyperactive-impulsive type has difficulty remaining seated when required to do so, blurts out answers to questions before they have been completed, and talks excessively (APA, 1994). Conduct disorder and oppositional defiant disorder can be concurrently diagnosed with ADHD, but conduct disorder and oppositional defiant disorder would not appear together as clinical dysfunctions.

Conduct disorders are those persistent behaviors in which adolescents engage that violate the basic rights of others and/or the norms of society (Gormly & Brodzinsky, 1993). Data from a 1984 U.S. Bureau of the Census report indicate that nearly half of the arrests for acts of vandalism, car thefts, burglary, and arson involved adolescents under the age of 18 (Gormly & Brodzinsky, 1993). The nature of these conduct-disordered behaviors are persistent and repetitive, while the consequences are more serious than those involved in a mischievous prank (Rapoport & Ismond, 1990). Rapoport and Ismond (1990) state that research indicates that predisposing factors for some form of conduct disorder may include economic factors, size of the family, and inconsistent or poor parenting. As a result of their deviant behaviors, these children experience academic failures and rejection from their peers; thus the path to delinquency widens. Gormly and Brodzinsky (1993) say: "Ultimately, these children identify with other deviant peers who encourage each other into more deliberate acts of aggression and violence" (p. 379). Although some researchers believe there is a clear link between deviant behavior and family, others do not think the causal link can be inferred. Peer influence has been concluded to be most highly related to status violation, that is, those behaviors that are not legal offenses because of the adolescent's minor status in society (e.g., truancy, running away from home, sexual promiscuity) (Gormly & Brodzinsky, 1993). Violent acts, such as fighting or possessing a weapon, and serious violations of the law, including burglary, were most significantly related to community poverty and external pressures, specifically high unemployment and a high crime rate (Gormly & Brodzinsky, 1993). Of interest, it has been concluded that most antisocial teenagers do not become antisocial adults; but when adults are criminals, the origins of this lifestyle usually can be traced to antisocial attitudes and behavior in childhood and adolescence. With oppositional defiant disorder, similar characteristics of attitude prevail, but there is no evidence of the violation of the basic rights of others, nor are major social rules and norms abandoned.

ODD, as defined by the *DSM-IV* (APA, 1994), is a disturbance of at least 6 months during which at least four of the following eight are present: (a) often loses temper, (b) often argues with adults, (c) often actively defies or refuses adult requests or rules, (d) often deliberately does things that annoy other people, (e) often blames others for his or her own mistakes, (f) is often touchy or easily annoyed by others, (g) is often angry and resentful, and (h) is often spiteful or vindictive. As mentioned previously, many similar characteristics are present in conduct disorder and ODD, but in the latter, they are present in a lesser, more socially acceptable form. ADHD has similar overlapping symptom traits: obstinacy, stubbornness, negativism, temper outbursts, lack of response to discipline, and so on (Rapoport & Ismond, 1990). The diagnosis of ODD is met only when the behavior is considerably more frequent than expected given comparisons with others of the same age and ability.

The *DSM-IV* (APA, 1994) includes specific, disruptive behaviors in children, often continuing into adolescence. The essential features of ODD are patterns of negativistic, hostile, disobedient, and defiant behaviors. The behaviors are devoid of the more serious violations of the basic rights of others as seen in conduct disorder. Generally, symptoms of ODD are more evident in interactions with adults and/or peers with whom the child or adolescent has maintained a relationship. Youngsters with this disorder are likely to manifest minimal dysfunction when examined clinically. Usually they do not regard themselves as oppositional or defiant, but justify their behaviors as a response to unreasonable circumstances. Typically, parents seek consultation, identifying the offspring as having a problem.

Consider this clinical scenario. Parents contact a mental health service provider because their 15-year-old son has become increasingly defiant during the past year. His most extreme behavior, according to them, has been leaving the house at night through a window. The frequency of this behavior has been three times in 2 weeks, all in association with a peer. The parents report loss of trust in their son, compounded by some destructiveness with personal possessions. The patient/client states that the parents are unreasonable in their expectations, set too many restrictions, and have no regard for his peer development. He justifies his frustration, anger, negativism, and defiance because of their attitude. He further blames his behavior problems on them for relocating without consideration of his needs. He expresses his moods openly and without modulation. This is particularly irritating to the father, who is extremely controlled, with a clear understanding of "how things should be done." Thus, the grounds are present for continued dysfunction in the family.

Associated features vary as a function of age and include low self-esteem, mood lability, low frustration tolerance, and temper outbursts. There may be use of illegal psychoactive substances, such as cannabis and alcohol. Use of tobacco is common. Retrospectively, ODD characteristics can be observed by 8 years of age, but precursors are believed to exist in early childhood. The *DSM-IV* (APA, 1994) notes that in males, a preschool problematic temperament existed, but few other factors are known that may predispose to this disorder. Many hypotheses exist, but no empirical facts have been substantiated. It is known that ODD is more common in males than in females before puberty, but gender differences do not maintain in postpubertal children (APA, 1987, 1994). There are estimates that 2% to 16% of the child/adolescent population has ODD.

In a study conducted by Cantwell and Baker (1989) that looked at the stability and natural history of *DSM-III-R* (APA, 1987) childhood disorders, oppositional disorder showed a natural history that was quite distinct from that of conduct disorder and from normal development. Oppositional disorder had the poorest recovery rate (7%) of all the behavioral psychiatric disorders. Unlike conduct disorder, oppositional disorder had a relatively high degree of stability (45%) over time. Those oppositional disordered children who developed other psychiatric illnesses at follow-up tended to have other behavioral disorders, either ADD alone or ADHD plus conduct disorder.

The ensuing discussion focuses on contributing factors to ODD from various theoretical formulations. In addition, empirical research findings are presented.

Contributing Factors

What constitutes problematic behavior in adolescents? That question has no agreed-upon answers from researchers, clinicians, parents, or adolescents. Problematic behavior has elements of negativism, rebellion, drug use, educational deficits, pregnancy, hostility, opposition, defiance, disobedience, marked carelessness, passive-aggressiveness, provocativeness, quarrelsomeness, resistance to change, running away, and teasing behavior, along with myriad other specific and authority-defined transgression behaviors. These behaviors create immediate social and family difficulties for the child and have the possibility, if preventive steps are not taken, of developing into more serious problems in adolescent adaptation.

Adolescent behavior problems have been studied for the past three to four decades, usually by isolating particular problems. More recently, researchers have been recognizing that problematic behaviors may coexist with other behaviors. Research by Donovan and Jessor (1985) illustrates this observation. They identified a syndrome of problem behaviors that included delinquent activities, drug use, and precocious sexual activity among junior and senior high school students. Data from retrospective reports revealed that engaging in one of the identified problem behaviors increases the probability that another problematic behavior will begin within the subsequent year. This finding suggests that the manifestation of the unique problem behavior likely emerges from a general pattern of difficulty in social development, rather than simply serving as a response to the rewards of a given behavior. Bell (1986) believes that to understand specific problem behaviors in adolescence, it is necessary to examine both the central developmental tasks and the behaviors that create the enduring risks of problems.

Among the most consistent correlates of adolescent problem behaviors are characteristics of the family and styles of interaction (Dumas & Gibson, 1989). Predictors of adolescent problematic behaviors are parental disinterest in the child and poor family management practices, such as providing inconsistent discipline to the child or adolescent. Maternal depression has also been directly correlated with behavior disorders in children (Dumas & Gibson, 1989). Thus, the environment has the capability of producing disruptive problematic behaviors in children and adolescents.

The above findings suggest that there is a complex family interaction dimension that plays an important role in adolescent behaviors. Offer (1969) presented attachment theory as a model to potentially account for much of this relationship, and suggested how family characteristics influence the problem behaviors of adolescents. A central premise of attachment theory is that children form internal working models of themselves in relation to others (Offer, 1969). Specifically, features of the attachment model assessed in 1-year-olds have been found to predict social competence at age 5 (Offer, 1969). It is inferred from these findings that an individual's attachment relationship mediates between family interactions in childhood and social competence later in the life span.

An explanation of hostile and/or maladaptive behavior that fits much of the available data on the correlates of adolescent problem behaviors is given by attachment theory. Within this theory, anger expression is considered a "natural" response of children to separation and/or loss of parental figures. Anger also results from real or perceived parental rejection (Materson, 1967). When parents continuously act in an inconsistent or rejecting manner, the children no doubt live lives of confusion, that is, they do not know about the physical or emotional availability of the parent. The child then experiences intense anger, which becomes a central feature of the parental interpersonal relationship. It is also noted that the anger can be displaced (Materson, 1967). The child's model for attachment relationships links the "poor" parenting in childhood to the deviant, rebellious, and hostile behavior in adolescence (Materson, 1967). The implication is that children whose parents do not meet their needs for security and emotional support form attachments characterized by feelings of anger and hostility and these perceptions are transferred to other people in their lives. Thus, their behaviors generalize, influencing social behaviors throughout their development and life span.

Another aspect relevant to understanding problem behaviors in adolescence is consideration of developmental striving-for-autonomy from parents and the simultaneous efforts to maintain a positive relationship with them (DiLalla, Mitchell, Arthur, & Pagliocca, 1988). A consistent tenet of most theories of autonomy and relatedness for adolescents is that their striving-for-autonomy optimally occurs in the context of a positive relationship (Murphey, Silbert, Coelho, Hamburg, & Greenberg, 1963). Allen, Aber, and Leadbeater (1990) report that adolescents viewed as the most socially competent by teachers and peers are those whose values reflect some autonomy from adult values. The independence is restricted, however, to relatively minor variations from adult expectations for the adolescents. These findings suggest that the optimal developmental path in adolescence is to seek autonomy, though not at the expense of the relationships with parents.

When autonomy and relatedness are considered along with attachment theory, an explanation emerges for the incidence of serious problem behaviors for certain groups of adolescents. The essential task of adolescence is to increase the degree of emotional, physical, and financial independence from parents. Although striving-for-autonomy is a part of normal adolescent development, those youngsters with insecure attachments are likely to expect or perceive that the parental relationships will be jeopardized. This strains the relationships with parents and ignites the sense of anger and insecurity implicit in some adolescents' attachments. When the expected developmental pressures for autonomy are combined with relationships with parents that are unable to withstand the pressures, a substantial risk of serious problem behaviors ensues (Allen et al., 1990).

Within psychodynamic theory, it is recognized that the parents are the most influential and meaningful people in an individual's life, until adolescence, at which time conflict is reactivated (Josselyn, 1971). Because the earliest and strongest emotional ties were to the parents, the intensification of all feelings and the channeling of sexual impulses along preestablished pathways creates a conflict for the adolescent. Love for the parent of the same sex carries an implication of a potential homosexual orientation, which is a culturally unacceptable response. At the same time, the intensity of feeling for the parent of the other sex violates the incest barrier. Furthermore, the pressure toward emancipation from family ties necessitates some mobilization of defenses against turning the strong emotions toward the parents; to do so would frustrate the goal of maturation, that is, becoming an adult in an adult society (Josselyn, 1971).

Psychodynamically, an adolescent abandons her childhood identity and struggles to structure a new one. This is compatible with her conceptualization of adulthood. In this task, adolescents strive to be independent, but overextend themselves, thereby becoming anxious and seeking the security of a dependent relationship. They try to assure themselves of their uniqueness by resorting to behavior similar to that of the negativistic 2-year-old. Adolescents cope with the reemergence of sexual urges by distancing themselves from their parents. They seek new ego ideals compatible with the concept of themselves as adults, abandoning archaic parts of their childhood ego ideal. Rebellion against aspects of their childhood superego also occurs as the adolescent explores new value systems formulated to what is considered an adult superego. At this time, behavior is based upon a primary preoccupation with self, rather than with other people or other activities. Childhood is past and adulthood is the future; the present is chaotic (Josselyn, 1971). This is one psychodynamic explanation of how adolescents contribute to their own oppositional behavior.

Genetic evidence is present for schizophrenia, depression, and several other behavior disorders (Schwartz & Johnson, 1985). No specific genetic evidence has been found for ODD in research. It is important to remember that the psychobiological system is partly responsible for behavior, but it acts in combination with the environment to produce individual differences.

Family conflict is a relatively new area of research (Mash & Barkley, 1989), and ODD is the first diagnostic category directly addressing parent-adolescent conflict. It is evident that the family plays a most significant role in factors that contribute to ODD. Foster and Robin (1988) posited that the child's transition into adolescence, with its concomitant biological, cognitive, and social changes, disrupts ongoing family patterns. The adolescent's increased requests for autonomy (again the major task of the adolescent years) precipitates this disruption. The family attempts to restructure its interactions with this changing and emerging member, but conflict results (Robin & Foster, 1989).

According to Robin and Foster (1989), there are numerous factors that determine whether the conflict becomes a significant problem for the family and the adolescent. Included among these factors are the family's problem-solving skills, their communication patterns, the belief systems of individual family members, and the structural and functional patterns that interrelate to each small component. Maladaptive patterns in any of the stated domains produce unresolved disputes, leading to recurring anger and further conflicts.

When the disagreements evolve, problem solutions and communication effectiveness are abandoned. Most families of ODD adolescents are not equipped with positive and productive problem-solving skills. They are unable to effectively and efficiently deal with the problematic situation. Communication skills facilitate the exchange of information among family members and are considered crucial to successful conflict resolution, but ODD families manifest poor communication skills with typical outcomes being misunderstanding, reciprocated negative exchanges, and angry expressions (Robin & Foster, 1989). Robin and Weiss (1980) compared families seeking treatment with nondistressed families and discovered that positive communication skills were seen more often in nondistressed families, with humor, approval, acceptance of responsibility, and supportiveness as key elements of positive communications.

Another factor that contributes to conflict between parents and children is cognition. Mash and Barkley (1989) say that thoughts influence interaction among family members by either facilitating or interfering with adaptive communication. For example, rigid, inflexible, and negatively biased thoughts about personal behavior (and/or other family members' actions) promote rigid, inflexible, and negative communications or reactions. When comparing distressed and nondistressed parents, the former more often endorsed beliefs supporting "perfectionism" (i.e., excessively high standards for the adolescent behavior) and "obedience" (i.e., excessive demands for the adolescent to unquestioningly follow parental demands). Distressed teens more strongly endorsed beliefs related to "fairness" (i.e., parental rules should always be reasonable according to the adolescent's standards) and "autonomy" (i.e., adolescents should be granted as much decision-making freedom as they wish) (Mash & Barkley, 1989).

The manner in which family members interact has been referred to as alignment (Mash & Barkley, 1989). Conflict can be initiated among family members when a "coalition" is formed. That is, two family members support each other against another member—for example, when two parents blame their family difficulties on an adolescent. In "triangulation," two disagreeing family members compete for the support of another family member, with the latter vacillating between the disagreeing parties (Mash & Barkley, 1989). Cross-generational coalitions lead to greater conflict because this parent-child pattern undermines the more adaptive Western societal expectation that parents work together. The parental goal of granting gradual autonomy to the developing adolescent within the constraints of flexible but consistent limits is violated in the cross-generation coalition. Triangulated patterns promote conflict because the two disputing members handle their disagreement indirectly through the third member, often implicitly allowing the third member to be the decision maker (Mash & Barkley, 1989). Family alignment is a significant contributing factor in parent-adolescent conflicts and the ultimate development of ODD. Research by Earls and Jung (1987) revealed a number of temperament characteristics of children that were significantly related to behavior problems. Some of these traits were activity level, adaptability, approach/withdrawal, intensity, persistence, and mood. They also found that marital discord was more related to behavior problems in boys than in girls. They concluded that, although certain temperamental characteristics are important precursors to the development of psychopathology, environmental characteristics may become more important in determining the persistence and course of the disorder once it has emerged (Earls & Jung, 1987).

Conger et al. (1991) tested the utility of a process model that related family economic difficulties to the antisocial behavior of early adolescents. There was support for the hypothesis that family economic problems influence hostility toward children and between spouses. The increase in hostility stems from the depression and hostile feelings the economically distressed adult is experiencing. Conger et al. (1991) suggested that the target of adult hostile behavior makes a difference in adolescent developmental processes. Parents who are preoccupied by finances and their disagreements with one another are likely to be too distracted by these issues to monitor and appropriately control the activities of their children. Parental conflict can create anxiety for early adolescents who are attempting to cope with significant social and biological changes in their lives, and then have to deal with the problematic and hostile behavior of parents (Reid & Patterson, 1989). As Labouvie and McGee (1986) noted, in such a situation, alcohol or drug use can assist the adolescent's coping effort by diminishing the negative emotions related to the stressful and unsure home environment and by promoting positive interactions with peers who are in similar circumstances.

Forehand, Middleton, and Long (1987) examined the effect divorce and a poor adolescent-parent relationship had on adolescent functioning. They found that the group in which there was a poor relationship with both parents was associated with poorer functioning than in other group comparisons. These results suggest that a good relationship with one parent is sufficient to prevent problems in school functioning. Parental divorce was associated with social and cognitive difficulties in adolescents compared with those from intact homes, who had higher grades and were perceived as more socially competent by teachers. When parents divorce, their use of effective monitoring and disciplinary procedures, as well as their positive relationship with their children, diminishes (Atkeson, Forehand, & Rickard, 1982). As a consequence, the social competence and cognitive performance of the child is likely to deteriorate.

Research has suggested that parental behavior affects substance use or deviant behaviors other than ODD by increasing the probability that adolescents will associate with disordered friends who are more likely to promote conduct problems (e.g., Elliott & Ageton, 1980; Reid & Patterson, 1989). The hostile and/or irritable parental behaviors, when directed toward adolescents, lead to hostile interactions between the parent and child and train the youngster in the effective use of these behaviors both through modeling and through trial-and-error learning (Reid & Patterson, 1989). This social learning process promotes a repertoire of coercive behaviors that is used outside the home and family, where the behaviors are considered socially inappropriate (Conger et al.,

1991). It is important to note that exposure to parent alcohol use is not essential for adolescent experimentation to occur.

The development of peer relationships and the capacity for useful work are important and influential factors that have the potential to contribute to or prevent oppositional behavior. Late childhood and adolescence marks the emergence of adult-style groups (Schwartz & Johnson, 1985). These groups range from informal crowds of friends to rigidly formal street gangs with specific rules of conduct. Peer friendships and groups, with their rules and norms, are the sources that often bring about conflict between parent and child. These associations can become dictating factors in children's lives. At times, the pressure or desire to conform to the group is greater than the parents' wishes and consequences. This is the time when autonomy and noncompliant behavior are primary objectives of the growing adolescent. Conformity to group norms (Schwartz & Johnson, 1985) and response to peer pressure have their maximum influence in the adolescent years.

Adolescence is the period when the capacity for work begins to emerge as a value. Work provides the individual with identity, a feeling of competence, usefulness, and self-esteem. The importance of the capacity to work on psychological well-being was reported by Vaillant and Vaillant (1981). In the sample of 456 men, the capacity to work as measured by income, job satisfaction, and the ability to remain employed was highly correlated with global measures of mental health. They also found that those teenagers who held part-time jobs, performed regular household tasks, and/or worked on extracurricular school projects were less likely to develop behavior disorders than were those youngsters who did not follow the capacity for work value. Failure to develop a capacity for work belief system is associated with the development of behavior disorders at later stages of life (Schwartz & Johnson, 1985).

Clinical Interventions

Approaches to child treatment have mimicked adult intervention schemes. Behavioral procedures have employed classical conditioning methods and the application of operant learning principles. Observational learning, as well as modification of maladaptive cognitions, which are presumed to be related to inappropriate modes of responding, are other behavioral techniques used with disordered children and adolescents. The wide range of behavioral approaches in use with child interventions include systematic desensitization, in vivo desensitization, modeling, implosive therapy, overcorrection procedures, bell and pad procedures, emotive imagery, cognitive behavior modification, token economies, contingency contracting, and time-out procedures. Some of these will be reviewed, keeping the ODD youngster as the focus.

Sarason, Johnson, and Siegel (1978) described the use of modeling procedures with incarcerated delinquents. Treatment was based on the notion that these children had difficulty functioning in an acceptable manner due in part to a lack of adaptive behaviors in their repertoire. The children participated in modeling sessions centering on specific problem areas. Observation of modeling scenes was followed by role-playing sessions. At a 5-year follow-up, differences in recidivism rates between subjects in the modeling and control groups were evident (Sarason et al., 1978). These findings indicate that modeling procedures can be used to teach or facilitate new adaptive behaviors in adolescents showing few such behaviors.

The operant approach to child behavior modification has been very effective (Phillips & Ray, 1980). It has been found valuable in increasing desirable behaviors in children displaying behavioral deficits as well as in decreasing maladaptive behaviors in those displaying behavioral excesses. In general, the operant approach to behavior modification is based largely on the premise that behavior is controlled by its consequences. Thus, behavior can be increased by arranging contingencies so that the behavior of interest is followed by positive reinforcement. Likewise, behavior can be weakened or eliminated through negative reinforcement or extinction.

Behavioral approaches have focused not only on overt observable behaviors but on cognitive processes as well. An assumption basic to this approach is that the negative self-statements and/or self-instructions generated by the individual are important contributors to maladaptive behaviors. These maladaptive cognitions can be positively modified to bring about desired behavioral responses (Schwartz & Johnson, 1985). The clinical utility of cognitive-behavioral approaches with children has been criticized (Hobbs, Moguin, & Tyroler, 1980) because there have been insufficient data to demonstrate that behavioral change is durable and generalizes to the nontreatment environment.

Token economies and contingency management systems are useful with behavior disordered adolescent populations. Coleman (1992) summarized research in this area and concluded that token economies were successful with adolescents in three ways: home-based reinforcement systems, group contingencies, and self-determined reinforcement. Home-based reinforcement systems have a powerful effect on behavior, when the parent and child agree on the targeted behaviors and the rewards in regard to successful compliance. Due to the influence of peers on adolescents, group contingencies can be successful, because reinforcement is dependent on the cooperation of every member of the group; if any member fails to exhibit the agreed-on behavior, then no one receives the reinforcement. Self-determined reinforcement allows children to choose from a parent-approved list or to negotiate reinforcers with the parent (Coleman, 1992).

Although child psychotherapy is most often conducted on an individual basis, many clinicians advocate treating children in groups (Schwartz & Johnson, 1985), an excellent context within which disordered children learn more adaptive ways of relating. The group also has a socializing influence on the overly aggressive and oppositional child, who ideally adopts more desirable ways of interacting. Greater generalization to the child's natural environment is expected because changes in group therapy result from actual interactions with other children rather than from simply talking about relationship issues. Although there are many testimonials to the effectiveness of group therapy, a review of the child group literature failed to yield supportive evidence for the group approach.

Family therapy maintains a high profile in dealing with the ODD child. After collecting sufficient assessment information, it is up to the therapist and family to formulate treatment goals, which are family and adolescent specific. Robin and Foster (1989) believe six to eight sessions weekly are sufficient for moderately distressed families. A time-limited initial contract is established with the family, specifying the goals, nature, and logistics of treatment. At the conclusion of the contract, the therapist and family assess the progress and make modifications as necessary (Robin & Foster, 1989). This procedure encourages family members to use their time efficiently and shows unwilling family members that their commitment is not a lifelong venture in therapy. The contract makes the desirable behaviors and goals observable to each member and provides the family with a "guideline" to follow when an impasse is reached.

Among the treatment elements that can be incorporated in a comprehensive family treatment plan are problem-solving communication training (PSCT) and cognitive restructuring. PSCT is a highly directive, skill-oriented intervention for teaching families to resolve specific disputes democratically and to communicate effectively about both the style and the substance of their interactions. In addition to presenting the family with a five-step outline of problem-solving steps, negative communication patterns are identified. Also, common issues of dispute are hierarchically ordered from least to most anger producing. The therapist guides the family by applying the problem-solving steps to one specific dispute per session. Negative communication patterns are targeted and corrected when they occur. To produce generalized change in the natural environment, the family members complete a variety of skill-building assignments between sessions, including written exercises, some problem-solving discussions, home communication exercises, and application of their new skills in daily interactions (Robin & Foster, 1989).

PSCT is divided into four stages: engagement, skill building, resolution of intense conflicts, and disengagement. During the engagement stage (usually about three 1-hour sessions), the therapist collects assessment information, establishes rapport, and negotiates a therapeutic contract. The skill-building stage emphasizes learning the five steps of problem solving and correcting deficient communication. Intense conflict resolution involves helping the family effectively deal with the most anger-provoking issues they encounter. The therapist is more concerned with engineering changes in basic interaction patterns and reaching resolutions than with skill acquisition itself. In the final stage, disengagement, the therapist gradually becomes less directive during discussions and schedules longer intervals between sessions. The family assumes greater responsibility for independent problem solving, and the therapist and family review strategies for preventing relapses. Therapy usually ends with an open-ended contract to return as needed in the future, with follow-up phone calls or booster sessions scheduled at either party's discretion (Mash & Barkley, 1989). Studies generally indicate that PSCT can produce positive results but that the outcomes can be quite variable.

Cognitive restructuring techniques teach families to become aware of, challenge, and correct distorted cognitions (Robin & Foster, 1989). The cognitive restructuring strategies implemented by Robin and Foster (1989) blend with Beck's collaborative empiricism and Ellis's rational-emotive therapy. Robin and Foster (1989) chose eight themes subsuming many of the unreasonable beliefs and misattributions expressed by families that constitute the usual cognitions targeted for change. The eight themes are love and approval, ruination, malicious intent, obedience, perfectionism, self-blame, fairness, and autonomy. For parents, the emphasis is on ruination, obedience, perfectionism, self-blame, and malicious intent. Adolescents' common irrational beliefs include fairness, ruination, malicious intent, and autonomy. The love and approval theme applies to both parents and children alike.

Two forms of cognitive restructuring are useful in treating parent-adolescent problems. The first is used primarily to relabel negative attributions attached to the causes of the other family member's behavior, that is, misattributions. The second is reserved for pervasive distortions that are central to family problems, notably, major cognitive distortions. Family members often make inferences about why others in the family behave as they do. Negative attributions induce unnecessary anger and limit problem solving.

When negative attributions are clearly verbalized, they can be treated like negative communication habits and changed through correction, instructions, modeling, and behavior rehearsal. When the attributions are not clearly verbalized, they can be elicited and corrected through either reframing or verification. With reframing, the therapist provides a family member with a benign alternative to the malevolent attribution. Verification involves asking the member to whom the intent is attributed to comment on its validity (Mash & Barkley, 1989).

The therapist uses a more structured strategy for dealing with major cognitive distortions. He or she follows six steps to help families correct serious cognitive distortions: (a) provide a rationale linking thoughts, feelings, and negative interaction; (b) identify the unreasonable belief; (c) challenge it; (d) suggest a more reasonable alternative; (e) design an experiment to disconfirm the unreasonable belief; and (f) prepare the family to conduct the experiment (Mash & Barkley, 1989). The purpose of the sixth step, conducting the experiment, is to help the family members understand the lack of logic involved in their cognitive distortion and thereby possibly enable them to incorporate the newly acquired positive cognitions into daily routines.

Cramerus (1990) has found it effective to interpret aggressive and negative adolescent behavior in terms of a deeply denied link of positive interaction with a powerful object (authority), which the patient believes can be bullied into abandoning a persecutory stance and coerced into providing restitution. Most ODD adolescents, regardless of gender, age, education, and social class, have responded to these interpretations with decreased hostility and defiance. Cramerus's approach assumes that adolescent symptoms of rage, defiance, and hostile devaluation of authority serve important defensive and restitutional ends that can be accepted by the patient following interpretation. He presumes that, for treatment to succeed, the patient must understand conflicting wishes and defenses, mourn narcissistic and object losses, and accept realistic limitations of the self and other. Only then can the adolescent work through the rage, vengefulness, defiance, and persistent sense of grievance and develop more effective ways to deal with the underlying longings, needs, and fears (Cramerus, 1990).

Recently, there has been a move toward training parents, usually mothers, to serve as therapists for their own children. It is possible that a parent trained to interact in more appropriate and therapeutic ways with the identified patient may also interact in a more appropriate manner with other children in the family. Resulting changes are expected to be more durable due to the extension of therapy into the home after formal treatment has ceased (Schwartz & Johnson, 1985). Procedures have ranged from client-centered approaches aiming to train parents to be more empathic, to behavioral approaches designed to train parents to become more effective in contingency management.

Inpatient

There is a lack of information concerning the treatment of ODD in acute inpatient facilities, such as hospitals, but there are data on the residential environments. These facilities vary greatly in terms of treatment, ranging from those offering essentially a 24-hour treatment milieu, to those providing little more than custodial care for residents. Typically, residential treatment programs consist of a unit where children reside 24 hours per day. The programs usually include the opportunity to attend school on a regular basis and to engage in a variety of therapeutic and recreational activities. Children in residential treatment are often seen in ongoing individual therapy by a mental health professional, and often the entire family is involved in treatment. The results indicate that even if positive changes result from treatment, they often are not maintained after the child is discharged from the treatment program (Schwartz & Johnson, 1985).

Prevention

Many of the pushes toward adolescent autonomy, as well as frustrations in seeking it, derive primarily from extrafamilial sources, such as schools, work settings, and peer groups. In addition, some of these influences may also act on parents, affecting their capacities to provide a secure base for their offspring (Ryan, Puig-Antich, Ambrosini, & Rabinovich, 1987). The bulk of research suggests that early preventive work can be effectively targeted at families, particularly if the interventions are comprehensive.

Preventive intervention with families is useful in addressing family management practices and mediating factors, such as socioeconomic status. Such factors have been related both to delinquency and to difficulty providing adequate child-rearing environments (Elliott & Ageton, 1980). Prevention and treatment efforts need to focus on providing contexts in which the adolescent gains autonomy while simultaneously developing strong, positive relationships with nonfamiliar peers and adults. Remediation can create social environments for adolescents that promote the development of models of attachment. The attachments occur when the adolescents' models of social relationships include functioning autonomously while maintaining strong and positive relationships (Bowlby, 1973, 1979).

Schools provide a promising site for such preventive interventions, given both their access to adolescents and the amount of time adolescents spend in them (Weissberg & Allen, 1986). There is an inverse relationship between adolescents' attachments to their schools and levels of delinquency (Fiqueira-McDonough, 1986). These findings suggest the value of designing schools and programs that allow adolescents to demonstrate their autonomy in ways other than by breaking rules, which jeopardizes their connection to school.

Parents and children can also prevent disruptive behaviors. There are three types of prevention—primary, secondary, and tertiary—for which the family can create different modes of functioning. The goal of primary prevention is eliminating the cause of a problem, thus preventing its occurrence. It is most successful when clear-cut etiological factors are identified and effective means of combating these factors are available. With ODD, this becomes very difficult because a multitude of factors is likely to contribute to the disruptive behaviors, and generally, there is no clear-cut, single contributing factor.

The goal of secondary prevention is the early identification and amelioration of problems, thereby preventing more serious disorders from developing. For example, psychological screening early in childhood can serve to uncover problems in the developing stages. This early identification needs to take place at an early age, before more serious difficulties develop.

Tertiary prevention involves limiting the aftereffects of psychopathology and is therefore closely related to the concept of rehabilitation (Schwartz & Johnson, 1985). The success of reducing the impact of the disturbance depends directly on the adequacy of treatment methods.

Programs designed to promote "positive mental health" through education about psychopathology and its causes have been promoted by governmental, charitable, and religious organizations and have taken forms ranging from an educational curriculum for schoolchildren (Forgays, 1978; Roen, 1967) to large-scale media campaigns. These efforts share the belief that the information conveyed will change attitudes and thereby prevent the development of psychopathology.

Conclusion

Oppositional defiant disorder is complex, and there is considerable overlap in symptoms with conduct disorder and attention-deficit/hyperactivity disorder. The incidence rate is unknown and treatment has used existing procedures rather than disorder-specific modalities. More research is needed on ODD to generate and substantiate treatment and prognostic directions. It does appear that early training for children who exhibit social interaction deficits and problem behaviors will result in reduced maladaptation and probable cessation of escalating disordered behavior. Parents are the most likely conduit for change, provided the youngster is invested in comparable goals.

References

Allen, J. P., Aber, J. L., & Leadbeater, B. J. (1990). Adolescent problem behaviors: The influence of attachment and autonomy. *Psychiatric Clinics of North America, 13*, 455-467.

American Psychiatric Association. (1987). *Diagnostic and statistical manual of mental disorders* (3rd ed., rev.). Washington, DC: Author.

American Psychiatric Association. (1994). *Diagnostic and statistical manual of mental disorders* (4th ed.). Washington, DC: Author.

Atkeson, B. M., Forehand, R., & Rickard, K. M. (1982). The effects of divorce on children. In B. B. Lahey & A. E. Kazdin (Eds.), *Advances in clinical child psychology* (Vol. 5, pp. 255-281). New York: Plenum.

Bell, R. Q. (1986). Age specific manifestations in changing psychosocial risk. In D. C. Farran & J. D. McKinney (Eds.), *The concept of risk in intellectual and psychosocial development* (pp. 169-185). New York: Academic Press.

Bowlby, J. (1973). *Attachment and loss: Vol. 2. Separation, anxiety and anger.* New York: Basic Books.

Bowlby, J. (1979). *The making and breaking of affectional bonds.* London: Tavistock.

Cantwell, D. P., & Baker, L. (1989). Stability and natural history of DSM-III childhood diagnoses. *Journal of the American Academy of Child and Adolescent Psychiatry, 28*, 691-700.

Coleman, M. C. (1992). Adolescents. In *Behavior disorders: Theory and practice* (2nd ed., pp. 249-282). Boston: Allyn & Bacon.

Conger, R. D., Lorenz, F. O., Elder, G. H., Melby, J. N., Simons, R. L., & Conger, K. J. (1991). A process model of family economic pressure and early adolescent alcohol use. *Journal of Early Adolescence, 11*, 430-449.

Cramerus, M. (1990). Adolescent anger. *Bulletin of the Menninger Clinic, 54*, 512-523.

DiLalla, L. F., Mitchell, C. M., Arthur, M. W., & Pagliocca, P. M. (1988). Aggression and delinquency: Family and environmental factors. *Journal of Youth and Adolescence, 17*, 233-246.

Donovan, J. E., & Jessor, R. (1985). Structure of problem behavior in adolescence and young adulthood. *Journal of Consulting and Clinical Psychology, 53*, 890-904.

Dumas, J. E., & Gibson, J. A. (1989). Behavioral correlates of maternal depressive symptomatology in conduct-disordered children. *Journal of Consulting and Clinical Psychology, 57*, 516-521.

Earls, F., & Jung, K. G. (1987). Temperament and home environment characteristics as causal factors in the early development of childhood psychopathology. *Journal of the American Academy of Child and Adolescent Psychiatry, 26,* 491-498.

Elliott, D. S., & Ageton, S. S. (1980). Reconciling race and class differences in self-reported and official estimates of delinquency. *American Social Revolution, 45,* 95-110.

Fiqueira-McDonough, J. (1986). School context, gender and delinquency. *Journal of Youth and Adolescence, 15,* 79-98.

Forehand, R., Middleton, K., & Long, N. (1987). Adolescent functioning as a consequence of recent parental divorce and the parent-adolescent relationship. *Journal of Applied Developmental Psychology, 8,* 305-315.

Forgays, J. (1978). A simulated home approach vs. locked ward therapy for chronic emotional disability. *Dissertation Abstracts International, 39,* 378.

Foster, S., & Robin, A. (1988). Family conflict and communication in adolescence. In E. Mash & L. Terdal (Eds.), *Behavioral assessment of childhood disorders* (2nd ed., pp. 717-775). New York: Guilford.

Gormly, A. V., & Brodzinsky, D. M. (1993). *Lifespan human development* (5th ed.). New York: Harcourt Brace Jovanovich.

Hobbs, S., Moguin, L., & Tyroler, M. (1980). Parameters of investigations of cognitive behavior therapy with children. *Catalog of Selected Documents in Psychology, 10,* 62-63.

Josselyn, I. M. (1971). *Adolescence.* New York: Harper & Row.

Kazdin, A. E. (1993). Adolescent mental health: Prevention and treatment programs. *American Psychologist, 48,* 127-141.

Labouvie, E. W., & McGee, C. R. (1986). Relation of personality to alcohol and drug use in adolescence. *Journal of Consulting and Clinical Psychology, 54,* 289-293.

Mash, E. J., & Barkley, R. A. (1989). *Treatment of childhood disorders.* New York: Guilford.

Materson, J. F. (1967). The symptomatic adolescent five years later: He didn't grow out of it. *American Journal of Psychiatry, 123,* 1338-1345.

Murphey, E. B., Silbert, E., Coelho, G. V., Hamburg, D. A., & Greenberg, I. (1963). Development of autonomy and parent-child interaction in late adolescence. *American Journal of Orthopsychiatry, 33,* 643-652.

Offer, D. (1969). *The psychological world of the teenager: A study of normal adolescent boys.* New York: Basic Books.

Phillips, J., & Ray, R. (1980). Behavioral approaches to childhood disorders. *Behavior Modification, 4,* 3-34.

Rapoport, J. L., & Ismond, D. R. (1990). *DSM-III-R training guide for diagnosis of childhood disorders.* New York: Brunner/Mazel.

Reid, J. B., & Patterson, G. R. (1989). The development of antisocial behaviour patterns in childhood and adolescence. Special Issue: Personality and aggression. *European Journal of Personality, 3,* 107-119.

Robin, A. L., & Foster, S. L. (1989). *Negotiating parent-adolescent conflict: A behavioral-family systems approach.* New York: Guilford.

Robin, A. L., & Weiss, J. G. (1980). Criterion-related validity of behavioral and self-report measures of problem-solving communication skills in distressed and non-distressed parent-adolescent dyads. *Behavioral Assessment, 2,* 339-352.

Roen, S. (1967). Teaching the behavioral sciences to children. *Child Study, 29,* 21-31.

Ryan, N., Puig-Antich, J., Ambrosini, P., & Rabinovich, H. (1987). The clinical picture of major depression in children and adolescents. *General Psychiatry, 44,* 854-861.

Sarason, I. G., Johnson, J. H., & Siegel, J. M. (1978). Assessing the impact of life changes: Development of the life experiences survey. *Journal of Consulting and Clinical Psychology, 46,* 932-946.

Schwartz, S., & Johnson, J. H. (1985). *Psychopathology of childhood.* New York: Pergamon.

Vaillant, G. F., & Vaillant, C. Q. (1981). Natural history of male psychological health: Work as a predictor of positive mental health. *American Journal of Psychiatry, 138,* 1433-1440.

Weissberg, R. P., & Allen, J. P. (1986). Promoting children's social skills and adaptive interpersonal behavior. In L. Michelson & B. Edelstein (Eds.), *Handbook of prevention* (pp. 153-175). New York: Plenum.

• CHAPTER 5 •

Anxiety Disorders

HARRY L. MILLS

In 1980, when the American Psychiatric Association published the *DSM-III,* anxiety disorders for both adults and children were formally disembedded from the theoretically overburdened territory of neurosis. The definition of *anxiety* became "apprehension, tension or uneasiness that stems from the anticipation of danger whether internal or external. . . . It may be focused on an object, situation or activity which is avoided (phobia) or unfocused (free floating anxiety)" (American Psychiatric Association [APA], 1980, p. 354). *DSM-III-R* (APA, 1987) included a subclassification of disorders characterized as Anxiety Disorders of Childhood and Adolescence. Three distinct disorders were considered unique to children: separation anxiety disorder, avoidant disorder, and overanxious disorder. *DSM-IV* (APA, 1994) eliminated the separate category, leaving only separation anxiety disorder as part of the disorders unique to infancy, childhood, and adolescence. In *DSM-IV,* the Anxiety Disorders section is applicable to children and teens as well as adults.

Although a clinically derived classification system holds popular appeal, empirically derived schemes such as those proposed by Achenbach (Achenbach, 1985; Achenbach & McConaughy, 1987) and Quay (Quay, 1972, 1977, 1979) are of significant value in understanding anxiety disorders. From extensive factor analytic studies of childhood disorders, two broad-band classifications have emerged: overcontrolled or internalizing disorders and undercontrolled or externalizing disorders. Anxiety manifests itself in problems of overcontrol. Employing the Child Behavior Checklist and other scales, Achenbach and McConaughy (1987) have identified broad-band characteristics that they characterize as internalizing disorders. This group includes problems within the self, such as unhappiness and fears. Syndromes that fall under the internalizing dimension include social withdrawal, depression, somatic complaints, and depressed withdrawal, depending on the age and sex of the child (Achenbach & McConaughy, 1987). The externalizing syndromes seem to involve little anxiety and include aggressive, destructive, delinquent, cruel, and hyperactive behavior patterns. One dimension seems to involve too much control, anxiety, and attendant dysphoria, and the other dimension, too little anxiety, self-control, and attending social dysfunction.

Definitions

Both anxiety and fear are experienced subjectively as dysphoric and aversive. Both involve the same types of physiological reactions, but *fear* is seen as a response to a genuine threat that disappears once the threat is removed. *Anxiety* represents a more enduring response to internal cues without obvious external threat. Anxiety may become associated with external objects or situations, however, and lead to fear for no apparent reason (Reed, Carter, & Miller, 1992).

The disorder specific to childhood in *DSM-IV* (APA, 1994) is *separation anxiety disorder.* The core feature is excessive anxiety concerning separation from significant others to whom the child is attached. When separated, the level of anxiety may reach the point of panic. The child exhibits unrealistic worry about harm to the attachment figure or a major calamity that would result in permanent separation. School refusal and refusal to go to sleep as well as persistent avoidance of being alone may be part of the presentation. Nightmares, somatic complaints, and clinging may also be present. The pattern described must take place well after developmentally expected stranger anxieties, which occur at approximately 8 months, and separation anxiety, which is common at 18 months (APA, 1987; Reed et al., 1992). In *DSM-III-R* (APA, 1987), *avoidant disorder* appeared under Anxiety Disorders of Children and Adolescence. It involved shrinking from contact with unfamiliar people while seeking contact with family or other familiar persons (e.g., peers). Such youngsters avoid contact with people they do not know to the point that social functioning and development were impaired. Anxiety with strangers may be so great that the children become uncommunicative and mute. In *DSM-IV,* children manifesting such symptoms must meet criteria for *social phobia.* In social phobia, persons are said to be fearful of situations in which they are evaluated by others or in which they may do something humiliating or embarrassing. Criteria have been modified to include children (APA, 1994; Kendall et al., 1992).

Generalized excessive anxiety and unrealistic worry were the hallmark features of *overanxious disorder* in *DSM-III-R.* Individuals may worry about the future or the past and tend to be extremely self-conscious. Routine visits to the doctor may lead to excessive worry. The adolescent is often very anxious about competence and about meeting the expectations of others. Somatic complaints (e.g., headaches or stomachaches) are very common, and no physical basis can be found (APA, 1987). Kendall et al. (1992) point out the overanxious youngsters' worry about cleanliness, keeping the rules, making appointments, and inquiry about situation danger create an illusion of maturity that can mask the distress they experience. In *DSM-IV,* such symptoms are classified under *generalized anxiety disorder.*

Panic disorder may also occur in children and adolescents. It is characterized by at least one panic episode that is unexpected and is not triggered by situations in which the person is the focus of attention (e.g., social phobia). Shaking, dyspnea, dizziness, palpitations, sweating, nausea, or abdominal distress and choking may be experienced during a panic attack. Although agoraphobic symptoms are very rare in children, they may develop in adolescence. Those symptoms include fear of being in places or situations from which escape might be difficult or embarrassing when away from home (APA, 1994).

According to Reed et al. (1992), *simple phobia* and *obsessive-compulsive disorder* are seen more frequently in children and adolescents than are the other anxiety disorders. The hallmark of simple phobia is disproportionate fear directed at a specific and well-circumscribed situation. The person is likely aware that the fear is out of proportion, and yet the reaction interferes with usual and appropriate functioning (Kendall et al., 1992; Reed et al., 1992).

Although *obsessive-compulsive disorder (OCD)* is thought to be comparatively rare in children and adolescents, it can be a severe disorder when it presents itself. Milby and Weber (1991) define the key terms:

> *Obsession*—an intrusive, repetitive thought, image or impulse. It is unacceptable, associated with subjective resistance and usually produces distress.
>
> *Compulsions*—a repetitive, stereotypical act, completely or partly unacceptable but regarded as excessive and/or exaggerated by the patient. It is accompanied by a subjective need to perform the act, often provokes long-term distress but usually reduces immediate distress. (p. 10)

Children and teens with *posttraumatic stress disorder (PTSD)* have experienced events that are outside the range of usual human experience and that would be distressing to anyone. Physical and sexual abuse, natural disasters, invasive medical procedures, and domestic violence are common examples. The victim tends to reexperience the event or events in recurrent dreams, memories, or play themes. There may be a numbing of general responsiveness or active avoidance of stimuli associated with the original trauma. High arousal manifests itself in hyposomnia, angry outbursts, and startle responses (Reed et al., 1992). Although considered an anxiety disorder, PTSD is beyond the scope of this chapter.

Incidence, Prevalence, and Comorbidity

Children often experience short-lived, transitory, and developmentally appropriate fears and anxieties that do not require professional intervention. The age of the child or developmental stage, however, must influence interpretation of an anxiety-based presentation. What is appropriate at one age may be a precursor to serious adjustment problems at another. These developmental issues often cloud interpretation of prevalence data (Kendall et al., 1992).

Much of the research on incident rates of children's fears is quite old and precedes the criterion-referenced diagnostic system *(DSM-III-R)* that arose in the 1980s. Recent studies by Ollendick and his associates (e.g., Ollendick, 1983; Ollendick, Matson, & Helsel, 1985) report an average of 11 fears for children between 8 and 11 years of age and 13 for children and adolescents between 7 and 18 years of age. Graziano and Mooney (1984) report that girls generally obtain higher fear scores than boys. Werry and Quay (1971), Richman, Stevenson, and Graham (1975), and Earls (1980) report from 12.8% to 16.5% of their sample with significant fears. Based on these studies, one might make the risky inference that from 5% to 16% of children experience intensive fears. Much more research is required.

Obsessive-compulsive disorder in children is rare. The highest incidence rates seem less than 2% of cases studied (Milby & Weber, 1991). A 1.2% incidence in 405 children seen in inpatient and outpatient settings was reported by Judd (1965). In a pool of 2,500 children, Adams (1972) also found a 1.2% incidence. Flament, Rapoport, Murphy, Berg, and Lake (1985) studied an entire school population of a New Jersey county and found a prevalence rate of .33% of the general adolescent population.

Although clinicians report that anxious youth often present with depressive symptoms, studies of the comorbidity with large samples are rare. Last, Strauss, and Francis (1987) found that one third of 22 children who presented with separation anxiety had a coexisting major depression. Bernstein and Garfinkel (1986) reported that of a sample of 26 teens with chronic school refusal, 16 were diagnosed with an anxiety disorder, and of that group, 81% had a coexisting major depression. Berney et al. (1981) found that 45% of school-phobic children exhibited signs of significant depression. *DSM-III* criteria were not used in that study, however. Strauss, Last, Herson, and Kazdin (1988) reported, in the best designed study to date, that 28% of the children with anxiety disorder also met *DSM-III* criteria for major depressive disorder.

Much more research will be required on incidence and prevalence using *DSM-III-R* criteria before generalizations can be made with confidence.

Contributing Factors

Infants have been observed to fear loud, unpredictable, sudden stimuli, loss of support, and high places (Ball & Tronick, 1971). Fear of strange people and novel objects becomes more evident as the child approaches the end of the first year (Bronson, 1972). Bowlby (1969) points out that infants show distress at separation from their caretaker. At around 6 months, the infant manifests anxiety to novel stimuli. At 6 months, fears of masks, dogs, and jacks-in-the-box also begin to emerge. These fears increase until 18 to 24 months and then decrease. Scarr and Salapatek (1970) found that children rated high on such fears at one point in time tend to be higher at a later date. This suggests that perhaps intensity of fear may be stable. Unlike earlier research (e.g., Agras, Chapin, & Oliveau, 1972), more recent research suggests fears and anxieties may be persistent (Reed et al., 1992), and Reed and associates report the following sources of anxiety at designated stages of development:

- From birth to 6 months, fears of excessive or unexpected sensory stimuli, loss of support, and loud noises are prevalent.
- From 6 to 9 months, fears of strangers and novel stimuli predominate.
- At the end of the first year, fears of separation, injury, or toilets are common.
- At the end of the second year, monsters, imaginary creatures, death, and robbers are dominant.
- By the end of the third year, dogs, large animals, and being alone arouse fearfulness.
- The end of the fourth year brings fears of darkness.
- School, injury, natural events, and social anxiety are predominant from ages 6 to 12.

Factor analysis of fears in children and adolescents yielded a five-factor structure according to Ollendick et al. (1985):

1. Fear of failure and criticism
2. Fear of the unknown
3. Fear of injury and small animals
4. Fear of danger and death
5. Medical fears

Kendall et al. (1992) suggest that humans respond with fear to naturally occurring signs of danger, such as loud noises, and that this might be seen as having adaptive value. Furthermore, survival may be enhanced by having attachment to familiar figures while fearing strangers. What may be normative or even adaptive at one age, however, may be maladaptive at a later stage. Such a developmental conceptualization suggests that child and adolescent anxiety disorders, and even their adult derivatives, may represent natural survival mechanisms gone awry. Although such speculation is intriguing, longitudinal research has yet to be conducted to support such notions.

Early Experiences

Speculation about prenatal influence in developing anxiety disorder far exceeds sound research, and thus no conclusions are clear. The level of influence and the types of parent-child interactions that are influential at different stages of development, however, have begun to be researched. Campbell (1986) provides an excellent summary of the interaction between development and parenting patterns, pointing out that caretaking behaviors of key attachment figures play an influential role. Bowlby (1973), among others, has speculated that when the attachment figure is available and responsive, the infant develops a sense of security and trust. Conversely, lack of availability and responsivity lead to heightened levels of anxiety and distress. Children's anxieties and fears are seen as developing normally out of biologically determined species-specific responses that lead to avoidance of possible hazards and to approach of protective figures (Campbell, 1986). As the youngster develops cognitive skills, the types of fears are transformed. At each stage, however, fears have survival value. They signal the need to protect oneself from harm. It is naive to assume, however, that such fears unreel themselves developmentally without influence from caretaker responses. The preschooler's fears of animals, the dark, or imaginary creatures are communicated to caretakers, and the caretaker response is likely to have influence. Furthermore, complex fear reactions, such as fear of strangers, are very much influenced by the way in which the stranger approaches (Rheingold & Eckerman, 1973). Females are less fear evoking than males (Brooks & Lewis, 1976). In short, there is variability in the level of the child's reaction to situations and strangers; there is variability in the social context and also in the nurturing reassuring response of attachment figures. Maternal responsiveness and accessibility have been shown to be associated with secure attachments, and securely attached infants are less anxious when exposed to events such as separation (Stayton, Ainsworth, & Main, 1973). Although it seems likely that parental influences on development of adolescent or adult anxiety disorder begin very early in development, the lack of longitudinal research leaves such contributions in the realm of intriguing speculation.

Genetic

Gittelman (1986) summarized evidence indicating that anxious behavior can be bred selectively in animals, and she reviewed available evidence supporting genetic influences in the development of anxiety disorders. Weissman, Leckman, Merikangas, Gammon, and Prusoff (1984) studied the psychiatric states of children of normal and depressed women and found the rate of anxiety symptoms much higher among the children of depressed/anxious individuals than among pure depressive and normal controls. The most common anxiety symptoms among the children involved separation anxiety. The type of anxiety disorder in the parent seemed a factor with the offspring of patients with panic disorder showing greater risk. Two additional studies by Berg, Butler, and Pritchard (1974) and Gittelman-Klein (1975) gave mixed support to the influence of heredity, with the Gittelman-Klein (1975) research lending limited support. There is also evidence supporting genetic influence in OCD. Elkins, Rapoport, and Lipsky (1980) reviewed the twin studies and found four that examined a total of 30 sets of twins, of which 24 showed concordance for OCD. Gittelman (1986b) pointed out that there are enough positive results to warrant systematic inquiry. Much more research is required, however.

Environment

Learning and conditioning theories about anxiety disorders have undergone considerable change since Watson's early formulations (Watson & Rayner, 1920). Demonstration of the simple respondent conditioning paradigm with Albert and furry objects has been challenged by subsequent failures at replication (Gray, 1971; Marks, 1969; Seligman, 1970) and by the clinical observation that many individuals with anxiety disorders do not present with history that justifies the theory. In addition, the following observations challenge traditional respondent conditioning theory:

1. Seligman (1970, 1971) has interpreted findings to indicate that natural selection has led humans to be genetically "prepared" to develop certain type of fears. All conditional stimuli are not the same. Furry objects, snakes, and spiders are more likely to evoke fear than are flowers and wooden blocks.
2. Fear can be transmitted vicariously without direct experience with the object of fear (Bandura & Rosenthal, 1966).
3. Rachman (1977) cities surveys, epidemiological studies, and observations by anthropologists that fears do not occur in patterns expected by traumatic interactions with objects and situations.
4. Rachman (1977) also points out that conditioned stimuli (CS) and unconditioned stimuli (UCS) pairings often do not result in acquired fear reactions. The CS being, for example, a furry, white rabbit and the UCS being a loud noise.
5. Eysenck (1976) has pointed out that fear responses do not diminish with repeated CS-only presentations.

In an excellent review of learning approaches to anxiety, Delprato and McGlynn (1984) propose a multifaceted framework for anxiety disorders. *Anxiety* is said to refer to an intricate composition of action modes, developmental origins, and maintaining conditions, all of which must be taken into account. Such a conceptualization runs counter to a unitary concept of fear and is much more compatible with research findings. Anxiety manifests itself within three distinct response systems: (a) overt motor behavior, (b) physiological, and (c) cognitive systems. A given patient's symptoms must be understood according to presentation within each of the three systems. Unlike traditional learning theory, Delprato and McGlynn (1984) insist that the developmental origins of an anxiety disorder may be in complex interaction that involves respondent or operant conditioning, modeling, and/or information transmission (e.g., instruction). And regardless of its origin, the disorder may be maintained through respondent, operant, modeling, or information learning processes.

Kendall et al. (1992) proposed a model for cognitive aspects of the development of an anxiety disorder in children and adolescents across time. In their formulation, the disorder begins with a behavioral event that is magnified because of heightened emotional intensity. At the culmination of the behavioral event, an explanation of the event is formulated. This is referred to as an attribution and is conceived as a relatively short-lived event. When multiple behavioral events and event outcomes follow the initial event, however, the youngster begins to develop a more precise anticipatory cognition or expectancy. Bandura (1977) described expectancies as being of two types: outcome expectancies and self-efficacy expectations. Expectancies develop, including expectation of catastrophic outcomes and expectation of an inability to cope with events, when situations of concern (e.g., the phobic object) present themselves. Without corrective experiences, the pattern may become something of a vicious circle, and the expectations evolve into consistent cognitive patterns (e.g., schemata) and attributional styles that are counterproductive. If this is the case, therapy must become a learning process to reduce support for dysfunctional schemas and construct new schema.

Family Interaction

The influence of parenting and family interaction patterns on the development of anxiety disorders has been the product of more speculation and clinical lore than research. Bowlby (1961) has suggested that separating from the mother early in life makes children vulnerable to later anxiety states. Research has not borne this out, however (Shepherd, Oppenheim, & Mitchell, 1971). In the case of obsessive-compulsive disorder, Rachman and Hodgson (1980) have observed that parental reaction to OCD are of two types: rejection and overindulgence. Studies of family characteristics of OCD youth have included Adams's (1973) study in which certain family characteristics were noted. These families:

1. Were highly verbal
2. Placed positive emphasis on etiquette
3. Valued social isolation or withdrawal
4. Emphasized cleanliness
5. Adhered to an instrumental morality
6. Derogated maleness

7. Practiced limited commitment (i.e., religion, politics, and social views)
8. Had a hoarding orientation toward money

Other researchers (e.g., Manchanda & Sharma, 1986; Tseng, 1973) have presented intriguing findings about the families of youngsters with OCD. Ambiguity characterizes research on family characteristics and other anxiety disorders.

Research on Effectiveness of Clinical Intervention

There remains a dearth of information on the value and effectiveness of the various forms of treatment for anxiety disorders in children and adolescents (Reed et al., 1992). As is the case with many other disorders, behavioral approaches represent the exception. Because of this, the primary focus of the remainder of this chapter will be on those approaches. Effective methods of intervention for child and adolescent anxiety disorders will be categorized as follows:

- Exposure
- Modeling
- Contingency management
- Cognitive-behavioral techniques
- Pharmacotherapy
- Family therapy

Representative research will be examined in each category.

Exposure Techniques

There are a variety of behavioral techniques that involve the key element of exposure. Systematic desensitization (Lazarus, 1959) and implosion therapy (Blagg & Yule, 1984) are among the common techniques appropriately included. Response prevention (Mills, Agras, Barlow, & Mills, 1973) is another. Exposure therapies have in common the presentation of the anxiety-provoking situation in imagination or in vivo, in either a graduated or an intensive fashion with or without incompatible or alternative coping responses such as relaxation. The supposed theoretical underpinnings for the approaches are far less important than an understanding of the clinical operations encompassed by the strategy or technique. Research on the role of relaxation training as a discrete technique has been neglected. It was introduced as a counterconditioning element as part of a desensitization procedure (Wolpe & Lazarus, 1966). It can also, however, be viewed as a coping device that provides for more intensive exposure and the cognitive changes that may attend such exposure. Regardless of the theoretical purpose, it should be an important starting point for effective clinical intervention. Morris (1973) and Cautela and Groden (1978) have reported shaping procedures to teach gradually longer periods of eye closing and methods of tensing or relaxing appropriate muscle groups. They also suggest use of toys of various types to promote effective learning. Morris and Kratochwill (1983) outline a detailed relaxation program for treatment of fears based on Jacobson's (1938) pioneering work. Once the child or adolescent develops basic proficiency in the office, practice homework is ordinarily given (Bergland & Chal, 1972; King, Hamilton, & Ollendick, 1988). The level of proficiency required depends in part on the use to which relaxation is to be put during subsequent treatment. Its use as a coping device in exposure to intensive anxiety-provoking situations requires a high level of skill. Koeppen (1974) originally reported, and Ollendick (1978) revised, relaxation techniques for children that are often called the "Turtle Techniques" because they employ imagery and a story involving a turtle. The scripts can be found in their entirety in Ollendick and Cerny (1981).

The first step in development of any exposure treatment is the development of an anxiety hierarchy. As Morris and Kratochwill (1991) point out, this is often done using index cards on which the parent, child, or adolescent writes the situations that provoke anxiety. The level of anxiety is then rated and the situations are placed in hierarchical order.

When desensitization is the selected strategy, the hierarchy is presented in imagination from the least distressing to the most distressing while the child tries to remain relaxed. Taylor (1972) and Miller (1972) have reported successful use of desensitization with school-related fears. Other successful uses of desensitization have been reported: Kushner (1965) with a fear of driving, Saunders

(1976) with motion sickness, and Obler and Terwilliger (1970) with fears of dogs or use of a public bus.

In vivo desensitization involves exposing the child or adolescent to progressively more distressing situations in reality rather than in imagination. Wilson and Jackson (1980), Waranch, Iwata, Wohl, and Nidiffer (1981), and Freeman, Roy, and Hemmick (1976) have reported successful use of in vivo desensitization with childhood fears.

One of the key factors in selection of imaginal versus in vivo desensitization is the age of the child. Morris and Kratochwill (1983) point out that children cannot form visual images until they are approximately 9 years of age. They suggest that imaginal desensitization should not be used until the children have reached at least that age.

There are a number of variations of systematic desensitization. Kondas (1967) and Barabasz (1973) have reported successful use of desensitization in small groups. Self-directed desensitization has been reported to be successful by Baker, Cohen, and Saunders (1973) and Rosen (1976). A creative variation that involves anxiety-inhibiting images in children called "emotive imagery" was first reported by Lazarus and Abramovitz (1962).

In treatment of OCD, exposure and response prevention have become a treatment of choice. Mills and his associates (Mills et al., 1973) were among the first to apply the technique to children. The child or teen is exposed to anxiety-arousing situations in vivo while the ritual provoked by the situation is prevented in some fashion. Foa, Steketee, and Milby (1980) and Steketee, Grayson, and Foa (1981) have demonstrated that response prevention is essential in conjunction with the exposure.

Flooding is a variation of exposure treatment described effectively by Marks (1975). Ollendick and Gruen (1972) describe a case study of flooding using imaginal stimuli associated with monster movies. Sreenivasan, Manocha, and Jain (1979) treated a severely dog-phobic 11-year-old using in vivo stimuli. The lack of adequate supporting research, however, has led investigators like Graziano (1978), Ollendick (1979), and Ollendick and Cerny (1981) to caution against indiscriminate use of these procedures. Given the lack of empirical support, the risks that attend such procedures are unacceptable.

Modeling

Treatment that results from the observation of another person performing the desired behavior has been referred to as *modeling* (e.g., Bandura, 1969; Kazdin & Wilson, 1978). In treatment of anxiety disorders, the paradigm involves a fearful observer who observes a model engaged in the behavior the person has a history of avoiding. Most agree with Bandura (1971) that the model should perform the avoided behavior in a graduated fashion.

Bandura, Grusec, and Menlove (1967) studied the effects of live modeling on the fear of dogs in children from 3 to 5 years of age. The children in modeling groups showed significantly more approach behavior than control groups. White and Davis (1974) examined the relative effectiveness of live modeling, observation/exposure only, and no treatment on dental treatment avoidance in children 4 to 8 years of age. Both the live model and exposure groups were significantly superior after treatment. Others have also reported success (Mann & Rosenthal, 1969; Ritter, 1968).

Symbolic modeling involves the presentation of the model through film, videotape, or imagination. Bandura and Menlove (1968) reported on the effects of filmed modeling on the dog-avoidant behavior of 48 children ages 3 to 5. Symbolic modeling was as effective as live modeling. Melamed and Siegel (1975) studied the effectiveness of symbolic modeling on reducing the anxiety level of youngsters facing hospitalization and surgery. Filmed modeling significantly reduced all measures of situational anxiety, and differences were maintained at follow-up. Melamed and her associates have demonstrated the effectiveness of symbolic modeling in a variety of situations (Melamed, Hawes, Heigy, & Glick, 1975; Melamed, Weinstein, Hawes, & Katin-Borland, 1975; Melamed, Yurcheson, Fleece, Hutcherson, & Hawes, 1978). An interesting variation on symbolic modeling involves reading stories to children on topics related to their particular fear (Fassler, 1985; Mikulas, Coffman, Dayton, Frayne, & Maier, 1985). Although discussion of the relative contribution of model characteristics, client characteristics, and modeling setting factors is beyond the scope of this chapter (see Melamed & Siegel, 1980, or Perry & Furukawa, 1986), it is important to distinguish between a *coping* versus a *mastery* performance by the model. Although research findings are hardly conclusive, most agree with Perry and Furukawa (1986) that the coping approach should receive primary consideration. This involves the model moving gradually from a performance that is similar to the patient/observer to the competency level that is the goal.

Variations on modeling procedures include *covert modeling* in which the child imagines that he or she is interacting with the feared stimulus, *participant modeling* in which the child observes the model and then actually practices the behavior pattern observed, and *graduated modeling* in which the complex behavior is broken down into its components by the model (Morris & Kratochwill, 1991).

Contingency Management

Positive reinforcement has been used alone and in combination with other behavioral therapy procedures to reduce various fears in a variety of settings (Conger & Keane, 1981; King et al., 1988). Leitenberg (Leitenberg & Callahan, 1973) employed a procedure called "reinforced practice" to reduce children's fear of darkness. Feedback was given regarding the exact time the children spent in a darkened room, and praise was given. Vaal (1973) reported on the use of a contingency contracting system in successful treatment of a school phobia. Various privileges and activities of choice were made dependent on meeting criterion/target behaviors. Other variations on the use of positive reinforcement have also been reported (Ayllon, Smith, & Rogers, 1970; Kellerman, 1980; Lazarus, Davison, & Polefka, 1965; Luiselli, 1977).

Shaping was reported by Tahmisian and McReynolds (1971) to have been used successfully to reduce school phobia in a 13-year-old girl. A variation on stimulus fading, in which the mother was gradually faded from the preschool setting for treatment of separation anxiety, was reported by Neisworth, Madle, and Goeke (1975). An extinction procedure, in which reinforcing conditions are removed, was reported to have been successfully used by Boer and Sipprelle (1970), Herson (1970), and Piersel and Kratochwill (1981).

Contingency management has been employed successfully with school phobia. Controlled studies have been rare, however, and the generalizability of the findings to more severe clinical presentations remains questionable. Little has changed since Carlson, Figueroa, and Lahey (1986) concluded that the apparent promise of reinforcement procedures has yet to be satisfactorily demonstrated in controlled research. The use of such procedures as a part of a treatment package continues to be common, however.

Cognitive-Behavioral Intervention

Kendall and Braswell (1985, p. 2) have pointed out that cognitive-behavioral approaches encompass a variety of techniques that build on a basic set of assumptions:

- Cognitive mediational processes are essential to ensure learning.
- Behavior, feelings, and thoughts are causally interrelated.
- Cognitive events such as expectations, self-statements, and attributions are important in understanding and predicting psychopathology.
- Behavioral and cognitive approaches are compatible.
- The key therapeutic tasks are to assess cognitive processes and design new learning experiences to remediate dysfunctional patterns.

One of the first cognitive-behavioral approaches, rational-emotive therapy (RET), was developed by Albert Ellis. Although it began as an adult application, it has more recently been extended to children and adolescents (Ellis, 1962, 1984). He presented the view that emotional difficulties were a result of irrational thoughts or beliefs. Several books have been published on applications of RET with children and adolescents (Bernard & Joyce, 1984; Ellis & Bernard, 1983). Research has been sparse, however. Bernard, Kratochwill, and Keefauver (1983) applied RET and self-instruction to reduce high-frequency hair pulling. Van der Ploeg-Stapert and Van der Ploeg (1986) evaluated a group treatment approach employing RET for reducing test anxiety in adolescents. Results showed significant reduction in anxiety.

Kanfer and his associates (Kanfer & Gaelick, 1986; Kanfer & Schefft, 1988) have formalized a self-control strategy that combines behavioral intervention with cognitive approaches. The child or adolescent is believed to have the capacity to learn to regulate his or her own behavior with the help of a therapist who acts in the role of instigator or motivator. The therapist teaches the client how, when, and where to use various cognitions to facilitate the learning of a new behavior pattern in relation to particular feared stimuli events or objects.

Kanfer, Karoly, and Newman (1975) compared the effectiveness of two types of verbal controlling responses on the reduction of children's fear of the dark. The competence treatment group learned sentences that emphasized their competence (e.g., I am a brave boy). A stimulus group learned sentences that reduced the aversive qualities of the fear situation (e.g., The dark is a fun place to be). The results suggested that learning to improve one's sense of competency with the help of a therapist acting in the role of instigator and motivator. The therapist teaches the client how, when, and where to use various cognitions to facilitate the learning of a new behavior pattern in relation to particular feared stimuli events or objects.

Another early contribution by Lazarus and Abramovitz (1962) has been characterized as emotive imagery. The child or adolescent is taught to focus on cognitive images that inhibit anxieties. Fictional characters (e.g., Superman) and fictional events (e.g., conquering the fear) are common materials for the imagery. For example, Jackson and King (1981) used the technique with a child whose fears of the dark, noises, and shadows followed a break-in by a prowler. The child's favorite character, Batman, was employed as a fantasy helper when the child was home in his room at night. Treatment was successful at termination and at 18-month follow-up. Meichenbaum and his associate pioneered the use of self-instruction training as a cognitive treatment strategy (e.g., Meichenbaum & Goodman, 1971). Treatment involves having the therapist model cognitive strategies. Meichenbaum (1986) describes the treatment as follows:

- An adult model performs the task while talking to herself out loud.
- The child or adolescent carries out the same task under the model's instruction.
- The child or adolescent then performs task while instructing himself out loud.
- The child or adolescent then whispers instructions to self.
- The child or adolescent finally performs the task while using silent self-instruction.

The self-instruction model has been employed successfully in the treatment of children's fears by Fox and Houston (1981) and Genshaft (1982).

Kendall (1985) has proposed distinguishing between cognitive distortions and cognitive deficiencies. Deficiencies involve an absence of thinking (e.g., in impulsive youngsters), and distortions refer to dysfunctional thoughts (e.g., If I fail, my mother will die). Anxious children and adolescents seem preoccupied with concerns about evaluations by self or others, and they seem to misperceive the demands of the environment. Thus, they add to their own stress level.

Kendall et al. (1991) described an integrated cognitive-behavioral strategy that attempts to teach children and teens to recognize signs of anxious arousal and then to let these signs serve as cues for alternative anxiety management strategies. The overall strategy at Temple University's Child and Adolescent Anxiety Disorder clinic involves the following elements:

- Coping modeling
- Identification and modification of anxious self-talk
- Exposure to anxiety-provoking situations
- Role-playing and contingent reward procedures
- Homework assignments (show that I can, or STIC)
- Affective education
- Awareness of bodily reactions and cognitive activities when anxious
- Relaxation procedures
- Graduated sequence of training tasks and assignments
- Application and practice of newly acquired skills in increasingly anxiety-provoking situations

The overall approach to intervention is described in *Anxiety Disorders in Youth: Cognitive-Behavioral Intervention* by Kendall et al. (1992). The book describes the sessions in some detail and thus can serve as something of a manual for clinicians seeking a comprehensive cognitive-behavioral approach to intervention.

Pharmacotherapy

Agents that have been tried in children and adolescents with anxiety disorders include neuroleptics, psychostimulants, antihistamines, anxiolytics, and antidepressants. Although neuroleptics have been used in anxiety states, Gittelman-Klein (1978) reviewed the literature and concluded there was little support for the use of neuroleptics in child and adolescent anxiety disorders. Since then, it generally has been conceded that neuroleptics are not a viable class of drugs for anxiety disorders due to irreversible side effects and the availability of safer alternatives. Although stimulants have been tried, Gittelman and Koplewicz (1986) pointed out that there is no evidence that stimulants are effective, and there is some evidence they may be contraindicated. The same authors go on to point out that evidence for the effectiveness of antihistamines is clearly wanting.

Antianxiety agents or anxiolytics are commonly used for anxiety symptoms in clinical settings. They are not useful for some patients (e.g., anxious manics), however, and may be inferior to alternatives, such as tricyclic antidepressants for some types of anxiety disorder (e.g., panic disorder). Although barbiturates are the oldest of the sedatives, Gittelman and Koplewicz (1986) point out that they are no longer a part of modern psychopharmacology. They have been replaced by the safer benzodiazepines. Although there is a large amount of information on treatment of adult anxiety disorders, the available literature on applications with children and adolescents is severely limited. This led Gittelman and Koplewicz (1986) to conclude that documentation of usefulness is lacking. This does, however, not rule out possible efficacy.

Antidepressants, on the other hand, have shown significant promise. Two tricyclic antidepressants have shown particular promise: imipramine and clomipramine. Imipramine has been found effective in inducing a return to school, in reducing other anxious symptomatology, and in providing for improvement in depressive symptoms. Gittelman-Klein and Klein (1971, 1973, 1980) and Bernstein, Garfinkel, and Borchardt (1987) studied the effects of alprazolam and caripramiase on overanxious disorder and found alprazolam significantly superior. Klein and Last (1989) have more recently questioned the efficacy of tricyclic medications with separation-anxious children in light of more recent unpublished research.

A newer drug that is chemically related to imipramine, clomipramine (Prozac) has been used with children and adolescents with obsessive-compulsive disorder. Rapoport, Elkins, and Mikkelsen (1980) and Flament et al. (1985) have obtained results supportive of the use of clomipramine in relieving obsessive-compulsive symptomatology.

Gittelman and Koplewicz (1986) have concluded that tricyclics seem to play a legitimate role in management of some severe, early anxiety disorders. Only two diagnoses, separation anxiety and obsessive-compulsive disorder, however, have been subjected to systematic scrutiny.

Family Therapy

Cognitive-behavioral approaches are quite compatible with systems models that posit that children are part of a network of activity. Family involvement is an essential element in treatment of anxiety disorders in children and adolescents. Mills et al. (1973) found that parental involvement was an important element in a successful response-prevention program. Kendall et al. (1992) enlist parental cooperation in the application of their cognitive-behavioral intervention. The focus of treatment, however, remains on the anxiety of the youngster. Kendall's approach (Kendall et al., 1992) is to encourage a spirit of collaborative problem solving in which family members can look at their behavior patterns, expectations, and attributions and how those may be contributing to the youth's presentation and the methods that must be developed. Within any family, this may include changing

The parent's unhelpful expectations of the child or adolescent
The child's or adolescent's expectations about him- or herself
The child's or adolescent's maladaptive beliefs
Patterns of attribution about the causes of behavioral outcomes

Within the framework of family intervention, Kendall et al. (1992) engage in role-playing, family brainstorming and problem solving, family relaxation training and evaluation, and reinforcement of appropriate patterns of behavior.

More traditional family therapy may also be an adjunct to effective treatment of anxiety disorders (e.g., Haley, 1976; Minuchin, 1974). Anxiety disorder symptoms may be conceived as part of a disturbed family system. For example, Harbin (1976) described strategic family therapy with a 16-year-old with a compulsion to redo homework. Treatment included a change in parental discipline and alteration of a hostile relationship between the child and the mother.

The lack of systematic research on the effectiveness of family therapy with anxiety-disordered children leaves the matter in the hands of individual clinicians and their level of comfort with these approaches. Experienced clinicians and Mills et al. (1973) caution, however, that to leave the family out of treatment may increase the risk of relapse.

Prevention

Like the weather, prevention is something about which there is a great deal of talk and pitifully little action. This, and the lack of methodological rigor, led Peterson, Zink, and Farmer (1992) to conclude that preventive efforts have a small constituency and continue to be underfunded and underresearched. Also, the lack of understanding of the specifics of etiology make preventive programs for specific problems (e.g., anxiety disorders) a highly speculative matter. The distinction between primary, secondary, and tertiary prevention in the medical sciences has been applied to mental health (Winett, Riley, King, & Altman, 1989). Primary prevention involves reducing the incidence of new cases of the target disorder, secondary prevention involves reducing the duration and severity of the disorder, and tertiary prevention involves reducing the severity and disability of the disorder. Although community mental health centers were to have addressed prevention as one of its primary missions, serious applications were few and results were disappointing.

Winett et al. (1989) have proposed an integration of community psychology and concepts of public health in addressing prevention on the heels of the failure of the original goals of community mental health. They propose that prevention intervention can take place at several levels, including at the level of the individual, at an interpersonal level (e.g., families or groups), at an organizational level (e.g., school), or an institutional level (e.g., day care licensing or entire school systems). They also point out that at any given level the approach may be either a passive waiting mode or an active interventionist mode.

Unfortunately, the state of research on the conditions that lead to psychological disorders makes an acquisition-oriented (Chassin, Presson, & Sherman, 1985) approach to prevention difficult. The same set of conditions (e.g., high stress and social isolation) may contribute to a wide variety of specific disorders (e.g., depression, anxiety, child abuse, or alcoholism). This makes some of the more general approaches to prevention applicable to anxiety disorders. Specific approaches remain extremely rare.

Affective education is one area for primary prevention that could influence both the development of depression and the development of anxiety disorders. Examples of such programs are the Human Development Program (Bessell & Palomares, 1970) and Developing Understanding of Self and Others, or DUSO (Dinkmeyer, 1970). Provided at an organizational level in elementary schools, such programs have targeted improved self-esteem, peer relationships, and motivation.

In addition, such affective education programs could be more effective in prevention of anxiety disorders if they addressed such skills as the following:

- Developing cue controlled relaxation skills
- Conquering fear (e.g., what to do when you are scared)
- Developing self-control
- Facing criticism constructively
- Stress management skills
- Thinking and feeling
- Problem solving under stress
- Improving self-esteem
- Going to sleep
- Solving problems versus worrying

Major stressful life events may be assured to contribute to an exacerbation of the symptoms of anxiety disorders. Parental divorce is clearly one such stress. Two of the best known models are the Divorce Adjustment Project: Children's Support Group (CSG) (Stolberg & Garrison, 1985) and the Children of Divorce Intervention Project (Pedro-Carroll & Cowen, 1985). Such programs are delivered in groups and often involve teaching and practicing cognitive-behavioral skills such as relaxation, problem solving, communication, and self-control. The gamelike approach often stimulates motivation for both children and parents.

Proposals made by Winett et al. and others that might contribute to prevention of anxiety disorders include the following:

- Improving parenting skills (e.g., love and support)
- Improving family support skills
- Training for child care workers
- Training for teachers
- Improving child care resources
- Programs for preparation for medical or dental procedures
- After-school programs
- Improved television programs for children
- Early identification of anxiety disorders and early intervention
- Early development of stress management skills

Without more research on the effectiveness of such programs, it must be said that prevention holds much in the way of promise that has yet to be realized. In the meantime, the attempt to correctly diagnosis and treat child and adult anxiety disorders continues.

References

Achenbach, T. M. (1985). *Assessment and taxonomy of child and adolescent psychopathology*. Beverly Hills, CA: Sage.

Achenbach, T. M., & McConaughy, S. H. (1987). *Empirically based assessment of child and adolescent psychopathology*. Newbury Park, CA: Sage.

Adams, J. (1972). Psychotherapy with obsessive children. *American Journal of Psychiatry, 128*, 1414-1417.

Adams, J. (1973). *Obsessive children*. New York: Brunner/Mazel.

Agras, W. S., Chapin, H. N., & Oliveau, D. C. (1972). The natural history of phobia. *Archives of General Psychiatry, 26*, 315-317.

American Psychiatric Association. (1980). *Diagnostic and statistical manual of mental disorders* (3rd ed.). Washington, DC: Author.

American Psychiatric Association. (1987). *Diagnostic and statistical manual of mental disorders* (3rd ed., rev.). Washington, DC: Author.

American Psychiatric Association. (1994). *Diagnostic and statistical manual of mental disorders* (4th ed.). Washington, DC: Author.

Ayllon, T., Smith, D., & Rogers, M. (1970). Behavioral management of school phobia. *Journal of Behavior Therapy and Experimental Psychiatry, 1*, 125-138.

Baker, B. L., Cohen, D. C., & Saunders, J. T. (1973). Self-direction desensitization for acrophobic behavior. *Research Therapy, 11*, 79-89.

Ball, W., & Tronick, E. (1971). Infant response to impending collision: Optical and real. *Science, 171*, 818-820.

Bandura, A. (1969). *Principles of behavior modification*. New York: Holt, Rinehart & Winston.

Bandura, A. (1971). Psychotherapy based upon modeling principles. In A. E. Bergin & S. L. Garfield (Eds.), Handbook of psychotherapy and behavior change (pp. 653-708). New York: John Wiley.

Bandura, A. (1977). Self-efficacy: Toward a unifying theory of behavioral change. Psychological Review, 84, 191-215.

Bandura, A., Grusec, J., & Menlove, F. (1967). Vicarious extinction of avoidance behavior. Journal of Personality and Social Psychology, 5, 16-23.

Bandura, A., & Menlove, F. (1968). Factors determining vicarious extinction of avoidance behavior through symbolic modeling. Journal of Personality and Social Psychology, 9, 99-108.

Bandura, A., & Rosenthal, T. L. (1966). Vicarious classical conditioning as a function of arousal level. Journal of Personality and Social Psychology, 3, 54-62.

Barabasz, A. (1973). Group desensitization of test anxiety in elementary schools. Journal of Psychology, 83, 295-301.

Berg, I., Butler, A., & Pritchard, J. (1974). Psychiatric illness in the mothers of school-phobic adolescents. British Journal of Psychiatry, 125, 466-467.

Bergland, B. W., & Chal, A. H. (1972). Relaxation training and a junior high behavior problem. School Counselor, 20, 288-293.

Bernard, M. E., & Joyce, M. R. (1984). Rational-emotive therapy with children and adolescents. New York: John Wiley.

Bernard, M. E., Kratochwill, T. R., & Keefauver, L. W. (1983). The effects of rational-emotive therapy and self-instructional training on chronic hair pulling. Cognitive Therapy in Research, 7, 273-280.

Berney, T., Kolvin, I., Bhate, S. R., Garside, R. F., Jeans, J., Kay, B., & Scarth, L. (1981). School phobia: A therapeutic trial with clomipramine and short term-outcome. British Journal of Psychiatry, 1138, 110-118.

Bernstein, G. A., & Garfinkel, B. D. (1986). School phobia: The overlap of affective and anxiety disorders. Journal of the American Academy of Child Psychiatry, 25, 235-241.

Bernstein, G. A., Garfinkel, B. D., & Borchardt, C. M. (1987). Imipramine versus alprazolam for school phobia. Paper presented at the annual meeting of the American Academy of Child and Adolescent Psychiatry, Washington, DC.

Bessell, H., & Palomares, U. (1970). Methods in human development: Theory manual and curriculum activity guide. San Diego, CA: Human Development Training Institute.

Blagg, N. R., & Yule, W. (1984). The behavioral treatment of school refusal-comparative study. Behavior Research and Therapy, 22, 119-127.

Boer, A. P., & Sipprelle, C. N. (1970). Elimination of avoidance behavior in the clinic and its transfer to the normal environment. Journal of Behavior Therapy and Experimental Psychiatry, 1, 169-174.

Bowlby, J. (1961). Childhood mourning and its implications for psychiatry. American Journal of Psychiatry, 118, 481-498.

Bowlby, J. (1969). Attachment and loss: Vol. 1. Attachment. New York: Basic Books.

Bowlby, J. (1973). Attachment and loss: Vol. 2. Separation. New York: Basic Books.

Bronson, G. W. (1972). Infants' reactions to unfamiliar persons and novel object. Monographs of the Society for Research in Child Development, 37(3, Serial No. 148).

Brooks, J., & Lewis, M. (1976). Infants' response to strangers: Midget, adult and child. Child Development, 47, 323-332.

Campbell, S. B. (1986). Developmental issues in childhood anxiety. In R. Gittelman (Ed.), *Anxiety disorders of childhood* (pp. 24-52). New York: Guilford.

Carlson, C. L., Figueroa, R. G., & Lahey, B. B. (1986). Behavior therapy for childhood anxiety disorders. In R. Gittelman (Ed.), *Anxiety disorders of childhood* (pp. 204-232). New York: Guilford.

Cautela, J. R., & Groden, J. (1978). *Relaxation: A comprehensive manual for adults, children, and children with special needs.* Champaign, IL: Research Press.

Chassin, L. A., Presson, C. C., & Sherman, S. J. (1985). Stepping backward in order to step forward: An acquisition-oriented approach to primary prevention. *Journal of Consulting and Clinical Psychology, 53,* 612-622.

Conger, J. C., & Keane, S. P. (1981). Social skills intervention in the treatment of isolated or withdrawn children. *Psychological Bulletin, 90,* 478-495.

Delprato, D. J., & McGlynn, F. D. (1984). Behavioral theories of anxiety disorders. In S. M. Turner (Ed.), *Behavioral theories and treatment of anxiety* (2nd ed., pp. 1-42). New York: John Wiley.

Dinkmeyer, D. (1970). *Developing understanding of self and others.* Circle Pines, MN: American Guidance Service.

Earls, F. (1980). The prevalence of behavior problems in three year old children: A cross cultural replication. *Archives of General Psychiatry, 37,* 1153-1157.

Elkins, R., Rapoport, J. L., & Lipsky, A. (1980). Obsessive compulsive disorder of childhood and adolescence: A neurological viewpoint. *Journal of the American Academy of Psychiatry, 19,* 511-524.

Ellis, A. (1962). *Reason and emotion in psychotherapy.* New York: Stuart.

Ellis, A. (1984). *Rational-emotive therapy and cognitive behavior therapy.* New York: Springer.

Ellis, A., & Bernard, M. (Eds.). (1983). *Rational-emotive approaches to the problems of childhood.* New York: Plenum.

Eysenck, H. J. (1976). The learning theory model of neurosis: A new approach. *Behavior Research and Therapy, 14,* 251-267.

Fassler, D. (1985). The fear of needles in children. *American Journal of Orthopsychiatry, 31,* 371-377.

Flament, M. F., Rapoport, J. L., Murphy, D. L., Berg, C. J., & Lake, C. R. (1985). Biochemical changes during clomipramine treatment of childhood obsessive-compulsive disorders. *Archives of General Psychiatry, 42,* 977-983.

Foa, E. B., Steketee, G., & Milby, J. B. (1980). Differential effects of exposure and response prevention in obsessive-compulsive washers. *Journal of Consulting and Clinical Psychology, 48,* 71-79.

Fox, J., & Houston, B. (1981). Efficacy of self-instructional training for reducing children's anxiety in an evaluative situation. *Behaviour Research and Therapy, 19,* 509-515.

Freeman, B. T., Roy, R. R., & Hemmick, S. (1976). Extinction of a phobia of physical examination in a 7-year-old mentally retarded boy: A case study. *Behavior Research and Therapy, 14,* 63-64.

Genshaft, J. L. (1982). The use of cognitive behavior therapy for reducing math anxiety. *School Psychology Review, 11,* 32-34.

Gittelman, R. (1986). Childhood anxiety disorders: Correlations and outcome. In R. Gittelman (Ed.), *Anxiety disorders of childhood* (pp. 101-125). New York: Guilford.

Gittelman, R., & Koplewicz, H. S. (1986). Pharmacotherapy of childhood anxiety disorders. In R. Gittelman (Ed.), *Anxiety disorders of childhood* (pp. 188-203). New York: Guilford.

Gittelman-Klein, R. (1975). Psychiatric characteristics of the relatives of school phobic children. In D. V. S. Sankan (Ed.), *Mental health in children* (Vol. 1, pp. 325-334). Westbury, NY: PSD Publications.

Gittelman-Klein, R. (1978). Psychopharmacotherapy treatment of anxiety disorders, mood disorders and Tourette's disorder in children. In M. A. Lipton, A. DiMascio, & K. F. Killam (Eds.), *Psychopharmacology: A generation of progress* (pp. 1471-1480). New York: Raven.

Gittelman-Klein, R., & Klein, D. F. (1971). Controlled imipramine treatment of school phobia. *Archives of General Psychiatry, 25,* 204-207.

Gittelman-Klein, R., & Klein, D. F. (1973). School phobia: Diagnostic considerations in the light of imipramine effects. *Journal of Nervous and Mental Disease, 156,* 199-215.

Gittelman-Klein, R., & Klein, D. F. (1980). Separation anxiety in school refusal and its treatment with drugs. In L. Hersov & I. Berg (Eds.), *Out of school* (pp. 321-341). New York: John Wiley.

Gray, J. (1971). *The psychology of fear and stress.* New York: McGraw-Hill.

Graziano, A. M. (1978). Behavior therapy. In B. B. Wolman, J. Egan, & A. O. Ross (Eds.), *Handbook of treatment of mental disorders in childhood and adolescence.* Englewood Cliffs, NJ: Prentice Hall.

Graziano, A., & Mooney, K. (1984). *Children and behavior therapy.* New York: Aldine.

Haley, J. (1976). *Problem-solving therapy.* San Francisco: Jossey-Bass.

Harbin, H. T. (1976). Cure by ordeal: Treatment of an obsessive-compulsive neurotic. *International Journal of Family Therapy, 1,* 324-332.

Herson, M. (1970). Behavior modification approach to a school-phobia case. *Journal of Clinical Psychology, 26,* 128-132.

Jackson, H. J., & King, N. J. (1981). The emotive imagery treatment of a child's traumatic-induced phobia. *Journal of Behavior Therapy and Experimental Psychiatry, 12,* 325-328.

Jacobson, E. (1938). *Progressive relaxation.* Chicago: University of Chicago Press.

Judd, L. L. (1965). Obsessive-compulsive neurosis in children. *Archives of General Psychiatry, 12,* 136-142.

Kanfer, F. H., & Gaelick, L. (1986). Self-management methods. In F. H. Kanfer & A. P. Goldstein (Eds.), *Helping people change* (3rd ed., pp. 283-345). Elmsford, NY: Pergamon.

Kanfer, F. H., Karoly, P., & Newman, A. (1975). Reduction of children's fear of the dark by confidence-related and situational threat-related verbal cues. *Journal of Consulting and Clinical Psychology, 43,* 251-258.

Kanfer, F. H., & Schefft, B. K. (1988). *The basics of therapy.* Champaign, IL: Search Press.

Kazdin, A. E., & Wilson, G. T. (1978). *Evaluation of behavior therapy: Issues, evidence, and research strategies.* Cambridge, MA: Ballinger.

Kellerman, J. (1980). Rapid treatment of nocturnal anxiety in children. *Journal of Behavior Therapy and Experimental Psychiatry, 11,* 9-11.

Kendall, P. C. (1985). Toward a cognitive-behavioral model of child psychopathology and a critique of related interventions. *Journal of Abnormal Child Psychology, 13,* 357-372.

Kendall, P. C., & Braswell, L. (1985). *Cognitive-behavioral therapy for impulsive children.* New York: Guilford.

Kendall, P. C., Chansky, T. E., Freidman, M., Kim, R., Kortlander, E., Sessa, F. M., & Siqueland, L. (1991). Treating anxiety disorders in children and adolescents. In P. C. Kendall (Ed.), *Child and adolescent therapy: Cognitive-behavioral procedures* (pp. 131-164). New York: Guilford.

Kendall, P. C., Chansky, T. E., Kane, M. T., Kim, R. S., Kortlander, E., Ronan, K. R., Sessa, F. M., & Siqueland, L. (1992). *Anxiety disorders in youth: Cognitive-behavioral intervention.* Boston: Allyn & Bacon.

King, N. J., Hamilton, D. I., & Ollendick, T. H. (1988). *Children's phobias: A behavioural perspective.* New York: John Wiley.

Klein, R. G., & Last, C. G. (1989). *Anxiety disorders in children.* New York: Russell Sage.

Koeppen, A. S. (1974). Relaxation training for children. *Journal of Elementary School Guidance and Counseling, 9,* 14-21.

Kondas, O. (1967). Reduction of examination anxiety and "stage fright" by group desensitization and relaxation. *Behaviour Research and Therapy, 5,* 275-281.

Kushner, M. (1965). Desensitization of a post-traumatic phobia. In L. P. Ullman & L. Krasner (Eds.), *Case studies in behavior modification* (pp. 193-195). New York: Holt, Rinehart & Winston.

Last, C., Strauss, C., & Francis, G. (1987). Comorbidity among childhood anxiety disorders. *Journal of Nervous and Mental Disease, 175,* 726-730.

Lazarus, A. A. (1959). The elimination of children's phobias by deconditioning. In H. J. Eysenck (Ed.), *Behavior therapy and the neurosis.* Oxford: Pergamon.

Lazarus, A. A., & Abramovitz, A. (1962). The use of "emotive imagery" in the treatment of children's phobias. *Journal of Mental Science, 108,* 191-195.

Lazarus, A. A., Davison, G. C., & Polefka, D. A. (1965). Classical and operant factors in the treatment of school phobia. *Journal of Abnormal Psychology, 70,* 225-229.

Leitenberg, H., & Callahan, E. J. (1973). Reinforcement practice and reductions of different kinds of fears in adults and children. *Behaviour Research and Therapy, 11,* 19-30.

Luiselli, J. K. (1977). Case report: An attendant-administered contingency management program for the treatment of toileting phobia. *Journal of Mental Deficiency Research, 21,* 283-288.

Manchanda, R., & Sharma, M. (1986). Parental discipline and obsessive-compulsive neurosis. *Canadian Journal of Psychiatry, 31,* 1-25.

Mann, J., & Rosenthal, T. L. (1969). Vicarious and direct counterconditioning of test anxiety through individual and group desensitization. *Behaviour Research and Therapy, 7,* 359-367.

Marks, I. (1969). *Fears and phobias.* New York: Academic Press.

Marks, I. M. (1975). Behavioral treatments of phobic and obsessive-compulsive disorders: A critical appraisal. In M. Hersen, R. M. Eisler, & P. M. Miller (Eds.), *Progress in behavior modification* (Vol. 1). New York: Academic Press.

Meichenbaum, D. (1986). Cognitive behavior modification. In F. H. Kanfer & A. P. Goldstein (Eds.), *Helping people to change* (3rd ed., pp. 346-380). Elmsford, NY: Pergamon.

Meichenbaum, D., & Goodman, J. (1971). Training impulsive children to talk to themselves: A means of developing self-control. *Journal of Abnormal Psychology, 77,* 115-126.

Melamed, B. G., Hawes, R. R., Heigy, E., & Glick, J. (1975). Use of filmed modeling to reduce uncooperative behavior of children during dental treatment. *Journal of Dental Research, 54,* 797-801.

Melamed, B. G., & Siegel, L. J. (1975). Reduction of anxiety in children facing hospitalization and surgery by use of filmed modeling. *Journal of Consulting and Clinical Psychology, 43,* 511-521.

Melamed, B. G., Weinstein, D., Hawes, R., & Katin-Borland, M. (1975). Reduction of fear related dental management problems using filmed modeling. *Journal of the American Dental Association, 90,* 822-826.

Melamed, B. G., Yurcheson, R., Fleece, E. L., Hutcherson, S., & Hawes, R. (1978). Effects of film modeling on the reduction of anxiety-related behaviors in individuals varying in level of previous experience in the stress situation. *Journal of Consulting and Clinical Psychology, 46,* 1357-1367.

Mikulas, W. L., Coffman, M. G., Dayton, D., Frayne, C., & Maier, P. L. (1985). Behavioral bibliotherapy and games for treating fear of the dark. *Child and Family Behavior Therapy, 7,* 1-7.

Milby, J. B., & Weber, A. (1991). Obsessive compulsive disorders. In T. R. Kratochwill & R. J. Morris (Eds.), *The practice of child therapy* (2nd ed.). Elmsford, NY: Pergamon.

Miller, P. M. (1972). The use of visual imagery and muscle relaxation in the counterconditioning of a phobic child: A case study. *Journal of Nervous and Mental Disease, 154,* 457-460.

Mills, H. L., Agras, W. S., Barlow, D. H., & Mills, J. R. (1973). Compulsive rituals treated by response prevention: An experimental analysis. *Archives of General Psychiatry, 28,* 524-529.

Minuchin, S. (1974). *Families and family therapy.* Cambridge, MA: Harvard University Press.

Morris, R. J. (1973). Shaping relaxation in the unrelaxed client. *Journal of Behavior Therapy and Experimental Psychiatry, 4,* 343-353.

Morris, R. J., & Kratochwill, T. R. (1983). *Treating children's fears and phobias: A behavioral approach.* Elmsford, NY: Pergamon.

Morris, R. J., & Kratochwill, T. R. (1991). Childhood fears and phobias. In T. R. Kratochwill & R. J. Morris (Eds.), *The practice of child therapy* (2nd ed., pp. 76-114). Elmsford, NY: Pergamon.

Neisworth, J. T., Madle, R. A., & Goeke, K. E. (1975). Errorless elimination of separation anxiety: A case study. *Journal of Behavioral Therapy and Experimental Psychiatry, 6,* 79.

Obler, M., & Terwilliger, R. F. (1970). Test effectiveness of systematic desensitization with neurologically impaired children with phobic disorders. *Journal of Consulting and Clinical Psychology, 34,* 314-318.

Ollendick, T. H. (1978). *Relaxation techniques with hyperactive, aggressive children.* Unpublished manuscript, Indiana State University.

Ollendick, T. H. (1979). Fear reduction techniques with children. In M. Herson, R. M. Eisler, & P. M. Miller (Eds.), *Progress in behavior modification* (Vol. 8). New York: Academic Press.

Ollendick, T. H. (1983). Reliability and validity of the revised Fear Survey Schedule for Children (FSSCR-R). *Behavior Research and Therapy, 21,* 685-692.

Ollendick, T. H., & Cerny, J. A. (1981). *Clinical behavior therapy with children.* New York: Plenum.

Ollendick, T. H., & Gruen, G. E. (1972). Treatment of a bodily injury phobia with implosive therapy. *Journal of Consulting and Clinical Psychology, 38,* 389-393.

Ollendick, T. H., Matson, J. L., & Helsel, W. J. (1985). Fears in childhood and adolescents: Normative data. *Behavior Research and Therapy, 23,* 465-467.

Pedro-Carroll, J. L., & Cowen, E. L. (1985). The children of divorce intervention program: An investigation of the efficacy of a school-based prevention program. *Journal of Consulting and Clinical Psychology, 53,* 603-611.

Perry, M. A., & Furukawa, M. J. (1986). Modeling methods. In F. H. Kanfer & A. P. Goldstein (Eds.), *Helping people change* (3rd ed., pp. 66-110). Elmsford, NY: Pergamon.

Peterson, L., Zink, M., & Farmer, J. (1992). Prevention of disorders in children. In C. E. Walker & M. C. Roberts (Eds.), *Handbook of clinical child psychology* (2nd ed., p. 951). New York: John Wiley.

Piersel, W. C., & Kratochwill, T. R. (1981). A teacher-implemented contingency management package to assess and test selective mutism. *Behavioral Assessment, 3,* 371-382.

Quay, H. C. (1972). Patterns of aggression, withdrawal and immaturity. In H. C. Quay & J. S. Werry (Eds.), *Psychophysiological disorders of childhood* (pp. 1-29). New York: John Wiley.

Quay, H. C. (1977). Measuring dimensions of deviant behavior: The Behavior Problem Checklist. *Journal of Abnormal Child Psychology, 5,* 277-289.

Quay, H. C. (1979). Classification. In H. C. Quay & J. S. Werry (Eds.), *Psychopathological disorders of childhood* (2nd ed., pp. 1-42). New York: John Wiley.

Rachman, S. J. (1977). The conditioning theory of fear acquisition: A critical examination. *Behaviour Research and Therapy, 15,* 375-387.

Rachman, S. J., & Hodgson, R. J. (1980). *Obsessions and compulsions.* Englewood Cliffs, NJ: Prentice Hall.

Rapoport, J., Elkins, R., & Mikkelsen, E. (1980). Clinical controlled trial of clomipramine in adolescents with obsessive-compulsive disorder. *Psychopharmacology Bulletin, 16,* 61-63.

Reed, L. J., Carter, B. D., & Miller, L. C. (1992). Fear and anxiety in children. In C. E. Walker & M. Roberts (Eds.), *Handbook of clinical child psychology* (2nd ed., pp. 237-260). New York: John Wiley.

Rheingold, H. L., & Eckerman, C. (1973). Fear of the stranger: A critical examination. In H. W. Reese (Ed.), *Advances in child development and behavior* (Vol. 8). New York: Academic Press.

Richman, N., Stevenson, J. E., & Graham, P. J. (1975). Prevalence of behavior problems in three year old children: An epidemiological study in a London borough. *Journal of Child Psychology and Psychiatry, 16,* 277-287.

Ritter, B. (1968). The group desensitization of children's snake phobias using vicarious and contact desensitization procedures. *Behaviour Research and Therapy, 6,* 1-6.

Rosen, G. (1976). *Don't be afraid: A program for overcoming your fears and phobias.* Englewood Cliffs, NJ: Prentice Hall.

Saunders, D. G. (1976). A case of motion sickness treated by systematic desensitization and *in vivo* relaxation. *Journal of Behavior Therapy and Experimental Psychiatry, 7,* 381-382.

Scarr, S., & Salapatek, P. (1970). Patterns of fear development during infancy. *Merrill-Palmer Quarterly, 16,* 53-90.

Seligman, M. E. P. (1970). On the generality of the laws of learning. *Psychological Review, 77,* 406-418.

Seligman, M. E. P. (1971). Phobias and preparedness. *Behavior Therapy, 2,* 307-320.

Shepherd, M., Oppenheim, B., & Mitchell, S. (Eds.). (1971). *Childhood behavior and mental health.* London: University of London Press.

Sreenivasan, V., Manocha, S. N., & Jain, V. K. (1979). Treatment of severe dog phobia in childhood by flooding: A case report. *Journal of Child Psychology and Psychiatry, 20,* 255-256.

Stayton, D. J., Ainsworth, M. D. S., & Main, M. B. (1973). Development of separation behavior in the first year of life: Protest, following and greeting. *Psychology, 9,* 213-225.

Steketee, G., Grayson, J. B., & Foa, E. B. (1981, August). *Effects of exposure and response prevention on obsessive-compulsive symptoms.* Paper presented at the American Psychological Association meeting, Los Angeles, CA.

Stolberg, A. L., & Garrison, K. M. (1985). Evaluating a primary prevention program of children of divorce. *American Journal of Community Psychology, 13,* 111-124.

Strauss, C. C., Last, C. G., Herson, M., & Kazdin, A. (1988). Association between anxiety and depression in children and adolescents with anxiety disorders. *Journal of Abnormal Child Psychiatry, 16,* 57-68.

Tahmisian, J., & McReynolds, W. (1971). The use of parents as behavioral engineers in the treatment of a school phobic girl. *Journal of Counseling Psychology, 18,* 225-228.

Taylor, D. W. (1972). Treatment of excessive frequency of urination by desensitization. *Journal of Behavior Therapy and Experimental Psychiatry, 3,* 311-313.

Tseng, W. (1973). Psychopathologic study of obsessive-compulsive neurosis in Taiwan. *Comprehensive Psychiatry, 14,* 139-140.

Vaal, J. J. (1973). Applying contingency contracting to a school phobic: A case study. *Journal of Behavior Therapy and Experimental Psychiatry, 4,* 371-373.

Van der Ploeg-Stapert, J. D., & Van der Ploeg, H. M. (1986). Behavioral group treatment of test-anxiety: An evaluation study. *Journal of Behavior Therapy and Experimental Psychiatry, 17,* 255-259.

Waranch, H. R., Iwata, B. A., Wohl, M. K., & Nidiffer, F. D. (1981). Treatment of retarded adults' mannequin phobia through *in vivo* desensitization and shaping approach responses. *Journal of Behavior Therapy and Experimental Psychiatry, 12,* 359-362.

Watson, J. B., & Rayner, P. (1920). Conditioned emotional reactions. *Journal of Experimental Psychology, 3,* 1-14.

Weissman, M. M., Leckman, J. F., Merikangas, K. R., Gammon, G. B., & Prusoff, B. A. (1984). Depression and anxiety disorders in parents and children. *Archives of General Psychiatry, 41*, 845-852.

Werry, J. S., & Quay, H. C. (1971). The prevalence of behavior symptoms in younger elementary school children. *American Journal of Orthopsychiatry, 41*, 136-143.

White, W. C., & Davis, M. T. (1974). Vicarious extinction of phobic behavior in early childhood. *Journal of Abnormal Child Psychology, 2*, 25-37.

Wilson, B., & Jackson, H. J. (1980). An *in vivo* approach to the desensitization of a retarded child's toilet phobia. *Australian Journal of Developmental Disabilities, 6*, 137-141.

Winett, R. A., Riley, A. W., King, A. C., & Altman, D. G. (1989). Prevention in mental health: A proactive-developmental-ecological perspective. In T. H. Ollendick & M. Hersen (Eds.), *Handbook of child psychopathology* (2nd ed., pp. 499-521). New York: Plenum.

Wolpe, J., & Lazarus, A. A. (1966). *Behavior therapy techniques.* Elmsford, NY: Pergamon.

• CHAPTER 6 •

Adolescent Drug Abuse: Contemporary Perspectives on Etiology and Treatment

RUTH BAUGHER PALMER

HOWARD A. LIDDLE

Adolescent drug abuse remains at seriously high rates, has dire short- and long-term consequences, and is correlated with numerous other high-risk behaviors. An overview of the current status of intervention research on adolescent drug abuse is provided. Particular emphasis is given to models that integrate family-systems approaches in the conceptualization and treatment of adolescent drug abuse because family processes have been documented as crucial to its etiology and course. Five conclusions are drawn that have implications for clinicians.

Status of Adolescent Drug Abuse

The United States has the *highest* rate of adolescent drug abuse among the world's industrialized nations (Falco, 1988). In the latest University of Michigan High School Survey, researchers produced an alarming finding: Substance abuse is increasing in the early

AUTHORS' NOTE: Completion of this chapter was supported by grants R01DA3714 and P50DA07697 from the National Institute of Drug Abuse to Howard A. Liddle.

adolescent population (Johnston, O'Malley, & Bachman, 1992). Significant proportional increases in the number of early adolescent substance users prompted the following warning: "This newest wave of adolescents entering the teen years may be at the vanguard of a reversal of previously improving conditions" (Johnston, 1993).

Information obtained from national surveys may underestimate the prevalence of substance abuse problems among adolescents. Prominent surveys rely on student data (Johnston et al., 1992) and so chronic absentees and high school dropouts are not included (an estimated 15% to 20% of students in this age group). Others (National Institute on Drug Abuse, 1988) track youth over the age of 12 residing in a household. Transient, runaway, and homeless youth, populations at extreme risk for drug abuse problems (Dryfoos, 1990; Schinke, Botvin, & Orlandi, 1991), are not included.

In addition, prevalence rates are but one indicator of severity. Many other issues contribute to severity of adolescent drug use, including age at first use, availability of adequate treatment, whether or not treatment is sought for drug abuse (and at what point), whether treatment is voluntary or mandated, and, of course, degree of impact of the specific drug of choice. Striking increases in drug use have been documented in the lower grades, with the age of first use lowering throughout the 1970s (Johnston et al., 1992). Severity of drug use among urban minority youth may be especially underestimated because until recently, this population has been largely overlooked in prevalence and intervention studies (Booth, Castro, & Anglin, 1990; Gibbs, 1984; Maddahian, Newcomb, & Bentler, 1985). This is especially unfortunate because there is evidence that inner-city, minority adolescents have limited access to early-intervention programs (Thompson & Simmons-Cooper, 1988) and are likely to participate in mandated rather than voluntary treatment, which often takes on a punitive rather than a supportive connotation (Thompson & Simmons-Cooper, 1988).

Consequences of Adolescent Drug Abuse

There is an emerging group of young people "at risk" for serious long-term consequences of substance abuse. Dryfoos (1990) estimated that 25% of 10- to 17-year-olds are at high risk because of delinquency and heavy drug use, and another 25% are at moderate risk due to experimentation with problem behaviors including drug use. Reports from other sources provide similar bleak estimates of adolescents at risk (Hechinger, 1992; Task Force on the Education of Young Adolescents, 1989; U.S. Congress, Office of Technology Assessment [OTA], 1991).

The human cost of adolescent drug abuse assumes several forms: Excessive use can result in future health problems, psychosomatic symptoms, ineffective school/work performance and/or subsequent reduced life opportunities, dysphoric emotional functioning, and impaired interpersonal relationships. Statistics of death, injury, and impairment document grim consequences of alcohol- and drug-related accidents, suicides, and homicides (Harris, 1985). Adolescents who use drugs are at risk for a variety of immediate and long-term health problems (Cohen, 1981; Newcomb & Bentler, 1988). Multiple substance use during adolescence results in greater incidence of crime, marital and job instability, and inadequate parenting capabilities (Kandel, 1990; Newcomb & Bentler, 1988).

The psychological and developmental sequelae are particularly tragic. Drugs retard social and emotional growth by preventing normal problem-solving experiences and their concomitant skill development (Baumrind & Moselle, 1985; Coombs, Paulson, & Palley, 1988). Milman, Bennett, and Hanson (1983) describe the developmental disruption: These youngsters "emerge from adolescence without having experienced it, without having addressed its tasks, without being able to carry into adulthood the legacy of conflicts resolved, obstacles overcome, fears conquered, social skills mastered, values defined, and relationships established" (p. 53). Consequences of this disrupted development include impaired interpersonal relationships and school failure, the aftermath of which is carried into adulthood. Adolescent drug users bypass the typical maturational sequence of school, work, and family formation and make the transition prematurely into adult roles of jobs and family without the necessary skills for success in such tasks (Newcomb, 1987). "Thus teenage drug users may develop a pseudomaturity that ill-prepares them for the real difficulties of adult life. As a consequence, they should evidence greater difficulty, if not failure, in these roles over time" (Newcomb & Bentler, 1988, p. 65). Chronic adolescent drug abuse, of course, has even more serious effects. It can begin a process that marginalizes these youth from any mainstream challenges, opportunities, or rewards.

Risk and Protective Factors
for Adolescent Drug Abuse

Available evidence indicates that adolescent substance abuse is the result of multiple factors that are social, intrapersonal, and developmental in nature (Gersick, Grady, Sexton, & Lyons, 1985; Hawkins, Lishner, Catalano, & Howard, 1986; Newcomb, Maddahian, Skager, & Bentler, 1987). Contemporary research in developmental psychopathology views outcomes in adolescence (adaptive or maladaptive) to be

> a result of the interaction between what an individual brings into this period (one's developmental trajectory) and the nature of the challenges and resources available during this period. This conception requires identifying (a) individual characteristics and capacities that could be considered strengths or weaknesses, (b) social resources available before the transition, (c) specific challenges (demands) that occur during adolescent transitions and the capacities and coping responses needed for adaptation, and (d) how developmental trajectories, challenges, and resources interact in determining outcome. (Ebata, Peterson, & Conger, 1990, p. 322)

This suggests a risk/protection framework for conceptualizing adolescent developmental functioning. Indeed, numerous researchers are adopting a risk-focused approach for understanding and intervening with many kinds of human problems, ranging from physical health issues to education. In recent years, this approach has been applied to adolescent drug abuse.

Hawkins, Catalano, and Miller (1992) present a comprehensive review of the risk/protective framework for adolescent drug abuse. They identify 17 risk factors that are divided into two categories: contextual factors and individual/interpersonal factors. The next section discusses conceptual frameworks of intervention for adolescent drug abuse. Each theory hypothesizes a different factor or factors to predict/explain drug abuse and thus targets them in concomitant intervention models. As apparent in the Hawkins et al. (1992) review, research has not yet identified a *single* causal factor. In fact, the number of risk factors is a more important predictor of adolescent substance abuse than any single risk factor, leading researchers to support a "multiple pathway" model of drug use (Bry, McKeon, & Pandina, 1982; Newcomb, Maddahian, & Bentler, 1986).

Correlates of adolescent drug abuse detail a dire clinical picture of youth at risk for numerous deleterious outcomes. Age at first use is an important correlate, with early initiation being a significant predictor of later and more heavy use (Bry et al., 1982; Kandel & Raveis, 1989; Newcomb et al., 1986). Doing poorly in school is another risk factor for substance abuse as well as for other problem behaviors in adolescence, such as delinquency and teen pregnancy (Dryfoos, 1990). Low self-esteem and low conventionality (i.e., lack of conformity, low religiosity) have also been linked to drug abuse (Bry et al., 1982; Newcomb et al., 1986). Family risk factors include parent and sibling modeling of substance abuse, poor relationships with parents, and inadequate child-rearing practices (Coombs & Paulson, 1988). Finally, associating with peers who use substances, having low resistance to their influences, and favoring peers' opinions over parents' and other adults are all risk markers for substance abuse (Dryfoos, 1990; Newcomb et al., 1986).

All of these, plus physiological vulnerabilities such as sensation seeking, low harm avoidance, and poor impulse control, are included under Hawkins et al.'s (1992) "individual and interpersonal" factors. "Contextual" factors they identify include (a) laws and norms favorable toward drug use behavior, (b) availability of drugs, (c) extreme economic deprivation, and (d) neighborhood disorganization. The more of these factors a teenager exhibits, the greater the risk for drug abuse. The risk/protective framework is metatheoretical; it can serve as a guide for researchers and practitioners of various theoretical persuasions.

Conceptual Frameworks for Intervention

Given the immediate and long-term consequences of adolescent drug abuse (Halikas, Weller, Morse, & Hoffman, 1983; Kandel, Davies, Karus, & Yamaguchi, 1986; Newcomb & Bentler, 1988; Shedler & Block, 1990) as well as the startling conclusion that within the area of adolescent drug abuse, treatment is the least understood and researched topic (Newcomb & Bentler, 1989), the need for additional knowledge about effective interventions is clear.

Presumably, treatment approaches are determined by their underlying theories about the etiology of adolescent drug abuse. Although the disease model of addiction is the basis for the most common form of drug abuse treatment, rarely have these interventions been subject to empirical evaluation (Institute of Medicine, 1990; Schinke et al., 1991). Moreover, existing studies on the disease model of addiction have not found evidence that treatment programs using this model prevent adolescent substance abuse (Allison & Hubbard, 1985).

Treatment studies of adolescent drug abuse are few, but some encouraging results have been found (Liddle & Dakof, in press). Most promising are those studies that have tested theory-driven models for the prevention and treatment of adolescent substance abuse. These include models based on social learning theory, problem behavior theory, social stress theory, and family-systems theory. Each of these theories will be briefly outlined along with their corresponding intervention models.

Social Learning Theory

Social learning theory (Bandura, 1977) posits that behavior is learned through a process of modeling and reinforcement. Individuals integrate and imitate behaviors they observe in others as well as the consequences of those actions. Substance abuse is conceptualized as socially learned and purposeful behavior (Rhodes & Jason, 1988a). Thus, researchers hypothesize that substance abuse can be prevented by helping adolescents develop skills that make them less susceptible to the social influences promoting substance abuse.

The social development model of Hawkins and colleagues (Hawkins & Weis, 1985) is grounded in social learning theory. It incorporates the concept of prosocial attachments as a buffer against adolescent problems such as conduct problems, school failure, and drug abuse. Several processes are hypothesized to produce bonds of attachment, commitment, and beliefs in the values of the social unit. These include (a) opportunities for involvement offered in each social unit, (b) skills used by people in the social unit, and (c) the reinforcements offered by that social unit (Catalano & Hawkins, 1996). Four elements of social bonding have been shown to protect and deter young people from drug abuse: strong attachments to parents, commitment to education, regular involvement in church activities, and belief in the conventional expectations, norms, and values of society (Hawkins et al., 1992). This model seeks to enhance these multiple prosocial bonds in an effort to cultivate values in youth that are antithetical to drug abuse.

Problem Behavior Theory

Jessor and Jessor (1977) conceptualize substance abuse to be one factor in a cluster of adolescent behaviors that make up a syndrome of problem behaviors. Drinking, smoking, drug use, delinquency, and precocious sexual activity are considered to be elements of a deviant adolescent lifestyle. In addition, deviance may involve certain nontraditional values, such as low religiosity, rebelliousness, and disregard for the law. Together, these attitudes and behaviors constitute a syndrome that is hypothesized to have the same etiology. This underlying tendency is determined by the interplay between behavior, personality, and the perceived social environment (Rhodes & Jason, 1988a). Problem behavior theory has been established in empirical studies (Donovan & Jessor, 1985; Donovan, Jessor, & Costa, 1988), replicated with additional populations, including ethnic minority students (Farrell, Danish, & Howard, 1992), and shown to have stability over time (Newcomb & McGee, 1991).

Drug use has been found to be a consistently strong indicator of deviance in general (McGee & Newcomb, 1992). Similar to social learning theory, problem behavior theory views substance abuse as functional behavior. It may fulfill some personal goal (e.g., facilitate admission to a peer group), or it may serve as a means of coping with failure, boredom, anxiety, or rejection (Jessor, 1984). Thus, deterring substance abuse requires that adolescents gain alternative means to accomplish these goals.

Several skills-based strategies have been tested that seek to enhance the social coping skills of youth to offset the pressures to use drugs and to provide alternative ways to establish effective interpersonal relationships (Botvin, Baker, Dusenbury, Tortu, & Botvin, 1990; Schinke & Gilchrist, 1984). These models have similar theoretical roots in social learning and problem behavior theories, and they use similar intervention strategies. Generic social and coping skills are targeted as well as domain-specific skills, knowledge, attitudes, and expectations about drugs. These models have demonstrated significant reductions in the use of one or more substances (Rhodes & Jason, 1988a; Schinke et al., 1991).

Social Stress Theory

Based on Albee's (1982) conceptualization of psychopathology, social stress theory posits risk for substance abuse to be a function of the stress level in an adolescent's life and the extent to which it is offset by positive attachments, coping skills, and resources (Rhodes & Jason, 1988a). In addition to individual and family variables such as social support and coping skills, the social stress model also seeks to address broader social variables that influence adolescent behavior (Rhodes & Jason, 1990). Among these environmental variables are community resources, role models, and opportunities.

Adolescent substance abuse is viewed as a long-term outcome of the transactions between the individual, significant others, and the social system. Thus, interventions are targeted not only at the individual adolescent but also at the ecological variables that influence substance abuse. In particular, prevention programs are aimed at the family, the school, the community, and the media (Rhodes & Jason, 1988a). Several studies have documented significant reductions in substance abuse as a result of comprehensive community-based programs (Johnson et al., 1990; Kim, 1982; Pentz et al., 1989; Rhodes & Jason, 1988b).

Family-Systems Theory

Although models based on each of the preceding theories are usually aimed at *preventing* adolescent substance abuse, family-based models typically are *treatment* focused. It is odd that families have seldom been included in prevention efforts, given the influence families have on adolescent behavior, including substance abuse involvement (Hawkins et al., 1992). Moreover, Bry (1985) found that when families are included in prevention programs, risk factors can be reduced, family management practices can be improved, and early signs of substance abuse problems can be reversed. In fact, some researchers conclude that when it is combined with other prevention targets, family involvement is the most successful means of drug abuse prevention (Dishion, Reid, & Patterson, 1988; Glynn & Haenlein, 1988a).

The past decade has witnessed an emerging interest in families in research on the etiology and treatment of adolescent substance abuse (Glynn & Haenlein, 1988b). Family-based theories have evolved from a focus on structural characteristics of the family such as birth order, family size, and family composition to dynamic characteristics of the family such as the parent-child relationship, parental modeling behavior (Glynn & Haenlein, 1988b), family adaptability, cohesion, and closeness (Friedman, Utada, & Morrisey, 1987). According to the family-systems perspective, these family processes are the core intervention targets.

Several family process variables have been implicated as correlates of adolescent drug abuse. There is widespread evidence that a positive relationship between parent(s) and child can serve as a protective buffer against involvement with drugs (Brook, Whiteman, Nomura, Gordon, & Cohen, 1988; Kandel, 1982; Wills, 1990). What appears to be crucial is the adolescent's perception of the presence of parental love and acceptance. In their absence, the teenager is more vulnerable to peer and societal influences to use drugs (Stein, Newcomb, & Bentler, 1987).

Family modeling of drug use has been found to be significantly related to adolescent use. Parent drug use has consistently been shown to influence children's decisions regarding drug use (Brook, Whiteman, & Gordon, 1983; Huba & Bentler, 1980; Newcomb, Huba, & Bentler, 1983). Of equal or greater importance, however, is perceived parental attitudes toward drug use. Adolescents who perceive their parents as having permissive views about drug abuse are more likely to use drugs than those who perceive their parents as holding nonpermissive views (McDermott, 1984). Relationships with other family members also affect substance use. Older siblings who are drug users can increase the likelihood of drug involvement by making substances available, initiating and engaging their younger siblings in drug use, and modeling attitudes approving of drug involvement (McKillip, Johnson, & Petzel, 1973; Needle et al., 1986).

Finally, family management strategies have been linked to adolescent substance abuse (Glynn & Haenlein, 1988b). Studies of parental style demonstrate how parental control strategies affect adolescent behavior, particularly in early and middle adolescence. Specifically, parents shape prosocial attitudes and behavior (and thus deter substance use) when they make clear behavioral expectations (such as demands for maturity and consistent monitoring of behavior) and implement consequences in a nonpunitive way (Baumrind, 1991; Block, Block, & Keyes, 1988; Coombs & Landsverk, 1988; Patterson,

1986; Shedler & Block, 1990). Conversely, discipline and supervision that is at either extreme—harsh, autocratic, and intrusive or permissive and neglectful—have been linked with adolescent drug use (Brook et al., 1988).

Intervention Studies:
Family Therapy With Adolescent Drug Abusers

As the research linking family processes and adolescent substance abuse grows, intervention studies have also been initiated that target family factors in treatment. Structural and strategic family therapy techniques have been among the most frequent interventions with adolescent substance abusers and their families (Szapocznik, Kurtines, Foote, & Perez-Vidal, 1983; Szapocznik et al., 1988). Szapocznik et al. (1983) compared conjoint structural-strategic family therapy (CFT) with one-person family therapy (OPFT) in treating adolescent substance abuse. Results indicated that both treatments were highly effective. The OPFT was not only as effective as the conjoint modality in bringing about significant improvement in behavior problem/drug abuse in youth, but also was as effective as conjoint in bringing about and maintaining significant improvements in family functioning. These results demonstrated that it is possible to change family interactions even when the whole family is not present. Thus, this model proves promising in addressing the extensive problem of getting families to come to treatment.

In a rare study on engagement of resistant families in treatment, Szapocznik et al. (1988) tested Strategic Structural Systems Engagement (SSSE) with an Engagement as Usual (EAU) condition. SSSE employs the same systemic and structural principles that are used in understanding and treating the family once it is in therapy to understand and treat the family's resistance to engagement. OPFT techniques were used with the family member who initiated therapy on the phone. Once the "symptom" of resistance was overcome and a family member agreed to come to therapy, the focus of treatment shifted to the presenting "symptom" of problem behavior and drug abuse. Findings of the two treatment methods (SSSE and EAU) were dramatic: More than 57% of the EAU families failed to engage in treatment; only 7.15% in the SSSE condition were lost from treatment. For families that completed both conditions, there were highly significant improvements in both the problematic adolescent's functioning and in family functioning, and these improvements were not significantly different across conditions. Thus, the critical distinction between the two was in their differential rate of retention.

This comprehensive program of research has resulted in significant contributions to the treatment of adolescent substance abuse by demonstrating how cultural variables can be synthesized within a model to enhance treatment engagement and outcome (Catalano et al., 1993). Szapocznik and his colleagues have used cultural knowledge in their treatment conceptualizations of specific clinical problems. They have then implemented that knowledge in the form of specific interventions in the therapy. The result has been a problem-specific and culturally sensitive model of treatment that has demonstrated excellent results with Hispanic populations.

The program of research at the Oregon Social Learning Center (OSLC) has implemented social learning principles in family treatment, specifically targeting parent management practices (Dishion, Patterson, & Kavanagh, 1992). They have articulated four empirically derived targets for effective family intervention: (a) parental monitoring practices, (b) adolescent's peer associates, (c) parental modeling of drug use, and (d) adolescent's level of skills and antisocial behavior (Dishion et al., 1988). Two approaches to intervening on these variables that represent the major outpatient intervention modalities in the field of adolescent drug use are parent training and peer training intervention. Parent training is based on social learning principles of child management. Based on 20 years of treating families with antisocial children, researchers at the OSLC have found promising results of parent management techniques with a variety of antisocial child behaviors, including substance abuse. Peer training interventions are skill-based models, often provided as prevention programs in school settings. Dishion et al. hypothesize that a more powerful treatment may be a *package* that combines family management training with a skills-based approach. Combination models of treatment have been developed and tested with success (Henggeler et al., 1986; Liddle, 1994).

Finally, as Dishion et al. (1988) suggest, models that integrate family-systems interventions with behavioral ones are emerging with promising results, demonstrating the efficacy of multicomponent treatment packages. In a small study, Bry, Conboy, and Bisgay

(1986) applied findings from adult literature on substance abuse treatment to the behavioral treatment of adolescent drug abusers and their families. Robin's (1981) problem-solving training was employed with variable but promising results. Three months of targeted family problem-solving training decreased drug use and school failure by the end of the 1¼-year follow-up.

Other integrative models have also demonstrated effectiveness with adolescent drug abusers and their families. A report by Lewis, Piercy, Sprenkle, and Trepper (1990) comparing the Purdue Brief Family Therapy model (PBFT) with family drug education showed that family therapy produced significant pre-post decreases in drug use, whereas drug education did not. PBFT integrates present-centered, problem-focused skills from structural, strategic, functional, and behavioral family therapies. Similarly, a treatment study by Joanning, Quinn, Thomas, and Mullen (1992) comparing family therapy with family drug education and adolescent group therapy found that the percentages of drug use for the three treatment conditions were 54%, 28%, and 16% for family therapy, education, and group therapy, respectively. Thus, the family-based conditions achieved the greatest effects.

Liddle et al. (1991) found similar results in a comparison of three treatments for adolescent substance abuse: Multidimensional Family Therapy (MDFT), Peer Group Therapy, and Multifamily Therapy. Liddle et al. (1991) found that 53% of youth receiving family therapy (MDFT) were hard drug users at pretest. At posttest, only 9% used hard drugs, and at 1-year follow-up, only 3% were using hard drugs. At termination, follow-up, or both, 81% of youth who got MDFT were either using no or very few substances; 47% were completely drug-free; and another 34% were using alcohol and/or marijuana once a week or less. Although all three of their compared treatments were at least somewhat effective in reducing adolescent drug abuse, MDFT provided the greatest decrease from pretreatment to posttreatment. Moreover, drop-out rates in MDFT were significantly lower than the rates in the other two conditions. As in the Szapocznik et al. (1988) study, this finding is especially significant because of growing recognition in the drug abuse field that attrition should be considered one of the more important outcome variables in intervention studies, given the intractable nature of substance abuse and the difficulty of retaining subjects in treatment (DeLeon & Jainchill, 1986). Similar retention results were found in

Friedman's (1989) comparison of family therapy with parent education for treatment of adolescent substance abuse. At follow-up evaluation 9 months posttreatment, both conditions showed significant improvement on numerous outcome criteria, including substance abuse (by more than 50% of the mean value of the Drug Severity Index scores). Although there was no significant difference between the two groups in degree of improvement on outcome measures, the family therapy condition enjoyed a much higher participation rate. In 93% of the family therapy cases, one or both parents remained in treatment, whereas only 67% of the parent education cases retained one or more parent. Again, given the field's concerns, the ability of family therapy models to engage and retain clients should be understood as one of the most promising findings for adolescent substance abuse treatment.

The Friedman (1989) investigation also demonstrates how empirically derived family therapy models can effectively treat related adolescent problems. In this study, the family therapy condition used the functional family therapy method of Alexander and Barton (1983), which has shown effectiveness with delinquent adolescents (Alexander, Barton, Schiavo, & Parsons, 1976). Thus, family therapy models targeting delinquency, an established correlate of adolescent drug abuse, may also offer promise with drug-abusing youth.

In all of the family-based models, family factors are targeted that have been linked to the etiology of adolescent substance abuse. Given that a 20-year literature review of treatment research (Kazdin, Bass, Ayers, & Rodgers, 1990) showed that family therapy was evaluated in only 4.1% of all the investigations, it is not surprising that there are relatively few studies of family therapy for adolescent substance abuse. Reviews of these intervention studies confirm the potential for family-based models, particularly those that are comprehensive in conceptualization and treatment delivery (Bry, 1988; Liddle & Dakof, in press).

Conclusions

Adolescent Drug Abuse Requires Multidimensional Conceptualizations and Interventions. Contemporary theory and research provide no simple explanation for adolescent drug abuse. Substance abuse in adolescence is understood within a multicausal, interactive framework that considers intrapersonal, interpersonal, and socio-cultural correlates. Thus, programs that intervene in multiple do-mains (i.e., individual, family, school, community) and address multiple targets (including the problem behavior itself and the precursors or correlates that heighten the risk) constitute state-of-the-art treatment. Hawkins et al.'s (1992) extensive review of research on risk and protective factors of adolescent drug abuse characterizes the current knowledge base:

> Most studies to date have focused on small subsets of identifiable risk factors for drug abuse. There is little evidence available regarding the relative importance and interactions of various risk factors in the etiology of drug abuse, although current studies are seeking to mea-sure a broader range of identified risk factors. At this time, it is difficult to ascertain, for instance, which risk factors or combinations of risk factors are most virulent, which are modifiable, and which are specific to drug abuse rather than generic contributors to adolescent problem behaviors. Current knowledge about the risk factors for drug abuse does not provide a formula for prevention, but it does point to potential targets for preventive intervention. (p. 65)

Consequently, interventions must be comprehensive in scope, tar-geting not only substance abuse directly but the concomitant prob-lem behaviors and their suspected etiological roots. Concerted efforts must be exerted to discern the psychological meanings and functions of drug abuse and other problem behaviors:

> This implies interventions that, in addition to specific, behavior-rele-vant information, attitudes, and skills, would orient toward the lifestyle organization of the separate risk behaviors, and therefore, toward alternative lifestyle choice. The general emphasis of such programs would be on health-promoting lifestyles that are relatively incompatible with the syndrome of risk behavior. (Jessor, 1984, p. 87)

The Course of Adolescent Drug Abuse Indicates a Progression From Problems Exhibited Long Before Adolescence. Longitudinal studies have facilitated further clarity on the developmental pathways leading to adolescent drug abuse. Early conduct problems (at pre-school) such as aggressiveness, irritability, and noncompliance have consistently been found to predict substance abuse (Hawkins et al.,

1986; Kellam, Brown, Rubin, & Ensminger, 1983) as well as other antisocial behavior in adolescence (Loeber, 1990). Several research programs have empirically derived models of deviant developmental trajectories that result in adolescent drug abuse. Patterson and colleagues (Loeber, 1990; Patterson, Reid, & Dishion, 1992) hypothesize that seemingly trivial coercive acts in early childhood are prototypes of more severe adolescent delinquent behaviors. Coercive acts are reinforced in home and school settings, and, over time, the child learns new coercive behaviors and becomes more proficient at using them to escape aversive situations. Family interactions are seen as integral to the course of this progression:

> A parent who is continually defeated in face-to-face discipline confrontations with a child will begin to feel there is no way to control the child's behavior. Eventually, the parent will stop monitoring what the child is doing. When the child's behavior is no longer being monitored by parents and teachers, the stage is set for learning about clandestine acts such as stealing, lying, truancy, experimenting with drugs, and spending time with antisocial peers. (Patterson et al., 1992, p. 29)

Thus, drug abuse is hypothesized to be part of a pattern of events wherein antisocial behavior is reinforced in multiple settings over a series of stages. The first stage consists of early coercive behavior that is reinforced by inadequate parenting practices, including inconsistent and poor monitoring. Second, the child's abrasive and noncompliant behavior results in disruption in academic skill acquisition and rejection by prosocial peers and adults (see also Dodge, Price, Bachorowski, & Newman, 1990). The child's social and academic failures at this stage lead him or her to seek out a supportive environment. In the third stage, the adolescent gravitates toward a deviant peer group in which drug use is common. Finally, severely lacking in skills and prosocial peer networks, the adolescent is at risk for long-term antisocial behavior as an adult (Patterson et al., 1992).

The social development model of Hawkins and colleagues provides a similar explanation of the etiology and course of adolescent drug use; it is also conceptualized in the context of the development of deviance as opposed to one of a unitary pathway to substance abuse. According to the social development model, deviance is produced by a weak, broken, or absent bond to the conventional order, including conventional individuals, activities, and beliefs (Hawkins et al., 1986):

> Behavior patterns will be more or less deviant depending on the types of opportunities and social influences to which one is exposed, the skillfulness with which one performs in various activities and interactions, and the relative balance of rewards one receives from participation in these activities. (p. 34)

As in Patterson and colleagues' model, the social development model identifies significant attachments (including families, schools, and peers) as settings for the development of prosocial or antisocial behavior, values, and skills, including drug use/nonuse behavior and attitudes.

The progression of drug abuse has important implications for prevention and treatment. We know from correlational data that school failure typically accompanies all of the problem behaviors (Dryfoos, 1990). We know from the developmental psychopathology literature that childhood aggression frequently precedes school difficulties (Loeber, 1990). We also know that childhood aggression occurs in the context of several family factors that place children at risk for conduct problems (Kazdin, 1987). Identifying and treating children who evidence aggressive behaviors and academic failure, as well as their families, may therefore be an important primary step in preventing substance abuse in adolescence (Dryfoos, 1990).

Multiple Targets of Intervention Can Be Identified From Studies of Risk Factors for Adolescent Drug Abuse. Because drug abuse appears to be multicausal in etiology and progresses with varying behaviors and in multiple contexts over time, numerous intervention targets are possible at different points in the developmental course. Cognitive processes, for example, are an important target for intervention. Coping skills, attributions about one's own competence, and interpretation of health-related information are all connected to adolescents' individual levels and styles of cognitive processing and subsequent drug attitudes and consumption.

Families are also key to alleviating adolescent drug abuse. The adolescent development literature tells us that detachment from parents makes teens vulnerable to negative peer influences (Kandel

& Andrews, 1987). Intervening with families to strengthen the parent-adolescent bond is crucial, and the developmental literature can guide us in this regard (Liddle, Schmidt, & Ettinger, in press). In addition to helping families cultivate developmentally appropriate attachment, there should be a complementary focus on developing appropriate parental influence (Liddle, 1994), in particular, discipline, monitoring, and reinforcement strategies. Families with high levels of warmth, democratic control, and psychological autonomy are most likely to produce teenagers who are competent and resistant to pressures to use drugs (Baumrind, 1991).

Developmentally Informed Interventions With Adolescents. Models must be individualized to the unique needs of the adolescent. There is great diversity among adolescents in terms of levels of ego functioning, social skills, and cognitive development. Developmental differences in adolescents' concepts of causality, emotion regulation, social perceptions, and perspective taking require therapeutic approaches that consider each child's unique abilities (Liddle & Schmidt, 1994). The matching of therapeutic efforts to the developmental needs of the adolescent is overlooked in the literature. Shirk (1988) identifies cognitive development to be a significant moderator of the therapy process: "Children at different ages bring markedly different cognitive repertoires and information processing capacities to the process of child psychotherapy. Consequently, their ability to communicate in and extract meaning from psychotherapy will be determined, in part, by their level of cognitive development" (p. 321).

Moreover, outcome research demonstrates greater improvement among adolescents whose treatment is matched to their individual cognitive style (Hester & Miller, 1988). Clinicians have multiple sources to assess adolescents' cognitive levels and hence their abilities to participate in therapeutic interventions. In addition to school records, testing results, and teachers' and parents' assessments of adolescents' cognitive capabilities and style, clinicians can learn by observation of the ways in which the adolescent reasons, communicates, strategizes, and remembers information (Liddle & Diamond, 1991).

Theory-Driven and Empirically Derived Interventions. Failure to anchor programs in a theoretical base and inadequate evaluation have been linked to ineffective outcomes with substance-abusing and delinquent youth (Stein, Garrett, & Christiansen, 1990). The proliferation of prevention and treatment approaches has not resulted in significant gains in reducing adolescent substance abuse (Tobler, 1986). Current outcome research reveals positive results of some models based on family-systems and behavior theories (Bry, 1988; Liddle & Dakof, in press). Integrative models that systematically combine interventions from various theoretical models are the wave of the future (Dishion et al., 1988). There is general agreement in intervention research that the most effective programs (a) are derived from an understanding of the causes and risk factors leading to the problem; (b) draw on theories and models of human behavior that direct the program's focus; (c) use intervention methods or techniques known to change behavior; and (d) monitor intervention implementation rigorously (Kazdin, 1993). Scales (1990) presents relevant recommendations for constructing and implementing such programs:

> Recognize the importance of the early childhood through early adolescent years, acknowledge the interconnectedness of these problems, and concentrate on strengthening coping skills, conditions that promote self-esteem and social support of various kinds, including increasing emphasis on simultaneous efforts with the adolescent as a whole person in an ecology of family, school, and community. (p. 423)

Although his recommendations are aimed at prevention in the generic sense, they are equally applicable to the prevention and treatment of adolescent substance abuse. For the one fourth to one half of our nation's youth who are at moderate to severe risk, we have much work to do to develop such programs to address their urgent needs.

In conclusion, several recommendations can be made. First, a multicausal, interactive framework is needed to sufficiently conceptualize the complex network of variables associated with adolescent drug abuse. Second, research on developmental psychopathology indicates the course of adolescent drug abuse to be a progression from problems exhibited long before adolescence. Third, targets for intervention include both the cognitive processes of the individual adolescent as well as the affective and behavioral realms of the family system. Fourth, interventions must be developmentally appropriate to the individual needs of the adolescent. Finally, interventions that have the most promise are theory driven and empirically derived.

References

Albee, W. (1982). Preventing psychopathology and promoting human potential. *American Psychologist, 32*, 150-161.

Alexander, J., & Barton, C. (1983). *Functional family therapy training manual*. Salt Lake City, UT: Western States Family Institute.

Alexander, J., Barton, C., Schiavo, R. S., & Parsons, B. V. (1976). Systems-behavioral intervention with families of delinquents: Therapist characteristics, family behavior, and outcome. *Journal of Consulting and Clinical Psychology, 44*, 656-664.

Allison, M., & Hubbard, R. L. (1985). Drug abuse treatment process: A review of the literature. *International Journal of Addictions, 20*, 1321-1345.

Bandura, A. (1977). *Social learning theory*. Englewood Cliffs, NJ: Prentice Hall.

Baumrind, D. (1991). The influence of parenting style on adolescent competence and substance abuse. *Journal of Early Adolescence, 11*, 56-95.

Baumrind, D., & Moselle, K. A. (1985). A developmental perspective on adolescent drug abuse. *Advances in Alcohol and Substance Abuse, 4*, 41-67.

Block, J., Block, J. H., & Keyes, S. (1988). Longitudinally foretelling drug usage in adolescence: Early childhood personality and environmental precursors. *Child Development, 59*, 336-355.

Booth, M. W., Castro, F. G., & Anglin, M. D. (1990). What do we know about Hispanic substance abuse? A review of the literature. In R. Glick & J. Moore (Eds.), *Drugs in Hispanic communities* (pp. 21-43). New Brunswick, NJ: Rutgers University Press.

Botvin, G. J., Baker, E., Dusenbury, L., Tortu, S., & Botvin, E. M. (1990). Preventing adolescent drug abuse through a multimodal cognitive-behavioral approach: Results of a 3-year study. *Journal of Consulting and Clinical Psychology, 58*, 437-446.

Brook, J. S., Whiteman, M., & Gordon, A. S. (1983). Stages of drug use in adolescence: Personality, peer, and family correlates. *Developmental Psychology, 19*, 269-277.

Brook, J. S., Whiteman, M., Nomura, C., Gordon, A. S., & Cohen, P. (1988). Personality, family, and ecological influences on adolescent drug use: A developmental analysis. In R. H. Coombs (Ed.), *The family context of adolescent drug use* (pp. 123-161). New York: Haworth.

Bry, B. H. (1985). Empirical foundations of family-based approaches to adolescent substance abuse. In T. J. Glynn, C. G. Leukefeld, & J. P. Ludford (Eds.), *Prevention of adolescent drug abuse* (DHE# [ADM]47, pp. 115-140). Rockville, MD: National Institute on Drug Abuse.

Bry, B. H. (1988). Family-based approaches to reducing adolescent substance use: Theories, techniques, and findings. In E. R. Rahdert & J. Grabowski (Eds.), *Adolescent drug abuse: Analyses of treatment research* (NIDA Research Monograph 77, DHHS Pub. No. [ADM]88-1523, pp. 39-68). Rockville, MD: National Institute on Drug Abuse.

Bry, B. H., Conboy, C., & Bisgay, K. (1986). Decreasing adolescent drug use and school failure: Long-term effects of targeted family problem-solving training. *Child and Family Behavior Therapy, 8,* 43-59.

Bry, B. H., McKeon, P., & Pandina, R. S. (1982). Extent of drug use as a function of number of risk factors. *Journal of Abnormal Psychology, 91,* 273-279.

Catalano, R. F., & Hawkins, J. D. (1996). The social development model: A theory of antisocial behavior. In J. D. Hawkins (Ed.), *Delinquency and crime: Current theories.* New York: Cambridge University Press.

Catalano, R. F., Hawkins, J. D., Krenz, C., & Gillmore, M., et al. (1993). Using research to guide culturally appropriate drug use prevention. *Journal of Consulting and Clinical Psychology, 61,* 804-811.

Cohen, S. J. (1981). *The substance abuse problems.* New York: Haworth.

Coombs, R. H., & Landsverk, J. (1988). Parenting styles and substance use during childhood and adolescence. *Journal of Marriage and the Family, 50,* 473-482.

Coombs, R. H., & Paulson, M. J. (1988). Contrasting family patterns of adolescent drug users and nonusers. In R. H. Coombs (Ed.), *The family context of adolescent drug use* (pp. 59-72). New York: Haworth.

Coombs, R. H., Paulson, M. J., & Palley, R. (1988). The institutionalization of drug use in America: Hazardous adolescence, challenging parenthood. In R. H. Coombs (Ed.), *The family context of adolescent drug use* (pp. 9-37). New York: Haworth.

DeLeon, G., & Jainchill, N. (1986). Circumstance, motivation, readiness, and suitability as correlates of treatment tenure. *Journal of Psychoactive Drugs, 18,* 203-208.

Dishion, T. J., Patterson, G. R., & Kavanagh, K. A. (1992). An experimental test of the coercion model: Linking theory, measurement, and intervention. In J. McCord & R. E. Tremblay (Eds.), *Preventing antisocial behavior* (pp. 253-282). New York: Guilford.

Dishion, T. J., Reid, J. B., & Patterson, G. R. (1988). Empirical guidelines for a family intervention for adolescent drug abuse. In R. H. Coombs (Ed.), *The family context of adolescent drug use* (pp. 189-224). New York: Haworth.

Dodge, K. A., Price, J. M., Bachorowski, J., & Newman, J. P. (1990). Hostile attributional biases in severely aggressive adolescents. *Journal of Abnormal Psychology, 99,* 385-392.

Donovan, J. E., & Jessor, R. (1985). Structure of problem behavior in adolescence and young adulthood. *Journal of Consulting and Clinical Psychology, 53,* 890-904.

Donovan, J. E., Jessor, R., & Costa, F. M. (1988). Syndrome of problem behavior in adolescence: A replication. *Journal of Consulting and Clinical Psychology, 56,* 762-765.

Dryfoos, J. G. (1990). *Adolescents at risk: Prevalence and prevention.* New York: Oxford University Press.

Ebata, A. T., Peterson, A. C., & Conger, J. J. (1990). The development of psychopathology in adolescence. In J. Rolf, A. S. Masten, D. Cicchetti, K. H. Nuechterlein, & S. Weintraub (Eds.), *Risk and protective factors in the development of psychopathology* (pp. 308-333). Cambridge, UK: Cambridge University Press.

Falco, J. (1988). *Preventing abuse of drugs, alcohol, and tobacco by adolescents* (Working paper for the Carnegie Council on Adolescent Development). Washington, DC: Carnegie Council on Adolescent Development.

Farrell, A. D., Danish, S. J., & Howard, C. W. (1992). Risk factors for drug use in urban adolescents: Identification and cross-validation. *American Journal of Community Psychology, 20,* 263-286.

Friedman, A. S. (1989). Family therapy vs. parent groups: Effects on adolescent drug abusers. *American Journal of Family Therapy, 17,* 335-347.

Friedman, A. S., Utada, A., & Morrisey, M. R. (1987). Families of adolescent drug abusers are "rigid": Are these families either "disengaged" or "enmeshed" or both? *Family Process, 26,* 131-148.

Gersick, K., Grady, K., Sexton, E., & Lyons, M. (1985). Personality and sociodemographic factors in adolescent drug use. In NIDA, *Drug use and the American adolescent* (U.S. DHHS, NIDA Research Monograph 38, pp. 39-45). Rockville, MD: National Institute on Drug Abuse.

Gibbs, J. T. (1984). Black adolescents and youth: An endangered species. *American Journal of Orthopsychiatry, 54,* 6-21.

Glynn, T. J., & Haenlein, M. (1988a). Managing adolescent behaviors at school: Implications for families. In R. H. Coombs (Ed.), *The family context of adolescent drug use* (pp. 225-243). New York: Haworth.

Glynn, T. J., & Haenlein, M. (1988b). Family theory and research on adolescent drug use: A review. In R. H. Coombs (Ed.), *The family context of adolescent drug use* (pp. 39-56). New York: Haworth.

Halikas, J. A., Weller, R. A., Morse, C. L., & Hoffman, R. G. (1983). Regular marijuana use and its effects on psychosocial variables: A longitudinal study. *Comprehensive Psychiatry, 24,* 229-235.

Harris, L. S. (1985). *Problems of drug dependence, 1984.* (Proceedings of the 46th Annual Scientific Meeting; Committee on Problems of Drug Dependence, Inc., NIDA Research Monograph 55, DHHS Pub. No. [ADM]85-1393). Rockville, MD: National Institute on Drug Abuse.

Hawkins, J. D., Catalano, R. F., & Miller, J. Y. (1992). Risk and protective factors for alcohol and other drug problems in adolescence and early adulthood: Implications for substance abuse prevention. *Psychological Bulletin, 112,* 64-105.

Hawkins, J. D., Lishner, D., Catalano, R., & Howard, M. (1986). Childhood predictors of adolescent substance abuse: Toward an empirically grounded theory. *Journal of Children in Contemporary Society, 8,* 11-48.

Hawkins, J. D., & Weis, J. G. (1985). The social development model: An integrated approach to delinquency prevention. *Journal of Primary Prevention, 6,* 73-97.

Hechinger, F. M. (1992). *Fateful choices: Healthy youth for the 21st century.* New York: Hill & Wang.

Henggeler, S. W., Rodick, D., et al. (1986). Multisystemic treatment of juvenile offenders: Effects on adolescent behavior and family interaction. *Developmental Psychology, 22*(1), 132-141.

Hester, R. K., & Miller, W. R. (1988). Empirical guidelines for optimal client-treatment matching. In E. R. Rahdert & J. Grabowski (Eds.), *Adolescent drug use: Analyses of treatment research* (NIDA Research Monograph Series 77, DHHS Pub. No. [ADM]88-1523, pp. 27-38). Rockville, MD: National Institute on Drug Abuse.

Huba, G. J., & Bentler, P. M. (1980). The role of peer and adult models for drug taking at different stages in adolescence. *Journal of Youth and Adolescence, 9,* 449-465.

Institute of Medicine. (1990). *Treating drug problems: A study of the evolution, effectiveness, and financing of public and private drug treatment systems* (Report by the Institute of Medicine Committee for the Substance Abuse Coverage Study, Division of Health Care Services). Washington, DC: National Academy Press.

Jessor, R. (1984). Adolescent development and behavioral health. In J. D. Matarazzo, S. M. Weiss, J. A. Herd, & N. E. Miller (Eds.), *Behavioral health: A handbook of health enhancement and disease prevention* (pp. 69-90). New York: John Wiley.

Jessor, R., & Jessor, S. L. (1977). *Problem behavior and psychosocial development: A longitudinal study of youth.* New York: Academic Press.

Joanning, H., Quinn, W., Thomas, F., & Mullen, R. (1992). Treating adolescent drug abuse: A comparison of family systems therapy, group therapy, and family drug education. *Journal of Marital and Family Therapy, 18,* 345-356.

Johnson, C. L., Pentz, M. A., Weber, M. D., Dwyer, J. H., Baer, N., MacKinnon, D. P., Hansen, W. B., & Flay, B. R. (1990). Relative effectiveness of comprehensive community programming for drug abuse prevention with high-risk and low-risk adolescents. *Journal of Consulting and Clinical Psychology, 58,* 447-456.

Johnston, L. D. (1993). University of Michigan, Ann Arbor, press release.

Johnston, L. D., O'Malley, P. M., & Bachman, J. G. (1992). Drug use, drinking, and smoking: National survey results from high school, college, and young adults populations 1975-1988 (National Institute on Drug Abuse). Washington, DC: Government Printing Office.

Kandel, D. (1982). Epidemiological and psychosocial perspectives on adolescent drug use. *Journal of the American Academy of Child Psychiatry, 21,* 328-347.

Kandel, D. (1990). Parenting styles, drug use, and children's adjustment in families of young adults. *Journal of Marriage and the Family, 52,* 183-196.

Kandel, D., & Andrews, K. (1987). Process of adolescent socialization by parents and peers. *International Journal of the Addictions, 22,* 319-342.

Kandel, D., Davies, M., Karus, D., & Yamaguchi, K. (1986). The consequences in young adulthood of adolescent drug involvement. *Archives in General Psychiatry, 43,* 746-754.

Kandel, D., & Raveis, V. H. (1989). Cessation of illicit drug use in young adulthood. *Archives of General Psychiatry, 46,* 109-116.

Kazdin, A. E. (1987). Treatment of antisocial behavior in children: Current status and future directions. *Psychological Bulletin, 102,* 187-203.

Kazdin, A. E. (1993). Adolescent mental health: Prevention and treatment programs. *American Psychologist, 48,* 127-141.

Kazdin, A. E., Bass, D., Ayers, W. A., & Rodgers, A. (1990). Empirical and clinical focus of child and adolescent psychotherapy research. *Journal of Consulting and Clinical Psychology, 58,* 729-740.

Kellam, S. G., Brown, C. H., Rubin, B. R., & Ensminger, M. E. (1983). Paths leading to teenage psychiatric symptoms and substance use: Developmental epidemiological studies in Woodlawn. In S. B. Guze, F. J. Earls, & J. E. Barrett (Eds.), *Childhood psychopathology and development* (pp. 17-47). New York: Raven.

Kim, S. (1982). Feeder area approach: An impact evaluation of a prevention project on student drug abuse. *International Journal of the Addictions, 17,* 305-313.

Lewis, R. A., Piercy, F. P., Sprenkle, D. H., & Trepper, T. (1990). Family-based interventions for helping drug-abusing adolescents. *Journal of Adolescent Research, 5,* 82-95.

Liddle, H. A. (1994). The anatomy of emotions in family therapy with adolescents. *Journal of Adolescent Research, 9,* 120-157.

Liddle, H. A., & Dakof, G. A. (in press). Family-based treatment for adolescent drug use: State of the science. In E. Rahdert et al. (Eds.), *Adolescent drug abuse: Assessment and treatment* (Research monograph). Rockville, MD: NIDA.

Liddle, H. A., Dakof, G. A., Parker, K., Diamond, G., Garcia, R., Barrett, K., & Hurwitz, S. (1991). *Effectiveness of family therapy versus multi-family therapy and group therapy: Results of the Adolescents and Families Project—a randomized clinical trial.* Manuscript submitted for publication.

Liddle, H. A., & Diamond, G. (1991). Adolescent substance abusers in family therapy: The critical initial phase of treatment. *Family Dynamics of Addiction Quarterly, 1,* 55-68.

Liddle, H. A., & Schmidt, S. (1994). Using the research literature on parenting to guide clinical practice. *Family Psychologist, 10,* 25-29.

Liddle, H. A., Schmidt, S., & Ettinger, D. (in press). Adolescent development research: Guidelines for clinicians. *Journal of Marital and Family Therapy.*

Loeber, R. (1990). Development and risk factors of juvenile antisocial behavior and delinquency. *Clinical Psychology Review, 10,* 1-41.

Maddahian, E., Newcomb, M. D., & Bentler, P. M. (1985). Single and multiple patterns of adolescent substance use: Longitudinal comparisons of four ethnic groups. *Journal of Drug Education, 15,* 311-326.

McDermott, D. (1984). The relationship of parental drug use and parents' attitude concerning adolescent drug use to adolescent drug use. *Adolescence, 19,* 89-97.

McGee, L., & Newcomb, M. D. (1992). General deviance syndrome: Expanded hierarchical evaluations at four ages from early adolescence to adulthood. *Journal of Consulting and Clinical Psychology, 60,* 766-776.

McKillip, J., Johnson, J. E., & Petzel, T. P. (1973). Patterns and correlates of drug use among urban high school students. *Journal of Drug Education, 3,* 1-12.

Milman, D. H., Bennett, A. A., & Hanson, M. (1983). Psychological effects of alcohol in children and adolescents. *Alcohol, Health and Research World, 7,* 50-53.

National Institute on Drug Abuse. (1988). *National Institute on Drug Abuse National Household Survey on drug abuse: Main findings 1985* (DHHS Pub. No. [ADM]88-1586). Washington, DC: Government Printing Office.

Needle, R., McCubbin, H., Wilson, M., Reineck, R., Lazar, A., & Mederer, H. (1986). Interpersonal influences in adolescent drug use: The role of older siblings, parents and peers. *International Journal of the Addictions, 21,* 739-766.

Newcomb, M. D. (1987). Consequences of teenage drug use: The transition from adolescence to young adulthood. *Drugs and Society, 1,* 25-60.

Newcomb, M. D., & Bentler, P. M. (1988). *Consequences of adolescent drug use: Impact on the lives of young adults.* Newbury Park, CA: Sage.

Newcomb, M. D., & Bentler, P. M. (1989). Substance use and abuse among children and teenagers. Special Issue: Children and their development: Knowledge base, research agenda, and social policy application. *American Psychologist, 44,* 242-248.

Newcomb, M. D., Huba, G. J., & Bentler, P. M. (1983). Mothers' influence on the drug use of their children: Confirmatory tests of direct modeling and mediational theories. *Developmental Psychology, 19*, 714-726.

Newcomb, M. D., Maddahian, E., & Bentler, P. M. (1986). Risk factors for drug use among adolescents: Concurrent and longitudinal analyses. *American Journal of Public Health, 76*, 525-531.

Newcomb, M., Maddahian, E., Skager, E., & Bentler, P. (1987). Substance abuse and psychosocial risk factors among teenagers: Associations with sex, age, ethnicity, and type of school. *American Journal of Drug and Alcohol Abuse, 13*, 413-433.

Newcomb, M. D., & McGee, L. (1991). Influence of sensation seeking on general deviance and specific problem behaviors from adolescence to young adulthood. *Journal of Personality and Social Psychology, 61*, 614-628.

Patterson, G. R. (1986). Performance models for antisocial boys. *American Psychologist, 41*, 432-444.

Patterson, G. R., Reid, J. B., & Dishion, T. J. (1992). *A social learning approach to family intervention: IV. Antisocial boys.* Eugene, OR: Castalia.

Pentz, M. A., Dwyer, J. H., MacKinnon, D. P., Flay, B., Hansen, W., & Johnson, C. A. (1989). A multi-community trial for primary prevention of adolescent drug abuse: Effects on drug use prevalence. *Journal of the American Medical Association, 261*, 3259-3266.

Rhodes, J. E., & Jason, L. A. (1988a). *Preventing substance abuse among children and adolescents.* New York: Pergamon.

Rhodes, J. E., & Jason, L. A. (1988b, March). *The Operation Snowball community-based substance abuse prevention program.* Invited paper presented at the First National Conference on Prevention Research Findings, Kansas City, MO.

Rhodes, J. E., & Jason, L. A. (1990). A social stress model of substance abuse. *Journal of Consulting and Clinical Psychology, 58*, 395-401.

Robin, A. L. (1981). A controlled evaluation of problem-solving communication training with parent-adolescent conflict. *Behavior Therapy, 12*, 593-609.

Scales, P. (1990). Developing capable young people: An alternative strategy of prevention programs. *Journal of Early Adolescence, 10*, 420-438.

Schinke, S. P., Botvin, G. J., & Orlandi, M. A. (1991). *Substance abuse in children and adolescents: Evaluation and intervention.* Newbury Park, CA: Sage.

Schinke, S. P., & Gilchrist, L. D. (1984). *Life skills counseling with adolescents.* Baltimore, MD: University Park Press.

Shedler, J., & Block, J. (1990). Adolescent drug use and psychological health: A longitudinal inquiry. *American Psychologist, 45*, 612-630.

Shirk, S. R. (1988). Conclusion: Cognitive development and child psychotherapy. In S. R. Shirk (Ed.), *Cognitive development and child psychotherapy: Perspectives in developmental psychology* (pp. 319-331). New York: Plenum.

Stein, J. A., Newcomb, M. D., & Bentler, P. M. (1987). An eight-year study of multiple influences on drug use and drug use consequences. *Journal of Personality and Social Psychology, 53*, 1094-1105.

Stein, S. L., Garrett, C. J., & Christiansen, D. (1990). Treatment strategies for juvenile delinquents to decrease substance abuse and prevent adult drug and alcohol dependence. In H. B. Milkman & L. I. Sederer (Eds.), *Treatment choices for alcoholism and substance abuse* (pp. 225-233). Lexington, MA: Lexington Books.

Szapocznik, J., Kurtines, W. M., Foote, F., & Perez-Vidal, A. (1983). Conjoint versus one personal family therapy: Some evidence for the effectiveness of conducting family therapy through one person. *Journal of Consulting and Clinical Psychology, 56,* 889-899.

Szapocznik, J., Perez-Vidal, A., Brickman, A., Foote, F., Santisteban, D., Hervis, O., & Kurtines, W. (1988). Engaging adolescent drug abusers and their families into treatment: A strategic structural systems approach. *Journal of Consulting and Clinical Psychology, 56,* 552-557.

Task Force on the Education of Young Adolescents. (1989). *Turning points: Preparing American youth for the 21st century.* Washington, DC: Carnegie Council on Adolescent Development.

Thompson, T., & Simmons-Cooper, C. (1988). Chemical dependency treatment and black adolescents. *Journal of Drug Issues, 18,* 21-31.

Tobler, N. S. (1986). Meta-analysis of 143 adolescent drug prevention programs: Quantitative outcome results of program participants compared to a control or comparison group. *Journal of Drug Issues, 16,* 537-567.

U.S. Congress, Office of Technology Assessment. (1991). *Adolescent health: Vol. 1. Summary and policy options* (Publication No. OTA-H-468). Washington, DC: Government Printing Office.

Wills, T. A. (1990). Social support and the family. In E. A. Blechman (Ed.), *Emotions and the family: For better or for worse* (pp. 75-98). Hillsdale, NJ: Lawrence Erlbaum.

• CHAPTER 7 •

Problem Sexual Behaviors in Adolescence

LISA TERRE
BARRY R. BURKHART

In the past several years, a parade of national study panels, task forces, and interest groups have expressed serious concern about the worsening problems of our nation's youth (e.g., Hamburg & Takanishi, 1989; Hendee, 1991; Kean, 1989; National Research Council, 1993; Weissberg, Caplan, & Harwood, 1991). Due, in part, to shifting social and economic circumstances that have unraveled traditional support networks, more youngsters find themselves struggling at earlier ages to cope with an unprecedented array of developmental hazards (Hamburg & Takanishi, 1989; Jackson & Hornbeck, 1989; Millstein, 1989; National Research Council, 1993; Ransome-Kuti, 1992). This chapter focuses on one set of challenges with wide-reaching implications for health and well-being: problem sexual behaviors, beginning with a discussion on sexual victimization (sexual abuse and rape) and then on consequences of high-risk sexual practices (sexually transmitted diseases, unplanned pregnancy).

Sexual Victimization

In this section, we examine the epidemiology and effects of sexual victimization in the lives of adolescents. Because the problems of sexuality in adolescents often do not coincide with the onset of puberty, however, we will broaden this review to include a brief overview of child sexual victimization. This is necessary for several reasons. Empirically, child sexual victimization precedes and often potentiates both general adolescent maladjustment as well as adolescent sexual victimization and victimizing. Pragmatically, despite their status as a high-risk group for victimization (Ageton, 1983) and victimizing (Barbaree, Hudson, & Seto, 1993; White & Koss, 1993), there is a relative absence of research about sexual victimization specific to the period of adolescence per se (Burkhart & Sherry, 1993). Finally, although the terms *childhood* and *adolescence* are intended to delineate distinct developmental stages, this distinction is much more apparent than real. It is not unusual, for example, for incestuous relations to begin in childhood and continue through early adolescence. In addition, there is increasing evidence that childhood sexual abuse predicts adolescent victimizing (Awad & Saunders, 1989; Pierce & Pierce, 1987) and victimization (Gidycz, Coble, Latham, & Layman, 1993). Thus, in both childhood and adolescence, the malevolent gauntlet of sexual abuse and victimization may represent a series of hurdles through which the adolescent must pass, often with all too little support from the adult world.

Prevalence

As Salter (1993), among others, has indicated, the phenomenon of sexual victimization and abuse has moved out of the academic into the public domain. Not a week goes by in which these issues are not introduced into the public consciousness through news media, television, or literature. Notwithstanding the media debate, there is an emerging consensus in the scientific literature about the prevalence of child/adolescent sexual victimization. As is often the case in science, however, it is a consensus defined as much by complexity as by clarity.

In her comprehensive review, Salter (1993) painstakingly outlines numerous methodological issues and their effects on estimates of prevalence. As Fromuth and Burkhart (1987, 1989) had previously demonstrated, methodological variations such as excluding non-contact offenses or including an age discrepancy as one of the criteria for abuse can have significant impact on estimates of prevalence rates. In addition, variations in methodology and sensitivity of the assessment procedures can markedly inhibit or enhance the accuracy of reports (Koss, 1990). Despite such complicating factors, Salter (1993) has argued that "the mass of data collected leaves little doubt that child sexual abuse is a substantial social problem" (p. 127). Furthermore, she notes that the best studies in terms of methodological tightness and sensitivity typically have the highest prevalence rates. For example, Russell's (1984, 1986) classic study, using trained interviewers and a sophisticated probability sampling procedure, found that 38% of women had an abusive contact offense before age 18. Wyatt (1985) similarly found that 45% of her sample were abused at the level of physical contact before age 18. Timmick (cited in Salter, 1993), using a less sensitive procedure (random digit dialing telephone interviews), found that 27% of women and 16% of men defined themselves as being sexually abused during childhood.

The majority of studies in the literature have focused on victimization occurring from childhood through adolescence. By requiring an age-discrepancy criterion (offender 5 or 10 years older than victim), however, peer victimization, the most frequent pattern of adolescent victimization, has been poorly evaluated. In studies where victimization by peers has been adequately sampled, however, it is clear that childhood victimization is first only chronologically, not numerically, as a stressor for adolescents.

Ageton (1983), in a comprehensive, prospective study, followed a nationwide probability sample of 1,725 male and female adolescents for 5 years (1976-1981). These adolescents were interviewed yearly, and during the final 3 years of the project (1978-1981), Ageton was able to gather relatively detailed data about experiences of victimization and perpetration for the girls and boys, respectively. Although Ageton's definition of sexual assault was relatively weak (e.g., all forced sexual behavior involving contact with the sexual parts of the body), her data were, nonetheless, compelling. In each of the 3 years of the study, Ageton found that between 5% and 11% of female adolescents experienced at least one sexual assault. Using a very conservative estimate based on the low end of the 95% confidence interval, Ageton predicted that between 700,000 and 1 million adolescents were victimized annually during the years of her study.

The data for the male adolescents were equally startling. Using the data from the face-to-face interview, Ageton found that from

2.2% to 3.8% of the sample acknowledged engaging in sexually assaultive behavior during each of the 3 years of the study. This translated into rates per 100,000 of 3,800 in 1978, 2,900 in 1979, and 2,200 in 1980. These figures probably should be seen as conservative in that males have demonstrated a reduced likelihood to report sexually assaultive behavior in face-to-face interviews relative to anonymous self-report (Koss & Oros, 1982).

Hall and Flannery (1984), using a random digit dialing telephone survey of 508 adolescents, found that 12% of the adolescent girls had been raped or sexually assaulted. Gidycz and Koss (1989), in a survey of young female adolescents (average age of 13), found that 55% percent had experienced at least one sexually aggressive act and 7.5% had been raped.

Finally, in a methodologically rigorous study, Koss (Koss, 1988; Koss, Gidycz, & Wisniewski, 1987) examined prevalence of sexual assault in a large ($N = 6,159$) sample of college students. Although the mean age of the subjects was 21 at the time of the survey, lifetime prevalence rates were obtained. These data have clear implications for understanding sexual assault in adolescents in that the mean age of rape victimization was 18 and the mean age for attempted rape was 17. The following prevalence rates were found for the sample of college women ($n = 3,107$): From age 14, 12% had experienced an attempted rape and 15% had been raped. Collapsing across all forms of sexually aggressive exposure, 54% had experienced at least one incident of sexual coercion.

Clearly, sexual victimization is a remarkably frequent pathogen for female adolescents. It is noteworthy that such a common stressor is so unacknowledged by schools, families, and, until recently, clinicians (Burkhart & Sherry, 1993).

The prevalence of sexual aggression among adolescent males is, perhaps, even less well measured than victimization among adolescent females. Using estimates of prevalence from several perspectives, however, it is clear that adolescent males are one of the groups most at risk for perpetration of sexual crimes (Murphy, Haynes, & Page, 1993; White & Koss, 1993). For example, 19% of all rapes and 20% of all other sexual offenses were committed by males under 19 years of age (cited in White & Koss, 1993). Moreover, Barbaree et al. (1993) suggested that, in addition to the estimated 20% of rapes committed by juveniles, between 30% and 50% of child sexual molestations are perpetrated by adolescent males.

Furthermore, Abel, Osborn, and Twigg (1993) found that untreated adolescent sex offenders not only continued their offense cycle into adulthood, they also accumulated significant numbers of victims throughout their adolescence and adulthood. For example, by age 45, for men who had begun to molest boys during adolescence, the *median* number of cumulative victims was more than 50.

In addition to child molestation and rape, peer-oriented sexual aggression also is a significant problem. In fact, by absolute count, sexual assault by known peers is the most prevalent form of sexual assault. In addition to the Ageton projects described earlier, several epidemiological surveys have highlighted the significance of this problem.

In the Koss study of college men (Koss et al., 1987), 24% of the sample ($n = 3,052$) acknowledged perpetrating some form of sexually aggressive behavior since age 14. Of these, more than 4% admitted to sexually aggressive behavior that met legal criteria for rape and an additional 3.2% admitted to attempted rape. Humphrey and White (cited in White & Koss, 1993) found that 6.4% of a sample of freshmen college men admitted to committing a rape since age 14 and prior to entering college. These data, along with the data from Ageton's project, are clear measures that sexual aggression has a high base rate during adolescence.

Effects of Sexual Abuse

The legacy of sexual abuse has been described as one of "depression and self-destructive behavior, anxiety, feelings of isolation and stigma, poor self-esteem, difficulty in trusting others, a tendency toward revictimization, substance abuse, and sexual maladjustment" (Browne & Finkelhor, 1986, p. 66). The complexity and broad range of effects are difficult to represent in this necessarily brief review. Readers interested in recent, comprehensive reviews of child sexual abuse effects should consult Kendall-Tackett, Williams, and Finkelhor (1993) or Lipovsky and Kilpatrick (1993).

As described by Browne and Finkelhor above, the effects of sexual abuse during childhood and adolescence are extensive (Briere & Runtz, 1988a, 1988b) and lasting (Bryer, Nelson, Miller, & Krol, 1987; Carmen, Rieker, & Mills, 1984). Furthermore, despite only recently receiving research attention, the effects of child sexual abuse appear to be more similar than different for males and females (Kendall-Tackett et al., 1993), at least for clinical samples (Fromuth & Burkhart, 1989).

Most research on effects of sexual abuse has grouped child and adolescent experiences or has assessed only young adolescent experiences. Research addressed specifically to effects of victimization in adolescents, however, echoes the findings of the child/adolescent literature (Burkhart & Sherry, 1993). The experience of sexual assault has both short-term (Gidycz & Koss, 1989) and long-term effects (Ageton, 1983; Gidycz et al., 1993) involving the classic psychological responses to trauma of fear, anxiety, depression, and decrements in social adjustment. In addition, a strong association between sexual assault and antisocial behavior, including drug abuse, has been demonstrated (Ageton, 1983; Dembo et al., 1989). Dembo et al. (1989), for example, found that the majority of adolescent females entering a detention center had been sexually victimized and that such history predicted drug abuse in a statistically developed causal model.

A critical developmental task of adolescence is defining one's sexuality. Though intuitively obvious, little research on the consequences of being sexually assaulted to the maturation process of sexual development in adolescents is available, with the exception of a link between early and later victimization (Ageton, 1983; Gidycz et al., 1993). Research more directly addressed to this area is needed as considerable clinical evidence suggests that adolescent victimization can alter the process of sexual development (Burkhart & Sherry, 1993).

Examination of the effects of sexual victimization has typically focused on the victim (Kendall-Tackett et al., 1993; Lipovsky & Kilpatrick, 1993). The effects on the perpetrator also deserve consideration, however. Despite the complexity of dealing with the spectrum of perpetrators from child abuse to stranger rape to acquaintance rape, there is one general finding that demands attention: Perpetration predicts perpetration. As illustrated by Abel's work (Abel & Rouleau, 1990; Abel et al., 1993), offenders who begin offending in adolescence typically continue offending as adults. This is true of both child sexual abuse perpetration as well as rape. Moreover, although the database is less extensive, it appears that this is also true of date or acquaintance rape. For example, Humphrey and White (cited in White & Koss, 1993) found that, of those adolescents who sexually assaulted someone during high school, 40% reported further sexually assaultive behavior during the first year of college. Moreover, there appears to be a high rate of comorbidity with adolescent perpetrators being involved in high rates of other sexual misconduct as well as other forms of psychopathology (Abel et al., 1993; Barbaree et al., 1993; Becker, Cunningham-Rathner, & Kaplan, 1986). The primary implication of such findings is clear: Prevention, both primary and secondary, must be a priority for policy decisions. Not providing effective treatment to an early adolescent offender is shortsighted and costly.

The traditional concern with the victimization-victimizer cycle is also of significance. A number of researchers have found that child sexual abuse victimization is a significant predicator for child sexual abuse perpetration (Becker et al., 1986). Rapists tend to have a lower base rate of child sexual abuse but often have higher rates of other forms of family pathology (Groth, 1977, 1979; Seghorn, Prentky, & Boucher, 1987). Lipovsky and Kilpatrick (1993) interpret these data to mean that sexual offending is determined by a complex web of factors, not simply an experience of child sexual abuse alone.

High-Risk Sexual Behaviors

Sexual maturation is a central characteristic of adolescence. As noted above, exploration of sexual identity issues and sexual experimentation gain ascendancy during this time. Yet, for too many youngsters, the mastery of these developmental milestones includes serious health-detrimental consequences such as sexually transmitted diseases and unplanned pregnancy (Cates, 1991; Friedman, 1992; Hendee, 1991). Unfortunately and somewhat counterintuitively, the risks associated with negotiating these developmental tasks appear to be increasing. Summarizing the current situation, Cates (1991) laments the 1990s as an unprecedented opportunity for risk reduction that has fallen far short of its potential in terms of results. Heightened awareness resulting from the AIDS crisis, which has riveted the nation's attention on "safe sex," should make this "the best of times," he argues, to successfully modify risky sexual practices. But, among teenagers, unhealthy behaviors and their sequelae show no immediate sign of remitting.

Indeed, an examination of historical trends reveals dramatic changes in the onset, frequency, and pattern of adolescent sexual activities. In addition to making their sexual debut at earlier ages, teenagers' rates of sexual activity, number of partners, and experimentation with high-risk sexual practices all are on the rise (Brooks-Gunn & Furstenberg, 1989; Cates, 1991; Friedman, 1992; National Research Council, 1993).

STD Overview and Prevalence

Although precise numbers vary somewhat across studies and samples, sexually transmitted diseases are at epidemic levels, and sexually active youth constitute the highest risk group for many of the 50 known STDs (Biro & Hillard, 1990; Cates, 1991; McCabe, Jaffe, & Diaz, 1993). It also has been estimated that approximately one fourth of students will contract an STD before high school graduation (Millstein, 1989). Among STDs with the greatest impact on adolescent health are chlamydia trachomatis, human papillomavirus, and HIV.

Chlamydial infections affect between 8% to 35% of sexually active adolescent females and 8% to 22% of adolescent males, many of whom are asymptomatic (Bell, 1990; Cromer, McLean, & Heald, 1992; Frost, Fawcett, & Sharp, 1989). Given these elevated levels, routine screening has been strongly recommended for all teenagers due to the possible reproductive sequelae of infection, including pelvic inflammatory disease and infertility/sterility (Cromer et al., 1992; Randolph & Washington, 1990).

Human papillomavirus (HPV) is estimated to affect between 38% to 53% of adolescents. Notwithstanding the wide variety of possible HPV manifestations, the infection frequently occurs in latent form, and many cases are believed to be undetected (Biro & Hillard, 1990). A relationship between HPV, cervical cancer, and other cytopathologic abnormalities has been noted (Becker et al., 1991; Koutsky et al., 1992).

Consistent with the upsurge in other venereal diseases, adolescent HIV is estimated to be doubling every 12 to 14 months (Boyer & Kegeles, 1991; Kipke, Futterman, & Hein, 1990). Although official figures indicate that teenagers currently represent about 1% of total AIDS cases, Kipke and colleagues (1990) argue that this proportion seriously underestimates the problem by excluding (a) asymptomatic youth, (b) those at early stages of the disease, and (c) individuals HIV-infected as teenagers who were not diagnosed with AIDS until later in life. In support of this assertion, recent studies on high-risk adolescent groups (e.g., homeless/runaways; incarcerated, drug addicted, or otherwise disenfranchised youth; and those residing in high-AIDS-prevalence communities) report pockets of substantially higher seroprevalence rates (Boyer & Kegeles, 1991; Cates, 1991; DiClemente, Brown, Beausoleil, & Lodico, 1993; DiClemente, Lanier, Horan, & Lodico, 1991; Kipke et al., 1990; McCabe et al., 1993; Rotheram-Borus & Koopman, 1991; Smith, McGraw, Crawford, Costa, & McKinlay, 1993).

Factors Contributing to STD Risk

Myriad factors at multiple levels interact in complex ways to heighten the risk of contracting a sexually transmitted disease during adolescence. What follows is a brief overview of the major STD risk factors that have been highlighted in recent research.

Sexual Activity and STDs. Sexual activity at younger ages has been associated with heightened STD vulnerability. Research consistently indicates that those initiating sexual activity earlier are prone to have more partners over a longer exposure interval and are more likely to have a history of sexually transmitted disease than their later onset counterparts (Boyer & Kegeles, 1991; Cates, 1991; Greenberg, Magder, & Aral, 1992). The youngest sexually active adolescents are not only the most likely to be involved in a variety of health-detrimental sexual practices (e.g., unprotected sex, multiple high-risk partners) but are also at highest risk for broader problem behaviors such as drug and alcohol use, school difficulties, and legal violations (Donovan, Jessor, & Costa, 1988; Durbin et al., 1993; Elster, Ketterlinus, & Lamb, 1990; Flora & Thoresen, 1988; Greenberg et al., 1992; Ketterlinus, Lamb, Nitz, & Elster, 1992).

Given the adverse consequences associated with very early sexual involvement, researchers have sought to better understand the factors precipitating teenage sexual behavior. Because the literature is voluminous, only a brief overview is contained herein (for comprehensive reviews, see, for example, two reports from the National Research Council on adolescent sexuality, pregnancy, and childbearing, 1987, and on adolescents in high-risk settings, 1993).

Overall, the data suggest that sexual initiation is multiply determined by a complex web of variables that may combine in distinctive ways for different adolescents. Despite the tendency to think
of teenagers in uniform terms, the precise mix of contributing
factors varies between youth representing different demographic
groups (such as age, gender, ethnicity, and SES) as well as within
these groups (Brooks-Gunn & Furstenberg, 1989; Fielding & Williams,
1991; Hardy, 1991; National Research Council, 1987; Sonenstein,
Pleck, & Ku, 1991; Winett, King, & Altman, 1989).

Among the *individual factors* identified as deterrents to sexual
initiation are social-cognitive reasoning abilities in the area of sexual
decision making, academic aspirations/achievement, and religious-
ness. Of interest, self-esteem has not consistently distinguished
earlier onset from later onset (Brooks-Gunn & Furstenberg, 1989;
Foster & Sprinthall, 1992; Green, Johnson, & Kaplan, 1992;
National Research Council, 1987; Turner, Irwin, Tschann, &
Millstein, 1993).

Biology also plays a role in the timing of sexual involvement. The
direct effects of early pubertal development (e.g., hormonal shifts),
however, are probably less powerful, in and of themselves, than the
indirect effects mediated through and amplified by social/contextual
factors, such as the reactions of significant others to obvious physical
changes (Brooks-Gunn & Furstenberg, 1989; Fielding & Williams,
1991; National Research Council, 1987; Turner et al., 1993).

Other *contextual factors* add to the mix as well. For instance,
nonintact family status (especially father-absent households), maternal history of early sexual experience, sexually active older
siblings, low levels of family religious participation, parental detachment, and lack of developmentally appropriate parental supervision all differentiate early from later initiators of sexual activity
(Brooks-Gunn & Furstenberg, 1989; National Research Council,
1987; White & DeBlassie, 1992; Winett et al., 1989; Wu &
Martinson, 1993; Young, Jensen, Olsen, & Cundick, 1991).

Family interaction patterns that advance adolescent social-cognitive abilities (e.g., "autonomy support" or "authoritative" child-
rearing styles) may be particularly relevant to forestalling sexual
behavior (Brooks-Gunn & Furstenberg, 1989; Dryfoos & Santelli,
1992; National Research Council, 1987, 1993; Turner et al., 1993).
Yet in and of themselves, parent-child relationships and communication about sexuality do not appear to exert straightforward,

simple influences on the timing of youngsters' sexual involvement, although they are generally considered to be important (Casper, 1990; Dryfoos & Santelli, 1992).

Broader *social influences* on adolescent sexual initiation (e.g., peers, media, societal values reflected in adult culture) also have received considerable attention (Fisher, 1988; Hahn, 1991; Males, 1992; Winett et al., 1989). The relative influence of different sociocultural factors remains controversial, however, and is probably mediated, at least in part, by the cumulative impact of other variables in the equation (Fielding & Williams, 1991; National Research Council, 1987; Smith et al., 1993). As an example, for some youth, major life contexts (e.g., schools, neighborhoods) are so malefic that they overwhelm personal or family assets (National Research Council, 1993). By contrast, for others, the impact of peers or media or additional sociocultural influences may be less destructive and, perhaps, more heavily counterbalanced by a preponderance of factors that help defer sexual involvement (National Research Council, 1987).

Individual Differences and STDs. Among sexually active teenagers, those who are youngest, who represent ethnic minority or other disenfranchised groups, and who reside in deteriorated communities are most vulnerable to STDs (Boyer & Kegeles, 1991; Flora & Thoresen, 1988). Other individual differences that may moderate adolescents' risk include STD knowledge, attitudes, and beliefs (Anderson et al., 1990; Becker & Joseph, 1988; Brooks-Gunn, Boyer, & Hein, 1988; DiClemente et al., 1993; Exner, Bahlburg, & Ehrhardt, 1992; Flora & Thoresen, 1988; Goldman & Harlow, 1993; Hobfoll, Jackson, Lavin, Britton, & Shepherd, 1993; Jemmott & Jemmott, 1992; Jemmott, Jemmott, Spears, Hewitt, & Cruz-Collins, 1992; Zimet et al., 1992; Zimet et al., 1993) as well as cognitive developmental abilities, such as abstract and future-oriented reasoning (Boyer & Kegeles, 1991; Winett et al., 1989; Zimet et al., 1993). Yet reported discrepancies between knowledge/attitudes and overt behaviors underscore the complex relationship of these variables to risky practices (e.g., DiClemente et al., 1993; Durbin et al., 1993; Kegeles, Adler, & Irwin, 1988). Nevertheless, the overall pattern of results clearly indicates the relevance of individual differences and the need for developmentally tailored, demographically sensitive approaches to modifying risk.

Drug use poses multiple hazards for STD transmission. In addition to the direct risks associated with IV drug use, more commonly used substances (e.g., alcohol, crack) may increase the likelihood of infection through careless sexual practices (Cates, 1991; Kipke et al., 1990; Kline & Strickler, 1993).

Sexual Abuse and STDs. Several recent studies indicate a correlation between prepubertal sexual victimization, risk-taking behaviors (e.g., substance abuse, early and multiple-partner sexual activity), and STDs in both males and females (Vermund, Alexander, Macleod, Kelley, & Alexander, 1990; Weber, Gearing, Davis, & Conlon, 1992; Zierler et al., 1991). In a similar vein, Males (1992) contends that adolescent venereal diseases are primarily the result of an overlooked but widespread pattern of sexual liaisons between young girls and adult men. He warns that failure to recognize the direct and indirect role of adult influences on adolescent STDs underlies the current failure to reduce infection rates. Given the very high prevalence of sexual abuse in children and adolescents (discussed above), the relationship between victimization and sexually transmitted diseases merits further investigation.

Biological Factors and STDs. In comparison with physically mature women, young adolescent girls, who are still in the process of physical development, may be particularly vulnerable to some STDs (e.g., chlamydia) and their complications (Brooks-Gunn et al., 1988; Cates, 1991; Shafer & Moscicki, 1991). Additional biological factors that heighten STD risk include (a) oral or genital ulcers and (b) other sexually transmitted diseases (Kline & Strickler, 1993; McCabe et al., 1993; Moss & Kreiss, 1990).

Family and STD Risk. As discussed with sexual initiation above, the adolescents who begin sexual activity earliest also tend to be most likely to engage in high-risk sexual practices and to acquire STDs. It is similarly clear that prior history of an STD does not predict subsequent prophylaxis and may, as noted above, represent a risk for additional infections (McCabe et al., 1993; O'Campo et al., 1992; Richert et al., 1993). Therefore, the family factors that predict early sexual debut are particularly relevant to heightened STD risk.

After the onset of sexual activity, however, consistent and effective use of barrier prophylaxes provides some disease protection.

In this regard, parental education and family support for young-sters' access to reproductive health care may enhance regular con-dom use (Cates, 1991; Dryfoos & Santelli, 1992; Fielding & Williams, 1991; National Research Council, 1987). For this reason, some school-based intervention advocates have concluded that parental involvement is critical to the success of these programs, which can serve to educate and empower parents to more effec-tively guide and support health-enhancing choices in their offspring (Dryfoos, 1991; Dryfoos & Santelli, 1992; Santelli et al., 1992).

Social Influences. In an effort to develop public health policy that encourages adolescent risk factor reduction at a time when self-reported condom use is very low (Langer, Zimmerman, Warheit, & Duncan, 1993), research has attempted to better understand social factors that affect the adoption of safer sex practices. Much of this work suggests that social comparisons, perceived reference group norms, and peer support for behavior change all influence the initiation and maintenance of reduced risk behaviors (DiClemente, 1991; Fisher, 1988; Kelly et al., 1991; Langer et al., 1993; Nelson, 1991). The media also have been frequently spotlighted as an agent of social influence. Yet compared with other developed countries, the United States has been slow to use the media in a widespread risk reduction campaign despite the health-detrimental social norms routinely depicted in youth-oriented entertainment media (Brooks-Gunn et al., 1988; Terre, Drabman, & Speer, 1991; Winett et al., 1989).

STD Intervention

Once detected, the technology for effective medical treatment of bacterial STDs is relatively straightforward. Many adolescents, however, lack a consistent source of health care (National Research Council, 1993) or may be reluctant to use services unless confiden-tiality is explicitly assured (Cheng, Savageau, Sattler, & DeWitt, 1993; Croft & Asmussen, 1993). Among those receiving health care, youngsters may be more prone to medication noncompliance than more mature patients, especially when the regimen is complex or extended over time (Cates, 1991). In recognition of these devel-opmental needs, adolescent medicine has emerged as a growing specialty, and school-based clinics are becoming increasingly common vehicles for service delivery (Lear, Gleicher, St. Germaine, & Porter, 1991; McCord, Klein, Foy, & Fothergill, 1993; National Research Council, 1993; Winter & Breckenmaker, 1991).

STD Prevention

Given that many of the most common STDs are viral infections for which no curative medication exists (Shafer & Moscicki, 1991), the primary focus of intervention has centered on prevention. Notwithstanding substantial effort, it is clear that, at the present time, sexual risk reduction programs still are in their infancy.

Optimal intervention design has been hampered by an accumulation of factors. For example, the nature, correlates, and natural history of adolescent sexual practices remain poorly understood, partially due to (a) the sensitive nature of research that seeks to ask schoolchildren indelicate questions about areas many adults find objectionable, as well as (b) broader problems inherent in the modification of behaviors for which the immediate consequences are pleasurable but the adverse consequences are delayed (similar, for instance, to eating high-fat diets and smoking) (see Bandura, 1986; Matarazzo, Weiss, Herd, Miller, & Weiss, 1984).

Moreover, despite a plethora of different programs, very few have been systematically evaluated and even fewer include other than self-report data. In their most recent report, the National Commission on AIDS (1993) emphasized the need for controlled treatment outcome research because

> we have not, as yet, pinpointed the elements in prevention programs for young adolescents that are necessary and sufficient to delay the age of first sexual intercourse, and to foster early and consistent use of barrier methods of contraception/disease prevention when intercourse is initiated. (pp. 18-19)

Kelly et al. (1991) present a strong case for the need to improve the state of current outcome measures. Self-reports are critical, they contend, and must be corroborated by other indexes of behavior change (e.g., communitywide shifts in STD incidence, condom purchasing patterns) so as to make firm conclusions about intervention effectiveness.

Nevertheless, conceptual and empirical advances are being made. It is now very clear that STD education enhances knowledge and may affect self-reported beliefs but yields inconsistent effects on actual behaviors (Brooks-Gunn et al., 1988; Brooks-Gunn & Furstenberg, 1989; Flora & Thoresen, 1988; Ford & Norris, 1993; Kegeles et al., 1988; Kirby, Barth, Leland, & Fetro, 1991; Ku, Sonenstein, & Pleck, 1992; Winter & Goldy, 1993). Moreover, given the substantial influence of demographic factors and sociocultural values on perceived risk, lifestyle, and treatment response, interventions targeting specific high-risk subgroups have gained increased empirical justification (Danielson, Marcy, Plunkett, Wiest, & Greenlick, 1990; Goldman & Harlow, 1993; Hobfoll et al., 1993; Jemmott & Jemmott, 1992; Kline & Strickler, 1993; Leland & Barth, 1992; Magana, 1991; Nelson, 1991; Quirk, Godkin, & Schwenzfeier, 1993; Schinke, Gordon, & Weston, 1990; Winett et al., 1989).

Some of the most innovative new programs are theory driven, such as an HIV risk reduction intervention using indigenous opinion leaders based on diffusion of innovation theory (Kelly et al., 1991) or efforts, informed by social learning theory, to enhance condom behavior-attitude correspondence by adding behavioral skills training (e.g., rehearsal and contingency planning) to traditional educational strategies (Winter & Goldy, 1993). There is a growing consensus, based on the precedent established in the modification of other health behaviors, however, that multilevel, multiprocess, theory-based programs will be necessary to effect any substantial, durable change (Bruhn, 1990; Flora & Thoresen, 1988; Winett et al., 1989).

Unplanned Pregnancy

Overview and Prevalence

Over the past decade, an enormous amount of evidence has documented adverse proximal and distal outcomes associated with adolescent pregnancy and childbearing. Young mothers suffer serious socioeconomic and personal hardship such as reduced probability of high school graduation and higher rates of poverty (Fielding

& Williams, 1991; Furstenberg, Levine, & Brooks-Gunn, 1990; Grogger & Bronars, 1993; National Research Council, 1987; Winett et al., 1989). Although it is now believed that in mothers older than 15, age may be a proxy for other confounding hazards (e.g., inadequate prenatal care, poor health habits), teenagers are at high risk for medical/birth complications, and their children may be more likely to develop cognitive and psychosocial problems (Christ et al., 1990; Furstenberg, Brooks-Gunn, & Chase-Lansdale, 1989; McAnarney, 1991; National Research Council, 1993). Unfortunately, in 1988, 11% of 15- to 19-year-olds had pregnancies, and in 1989, more than one-half million children were born to teenage mothers (Henshaw, 1993; National Research Council, 1993).

Despite broad consensus on the seriousness of the problem, U.S. rates of adolescent pregnancy, childbearing, and abortion (particularly for girls under age 15) outpace those of most other developed countries, even though sexual activity rates are comparable (Creatsas et al., 1991; Hardy, 1991; National Research Council, 1987; Westoff, 1988). After an exhaustive review of research and intervention efforts, the National Research Council (1987) issued a report that concluded on this note:

> Despite the magnitude of human and monetary resources that have been directed at tackling the problems . . . we have found only limited documentation of successful program models for pregnancy prevention and for the support and care of pregnant and parenting teenagers and their children. (pp. 3, 257)

Regrettably, the situation shows no immediate sign of improving (Hobfoll et al., 1993; National Research Council, 1993; Williams, 1991).

Contributing Factors

As is the case with sexually transmitted diseases, adolescent pregnancy results from the complex interaction of multiple influences at various choice points, beginning at sexual initiation (National Research Council, 1987; Winett et al., 1989). Once the sexual involvement option is engaged, the issue of contraception becomes prepotent. Although there exists an impression that contraceptive use may be increasing, as many as one half of sexually active youth acknowledge unprotected intercourse, and rates of teenage pregnancy and abortion continue unabated (e.g., National Research Council, 1993).

Unfortunately, current understanding of adolescent contraception is somewhat skewed because the bulk of extant research has, with a few exceptions (e.g., Marsiglio, 1993; Marsiglio & Shehan, 1993; Stone & Waszak, 1992), excluded consideration of male partners. With that caveat, some factors associated in the literature with "adolescent" contraception follow.

Individual. Sociodemographic influences on adolescent contraception are similar to those contributing to early sexual initiation. That is, regular and effective contraception covaries with older age at sexual initiation, better education, higher SES, identification with traditional middle-class values, social-cognitive decision-making skills associated with abstract thinking abilities, and academic aspirations/achievement (Casper, 1990; Foster & Sprinthall, 1992; Green et al., 1992; National Research Council, 1987; Plotnick, 1992; Swenson, 1992; Williams, 1991).

Biological. Secular trends toward declining ages of puberty serve to underscore the heterogeneity of youth included under the "adolescent" rubric (Friedman, 1992; Hardy, 1991). Because physical maturity outpaces cognitive and emotional development, sexually active early-maturers (who may be preteenage) represent a special high-risk group for inadequate contraceptive practices and many other adverse consequences of premature sexual involvement (Hardy, 1991; Howard & McCabe, 1990).

Family stress, disorganization, and dysfunction (especially involving child sexual abuse) have all been repeatedly associated with adolescent pregnancy (Boyer & Fine, 1992; Swenson, 1992; Wu & Martinson, 1993). By contrast, maternal education and positive mother-daughter communications that provide birth control information and encouragement may bode well for more effective contraceptive practices in daughters (Casper, 1990; National Research Council, 1987).

Social Influences. For some girls, parental influence may be eclipsed by a barrage of more salient factors at other levels. For instance, adolescent females often yield responsibility for pregnancy prevention to their partners. Yet the few existing male-oriented studies suggest boys may be less well informed about contraceptive options than their female counterparts and, in some cases, may view pregnancy as evidence of their masculinity (Brooks-Gunn & Furstenberg, 1989; Eisen, Zellman, & McAlister, 1990; Fielding & Williams, 1991; Marsiglio, 1993).

In recent days, the national dialogue on adolescent pregnancy has spotlighted a different level of social influences: community characteristics and public policy efforts. In support of this focus, substantial empirical evidence indicates that deteriorated communities, lacking social and economic opportunity, represent serious detriments to healthy growth and development (National Research Council, 1993). These high-risk settings may affect contraceptive choices and unplanned pregnancy by (a) creating an "underclass" or disenfranchised group that feels powerless and alienated from mainstream middle-class values (Westoff, 1988; Williams, 1991) and (b) reducing the costs of contraceptive risk taking when considered against the backdrop of more salient day-to-day stressors (Grady, Klepinger, & Billy, 1993; National Research Council, 1993; Westoff, 1988). Although controversial (National Research Council, 1987; Rank, 1989), research examining welfare, abortion, and family planning policies suggests that pregnancy and its resolution may be influenced by the immediate incentives associated with social policy parameters (Lundberg & Plotnick, 1990), and that some social programs designed to help the disadvantaged (e.g., AFDC) may have had unintended, but nevertheless corrosive, effects on both the family and the community (National Research Council, 1987, 1993).

Prevention

When the National Research Council (1987) first issued its report on adolescent pregnancy, it considered three broad types of preventive programs: (a) efforts to enhance knowledge or influence attitudes (e.g., sex/family life education, assertiveness/decision-making training, family communication, teenage theater, and other media approaches), (b) programs to provide access to contraception (e.g., condom distribution programs, school-based clinics, pregnancy testing and counseling, hotlines), and (c) programs to enhance life options (e.g., life planning, role model and mentoring programs, programs to improve school performance, youth employment programs, coalitions, and interest groups). Despite the National Research Council's conclusion that none had demonstrated more than limited impact on teenage fertility, it set prevention as the highest, most cost-effective priority.

Since that time, substantial research and program evolution has occurred (Blau & Gullotta, 1993). Contemporary efforts tend to be theory driven and informed by group interventions modeled after broader risk reduction efforts (e.g., cardiovascular disease). Yet the best approach to successfully forestall adolescent pregnancy has not yet been identified. Generally speaking, however, programs designed to help teenagers postpone sexual onset have tended to report higher success rates than those aimed at reducing sexual activity or increasing regular contraceptive use among sexually active youth (Eisen et al., 1990; Howard & McCabe, 1990; Kirby, Barth, et al., 1991; Kirby et al., 1993; Kirby, Waszak, & Ziegler, 1991).

Consistent with what has been learned from the modification of other health behaviors, the most promising new programs are truly comprehensive. For instance, using a school/community approach with a "barrage of multiple interventions" (e.g., decision making, communication skills, education, community awareness activities) with the assistance of multiple media channels aimed at parents, teachers, clergy, community leaders, and public school children, Vincent, Clearie, and Schluchter (1987) documented a sustained decline in adolescent pregnancies 2 years postintervention relative to surrounding control communities. Both successes and problems replicating the Vincent et al. program will further refine current understanding of the critical processes involved and help fine-tune the intervention itself.

In addition to advances in the area of primary prevention, programs to provide short-term support for pregnant and parenting teenagers have shown some success in promoting academic retention and delaying repeat pregnancy (O'Sullivan & Jacobsen, 1992; Ross, Jones, & Musick, 1992; Seitz, Apfel, & Rosenbaum, 1991; Warrick, Christianson, Walruff, & Cook, 1993). Yet overenthusiasm for these support programs must be tempered by recognition of their inherently transient nature and necessarily limited range of influence (National Research Council, 1987, 1993).

References

Abel, G. G., Osborn, C. A., & Twigg, D. A. (1993). Sexual assault through the life span: Adult offenders with juvenile histories. In H. E. Barbaree, W. L. Marshall, & S. M. Hudson (Eds.), *The juvenile sex offender* (pp. 104-117). New York: Guilford.

Abel, G. G., & Rouleau, J. L. (1990). The nature and extent of sexual assault. In W. L. Marshall, D. R. Laws, & H. E. Barbaree (Eds.), *Handbook of sexual assault: Issues, theories and treatment of the offender* (pp. 9-21). New York: Plenum.

Ageton, S. S. (1983). *Sexual assault among adolescents.* Lexington, MA: D. C. Heath.

Anderson, J., Kann, L., Holtzman, D., Arday, S., Truman, B., & Kolbe, L. (1990). HIV/AIDS knowledge and sexual behavior among high school students. *Family Planning Perspectives, 22*(6), 252-255.

Awad, G. A., & Saunders, E. (1989). Adolescent child molesters: Clinical observations. *Child Psychiatry and Human Development, 19,* 195-206.

Bandura, A. (1986). *Social foundations of thought and action: A social cognitive theory.* Englewood Cliffs, NJ: Prentice Hall.

Barbaree, H. E., Hudson, S. M., & Seto, M. C. (1993). Sexual assault in society: The role of the juvenile offender. In H. E. Barbaree, W. L. Marshall, & S. M. Hudson (Eds.), *The juvenile sex offender* (pp. 1-24). New York: Guilford.

Becker, J. V., Cunningham-Rathner, J., & Kaplan, M. S. (1986). Adolescent sexual offenders: Demographics, criminal and sexual histories, and recommendations for reducing future offenses. Special Issue: The prediction and control of violent behavior: II. *Journal of Interpersonal Violence, 1,* 431-445.

Becker, M., & Joseph, J. (1988). AIDS and behavioral change to reduce risk: A review. *American Journal of Public Health, 78,* 394-410.

Becker, T., Wheeler, C., McGough, N., Jordan, S., Dorin, M., & Miller, J. (1991). Cervical papillomavirus infection and cervical dysplasia in Hispanic, Native American, and non-Hispanic white women in New Mexico. *American Journal of Public Health, 81,* 582-586.

Bell, T. (1990). Chlamydia trachomatis infections in adolescents. *Medical Clinics of North America, 74,* 1225-1233.

Biro, F., & Hillard, P. (1990). Genital human papillomavirus infection in adolescents. *Medical Clinics of North America, 74,* 1235-1249.

Blau, G. M., & Gullotta, T. P. (1993). Promoting sexual responsibility in adolescents. In T. P. Gullotta (Ed.), *Adolescent sexuality* (pp. 181-203). Newbury Park, CA: Sage.

Boyer, C., & Kegeles, S. (1991). AIDS risk and prevention among adolescents. *Social Science and Medicine, 23*(1), 11-23.

Boyer, D., & Fine, D. (1992). Sexual abuse as a factor in adolescent pregnancy and child maltreatment. *Family Planning Perspectives, 24*(4), 4-11.

Briere, J., & Runtz, M. (1988a). Symptomatology associated with childhood sexual victimization in a non-clinical adult sample. *Child Abuse & Neglect, 12,* 51-59.

Briere, J., & Runtz, M. (1988b). Post sexual abuse trauma. In G. E. Wyatt & G. J. Powell (Eds.), *Lasting effects of child sexual abuse* (pp. 85-99). Newbury Park, CA: Sage.

Brooks-Gunn, J., Boyer, C., & Hein, K. (1988). Preventing HIV infection and AIDS in children and adolescents. *American Psychologist, 43,* 958-964.

Brooks-Gunn, J., & Furstenberg, F. (1989). Adolescent sexual behavior. *American Psychologist, 44,* 249-257.

Browne, A., & Finkelhor, D. (1986). The impact of child sexual abuse: A review of the research. *Psychological Bulletin, 99,* 66-77.

Bruhn, J. (1990). A community model for AIDS prevention. *Family & Community Health, 13*(2), 65-77.

Bryer, J. B., Nelson, B. A., Miller, J. B., & Krol, P. A. (1987). Childhood sexual and physical abuse as factors in adult psychiatric illness. *American Journal of Psychiatry, 144,* 1426-1430.

Burkhart, B. R., & Sherry, A. (1993). Sexual victimization in adolescents. *Advances in Medical Psychotherapy, 6,* 171-183.

Carmen, E. H., Rieker, P. P., & Mills, T. (1984). Victims of violence and psychiatric illness. *American Journal of Psychiatry, 141,* 378-383.

Casper, L. (1990). Does family interaction prevent adolescent pregnancy? *Family Planning Perspectives, 22*(3), 109-114.

Cates, W. (1991). Teenagers and sexual risk taking: The best of times and the worst of times. *Journal of Adolescent Health, 12,* 84-94.

Cheng, T., Savageau, J., Sattler, A., & DeWitt, T. (1993). Confidentiality in health care: A survey of knowledge, perceptions, and attitudes among high school students. *Journal of the American Medical Association, 269,* 1404-1407.

Christ, M., Lahey, B., Frick, P., Russo, M., McBurnett, K., Loeber, R., Stouthamer-Loeber, M., & Green, S. (1990). Serious conduct problems in the children of adolescent mothers: Disentangling confounded correlations. *Journal of Consulting and Clinical Psychology, 58,* 840-844.

Creatsas, G., Goumalatsos, N., Deligeoroglou, E., Karagitsou, T., Calpaktsoglou, C., & Arefetz, N. (1991). Teenage pregnancy: Comparison with two groups of older pregnant women. *Journal of Adolescent Health, 12,* 77-81.

Croft, C., & Asmussen, L. (1993). A developmental approach to sexuality education: Implications for medical practice. *Journal of Adolescent Health, 14,* 109-114.

Cromer, B., McLean, C., & Heald, F. (1992). A critical review of comprehensive health screening in adolescents. *Journal of Adolescent Health, 13*(2), 1S-64S.

Danielson, R., Marcy, S., Plunkett, A., Wiest, W., & Greenlick, M. (1990). Reproductive health counseling for young men: What does it do? *Family Planning Perspectives, 22*(3), 115-121.

Dembo, R., Williams, L., LaVoie, L., Berry, E., Getreu, A., Wish, E. D., Schmeidler, J., & Washburn, M. (1989). Physical abuse, sexual victimization, and illicit drug use: Replication of a structural analysis among a new sample of high-risk youths. *Violence and Victims, 4*(2), 101-120.

DiClemente, R. (1991). Predictors of HIV-preventive sexual behavior in a high-risk adolescent population: The influence of perceived peer norms and sexual communication on incarcerated adolescents' consistent use of condoms. *Journal of Adolescent Health, 12,* 385-390.

DiClemente, R., Brown, L., Beausoleil, N., & Lodico, M. (1993). Comparison of AIDS knowledge and HIV-related sexual risk behaviors among adolescents in low and high AIDS prevalence communities. *Journal of Adolescent Health, 14,* 231-236.

DiClemente, R., Lanier, M., Horan, P., & Lodico, M. (1991). Comparison of AIDS knowledge, attitudes, and behaviors among incarcerated adolescents and a public school sample in San Francisco. *American Journal of Public Health, 81,* 628-630.

Donovan, J., Jessor, R., & Costa, F. (1988). Syndrome of problem behavior in adolescence: A replication. *Journal of Consulting and Clinical Psychology, 56*, 762-765.

Dryfoos, J. (1991). Preventing high risk behavior. *American Journal of Public Health, 81*, 157-158.

Dryfoos, J., & Santelli, J. (1992). Involving parents in their adolescents' health: A role of school clinics. *Journal of Adolescent Health, 13*, 259-260.

Durbin, M., DiClemente, R., Siegel, D., Krasnovsky, F., Lazarus, N., & Camacho, T. (1993). Factors associated with multiple sex partners among junior high school students. *Journal of Adolescent Health, 14*, 202-207.

Eisen, M., Zellman, G., & McAlister, A. (1990). Evaluating the impact of a theory-based sexuality and contraceptive education program. *Family Planning Perspectives, 22*(6), 261-271.

Elster, A., Ketterlinus, R., & Lamb, M. (1990). Association between parenthood and problem behavior in a national sample of adolescents. *Pediatrics, 85*, 1044-1050.

Exner, T., Bahlburg, H., & Ehrhardt, A. (1992). Sexual self control as a mediator of high risk sexual behavior in a New York city cohort of HIV+ and HIV-gay men. *Journal of Sex Research, 29*, 389-406.

Fielding, J., & Williams, C. (1991). Adolescent pregnancy in the United States. *American Journal of Preventive Medicine, 7*(1), 47-52.

Fisher, J. (1988). Possible effect of reference group-based social influence on AIDS-risk behavior and AIDS prevention. *American Psychologist, 43*, 914-920.

Flora, J., & Thoresen, C. (1988). Reducing the risk of AIDS in adolescents. *American Psychologist, 43*, 965-970.

Ford, K., & Norris, A. (1993). Knowledge of AIDS transmission, risk behavior, and perceptions of risk among urban, low-income, African-American and Hispanic youth. *American Journal of Preventive Medicine, 9*, 297-306.

Foster, V., & Sprinthall, N. (1992). Developmental profiles of adolescents and young adults choosing abortion: Stage sequence, decalage, and implications for policy. *Adolescence, 27*(107), 655-673.

Friedman, H. (1992). Changing patterns of adolescent sexual behavior: Consequences for health and development. *Journal of Adolescent Health, 13*, 345-350.

Fromuth, M. E., & Burkhart, B. R. (1987). Childhood sexual victimization among college men: Definitional and methodological issues. *Violence and Victims, 2*, 241-253.

Fromuth, M. E., & Burkhart, B. R. (1989). Long-term psychological correlates of childhood sexual abuse in two samples of college men. *Child Abuse & Neglect, 13*, 533-542.

Frost, H., Fawcett, K., & Sharp, J. (1989). Adolescent sexual behavior: A model for behavioral strategies. *Behavior Therapist, 12*(10), 239-242.

Furstenberg, F., Brooks-Gunn, J., & Chase-Lansdale, L. (1989). Teenaged pregnancy and childbearing. *American Psychologist, 44*, 313-320.

Furstenberg, F., Levine, J., & Brooks-Gunn, J. (1990). The children of teenage mothers: Patterns of early childbearing in two generations. *Family Planning Perspectives, 22*(2), 54-61.

Gidycz, C. A., Coble, C. N., Latham, L., & Layman, M. J. (1993). Sexual assault experience in adulthood and prior victimization experiences: A prospective analysis. *Psychology of Women Quarterly, 17*, 151-168.

Gidycz, C. A., & Koss, M. P. (1989). The impact of adolescent sexual victimization: Standardized measures of anxiety, depression, and behavioral deviancy. *Violence and Victims, 4,* 139-149.

Goldman, J., & Harlow, L. (1993). Self-perception variables that mediate AIDS-preventive behavior in college students. *Health Psychology, 12*(6), 489-498.

Grady, W., Klepinger, D., & Billy, J. (1993). The influence of community characteristics on the practice of effective contraception. *Family Planning Perspectives, 25,* 4-11.

Green, V., Johnson, S., & Kaplan, D. (1992). Predictors of adolescent female decision making regarding contraceptive usage. *Adolescence, 27*(107), 613-632.

Greenberg, J., Magder, L., & Aral, S. (1992). Age at first coitus: A marker for risky sexual behavior in women. *Sexually Transmitted Diseases, 19,* 331-334.

Grogger, J., & Bronars, S. (1993). The socioeconomic consequences of teenage childbearing: Findings from a natural experiment. *Family Planning Perspectives, 25,* 156-161, 174.

Groth, A. N. (1977). The adolescent sexual offender and his prey. *International Journal of Offender Therapy and Comparative Criminology, 21,* 249-254.

Groth, A. N. (1979). *Men who rape: The psychology of the offender.* New York: Plenum.

Hahn, R. (1991). What should behavioral scientists be doing about AIDS? *Social Science & Medicine, 33*(1), 1-3.

Hall, E. R., & Flannery, P. J. (1984). Prevalence and correlates of sexual assault experiences in adolescents. *Victimology, 9,* 398-406.

Hamburg, D., & Takanishi, R. (1989). Preparing for life: The critical transition of adolescence. *American Psychologist, 44,* 825-827.

Hardy, J. (1991). Pregnancy and its outcome. In W. R. Hendee (Ed.), *The health of adolescents* (pp. 250-281). San Francisco: Jossey-Bass.

Hendee, W. R. (Ed.). (1991). *The health of adolescents.* San Francisco: Jossey-Bass.

Henshaw, S. (1993). Teenage abortion, birth and pregnancy statistics by state, 1988. *Family Planning Perspectives, 25,* 122-126.

Hobfoll, S., Jackson, A., Lavin, J., Britton, P., & Shepherd, J. (1993). Safer sex knowledge, behavior, and attitudes of inner-city women. *Health Psychology, 12,* 481-488.

Howard, M., & McCabe, J. (1990). Helping teenagers postpone sexual involvement. *Family Planning Perspectives, 22,* 21-26.

Jackson, A., & Hornbeck, D. (1989). Educating young adolescents. *American Psychologist, 44,* 831-836.

Jemmott, L., & Jemmott, J. (1992). Increasing condom use intentions among sexually active black adolescent women. *Nursing Research, 41,* 273-279.

Jemmott, J., Jemmott, L., Spears, H., Hewitt, N., & Cruz-Collins, M. (1992). Self-efficacy, hedonistic expectations and condom use intentions among inner city black adolescent women: A social cognitive approach to AIDS risk behavior. *Journal of Adolescent Health, 13,* 512-519.

Kean, T. (1989). The life you save may be your own: New Jersey addresses prevention of adolescent problems. *American Psychologist, 44,* 828-830.

Kegeles, S., Adler, N., & Irwin, C. (1988). Sexually active adolescents and condoms: Changes over one year in knowledge, attitudes, and use. *American Journal of Public Health, 78,* 460-461.

Kelly, J., St. Lawrence, J., Diaz, Y., Stevenson, L., Hauth, A., Brasfield, T., Kalichman, B., Smith, J., & Andrew, M. (1991). HIV risk behavior reduction following intervention with key opinion leaders of population: An experimental analysis. *American Journal of Public Health, 81,* 168-171.

Kendall-Tackett, K. A., Williams, L. M., & Finkelhor, D. (1993). Impact of sexual abuse on children: A review and synthesis of recent empirical studies. *Psychological Bulletin, 113,* 164-180.

Ketterlinus, R., Lamb, M., Nitz, K., & Elster, A. (1992). Adolescent nonsexual and sex-related problem behaviors. *Journal of Adolescent Research, 7,* 431-456.

Kipke, M., Futterman, D., & Hein, K. (1990). HIV infection and AIDS during adolescence. *Medical Clinics of North America, 74,* 1149-1167.

Kirby, D., Barth, R., Leland, N., & Fetro, J. (1991). Reducing the risk: Impact of a new curriculum on sexual risk-taking. *Family Planning Perspectives, 23,* 253-263.

Kirby, D., Resnick, M., Downes, B., Kocher, T., Gunderson, P., Potthoff, S., Zelterman, D., & Blum, R. (1993). The effects of school-based health clinics in St. Paul on school-wide birthrates. *Family Planning Perspectives, 25,* 12-21.

Kirby, D., Waszak, C., & Ziegler, J. (1991). Six school-based clinics: Their reproductive health services and impact on sexual behavior. *Family Planning Perspectives, 23,* 6-16.

Kline, A., & Strickler, J. (1993). Perceptions of risk for AIDS among women in drug treatment. *Health Psychology, 12, 313-323.*

Koss, M. P. (1988). Hidden rape: Sexual aggression and victimization in a national sample in higher education. In A. W. Burgess (Ed.), *Rape and sexual assault II* (pp. 3-26). New York: Garland.

Koss, M. P. (1990). Violence against women. *American Psychologist, 45,* 374-380.

Koss, M. P., Gidycz, C. A., & Wisniewski, N. (1987). The scope of rape: Incidence and prevalence of sexual aggression and victimization in a national sample of higher education students. *Journal of Consulting and Clinical Psychology, 55,* 162-170.

Koss, M. P., & Oros, C. (1982). The sexual experience survey: A research instrument investigating sexual aggression and victimization. *Journal of Consulting and Clinical Psychology, 50,* 455-457.

Koutsky, L., Holmes, K., Critchlow, C., Stevens, C., Paavonen, J., Beckmann, A., DeRouen, T., Galloway, D., Vernon, D., & Kiviat, N. (1992). A cohort study of the risk of cervical intraepithelial neoplasia grade 2 or 3 in relation to papillomavirus infection. *New England Journal of Medicine, 327*(18), 1272-1278.

Ku, L., Sonenstein, F., & Pleck, J. (1992). The association of AIDS education and sex education with sexual behavior and condom use among teenage men. *Family Planning Perspectives, 24,* 100-110.

Langer, L., Zimmerman, R., Warheit, G., & Duncan, R. (1993). Decision-making orientation and AIDS-related knowledge, attitudes, and behaviors of Hispanic, African-American, and white adolescents. *Health Psychology, 12,* 227-234.

Lear, J., Gleicher, H., St. Germaine, A., & Porter, P. (1991). Reorganizing health care for adolescents: The experience of the school-based adolescent health care program. *Journal of Adolescent Health, 12,* 450-458.

Leland, N., & Barth, R. (1992). Gender differences in knowledge, intentions, and behaviors concerning pregnancy and sexually transmitted disease prevention among adolescents. *Journal of Adolescent Health, 13,* 589-599.

Lipovsky, J. A., & Kilpatrick, D. G. (1993). The child sexual abuse victim as an adult. In W. O'Donohue & J. H. Geer (Eds.), *The sexual abuse of children: Clinical issues* (Vol. 2, pp. 430-476). Hillsdale, NJ: Lawrence Erlbaum.

Lundberg, S., & Plotnick, R. (1990). Effects of state welfare, abortion, and family planning policies on premarital childbearing among white adolescents. *Family Planning Perspectives, 22,* 246-251.

Magana, J. (1991). Sex, drugs, and HIV: An ethnographic approach. *Social Science & Medicine, 33*(1), 5-9.

Males, M. (1992). Adult liaison in the "epidemic" of "teenage" birth, pregnancy, and venereal disease. *Journal of Sex Research, 29*(4), 525-545.

Marsiglio, W. (1993). Adolescent males' orientation toward paternity and contraception. *Family Planning Perspectives, 25,* 22-31.

Marsiglio, W., & Shehan, C. (1993). Adolescent males' abortion attitudes: Data from a national survey. *Family Planning Perspectives, 25,* 162-169.

Matarazzo, J., Weiss, S., Herd, J., Miller, N., & Weiss, S. (Eds.). (1984). *Behavioral health: A handbook of health enhancement and disease prevention.* New York: John Wiley.

McAnarney, E. (1991). Commentary on teenage pregnancy: Comparison with two groups of older pregnant women. *Journal of Adolescent Health, 12,* 82-83.

McCabe, E., Jaffe, L., & Diaz, A. (1993). Human immunodeficiency virus seropositivity in adolescents with syphilis. *Pediatrics, 92,* 695-698.

McCord, M., Klein, J., Foy, J., & Fothergill, K. (1993). School-based clinic use and school performance. *Journal of Adolescent Health, 14,* 91-98.

Millstein, S. (1989). Adolescent health. *American Psychologist, 44*(3), 837-842.

Moss, G., & Kreiss, J. (1990). The interrelationship between human immunodeficiency virus infection and other sexually transmitted diseases. *Medical Clinics of North America, 74,* 1647-1660.

Murphy, W. D., Haynes, M. R., & Page, I. J. (1993). Adolescent sex offenders. In W. O'Donohue & J. H. Geer (Eds.), *The sexual abuse of children: Clinical issues* (Vol. 2, pp. 394-429). Hillsdale, NJ: Lawrence Erlbaum.

National Commission on AIDS. (1993). *Behavioral and social sciences and the HIV/AIDS epidemic.* Washington, DC: Author. (Available from the CDC, National AIDS Clearinghouse, P.O. Box 6003, Rockville, MD 30849, 1-800-458-5231)

National Research Council. (1987). *Risking the future: Adolescent sexuality, pregnancy, and childbearing.* Washington, DC: National Academy Press.

National Research Council. (1993). *Losing generations: Adolescents in high risk settings.* Washington, DC: National Academy Press.

Nelson, E. (1991). Sexual self-defense versus the liaison dangereuse: A strategy for AIDS prevention in the '90s. *American Journal of Preventive Medicine, 7,* 146-149.

O'Campo, P., Deboer, M., Faden, R., Kass, N., Gielen, A., & Anderson, J. (1992). Prior episode of sexually transmitted disease and subsequent sexual risk-reduction practices: A need for improved risk-reduction interventions. *Sexually Transmitted Diseases, 19,* 326-330.

O'Sullivan, A., & Jacobsen, B. (1992). A randomized trial of a health care program for first-time adolescent mothers and their infants. *Nursing Research, 41,* 210-215.

Pierce, L. H., & Pierce, R. L. (1987). Incestuous victimization by juvenile sex offenders. *Journal of Family Violence, 2*, 351-364.

Plotnick, R. (1992). The effects of attitudes on teenage premarital pregnancy and its resolution. *American Sociological Review, 57*, 800-811.

Quirk, M., Godkin, M., & Schwenzfeier, E. (1993). Evaluation of two AIDS prevention interventions for inner-city adolescent and young adult women. *American Journal of Preventive Medicine, 9*, 21-26.

Randolph, A., & Washington, E. (1990). Screening for chlamydia trachomatis in adolescent males: A cost-based decision analysis. *American Journal of Public Health, 80*, 545-550.

Rank, M. (1989). Fertility among women on welfare: Incidence and determinants. *American Sociological Review, 54*, 296-304.

Ransome-Kuti, O. (1992). Keynote address at the Fifth Congress of the International Association for Adolescent Health. *Journal of Adolescent Health, 13*, 342-344.

Richert, C., Peterman, T., Zaidi, A., Ransom, R., Wroten, J., & Witte, J. (1993). A method for identifying persons at high risk for sexually transmitted infections: Opportunity for targeting intervention. *American Journal of Public Health, 83*, 520-524.

Ross, H., Jones, E., & Musick, J. (1992). Comparing outcomes in a statewide program for adolescent mothers with outcomes in a national sample. *Family Planning Perspectives, 24*, 66-71.

Rotheram-Borus, M., & Koopman, C. (1991). Sexual risk behaviors, AIDS knowledge, and beliefs about AIDS among runaways. *American Journal of Public Health, 81*, 206-208.

Russell, D. (1984). *Sexual exploitation: Rape, child sexual abuse, and workplace harassment.* Beverly Hills, CA: Sage.

Russell, D. E. H. (1986). *The secret trauma: Incest in the lives of girls and women.* New York: Basic Books.

Salter, A. C. (1993). Epidemiology of child sexual abuse. In W. O'Donohue & J. H. Geer (Eds.), *The sexual abuse of children: Theory and research* (Vol. 1, pp. 108-138). Hillsdale, NJ: Lawrence Erlbaum.

Santelli, J., Alexander, M., Farmer, M., Papa, P., Johnson, T., Rosenthal, B., & Hotra, D. (1992). Bringing parents into school clinics: Parent attitudes toward school clinics and contraception. *Journal of Adolescent Health, 13*, 269-274.

Schinke, S., Gordon, A., & Weston, R. (1990). Self-instruction to prevent HIV infection among African-American and Hispanic-American adolescents. *Journal of Consulting and Clinical Psychology, 58*, 432-436.

Seghorn, T. K., Prentky, R. A., & Boucher, R. J. (1987). Childhood sexual abuse in the lives of sexually aggressive offenders. *Journal of the American Academy of Child and Adolescent Psychiatry, 26*, 262-267.

Seitz, V., Apfel, N., & Rosenbaum, L. (1991). Effects of an intervention program for pregnant adolescents: Educational outcomes at two years postpartum. *American Journal of Community Psychology, 19*, 911-930.

Shafer, M., & Moscicki, A. (1991). Sexually-transmitted diseases. In W. R. Hendee (Ed.), *The health of adolescents* (pp. 211-249). San Francisco: Jossey-Bass.

Smith, K., McGraw, S., Crawford, S., Costa, L., & McKinlay, J. (1993). HIV risk among Latino adolescents in two New England cities. *American Journal of Public Health, 83*, 1395-1399.

Sonenstein, F., Pleck, J., & Ku, L. (1991). Levels of sexual activity among adolescent males in the United States. *Family Planning Perspectives, 23*, 162-167.

Stone, R., & Waszak, C. (1992). Adolescent knowledge and attitudes about abortion. *Family Planning Perspectives, 24*, 52-57.

Swenson, I. (1992). A profile of young adolescents attending a teen family planning clinic. *Adolescence, 27*(107), 647-653.

Terre, L., Drabman, R., & Speer, P. (1991). Health-relevant behaviors in media. *Journal of Applied Social Psychology, 21*(16), 1303-1319.

Turner, R., Irwin, C., Tschann, J., & Millstein, S. (1993). Autonomy, relatedness, and the initiation of health risk behaviors in early adolescence. *Health Psychology, 12*, 200-208.

Vermund, S., Alexander, R., Macleod, S., Kelley, K., & Alexander, R. (1990). History of sexual abuse in incarcerated adolescents with gonorrhea or syphilis. *Journal of Adolescent Health Care, 11*, 449-452.

Vincent, M., Clearie, A., & Schluchter, M. (1987). Reducing adolescent pregnancy through school and community-based education. *Journal of the American Medical Association, 257*(24), 3382-3386.

Warrick, L., Christianson, J., Walruff, J., & Cook, P. (1993). Educational outcomes in teenage pregnancy and parenting programs: Results from a demonstration. *Family Planning Perspectives, 25*, 148-155.

Weber, F., Gearing, J., Davis, A., & Conlon, M. (1992). Prepubertal initiation of sexual experiences and older first partner predict promiscuous sexual behavior of delinquent adolescent males: Unrecognized child abuse? *Journal of Adolescent Health, 13*, 600-605.

Weissberg, R., Caplan, M., & Harwood, R. (1991). Promoting competent young people in competence-enhancing environments: A systems-based perspective on primary prevention. *Journal of Consulting and Clinical Psychology, 59*, 830-841.

Westoff, C. (1988). Unintended pregnancy in America and abroad. *Family Planning Perspectives, 20*, 254-261.

White, J. W., & Koss, M. P. (1993). Adolescent sexual aggression within heterosexual relationships: Prevalence, characteristics, and causes. In H. E. Barbaree, W. L. Marshall, & S. M. Hudson (Eds.), *The juvenile sex offender* (pp. 182-202). New York: Guilford.

White, S., & DeBlassie, R. (1992). Adolescent sexual behavior. *Adolescence, 27*(105), 183-191.

Williams, L. (1991). Determinants of unintended childbearing among ever-married women in the United States: 1973-1988. *Family Planning Perspectives, 23*, 212-221.

Winett, R., King, A., & Altman, D. (1989). *Health psychology and public health: An integrative approach.* New York: Pergamon.

Winter, L., & Breckenmaker, L. (1991). Tailoring family planning services to the special needs of adolescents. *Family Planning Perspectives, 23*, 24-30.

Winter, L., & Goldy, S. (1993). Effects of prebehavioral cognitive work on adolescents' acceptance of condoms. *Health Psychology, 12*, 308-312.

Wu, L., & Martinson, B. (1993). Family structure and the risk of a premarital birth. *American Sociological Review, 58*, 210-232.

Wyatt, G. E. (1985). The sexual abuse of Afro-American and white-American women in childhood. *Child Abuse & Neglect, 9*, 507-519.

Young, E., Jensen, L., Olsen, J., & Cundick, B. (1991). The effects of family structure on the sexual behavior of adolescents. *Adolescence, 26*(104), 977-986.

Zierler, S., Feingold, L., Laufer, D., Velentgas, P., Gordon, I., & Mayer, K. (1991). Adult survivors of childhood sexual abuse and subsequent risk of HIV infection. *American Journal of Public Health, 81*, 572-575.

Zimet, G., Bunch, D., Anglin, T., Lazebnik, R., Williams, P., & Krowchuk, D. (1992). Relationship of AIDS-related attitudes to sexual behavior changes in adolescents. *Journal of Adolescent Health, 13*, 493-498.

Zimet, G., DiClemente, R., Lazebnik, R., Anglin, T., Ellick, E., & Williams, P. (1993). Changes in adolescents' knowledge and attitudes about AIDS over the course of the AIDS epidemic. *Journal of Adolescent Health, 14*, 85-90.

CHAPTER 8

Eating Disorders

ROBERT J. WEINSTEIN

Overview and History

Eating disorders as a diagnostic category of adolescent psycho-pathology represent one of the more complex examples of the interplay between the individual, family, and larger sociocultural systems in which the adolescent attempts to persevere. From the outset, the fact that the vast majority of adolescents afflicted by these disorders are female (90% to 96%) suggests a susceptibility to these behaviors that is likely rooted in gender-specific roles whose origins lie within cultural beliefs held by individuals and families. This chapter attempts to briefly summarize the field of eating disorders as a behavior of concern in adolescents and, more specifically, a severe and potentially deadly psychiatric disorder. The multifaceted roots of this illness will be explored from various theoretical frameworks.

Definitions

According to the *Diagnostic and Statistical Manual of Mental Disorders* (fourth edition; *DSM-IV*), the two major types of eating disorders are anorexia nervosa (AN) and bulimia nervosa (BN). A third category in the *DSM-IV*, Eating Disorder Not Otherwise Specified (ED-NOS), is used for what are determined to be atypical eating disorders.

The diagnostic criteria for anorexia nervosa as defined by the *DSM-IV* (American Psychiatric Association, 1994) are as follows:

> A. Refusal to maintain body weight at or above a minimally normal weight for age and height (e.g., weight loss leading to maintenance of body weight less than 85% of that expected; or failure to make expected weight gain during period of growth, leading to body weight less than 85% of that expected).
>
> B. Intense fear of gaining weight or becoming fat, even though underweight.
>
> C. Disturbance in the way in which one's body weight or shape is experienced, undue influence of body weight or shape on self-evaluation, or denial of the seriousness of the current low body weight.
>
> D. In postmenarcheal females, amenorrhea, i.e., the absence of at least three consecutive menstrual cycles. (A woman is considered to have amenorrhea if her periods occur only following hormone, e.g., estrogen, administration.) (pp. 544-545)

On examination of these criteria, the predominant symptoms of the illness and target symptoms of various treatment perspectives and techniques can be clarified. In examining Criterion A, it is important to note that the critical factor of 15% below expected weight, as determined by expected weight for age and height, represents a change from the factor of 25% below expected weight used in a previous diagnostic manual (*DSM-III*) (American Psychiatric Association, 1980). This change to a lower weight threshold for the diagnosis of AN arose due to the potentially life-threatening medical complications that may occur with significant weight loss and the need for earlier diagnosis and treatment.

Criteria B and C delineate the characteristic of eating disorders that is often the most refractory to treatment interventions, namely, body image distortion. Individuals with eating disorders are typically unable to view their body shape and size in a realistic way, and will greatly distort the physical dimensions of some part or often all parts of their bodies. This phenomenon has been well documented through various verbal and nonverbal assessment techniques (Lindholm & Wilson, 1988).

Criterion D describes the medical condition known as amenorrhea, diagnosed when a female misses three consecutive menstrual cycles (assuming other possible biological etiologies have been ruled out). This criterion becomes more problematic when attempting to diagnose younger females whose onset of menses may have not naturally occurred, even if functioning in a healthy state. What is typically done in this situation is an assessment of the expected time of the onset of menses, based on family history. Although amenorrhea is the sole medical sequela of starvation discussed in the diagnostic criterion, there are a number of other potentially severe medical conditions seen in AN that must be assessed and treated when working with the disorder. These will be discussed further in later sections of this chapter.

The *DSM-IV* also separates and delineates AN into two subtypes: Restricting Type and Binge-Eating/Purging Type. This updated classification is important for understanding the clinical presentation of AN. The more traditional conception of the anorexic patient is a female who severely restricts her daily caloric intake and through this behavior reaches and/or maintains a critically low body weight. This is what has been termed AN, Restricting Type. The other type of AN is termed Binge-Eating/Purging Type, in which individuals, during an episode of AN, regularly engage in binge-eating or purging behaviors such as self-induced vomiting or misuse of laxatives, diuretics, or enemas. These behaviors represent another way to lose weight or maintain a low body weight (American Psychiatric Association, 1994).

The *DSM-IV* diagnostic criteria (American Psychiatric Association, 1994) for bulimia nervosa are as follows:

A. Recurrent episodes of binge eating. An episode of binge eating is characterized by both of the following:

  (1) eating, in a discrete period of time (e.g., within any 2-hour period), an amount of food that is definitely larger than most people would eat during a similar period of time and under similar circumstances

  (2) a sense of lack of control over eating during the episode (e.g., a feeling that one cannot stop eating or control what or how much one is eating)

B. Recurrent inappropriate compensatory behavior in order to prevent weight gain, such as self-induced vomiting; misuse of laxatives, diuretics, enemas, or other medications; fasting; or excessive exercise.

C. The binge eating and inappropriate compensatory behaviors both occur, on average, at least twice a week for 3 months.

D. Self-evaluation is unduly influenced by body shape and weight.

E. The disturbance does not occur exclusively during episodes of Anorexia Nervosa. (pp. 549-550)

The defining symptom of BN is, as described in diagnostic criteria A-C, the binge/purge cycle. Bingeing occurs when an individual rapidly consumes a large amount of food in a short period of time, with an intense out-of-control feeling associated with the behavior. Purging occurs through the use of various behaviors whose goal is to rapidly rid the body of the calories taken in during the binge, attempting to avoid weight gain. These various behaviors may include self-induced vomiting by the use of a finger or other implement forced down the throat; ingestion of syrup of ipecac to induce vomiting; the use of laxatives, diuretics, diet pills, water pills, and/or enemas to induce rapid excretion of calories; and/or intense exercise to rapidly burn calories. Any single or combined use of the above described behaviors carries with it significant risk for medical complications.

Criterion D describes body image difficulties, similar to those characterized in AN. A critical error made somewhat frequently when assessing an individual for BN is a preconceived notion that patients with eating disorders are at low weight. On the contrary, it is critical to understand that people with BN may fall at any and all ranges of the weight spectrum: underweight, normal or average weight, overweight, or obese. If the diagnosis is made based solely on weight, a large proportion of individuals with BN will be missed. This fact makes identification of individuals with BN more difficult than those with AN. The initial history taken in an eating disorders evaluation must include direct questions concerning the use of each of the techniques of purging mentioned above.

DSM-IV also delineates two subtypes of BN: Purging Type and Nonpurging Type. Bulimia nervosa, Purging Type, is the more commonly seen presentation, in which the individual regularly engages in the above described purging behaviors such as self-induced vomiting or the misuse of laxatives, diuretics, or enemas. The Nonpurging Type of bulimia nervosa refers to individuals who use other inappropriate compensatory behaviors such as excessive exercise or fasting but do not regularly engage in self-induced vomiting or the misuse of laxatives, diuretics, or enemas (American Psychiatric Association, 1994).

Incidence and Prevalence

There has been a significant increase in studies of the incidence and prevalence of eating disorders in countries throughout the world. Eckert (1985) found the age of onset to lie between 12 and 25 years, with significant peaks at ages 14 and 18 years. The *DSM-IV* summarizes the prevalence studies of AN as ranging from 0.5% to 1.0% in late adolescent and young adult females (American Psychiatric Association, 1994). For BN, the *DSM-IV* reports the prevalence to be approximately 1% to 3% in adolescent and young adult females. Prevalence studies in school-aged female children have suggested a range of approximately 1 in 100 to 1 in 155 being at risk for AN (Crisp, Palmer, & Kalucy, 1976; Nylander, 1971). For BN, a range of 54% to 86% of school-aged females were found to practice binge eating, and of this group, 5% to 20% met the criteria for a *DSM-III-R* diagnosis of BN (Harper-Giuffre, 1992).

In terms of sex ratio, 90% to 96% of eating disordered patients are females (Harper-Giuffre, 1992). In addition, the prevalence rate of eating disorders among males is significantly less than in females. It is difficult to clarify, however, whether this represents an actual lower prevalence rate or whether males experience more difficulty identifying themselves with a predominantly female disorder.

Research on Contributing Factors

Internal Factors

Hilde Bruch's (1970, 1973, 1978) pioneering work on AN is perhaps the first and most notable discussion of the individual factors that contribute to the development of eating disorders. Using a psychoanalytic framework, Bruch described the anorexic patient as struggling with issues rooted in preoedipal development, demonstrating deficits in self-identity and autonomy (Swift, 1991). Bruch related these deficits to a mother's inability to respond in an appropriate and supportive manner to the young child's needs (Bruch, 1973). In examining the causes of BN, self-psychology theorists such as Sugarman (1991) and Sands (1991) discuss how adolescent females who have experienced conflictual and nongratifying early relationships with their mothers (which Sugarman feels is often due to psychopathology in the mother) use bingeing and purging as a way to act out aggressive impulses on their developing bodies, which at that point begin to resemble their mother's body. Sands (1991) describes the increased capabilities of bulimic patients to dissociate, viewing the binge/purge behavior as a split-off ego state or dissociative state. A number of other psychoanalytic and psychodynamic theorists have used these seminal works as a starting point for further examination, including Selvini-Palazzoli (1974), Johnson and Connors (1987), and Goodsitt (1985).

There have been several personality features commonly seen in eating disorder patients. To others (including family), these girls will often present as good to excellent students, popular with their peers, good athletes, who are apparently successful in the majority of their endeavors. When asked specifically about emotional issues, however, adolescents with AN will typically describe themselves as perfectionistic, shy, obsessive, extremely dependent on others for approval (i.e., parents, friends, siblings), and possessing extremely low self-esteem and poor self-concept (Harper-Giuffre, 1992). Intense feelings of self-deprecation and self-loathing are often described by these individuals. In addition to much overlap with the above-mentioned personality characteristics of persons with AN, Harper-Giuffre (1992) describes bulimics as struggling with interpersonal sensitivity, self-criticalness, competitiveness, affective instability, and, in some individuals, difficulty with sex role identity. In some eating disorder patients, a history of weight disturbances during childhood and/or adolescence may be present.

A controversial topic in examining factors contributing to the development of eating disorders is sexual abuse. Research in this area has yielded conflicting results. Several studies have found that approximately 30% to 50% of adult women with eating disorders report a history of unwanted sexual experiences at varying ages (Waller, 1992). There also appears to be a relationship between unwanted sexual experiences and the nature of an eating disorder. Bulimic patients report a higher incidence of unwanted sexual experiences than anorexic patients. In addition, the spectrum from purely restrictive anorexics to bulimics who actively binge and purge is positively correlated with an increasing frequency of reported unwanted sexual experiences (Waller, 1992). Folsom and her colleagues (Folsom et al., 1993), however, found that the rates of reported sexual abuse in an eating disorder population do not differ significantly from those of a general psychiatric population. Therefore, it is difficult to determine any possible causal link between sexual abuse and eating disorders.

Biological Factors

In addition to psychosocial factors, biological/genetic factors that may contribute to the development of eating disorders have been examined. Studies find concordance rates of 50% for monozygotic twins versus 10% for dizygotic twins (Harper-Giuffre, 1992). In examining families with a member diagnosed with an eating disorder, studies have found rates for a relative diagnosed with an eating disorder to range between 2.0% and 7.3% (Woodside, 1993). More significant, Strober, Morrell, Burroughs, Salkin, and Jacobs (1985) found that the risk for a female relative of an eating disorder patient to develop an eating disorder was five times that for a control group. Woodside (1993) summarizes these findings as pointing to eating disorders being familial, with rates elevated compared with control populations. A family history of weight problems (most typically obesity), alcoholism, and/or affective illness has also been found to be positively related to the diagnosis of eating disorders (Harper-Giuffre, 1992).

Family Factors

The role of the family in the development of eating disorders has also been examined by a number of theorists. Much of this work has sought to identify a distinctive familial pattern of functioning for eating disorders, and several different patterns have been proposed. Kog and Vandereycken (1989) reviewed the various perspectives taken by family researchers and theorists, and found studies that have implicated the relative influence of mothers, fathers, siblings, grandparents, and general attitudes of parents in the development of eating disorders in children. Psychodynamic theorists such as Bruch (1970, 1973, 1978) view early dysfunctional relationships with the mother as being at the root of the development of an eating disorder. Other theorists such as Maine (1991) view the emotional unavailability of the father as a causal factor in the development of an eating disorder. Kog and Vandereycken (1989) summarize research on what are viewed as "typical" attitudes attributed to parents of eating disordered children, including expectations for high achievement, success, and conformity as well as certain beliefs concerning physical appearance. Minuchin and his colleagues (Minuchin, Rosman, & Baker, 1978; Minuchin et al., 1975) have used structural family theory to describe a "psychosomatic family constellation" that functions together with a physiologically susceptible child to be at the root of the development and maintenance of a psychosomatic illness such as AN.

Sociocultural Factors

Perhaps the most controversial set of factors that contributes to the development of eating disorders is sociological or sociocultural-based beliefs about body shape and size. Much has been written about the cultural pressures that females experience around all aspects of their physical appearance. These pressures have been intensified in our culture by the multibillion-dollar diet/weight loss industry, which, in combination with the popular press and fashion industry, defines how a woman's body *should* appear. The shape and dimensions of the "ideal" woman's body have changed drastically over time, from the full-figured woman portrayed in the art of the late nineteenth century, through the emaciated appearance of Twiggy in the 1960s, into the muscular, thin, well-defined athletic body of the 1980s, to return to the "waif" look of the 1990s, as described in the September 20, 1993, cover story of *People* magazine titled "How Thin Is Too Thin?" (Lague et al., 1993).

In examining body measurements of *Playboy* magazine centerfolds and Miss America Pageant contestants, as well as the frequency of "diet for weight loss" articles in women's magazines over the past 30 years, Wiseman, Gray, Mosimann, and Ahrens (1992) found significant changes in the cultural expectations for women's bodies. From 1979 to 1988, both the centerfolds and the contestants were at body weights 13% to 19% below expected weights for age, and a clear pattern of decreasing weight was found in the Miss America contestants from 1979 to 1988. The authors also found a significant increase in the number of dieting articles found in popular women's magazines over the past 30 years.

This example of the current culture's overemphasis and overvaluation of weight and body appearance is clearly mirrored in the proliferation of eating disorders in the United States and other industrialized countries. In the upcoming discussion of treatment strategies for eating disorders, it is essential to take into account the intense cultural pressures impinging on a female attempting to recover from these disorders.

Research on the Effectiveness
of Clinical Interventions

As evidenced in the previous discussion of diagnostic criteria for AN and BN, these disorders cannot be viewed merely as a problem affecting emotional functioning. Rather, the potential *physical* sequelae of eating disorders may be and often are life threatening. Although the upcoming discussion of therapeutic interventions will separate techniques and levels of treatment as distinct entities, it is most often the case that eating disorder patients require a multimodal approach to treatment. It is often necessary to combine several techniques and interventions to effectively and adequately treat these disorders. The division of this discussion of techniques is merely for didactic purposes.

Outpatient Treatment

Individual Interventions. The origins of individual outpatient treatment of eating disorders lie in psychodynamic theory and, more specifically, in the self-psychology paradigm exemplified in Kohut's work (Kohut, 1971). In discussing treatment, AN is viewed as a disorder of the self (Goodsitt, 1985). Treatment is focused on the therapist's "filling in the deficits of the patient's self" (Goodsitt, 1985, p. 56). The therapist's role is to manage the transference rather than interpret it. Working in this way, the therapist must be active and flexible, with the ability to adapt to the current level of functioning of the patient. The therapist must also function to help the patient regulate anxiety and tension. The therapist must understand and anticipate this anxiety, and as best as possible soothe the patient. This is often achieved through a didactic approach, educating the patient about the realities of how the digestive system works and how fat and calories are processed by the body (Goodsitt, 1985).

Sands (1991) uses the concept of dissociation to understand and treat bulimic patients. She describes bulimia as a split-off self state, forming what she terms the *bulimic self*. In treatment, the therapeutic relationship must support and empathize with this split-off self state, and provide a setting in which to understand the hidden needs of this "self" (Sands, 1991). In this way, therapy can focus on developing other healthier, more appropriate ways to meet these needs.

In addition to psychodynamic strategies, many theorists have investigated the utility of behavioral and cognitive-behavioral interventions. In her review of behavioral treatment of AN, Halmi (1985) notes that there have been very few studies involving the outpatient treatment of AN solely using behavioral techniques. She notes that the vast majority of these studies involve treatment in an inpatient setting, and more specifically involve the use of behavioral interventions in combination with other treatment modalities (i.e., medication, milieu treatment, cognitive-behavioral treatment, family treatment) (Halmi, 1985). Some studies, however, have looked exclusively at behavioral treatment of AN in an outpatient setting. In a study comparing behavioral and cognitive-behavioral treatment of BN in a group setting, Wolf and Crowther (1992) found positive results using behavioral treatment focused on the identification and modification of antecedents and consequences to bulimic episodes. More specifically, in comparison with a matched, wait-list control group, the authors demonstrated significant reductions in the frequency of binge eating and use of various purging techniques, significant reductions in reported body dissatisfaction, and an increase in feelings of adequacy, security, and control (Wolf & Crowther, 1992). It is important to note that these interventions were short term (8 weeks), and 3-month follow-up data indicate significant relapse rates, demonstrating the need for ongoing treatment.

The relative effectiveness of cognitive-behavioral interventions with BN have been closely examined in the work of Fairburn and his colleagues (Fairburn, 1985, 1988; Fairburn et al., 1991; Fairburn, Kirk, O'Connor, & Cooper, 1986). These techniques involve a time-limited intervention in which patient and therapist work in a collaborative way to gain symptomatic control as well as to change the faulty cognitions that are present in patients with BN (Fairburn, 1985). Treatment is divided into three stages. The first stage involves targeting the establishment of some control over bingeing and purging behaviors. The second stage focuses on the identification and modification of faulty cognitions. The third stage hones in on developing ways in which to maintain these changes (Fairburn, 1985). These goals are achieved through the use of techniques such as self-monitoring, stimulus control, examination of the function of symptoms, and cognitive restructuring.

In contrast to psychotherapeutic interventions, there has been a proliferation of research studies examining biochemical interventions with eating disorders. Garfinkel and Garner's (1987) book on the use of medication with eating disorders contains chapters discussing the possible use of practically all categories of psychoactive medications in the treatment of eating disorders. The majority of current research and the most common clinical practice, however, have focused on the use of various types of antidepressants in the treatment of AN and BN. In differentiating the use of medication with anorexic patients versus bulimic patients, Herzog, Heller, Strober, Yeh, and Pai (1992), surveying professionals who treat eating disorders, found a trend toward using medication more frequently with bulimic patients than with anorexic patients.

Recent research has examined the relationship between eating patterns and the levels of the neurotransmitter serotonin in the brain. With the development of medications that specifically target levels of serotonin, such as fluoxetine (Prozac), studies have found significant positive effects on the frequency of bingeing and purging in bulimics at certain dosages (Fluoxetine Bulimia Nervosa Collaborative [FBNC] Study Group, 1992; Goldbloom, 1987). New medications similar to Prozac such as sertraline (Zoloft) and paroxetine (Paxil) have also been increasingly used with eating disorder patients. Given evidence of substantial overlap between eating disorders and affective disorders, the use of more traditional tricyclic antidepressants such as amitriptyline, desipramine, and imipramine is also common (Herzog & Brotman, 1987). A significant benefit in the use of the serotonin-targeting medications is the likelihood of significantly fewer side effects. Given the possible medical sequelae of eating disorders, this situation is highly favorable. There is also some evidence that the use of short-acting benzodiazepines such as lorazepam (Ativan) and oxazepam (Serax) administered before meals may help patients who experience overwhelming anxiety during meals (Anderson, 1987). Overall, there is a lack of well-controlled double-blind studies examining the use of other psychoactive medications with eating disorders, but clinical use of antidepressant and anxiolytic medications is often thought of as an important component in treatment.

Family Interventions. As noted previously, family functioning has been examined as a possible contributing factor in the development of eating disorders. Following from this, there has been significant focus on family interventions in the treatment of eating disorders.

Minuchin and his colleagues (Minuchin et al., 1975; Minuchin et al., 1978) have developed and implemented theories and techniques of structural family therapy to treat what they term *psychosomatic families* (eating disorders, diabetes, asthma). This well-established school of family therapy views the *structure* and *process* of family interactions and relationships as the focus of therapy. The therapist views the eating disorder as a *symptom* of family pathology. At the core of this treatment is the therapist using his or her position of power in the therapy room to enter the family system at various points, unbalance the current structure of the family, and maintain this state of unbalance until the family structure shifts to support the new, healthier family pattern. A unique assessment technique that this school of family therapy uses, for the initial evaluation, is to have the family actually eat a meal with the therapist in the therapy room. This provides the therapist with the actual experience of the family dynamic around the symptom (Minuchin et al., 1978).

At about the same time that Minuchin was developing his theoretical framework, Selvini-Palazzoli (1974) was also developing a family-based systemic model for the treatment of eating disorders. Similar to Minuchin, Selvini-Palazzoli felt that the eating disorder was rooted in family psychopathology. For her, the role of the therapist is to search for and make explicit the underlying secret rules that perpetuate family dysfunction and to work on redefining these rules in a more functional manner.

The previously described structural and systemic schools of family therapy represent the major initial work in the field. Minuchin and Selvini-Palazzoli's interventions have been expanded on by many clinicians, including Vandereycken and his colleagues, who more recently have attempted to combine various techniques and use a more eclectic approach. Vandereycken and Vanderlinden (1989) propose a *behaviorally oriented family approach* when treating eating disorder patients in the outpatient setting. The goals of this intervention are to emphasize the responsibility of the patient for her own health and recovery, to provide parents with concrete tasks to perform at home to decrease their anxiety and feelings of helplessness, and to avoid self-defeating power struggles by "neutralizing the problem of food refusal or threatening weight loss" (Vandereycken & Vanderlinden, 1989, p. 233).

In this behaviorally oriented family paradigm, the therapist may function in a supportive/empathic role at certain times, and may become challenging and confrontational at other times. Behavioral contracting is used around specific weight and caloric intake issues, thereby placing the responsibility on the patient for weight gain, and removing the family from this power struggle. The other specific goal is to normalize the interactions and behaviors regarding food issues in the home, thereby replacing the maladaptive eating habits the eating disorder has likely brought about at home (Vandereycken & Vanderlinden, 1989).

Inpatient Treatment

Throughout this discussion, the potential severity of the medical sequelae of eating disorders has been emphasized. In addition, the need for a multimodal, multidisciplinary approach to the treatment of eating disorders has been addressed. When a patient becomes medically and/or psychiatrically compromised to the point at which her life is assessed to be at risk, inpatient hospitalization becomes necessary and critical. This determination may originate from the patient's pediatrician/family practitioner, from the therapist knowledgeable of the medical sequelae, or often from a consultation among the treating professionals. When the intensity of outpatient treatment is assessed to be inadequate for the level of severity of symptoms, this step becomes essential.

It is also important to evaluate the initial level of treatment necessary during intake/evaluation. During the first session, an accurate assessment of both medical and psychiatric functioning must be completed. It is a good rule of thumb to request that the patient have a complete physical examination by a physician, which may include a blood count, electrolytes, EKG, or other diagnostic procedures deemed necessary by the physician. It is important to obtain this level of evaluation at the outset of treatment to prevent the development of any new or exacerbation of any ongoing medical problems. Significant medical findings may also direct the initial recommendation for the level of intervention.

From a medical perspective, deterioration in vital signs (i.e., bradycardia, hypothermia, hypotension), changes in electrolyte balance, changes in cardiac status as determined by an EKG or other diagnostic procedure, significant gastrointestinal symptoms such as hematemesis, or an overall perceived deterioration in medical functioning are typical examples of symptoms necessitating an inpatient admission (Kennedy & Shapiro, 1993). For bulimic patients, an escalation in the frequency of binge/purge episodes, or in anorexic patients, ongoing weight loss, might also necessitate an inpatient admission. Psychiatrically, it is often the level of depression/suicidality that necessitates an inpatient admission for an eating disorder patient.

The obvious and primary goal of an inpatient admission is to provide the most intensive, 24-hour, multimodal treatment for the patient. Throughout the country, many specialized eating disorder treatment programs have been developed to target the specific needs of the eating disorder patient. When this type of program is not available, admission to a general child/adolescent psychiatric unit or sometimes a pediatric unit in a medical hospital is suggested. It is becoming increasingly evident, however, that medical and/or general psychiatric units may not have the resources to provide the multimodal treatment that is recommended when working with eating disorder patients.

Once on an inpatient unit, the focus of treatment should be to stabilize the patient's medical and/or psychiatric symptoms through the use of behaviorally focused interventions. At this point in treatment, close contact between the medical and psychiatric professionals is essential. Monitoring of the patient's vital signs, cardiac status, and daily caloric intake is likely to be critical (Kennedy & Shapiro, 1993). Close supervision and limitations around eating and bathroom use may also be essential to avoid maladaptive behaviors such as hiding food and/or purging after eating. This is also likely to be a time for a psychiatric evaluation for a possible trial of medication, if determined as necessary by the treatment team. For children and adolescents, significant family involvement in treatment is strongly recommended.

Currently in the United States, there is a movement toward the use of partial hospital programs (PHP) or day treatment programs in psychiatric treatment. The goal of this type of intervention is to provide intensive treatment in a less restrictive setting than an inpatient unit. Typically, patients attend these programs for several hours per day but return home each evening and on weekends. For eating disorder patients, this provides an effective way to monitor some portion of the individual's daily caloric intake, provide intensive individual, group, and/or family treatment on a daily basis, and immediately focus on the individual's functioning at home each evening, with the goal being the patient reaching a level of functioning that permits her to return to less intense, less demanding outpatient treatment. For further discussion of this treatment, an extensive model for the day treatment of eating disorder patients has been developed at the Toronto General Hospital and is described in a monograph (Piran & Kaplan, 1990).

In an inpatient setting, a group therapy, short-term focus may be the most effective form of treatment. The longer term nature of traditional individual psychotherapy is becoming less consistent with the move toward shorter inpatient stays. Group psychotherapy then becomes the modality of choice as a way to target eating disorder symptoms, both directly with each individual patient and indirectly through her fellow group members. A group focus additionally provides a sense of support and diminishes feelings of isolation so commonly experienced by these patients. With the goal of short-term stabilization, beginning possibly in an inpatient setting and using a transfer to a PHP as a "step-down" level of treatment, the patient can improve her condition to the point at which she can return to her previous level of functioning, including an ability to effectively benefit from some more traditional outpatient interventions (Kennedy & Shapiro, 1993).

For the minority of patients who do not respond to the intensity of an inpatient or PHP setting, or who are not able to show effective progress when discharged to home, a recommendation for transfer to a therapeutic residential setting may be necessary. Again, there are very few residential settings that specifically focus on the treatment of eating disorders. More general psychiatric residential settings are, however, beginning to include protocols for eating disorder patients. In examining a referral to a residential setting, the ability of the setting to provide appropriate medical and psychiatric backup is critical.

Nontraditional Treatment

There has been a recent increase in the number of self-help groups available for persons with eating disorders. Support groups often can be an effective adjunct to more traditional treatment strategies (Enright, Butterfield, & Berkowitz, 1985). These groups may differ significantly in makeup, group membership, structure, and perspective. Groups may be "open" or "closed," not requiring or requiring a commitment to attend on a regular basis, respectively. Some groups have a professionally trained facilitator or group leader, whereas others may be leaderless. Other group leaders may be persons who have recovered from an eating disorder, following the model often used in chemical dependency treatment.

There has been recent discussion of applying the 12-step model used in the treatment of other addictions to eating disorders. Overeaters Anonymous is a 12-step program that focuses on certain types of eating problems. Johnson and Sansone (1993) have taken the traditional 12-step model of the Alcoholics Anonymous program and modified the 12 steps to apply to recovery from eating disorders. Johnson has developed a program whose focus is to treat chronic eating disorder patients who have not responded to traditional treatment techniques. The program resembles a therapeutic community in which patients are required to move to the area and make a minimum of a 1-year commitment to the program (Johnson, 1992).

Prevention of Eating Disorders

Eating disorders represent a significant and growing problem in the current culture. Prevention is a critical aspect in examining this type of problem. Education is an essential component of prevention. Parents, physicians, teachers, coaches, and other adults with whom children and adolescents have contact must understand the impact of their own eating habits and attitudes toward body image on younger individuals. The pressure that high school coaches may and often do place on teenagers regarding their weight, or the need to reach certain weight goals to participate on athletic teams, often has significant psychological ramifications. How physicians talk to their younger patients about weight issues may also have significant effects on children's and adolescents' thoughts and behaviors. Parents who chronically diet, compulsively exercise, or constantly focus on weight loss may potentially provide a poor role model for children and/or adolescents. Parents must convey to their children that self-esteem and self-concept is not solely based on physical appearance. It is critical to teach children and adolescents that human bodies significantly differ in shape and size.

Education of all adults who play a significant role for children and adolescents around healthy eating patterns is one of the most effective ways to prevent eating disorders. Also, parents, physicians, and school officials should understand and be able to identify early signs of eating disordered behavior such as large weight losses or fluctuations, significant restriction of daily caloric intake, obsessive discussion or compulsive behaviors around weight and/or eating behaviors, or general changes in the health status of a previously healthy adolescent.

An understanding of the cultural pressures that teenage girls experience about weight and body image permits adults to effectively discuss these issues in an open forum. In this way too, adults can provide effective role models through their own thoughts and behaviors around food and weight, placing the individuals most able to prevent the development of eating disorders in a position that facilitates this goal.

References

American Psychiatric Association. (1980). *Diagnostic and statistical manual of mental disorders* (3rd ed.). Washington, DC: Author.

American Psychiatric Association. (1994). *Diagnostic and statistical manual of mental disorders* (4th ed.). Washington, DC: Author.

Anderson, A. E. (1987). Use and potential misuses of antianxiety agents in the treatment of anorexia nervosa and bulimia nervosa. In P. E. Garfinkel & D. M. Garner (Eds.), *The role of drug treatments for eating disorders* (pp. 64-66). New York: Brunner/Mazel.

Bruch, H. (1970). Psychotherapy in primary anorexia nervosa. *Journal of Nervous and Mental Diseases, 150,* 51-66.

Bruch, H. (1973). *Eating disorders: Obesity, anorexia nervosa, and the person within.* New York: Basic Books.

Bruch, H. (1978). *The golden cage.* Cambridge, MA: Harvard University Press.

Crisp, A. H., Palmer, R. L., & Kalucy, R. S. (1976). How common is anorexia nervosa? A prevalence study. *British Journal of Psychiatry, 218,* 549-554.

Eckert, E. D. (1985). Characteristics of anorexia nervosa. In J. E. Mitchell (Ed.), *Anorexia nervosa and bulimia: Diagnosis and treatment* (pp. 3-29). Minneapolis: University of Minnesota Press.

Enright, A. B., Butterfield, P., & Berkowitz, B. (1985). Self-help and support groups in the management of eating disorders. In D. M. Garner & P. E. Garfinkel (Eds.), *Handbook of psychotherapy for anorexia nervosa and bulimia nervosa* (pp. 491-512). New York: Guilford.

Fairburn, C. G. (1985). Cognitive-behavioral treatment for bulimia. In D. M. Garner & P. E. Garfinkel (Eds.), *Handbook of psychotherapy for anorexia nervosa and bulimia nervosa* (pp. 160-192). New York: Guilford.

Fairburn, C. G. (1988). The current status of the psychological treatments for bulimia nervosa. *Journal of Psychosomatic Research, 32,* 635-645.

Fairburn, C. G., Jones, R., Peveler, R. C., Carr, S. J., Solomon, R. A., O'Connor, M., Burton, J., & Hope, R. A. (1991). Three psychological treatments for bulimia nervosa: A comparative trial. *Archives of General Psychiatry, 48,* 463-469.

Fairburn, C. G., Kirk, J., O'Connor, M., & Cooper, P. (1986). A comparison of two psychological treatments for bulimia nervosa. *Behaviour Research and Therapy, 24,* 629-643.

Fluoxetine Bulimia Nervosa Collaborative (FBNC) Study Group. (1992). Fluoxetine in the treatment of bulimia nervosa. *Archives of General Psychiatry, 49,* 139-147.

Folsom, V., Krahn, D., Nairn, K., Gold, L., Demitrack, M. A., & Silk, K. R. (1993). The impact of sexual and physical abuse on eating disordered and psychiatric symptoms: A comparison of eating disordered and psychiatric inpatients. *International Journal of Eating Disorders, 13,* 249-258.

Garfinkel, P. E., & Garner, D. M. (1987). *The role of drug treatments for eating disorders.* New York: Brunner/Mazel.

Goldbloom, D. S. (1987). Serotonin in eating disorders: Theory and therapy. In P. E. Garfinkel & D. M. Garner (Eds.), *The role of drug treatment for eating disorders* (pp. 124-149). New York: Brunner/Mazel.

Goodsitt, A. (1985). Self psychology and the treatment of anorexia nervosa. In D. M. Garner & P. E. Garfinkel (Eds.), *Handbook of psychotherapy for anorexia nervosa and bulimia nervosa* (pp. 55-82). New York: Guilford.

Halmi, K. A. (1985). Behavioral management for anorexia nervosa. In D. M. Garner & P. E. Garfinkel (Eds.), *Handbook of psychotherapy for anorexia nervosa and bulimia nervosa* (pp. 147-159). New York: Guilford.

Harper-Giuffre, H. (1992). Overview of eating disorders. In H. Harper-Giuffre & K. R. MacKenzie (Eds.), *Group psychotherapy for eating disorders* (pp. 3-28). Washington, DC: American Psychiatric Association.

Herzog, D. B., & Brotman, A. W. (1987). Use of tricyclic antidepressants in anorexia nervosa and bulimia nervosa. In P. E. Garfinkel & D. M. Garner (Eds.), *The role of drug treatments for eating disorders* (pp. 36-58). New York: Brunner/Mazel.

Herzog, D. B., Heller, M. B., Strober, M., Yeh, C., & Pai, S. Y. (1992). The current status of treatment for anorexia nervosa and bulimia nervosa. *International Journal of Eating Disorders, 12,* 215-220.

Johnson, C. L. (1992, May). *Contemporary issues in the treatment of eating disorders.* Symposium presented at Elmcrest Psychiatric Institute, Portland, CT.

Johnson, C. L., & Connors, M. (1987). *The etiology and treatment of bulimia nervosa: A biopsychosocial perspective.* New York: Basic Books.

Johnson, C. L., & Sansone, R. A. (1993). Integrating the twelve-step approach with traditional psychotherapy for the treatment of eating disorders. *International Journal of Eating Disorders, 14,* 121-134.

Kennedy, S. H., & Shapiro, C. (1993). Medical management of the hospitalized patient. In A. S. Kaplan & P. E. Garfinkel (Eds.), *Medical issues and the eating disorders: The interface* (pp. 213-238). New York: Brunner/Mazel.

Kog, E., & Vandereycken, W. (1989). The speculations: An overview of theories about eating disorder families. In W. Vandereycken, E. Kog, & J. Vanderlinden (Eds.), *The family approach to eating disorders* (pp. 7-24). New York: PMA Publishing.

Kohut, H. (1971). *The analysis of the self.* New York: International Universities Press.

Lague, L., Lynn, A., Armstrong, L., Sheff-Cahan, V., Saveri, G., & Healy, L. S. (1993, September 20). How thin is too thin? *People, 40*(12), 74-80.

Lindholm, L., & Wilson, G. T. (1988). Body image assessment in patients with bulimia nervosa and normal controls. *International Journal of Eating Disorders, 7,* 527-539.

Maine, M. (1991). *Father hunger: Fathers, daughters, & food.* Carlsbad, CA: Gurze.

Minuchin, S., Baker, L., Rosman, B. L., Liebman, R., Milman, L., & Todd, T. C. (1975). A conceptual model of psychosomatic illness in children: Family organization and family therapy. *Archives of General Psychiatry, 32,* 1031-1038.

Minuchin, S., Rosman, B., & Baker, L. (1978). *Psychosomatic families: Anorexia nervosa in context.* Cambridge, MA: Harvard University Press.

Nylander, I. (1971). The feeling of being fat and dieting in a school population: Epidemiologic, interview investigation. *Acta Sociomedica Scandinavica, 3,* 17-26.

Piran, N., & Kaplan, A. S. (1990). *A day hospital group treatment program for anorexia nervosa and bulimia nervosa.* New York: Brunner/Mazel.

Sands, S. (1991). Bulimia, dissociation, and empathy: A self-psychological view. In C. Johnson (Ed.), *Psychodynamic treatment of anorexia nervosa and bulimia* (pp. 34-67). New York: Guilford.

Selvini-Palazzoli, M. (1974). *Self-starvation.* New York: Jason Aronson.

Strober, M., Morrell, W., Burroughs, J., Salkin, B., & Jacobs, C. (1985). A controlled family study of anorexia nervosa. *Journal of Psychiatric Research, 19,* 239-246.

Sugarman, A. (1991). Bulimia: A displacement from psychological self to body self. In C. Johnson (Ed.), *Psychodynamic treatment of anorexia nervosa and bulimia* (pp. 3-33). New York: Guilford.

Swift, W. J. (1991). Bruch revisited: The role of interpretation of transference and resistance in the psychotherapy of eating disorders. In C. Johnson (Ed.), *Psychodynamic treatment of anorexia nervosa and bulimia* (pp. 51-67). New York: Guilford.

Vandereycken, W., & Vanderlinden, J. (1989). A family-oriented strategy in outpatient treatment. In W. Vandereycken, E. Kog, & J. Vanderlinden (Eds.), *The family approach to eating disorders* (pp. 227-238). New York: PMA Publishing.

Waller, G. (1992). Sexual abuse and bulimic symptoms in eating disorders: Do family interaction and self-esteem explain the links? *International Journal of Eating Disorders, 12,* 235-240.

Wiseman, C. V., Gray, J. J., Mosimann, J. E., & Ahrens, A. H. (1992). Cultural expectations of thinness in women: An update. *International Journal of Eating Disorders, 11,* 85-90.

Wolf, E. M., & Crowther, J. H. (1992). An evaluation of behavioral and cognitive-behavioral group interventions for the treatment of bulimia nervosa in women. *International Journal of Eating Disorders, 11*, 3-15.

Woodside, D. B. (1993). Genetic contributions to eating disorders. In A. S. Kaplan & P. E. Garfinkel (Eds.), *Medical issues and the eating disorders* (pp. 193-212). New York: Brunner/Mazel.

CHAPTER 9

Adolescent Suicide and Depression

GARY M. BLAU

Linda sat at the edge of her bed. She stared blankly at the bottle of sleeping pills in her left hand and the bottle of bourbon in her right. A tear trickled down her cheek as she thought about the recent breakup with her boyfriend, her falling grades, and her fear of being pregnant. She felt worthless and insignificant. She wanted to talk with her mother, but at 15, Linda felt isolated and alone. She barely saw either of her parents since their divorce. Her father had his new girlfriend. Her mother was busy with her new job and caring for her little brother. An overwhelming sense of despair fell on her. She felt trapped and helpless. Like a caged tiger, there was no escape. She remembered feeling sad. She remembered feeling pressure. Now she just felt numb. She couldn't bear the pain of another day. Nothing seemed worthwhile. She looked again at the contents of each hand. She closed her eyes, and . . .

Statistics

Suicide is the third leading cause of death among young people between the ages of 15 and 24, surpassed only by accidents and homicides (Holinger & Offer, 1982; McGinnis, 1987). Between 1960 and 1984, the suicide rate for this age group more than doubled, from 5.2 to 12.3 per 100,000. The rate has tripled since 1950. Each year, more than 5,000 teenagers commit suicide. Berman and Carroll (1984) and Berman (1987) report that there were

5,200 adolescent suicides in 1980, accounting for 11% of all deaths among 15- to 24-year-olds. In 1988, Holinger (1990) reported 15,458 "identified" suicide attempts for the 10- to 19-year-old population. These statistics were based on information obtained when youngsters came to the attention of the medical system (through the emergency room), and these attempts resulted in 18,530 days of hospitalization. Many suicide attempts, however, do not result in hospitalization, and statistics for these attempts (or gestures) are difficult to obtain. Spence (1986) estimates that more than 1,000 children and adolescents try to kill themselves every day. More specifically, Nazario (1994) estimates that adolescent females account for 300,000 suicide attempts each year and that adolescent males account for 100,000 attempts.

Statistics on adolescent suicide are indeed alarming, and several national studies have provided compelling information. Ross (1985), in a study with high school students from three separate communities, found that between 7% and 13% reported at least one suicide attempt. Nearly 53% of the high school students responding to the survey said they have seriously considered suicide at some time in their lives; 46% said they knew a young person who has tried to commit or committed suicide (Mental Health Association of Alabama, 1988). Of further concern is the finding that children aged 10 to 14 are killing themselves three times more often than they did 20 years ago.

The purpose of this chapter is to provide a brief overview of adolescent suicide, focusing on some of the factors that may increase the chances of a suicide attempt as well as strategies to intervene and prevent the tragedy of adolescent suicide.

Introduction

Adults often view adolescence as a time for being carefree and without responsibility. A youngster is expected to be full of life, energy, and hope. Given the above statistics, however, this is obviously not the case. Adolescence is also a time of great transition and rapid change. Teenagers must give up their dependence and become autonomous, they must develop an individual identity, and they must adjust to the physiological, cognitive, and emotional changes that occur. Thus, instead of being cheerful and lighthearted, adolescents are marked by storm and stress (Adams & Gullotta, 1989).

What kind of person commits suicide? What are the risk factors to be concerned about? Too often, people believe that only "crazy" people attempt suicide, and that successful or popular people are immune to such drastic action. In reality, however, this is not the case. Anyone can and does commit suicide. Therefore, predicting whether someone is suicidal is difficult. Many myths, however, abound regarding adolescent suicide. One myth is that teenagers who talk about killing themselves do not actually do it (Allen, 1987). This is one of the most tragic myths because verbal statements about a wish to die are clearly meaningful and should not be ignored. As many as 60% of persons who commit suicide have made a prior statement as to their intent, and according to Giovacchini (1981), these prior statements are a desperate cry for help. Another myth is that talking to an adolescent about suicide will make him or her complete the act. Because most teenagers have considered suicide at one time or another, talking about suicide, contrary to popular opinion, does not "plant the seed." Rather, open communication about suicide may prevent an attempt by showing the teens that they are cared for or allowing the youths to express their intent and therefore be amenable to intervention.

Another myth is that suicidal youth are intent on dying. Most suicidal teens are undecided about death and instead view death as a way to avoid suffering (Schneidman, 1987). Yet another myth is that once a youth is suicidal, he or she will remain suicidal forever (McGuire, 1984). In actuality, most teens who wish to kill themselves are only suicidal for a brief period, and if they can be supported during this crisis, they do not necessarily remain suicidal. Finally, although there are many other myths (e.g., all suicidal youth are mentally ill), one myth that is particularly troublesome is the belief that a "suicidal-type" person exists. All kinds of youth attempt to end their lives regardless of their background and characteristics. This makes predicting youth suicide difficult and points to a complex set of risk factors that must be evaluated when working with a potentially suicidal teen (Hicks, 1990).

Notwithstanding the myths, there is no one risk factor that, if present, causes suicide. Rather, academicians and practitioners have put forth a list of potential risk factors that indicate increased probability of a suicide attempt. Many authors separate risk factors into general and specific categories (Allen, 1987; Spence, 1986). General categories include gender, minority status, societal conditions, family dysfunction, and psychiatric impairment (e.g., drug and alcohol abuse, depression). Specific risk factors include high expectations, loss of boy- or girlfriend, poor academic performance and failure to achieve, pregnancy, change in residence or loss of social support, death of a family member, divorce or separation of parents, and sexual or physical abuse.

General Risk Factors

Gender

According to Spence (1986), Berman (1987), and Nazario (1994), females are more than twice as likely to attempt suicide, but males are four times as likely to be successful. The typical *completed* suicide in adolescence is a male using a gun, and the typical adolescent *attempter* is a female ingesting pills. This sex-specific choice of method appears to be one of the main reasons that males have been considered at higher risk for completed suicides as compared with females, but that females are considered at higher risk for a suicide attempt (Berman, 1987).

Minority Status

Another factor to consider is minority status. Although the suicide rate for minorities is reportedly lower than that of the white majority, more than 25% of completed suicides in the African American population are aged 15 to 24. In addition, the greatest increase in suicide rates in the past decade has been for young black males (Berman, 1987). Reasons for this include feelings of powerlessness and oppression that often pervade the young minority individuals' growth and development.

Societal Conditions

Compared with living in affluent communities, living in economically depressed areas appears to increase the chances for suicide among teenagers (Muldoon, 1987). Stress caused by poverty can lead to the feelings of helplessness and hopelessness that are often reported by adolescents who attempt suicide. In addition, increasing poverty also gives rise to increasing crime and delinquent behavior. This is significant in that youth identified as delinquent are more likely to attempt or commit suicide. Miller, Chiles, and Barnes (1982), studying 150 delinquent adolescents at a youth correctional facility in Washington State, found that 20% of their sample (of 13- to 15-year-olds) had previously attempted suicide. These researchers also found that delinquents who are detained in adult facilities are at greater risk. In fact, the U.S. Department of Justice, as reported by Berman (1987), found that the suicide rate for juveniles in adult jails is five times greater than that for youth in the general population. Berman and Cohen-Sandler (1982) outlined a sample of indicators of societal change affecting the adolescent population. Increases in the number of children from divorced families, births to unmarried teens, homelessness, and violence all serve to increase the risk of adolescent suicide.

Family Dysfunction

Another factor, and perhaps the most researched, focuses on family and parental dynamics. As adolescents are often caught between childhood and adulthood, their ability to separate, develop a unique sense of self, and move toward self-sufficiency is important. Parental behaviors affect teenagers' ability to navigate this transition, and researchers (e.g., McKenry, Tishler, & Kelly, 1982; Tishler & McKenry, 1982) have identified that parents of suicidal adolescents more often engage in overt conflicts and have significant psychological problems (ranging from depression to drug and alcohol abuse). In fact, although suicidal tendencies in teenagers do not necessarily indicate family problems, parental or sibling emotional disorders (especially drug and alcohol addiction) have been highly correlated with adolescent suicide attempts and may play an important role in a teenager's decision to end his or her life (Garfinkel, Froese, & Hood, 1982).

Psychiatric Impairment: Drug/Alcohol Abuse

Drugs and alcohol often play a major role in suicide and suicide attempts (McKenry, Tishler, & Kelly, 1983; Muldoon, 1987). Shafii, Corrigan, Whittinghill, and Derrick (1985), in their review of 20 completed suicides, found that 70% of the suicide victims were frequent users of drugs and alcohol. Schwartz, Hoffman, and Jones (1987), in a study of 35 teens hospitalized for drug abuse, found that 20% had attempted suicide. McKenry et al. (1983) interviewed 46 youths who had attempted suicide and found that 43% had serious drug problems. Muldoon (1987) suggests that these data reveal a marked correlation between drug and alcohol abuse and adolescent suicide. In fact, Muldoon writes that every adolescent drug abuser must be considered at greater risk for suicide, and that every suicidal youth must be considered at greater risk for substance abuse.

Psychiatric Impairment: Depression

Of all risk factors, depression has received the most attention. Some professionals believe that suicidal persons are nearly always depressed (Allen, 1987). Feelings of hopelessness, helplessness, despair, and pessimism give rise to suicidal thoughts and actions. Not all suicidal persons are depressed, however, and not all depressed persons are suicidal (Glaser, 1981). A suicidal tendency may stem from other reasons. For example, attention getting (rather than hopelessness and despair) or revenge may be the primary motive. To put it simply, although depression is still considered the best predictor for a potential suicide, suicide and depression are not synonymous (Allen, 1987).

The fact remains, however, that depression can be a contributing factor in suicide and suicide attempts. Its importance emerges in almost every study of adolescent suicide (Muldoon, 1987). Crumley (1979), in a study of 40 adolescents hospitalized after a suicide attempt, found that 80% were diagnosed with some form of depressive disorder. The following four themes have been identified as significant in the depression-suicide correlation:

- Exaggerated feelings of worthlessness and low self-esteem
- Feelings of powerlessness and external locus of control (i.e., feeling like nothing one does will make a difference)
- A negative view of the world
- A negative view of the future

Although all people, especially teenagers, experience the above four themes at one time or another, for depressed or suicidal teens, these feelings dominate their lives. It is not so much that the adolescent wants to die but that he or she wants to stop the pain of the negative feelings, and therefore suicide becomes an option. Fortunately, as stated earlier, depression alone does not cause suicide. Adolescents who have been depressed for several years may not even attempt suicide. Long-standing problems, such as depression, drug/alcohol abuse, and family dysfunction, however, increase the likelihood that a teen will attempt suicide.

Specific Risk Factors

Although long-standing problems increase a teen's vulnerability to suicide, some immediate crisis, especially if the crisis involves embarrassment or humiliation, typically occurs just before a suicide attempt. Many studies have attempted to identify specific characteristics or events that give rise to suicidal behavior (Garfinkel et al., 1982; McKenry et al., 1982; Miller et al., 1982). Unfortunately, these high-stress events are individual specific and therefore harder to predict. What is upsetting to one teenager is not to another, and individual perception, coping style, and history must be taken into account when identifying specific risk factors.

Specific risk factors that may intensify long-standing problems include the following: an argument or intense conflict with a significant adult or peer, intoxication, pregnancy, breakup of a relationship, severe disappointments in school or athletics, suicide attempt by someone the teen knows, death of a loved one, separation/divorce of parents, injury/illness of self or loved one, remarriage of a parent, and change in residence.

Determining Risk

Although no one can perfectly predict or prevent every suicide attempt, there are certain warning signs that, if present, warrant further exploration. Nazario (1994) has listed 12 such "early-warning" signs and they include:

- A suicide threat or comment regarding a desire to die

- Preoccupation with death
- Impulsive behavior
- Prolonged sadness or loss of family
- Cutting off friends or favorite activities
- Deterioration of school performance
- Change in eating or sleeping habits
- Intense feelings of guilt or shame
- Feelings of not being appreciated
- Abuse of alcohol or drugs
- Previous suicide attempts
- Giving away prized possessions

The final determination of whether a teenager is actively suicidal must come from a trained and qualified health care professional. Any of the above risk factors, either alone or in combination, only provides a clue about suicidal intent. Qualified professionals analyze the individual's statements and behaviors further to determine the degree to which the person is at risk of injuring him- or herself. The professional often attempts to evaluate the following characteristics of the potentially suicidal adolescent:

- Previous threats
- Previous attempts
- Specificity of plan
- Availability of means
- Lethality of means
- Rescue resources available
- Accumulation of signs and stressors
- History of suicide in the family
- View of suicide and death

Clinical interviewing has been the traditional strategy to determine risk with a suicidal adolescent (Hicks, 1990). If a youth admits being at risk, follow-up questions are imperative. Hicks (1990) recommends that a clinical interview for suicide risk begin with the question: "How would you harm yourself?" If the teenager has a plan, the next step is to query the details. Miller (1984) has suggested the S-L-A-P method of questioning (S = "specificity" of plan, L = "lethality" of plan, A = "availability" of the proposed suicide implement, P = "proximity" of helping resources). Of course, this quick method of questioning is only a guideline and Hicks (1990) suggests four additional factors that can be added to assess the level of suicidal risk. An acronym to assist with remembering these factors is D-I-R-T. The D stands for "dangerous" and reminds the interviewer to assess the risk of previous attempts and the current plan. The I stands for "impression," which connotes the individual's intent and perception about what he or she is doing. The R stands for "rescue" and identifies whether there are any opportunities within the suicide plan for rescue. If the chances for rescue are poor, the risk is greater. Finally, the T stands for "timing" and suggests that the current danger is higher if the timing of previous attempts was recent. Interviewing a potentially suicidal teen using the above-mentioned format will help determine the nature of the risk factors and the most appropriate strategies to provide safety and save a young person's life.

In addition to interviewing an adolescent, there are also standardized evaluation instruments that have been developed to assist professionals in making judgments about a teenager's dangerousness.

Assessment

Considerable effort has been given to the development of instruments that can assist in the prediction of suicide. Many of these assessment devices use lists of specific warning signs as well as general factors. Responses to the combinations of these predictors are then evaluated to determine the degree of suicidal risk for the individual. Correlations between specific behavioral acts and suicide attempts have been generated in several studies (Johnson, 1985; Rohn, Sarles, Kenny, Reynolds, & Heald, 1977). The suicidal attempter will often provide signs, especially if he or she wishes to be rescued. These signs may include a preoccupation with death and dying, giving away prized possessions, making a will, verbal discussions of death and suicide, changes in sleeping or eating habits, withdrawal from friends and family, major behavioral changes such as poor school performance or dropping out of activities, mood changes or bursts of anger, recent suicide attempts, and sudden euphoric or whirlwind activity following a period of depression.

DIRECT FACTORS (INDICATIONS)

HIGH DEGREE OF RISK   LOW DEGREE OF RISK

high _____ low

awareness of/identification with a
peer suicide (attempted or completed)

high _____ low

family history of depression or suicide

high _____ low

presence of predisposing personality features and styles

—impulsive   —compulsive (rigid)
—risk-taking or self-destructive
—conduct disorder, borderline, or antisocial

high _____ low

level of substance abuse (relates to impulsivity and means)

high _____ low

duration, frequency, specificity,
& lethality of thoughts, plan, gesture, attempt

high _____ low

presence of seasonal or anniversary factors

high _____ low

history of aggression

high _____ low

access to means

high _____ low

number and intensity of precipitating factors and stressors

high _____ low

intentionality

high _____ low

degree of depression

high _____ low

sense of hopelessness (a better predictor than depression)

high _____ low

pronounced changes in mood, behavior, or energy level

high _____ low

presence of "termination behaviors"
(e.g., giving away special belongings)

Figure 9.1. Assessment of Suicidal Risk: Indications
SOURCE: Child and Family Agency of Southeastern Connecticut, Inc.
NOTE: Remember that 75% to 80% of serious attempters give clear warnings.

INVERSE FACTORS (CONTRAINDICATIONS)

HIGH DEGREE OF RISK   LOW DEGREE OF RISK

low _____ high
          interpersonal connectedness/ability
          and willingness to use supports

low _____ high
          ability to plan alternative problem-solving
          strategies/sense of empowerment

low _____ high
          ability to discriminate between situations that
          would or would not lead to suicidal death

low _____ high
          clarity of concepts regarding death
          (e.g., regarding permanence and finality)

low _____ high
          willingness to contract to not commit suicide

low _____ high
          ability to self-reinforce and accept others' confirmation

Figure 9.2. Assessment of Suicidal Risk: Contraindications
SOURCE: Child and Family Agency of Southeastern Connecticut, Inc.

An example of a clinically based suicide risk assessment instrument can be found in Figures 9.1 and 9.2. This assessment instrument, developed and used at Child and Family Agency of Southeastern Connecticut, was designed to determine an individual's intent and risk for suicide (Calvert, 1990). If several categories indicate a "high degree of risk," then plans must be made to protect the individual from injuring him- or herself.

More recently, a number of standardized suicide assessment scales have been developed. Perhaps the most notable of the suicide assessment inventories has been developed by William Reynolds. As a researcher and clinician, Reynolds (1988, 1989a, 1989b, 1992) has developed several assessment tools that measure depression and suicidal ideation in children and adolescents. The *Suicidal Ideation Questionnaire (SIQ)* and the *Suicidal Behavior History Form (SBHF)* are two examples for adolescents. The SIQ was developed to assess the frequency of suicidal thoughts in adolescents, and the SBHF provides more detailed information about the nature of previous suicide attempts and characteristics related to the seriousness of the behavior. Each scale takes approximately 10 minutes to administer (the SBHF could take up to 30 minutes), and both purport to provide formal information about suicide risk. Reliability and validity information have yielded impressive results, and the scales can be used for research or in clinical, school, correctional, medical, and other settings in which suicidal behavior is a potential risk.

Suicide Attempts

A variety of studies have investigated people who have had unsuccessful suicide attempts. The most notable is described by Hawton, Cole, O'Grady, and Osborn (1982). These authors evaluated 50 adolescents who were rescued following a substantial overdose. The adolescents responded to questions about their feelings preceding their attempts and about their specific reasons and motivations. In addition, mental health professionals involved with suicidal adolescents were asked their opinion. According to the results, most adolescents felt particularly angry or lonely just prior to a suicide attempt. Of interest, however, was that older adolescents (16-18) indicated that they had been worried about the future. Having failed in life and feeling ashamed were two other responses for why youngsters would want to take their own lives.

To investigate specific reasons for suicide, clinical assessors developed a list of eight hypothesized intentions for an attempt. The adolescent and the clinical assessors then rated the behaviors listed. The percentages and correlations indicated significant agreement between the ratings. Clinicians and adolescents both indicated three prominent reasons for a suicide attempt. One was to get relief from a terrible state of mind. The second was to escape for a while from an impossible situation, and the third was to make people understand how desperate they felt.

One striking difference between the adolescents' choices and those of the clinicians was that the clinicians believed that the adolescents' reasons were more punitive and manipulative. They differed on three specific questions. The first was to make people sorry for the way they were treating the youth. The second was to try to influence a person or persons or get them to change their minds, and the third was to seek help from someone. Of interest, this difference was also found in a study by Bancroft et al. (1979) and may reflect the adolescent's desire to avoid admitting to negative reasons as the basis for a suicide attempt.

Treatment

Once an adolescent has made an unsuccessful suicide attempt, or has been evaluated to be at high risk of a suicide attempt, intervention is clearly warranted. According to Hicks (1990), suicidal youth must be considered in crisis. Suicidal youth rarely give intervenors the luxury of time to develop plans. As a result, suicidal youth need an immediate response, and many authors have suggested a crisis intervention model (Gispert, Wheeler, Marsh, & Davis, 1985; Sawicki, 1988). Hicks (1990) describes Caplan's (1964) four-phase crisis model as it relates to teen suicide. In phase 1, the "initial" phase, the youth is beginning to feel tension and may appear anxious and confused. At this point, the intervenor should gently confront the teen about his plans and identify other avenues for coping. Often, the youth is more willing to accept help during this phase, which allows an opportunity to deescalate any potential suicidal crisis. The second phase is referred to as the "escalation" phase. If the youth believes that she has no coping abilities (or that she has nothing to live for), her functioning becomes more disorganized. Again, the intervenor can assist with the development of coping strategies as well as monitor the potential risk for suicide. In the third phase, referred to as "redefinition," the youth will either redefine the problem into satisfactory terms or resign himself to failure. This phase represents a crossroads for the teen, and the outcome is either the successful resolution of his problem or movement into the fourth phase. This phase, called "dysfunction," occurs when the problem is not resolved or is avoided. At this time, the youngster may feel "at the breaking point," and should be considered at high risk for suicide. The youth's self-destructive impulses are readily apparent and more intrusive safety measures should be exercised (e.g., hospitalization).

During a suicidal crisis, and during any postsuicidal interventions, the goal of treatment is to broaden the suicidal youth's perspective such that she recognizes other possible options, one of which is life. Although a teenager may be admitted to a hospital or require full-time supervision for a brief period, it is important to note that the majority of adolescents who make a suicide attempt have a relatively good postsuicide adjustment. In fact, repeat attempts only occur in 10% of the population 1 full year after the initial suicide attempt (Hawton, O'Grady, & Osborn, 1982). The remaining 90% do not make another attempt within a year. Hawton et al. (1982) state that the majority of adolescent suicide attempters improve their functioning within 1 month of an attempt. For those who continue to experience major difficulties, problems in mental and physical health, marital dysfunction, and criminality have been associated.

Longer term treatment for individuals with issues of suicide reflect the current approaches in mental health and medical interventions (Miller & Collier, 1982). There are few special techniques or guidelines, except those that address immediate crisis intervention. Peck (1982) states that treatment of suicidal adolescents is essentially the same as that for other disturbed young people. Psychological, social, and pharmacological approaches may be used singly or in combination. Although hospital, partial hospital, or residential settings are used for some interventions (particularly during the initial crisis), outpatient services are more typical.

A variety of psychotherapeutic approaches may be used to work with suicidal teenagers. Cognitive, cognitive-behavioral, analytical, and family therapies are typical treatment methods (Rotheram-Borus, Piacentini, Miller, Graae, & Castro-Blanco, 1994). In addition, the use of medication (e.g., antidepressants) is not uncommon as part of a treatment regimen. Although medications have not been found particularly useful during a suicidal state, they may be quite beneficial to help reduce an underlying disorder, such as depression (Pfeffer, 1978). Used correctly, and in conjunction with other forms of therapy, antidepressant medication can be an important component in the successful adjustment following a suicide attempt.

Prevention

Instead of focusing attention on adolescents who are suicidal or who have made suicide attempts, many authors have advocated enhanced prevention services (Johnson, 1985; Mental Health Association of Alabama, 1988; Ross, 1980). Perhaps potential crisis situations can be avoided if adolescents are provided with programs aimed at suicide prevention. Johnson (1985) states that there are two types of prevention efforts. The first focuses on the individual. Educational, problem-solving, and decision-making programs are offered to individuals or groups to increase adolescents' competency and reduce the likelihood of a suicide attempt.

An example of an individually focused method is the Mental Health Association of Alabama's (1988) *Teenage Suicide Prevention*. This manual contains a five-session curriculum designed to teach young people about suicide. Topics such as reasons for suicide, myths and facts about suicide, values clarification, risk factors, and how to intervene if a friend is suicidal are included. In the section of the curriculum on intervention, teenagers are taught specific things to consider if someone they know becomes suicidal. They are taught to trust their instincts and suspicions: If you think someone is suicidal, take her seriously; let the person know someone cares about her well-being; be a good listener; talk freely and ask direct questions about her intentions; encourage her to get help as soon as possible, and let the person know that her problem cannot be kept a secret; take seriously every complaint and feeling the person expresses; do not moralize, sermonize, or debate the right or wrong of suicide; and do not leave the person alone if she is at high risk. These types of programs have become more widespread and are believed to be effective in reducing the probability that a suicide attempt will occur (Johnson, 1985). Individually focused youth suicide prevention may also be more comprehensive than simply preventing death by suicide. Many youngsters are more at risk because of low self-esteem and poor problem-solving skills. Thus, prevention efforts geared toward improving self-image and increasing positive decision-making abilities may also be effective in reducing adolescent suicide.

The second type of prevention effort has been labeled systemic or ecological (Hicks, 1990; Spence, 1986). These efforts focus on the role of schools in enhancing adolescent health and development, and the role of community and society in reducing the stressors (e.g., poverty, prejudice) that may be associated with motivation to commit suicide. Hicks (1990) writes that effective suicide prevention strategies not only include an individually based curriculum (e.g., improving problem solving, teaching how to identify suicidal behavior in peers) but also include training for parents, teachers, and other school personnel (e.g., social workers, crisis team members). Furthermore, such efforts should include community outreach so that the issues of teen suicide are brought into awareness. Educating the community allows supportive services to increase and provides a foundation of community involvement in the problems of teenagers (Sawicki, 1988). Unfortunately, despite these efforts, society continues to use denial and often blames the victims (or the victims' parents) when a suicide occurs.

Across the country, there have been substantial efforts to prevent youth suicide. The Connecticut legislature, for example, in November 1989, enacted Public Act No. 89-191—An Act Concerning the Prevention of Youth Suicide. This legislation stipulated the development of an Advisory Board, comprised of representatives from designated state agencies, service providers, educators, students, and parents, that served in an advisory capacity to the State Department of Children and Families (known at that time as the Department of Children and Youth Services). From its inception, the Advisory Board began establishing goals and areas of responsibility, and within 3 months had developed 11 action plans that focused on youth suicide prevention. Examples of the Advisory Board's goals included increasing public awareness about teenage suicide, developing a statewide training curriculum designed to prevent and intervene in youth suicide situations, ensuring that all communities had the capacity to respond to suicidal youth via crisis intervention and treatment services, and establishing a coordinated system to collect, analyze, and disseminate data regarding youth suicide and youth suicide prevention efforts.

To accomplish these goals, the Advisory Board focused on four action areas: legislation, training, public awareness, and data collection, and many significant accomplishments have occurred. One such accomplishment was to reduce barriers for at-risk youth to obtain services. The Advisory Board, in conjunction with a state senator, proposed legislation that would allow minors access to mental health treatment without parental consent. Although the bill failed to pass in 1991, it was successful in 1992, and An Act Concerning Outpatient Mental Health Treatment for Minors and Defining Community Health Centers went into effect in October 1992. In response to the passing of the bill, the Advisory Board established guidelines and criteria for the treatment of youth without parental consent, and is now investigating how the law has affected youth suicide prevention.

The Advisory Board has also been successful in the development of training materials. Guidelines for training school personnel in suicide prevention were distributed to all school systems, K-12 curriculum guidelines for teaching about suicide prevention were established and approved by the State Department of Education, and procedures to review police departments' crisis intervention training were brought into existence. These goals and more are the hallmark of suicide prevention efforts, and Connecticut is not alone in these endeavors. Alabama, Florida, Maryland, and New Jersey, to name a few, have also developed training curricula, and suicide prevention efforts continue to expand.

The commitment of state agencies, legislators, service providers, students, and parents to address issues of youth suicide is a crucial first step in the development of successful prevention efforts. Developing comprehensive strategies is next. The causes of adolescent suicide are complex and multifaceted, and prevention and intervention strategies must be the same. Fortunately, in many parts of the country, suicide prevention is being taken seriously and tragedies are being avoided. What is clear, based on extensive literature and clinical experience, is that suicidal behavior is a communication of pain and suffering. Now, more than ever, society must increase its awareness of the underlying issues that are often the precursors to needless loss of life. Teenage depression, substance abuse, poverty, and racial and ethnic prejudice are just a few of the problems that face today's adolescent. Society can no longer afford to look away. Isn't a teenager's life more important?

References

Adams, G., & Gullotta, T. P. (1989). *Adolescent life experiences.* Pacific Grove, CA: Brooks/Cole.

Allen, B. P. (1987). Youth suicide. *Adolescence, 22*(86), 273-288.

Bancroft, J., Hawton, K., Simkin, S., Kingston, B., Cumming, C., & Whitewell, D. (1979). The reasons people give for taking overdoses: A further inquiry. *British Journal of Medical Psychology, 52,* 353-365.

Berman, A. L. (1987). The problem of adolescent suicide. *Division of Child, Youth, and Family Services Newsletter, 10*(2), 1-5.

Berman, A. L., & Carroll, T. (1984). Adolescent suicide: A critical review. *Death Education, 8,* 53-64.

Berman, A. L., & Cohen-Sandler, R. (1982). Childhood and adolescent suicide research: A critique. *Crisis, 3,* 3-15.

Calvert, R. (1990). *Assessment of suicidal risk.* New London, CT: Child and Family Agency of Southeastern Connecticut, Inc.

Caplan, G. (1964). *Principles of preventive psychiatry.* New York: Basic Books.

Crumley, F. E. (1979). Adolescent suicide attempts. *Journal of the American Medical Association, 241*(22), 1022-1027.

Garfinkel, B. D., Froese, A., & Hood, J. (1982). Suicide attempts in children and adolescents. *American Journal of Psychiatry, 139,* 1257-1261.

Giovacchini, P. (1981). *The urge to die.* New York: Macmillan.

Gispert, M., Wheeler, K., Marsh, L., & Davis, M. S. (1985). Suicidal adolescents: Factors in evaluation. *Adolescence, 20,* 753-762.

Glaser, K. (1981). Psychopathological patterns in depressed adolescents. *American Journal of Psychotherapy, 35,* 368-382.

Hawton, K., Cole, D., O'Grady, J., & Osborn, M. (1982). Motivational aspects of deliberate self-poisoning in adolescents. *British Journal of Psychiatry, 141,* 286-291.

Hawton, K., O'Grady, J., & Osborn, M. (1982). Adolescents who take overdoses: Their characteristics, problems, and contacts with helping agencies. *British Journal of Psychiatry, 140,* 118-123.

Hicks, B. B. (1990). *Youth suicide: A comprehensive manual for prevention and intervention.* Bloomington, IN: National Educational Service.

Holinger, P. (1990). The causes, impact, and preventability of childhood injuries in the United States: Childhood suicide in the United States. *American Journal of Diseases of Children, 144,* 670-676.

Holinger, P., & Offer, D. (1982). Prediction of adolescent suicide: A population model. *American Journal of Psychiatry, 139,* 302-307

Johnson, W. Y. (1985). Classroom discussion of suicide: An intervention tool for the teacher. *Contemporary Education, 56*(2), 636-638.

McGinnis, J. M. (1987). Suicide in America: Moving up the public agenda. *Suicide and Life Threatening Behavior, 17*(1), 15-23.

McGuire, D. (1984). Childhood suicide. *Child Welfare, 63*(1), 17-26.

McKenry, P., Tishler, C., & Kelly, C. (1982). Adolescent suicide: A comparison of attempters and non-attempters in an emergency room population. *Clinical Pediatrics, 21,* 266-270.

McKenry, P., Tishler, C., & Kelly, C. (1983). The role of drugs in adolescent suicide attempts. *Suicide and Life-Threatening Behavior, 13,* 210-214.

Mental Health Association of Alabama. (1988). *Teenage suicide prevention.* Montgomery: Alabama Department of Public Health.

Miller, G., & Collier, J. (1982). Family treatment approaches to suicidal children and adolescents. *Journal of the American Academy of Child Psychiatry, 8,* 491-498.

Miller, M. (1984). *Training workshop manual.* San Diego, CA: Suicide Information Center.

Miller, M. L., Chiles, J. A., & Barnes, V. E. (1982). Suicide attempters within a delinquent population. *Journal of Consulting and Clinical Psychology, 50,* 491-498.

Muldoon, J. A. (1987). *Adolescent suicide: Identification and intervention*. Minneapolis, MN: Community Intervention, Inc.

Nazario, T. A. (1994). What parents should know about teenage suicide. *Child Welfare Report, 2*(6), 1-8.

Peck, M. (1982). Youth suicide. *Death Education, 6*, 29-47.

Pfeffer, C. (1978). Psychiatric hospital treatment of suicidal children. *Suicide and Life Threatening Behavior, 8*, 150-160.

Reynolds, W. M. (1988). *Suicidal Ideation Questionnaire (SIQ)*. Lutz, FL: Psychological Assessment Resources.

Reynolds, W. M. (1989a). *Reynolds Adolescent Depression Scale (RADS)*. Lutz, FL: Psychological Assessment Resources.

Reynolds, W. M. (1989b). *Reynolds Child Depression Scale (RCDS)*. Lutz, FL: Psychological Assessment Resources.

Reynolds, W. M. (1992). *Suicidal Behavior History Form (SBHF)*. Lutz, FL: Psychological Assessment Resources.

Rohn, R., Sarles, R., Kenny, T., Reynolds, B., & Heald, F. (1977). Adolescents who attempt suicide. *Journal of Pediatrics, 90*, 636-638.

Ross, C. P. (1980). Mobilizing schools for suicide prevention. *Suicide and Life Threatening Behavior, 10*, 239-243.

Ross, C. P. (1985). Teaching children the facts of life and death: Suicide prevention in the schools. In M. L. Peck, N. L. Farberow, & R. E. Litman (Eds.), *Youth suicide*. New York: Springer.

Rotheram-Borus, M. J., Piacentini, J., Miller, S., Graae, F., & Castro-Blanco, D. (1994). Brief cognitive-behavioral treatment for adolescent suicide attempters and their families. *Journal of the American Academy of Child and Adolescent Psychiatry, 33*, 508-517.

Sawicki, S. (1988). Effective crisis intervention. *Adolescence, 23*, 83-89.

Schneidman, E. S. (1987). At the point of no return. *Psychology Today, 3*, 55-58.

Schwartz, R. H., Hoffman, N. G., & Jones, R. (1987). Behavioral, psychosocial, and academic correlates of marijuana usage in adolescence. *Clinical Pediatrics, 26*, 214-220.

Shafii, M., Corrigan, S., Whittinghill, J. R., & Derrick, A. (1985). Psychological autopsy of completed suicide in children and adolescents. *American Journal of Psychiatry, 142*(9), 406-414.

Spence, W. (1986). *Suicide can be prevented*. Waco, TX: WRS Group Incorporated.

Tishler, C., & McKenry, P. (1982). Parental negative self image and adolescent suicide attempters. *Journal of the American Academy of Child Psychiatry, 21*, 404-408.

CHAPTER 10

The Neurobiology of Schizophrenia

DEEPAK CYRIL D'SOUZA

JOHN HARRISON KRYSTAL

Broadly, schizophrenia is a complex psychiatric syndrome that presents in early adulthood as an acute psychotic episode, preceded by warning symptoms, and followed by periods of psychosis and accompanying decline in most areas of functioning. The signs and symptoms of schizophrenia are varied and encompass almost every area of behavior and cognition: emotion, motor function, attention, executive function, speech and language, volition, and perception. Schizophrenia frequently leads to social, vocational, and economic impairment and has a devastating impact on patients, their families, and society. The lifetime prevalence is about 1%, and it costs society more than the financial burden of cancer. Although the concept of schizophrenia has been defined with a reasonable degree of agreement, it is continuously undergoing refinement even today. It is important to recognize that the current concept of schizophrenia is provisional and based on a need to achieve consensus about a definition rather than on an understanding of pathophysiology or etiology. The following section will attempt to trace the concept of schizophrenia as it has evolved into what it is today.

History

Although the signs and symptoms of schizophrenia have been mentioned in texts since antiquity, it was only at the turn of this century that schizophrenia was recognized and investigated as a distinct clinical syndrome. The first comprehensive definition of schizophrenia was published in 1919 by the German psychiatrist Emil Kraeplin in his treatise *Dementia Praecox and Paraphrenia* (Kraeplin, 1919/1971). In this influential account, which is referred to even today, Kraeplin called schizophrenia *dementia praecox* (early-occurring dementia) and considered it an endogenous syndrome with a chronic, relapsing, unremitting chronic course resulting in severe disability without recovery. Kraeplin hypothesized that dementia praecox involved a failure of integration of volition, affect, and cognition. Today, Kraeplin's schizophrenia probably fits best with the *Diagnostic and Statistical Manual's (DSM-IV)* diagnosis of Chronic Schizophrenia. The Swiss psychiatrist Eugene Bleuler, who was influenced by the work of Sigmund Freud, proposed a much broader concept of schizophrenia based primarily on signs and symptoms rather than course and outcome. Bleuler, who coined the term *schizophrenia,* proposed that disorder of the formulation and expression of thought was the fundamental symptom of schizophrenia. Bleuler wrote in 1950:

> By the term "dementia praecox" or "schizophrenia" we designate a group of psychoses whose course is at times chronic, at times marked by intermittent attacks, and which can stop or retrograde at any stage, but does not permit a full restitutio ad integrum. The disease is characterized by a specific type of alteration of thinking, feeling and relation to the external world which appears nowhere else in this particular fashion.

He also identified four cardinal symptoms of schizophrenia (the four As as they have been termed)—autism, ambivalence, abnormal thoughts, and abnormal affect—and considered psychotic symptoms such as hallucinations and delusions as accessory symptoms. The influence of Kraeplin and Bleuler led to a schism over the diagnosis and conceptualization of schizophrenia. The Swiss-American camp, influenced by Bleuler and Freud, emphasized the cardinal symptoms, sometimes without the same emphasis on frank psychotic symptoms, resulting in an overinclusive diagnostic scheme. The British and non-Swiss continental group were much more exclusive and conservative in diagnosis. These two schools of thought resulted in great divergence in the estimates of the incidence and prevalence of schizophrenia; therefore, the Cross-National Study of Diagnosis of Mental Disorders conducted in the 1960s showed that the greater incidence of schizophrenia as an admitting diagnosis in psychiatric hospitals in the United States, as compared with Britain, was in fact a result of overdiagnosis by U.S. psychiatrists based on overinclusiveness. These discrepancies were confirmed by the U.S./U.K. study (Cooper et al., 1972; Kendell, Cooper, & Goulay, 1971) and the International Pilot Study of Schizophrenia (World Health Organization, 1973). Kurt Schneider, an important influence on the conceptual history of schizophrenia, emphasized specific types of psychotic symptoms that he believed to occur only in schizophrenia. He termed these *first rank symptoms* because of their first rank importance in diagnosing schizophrenia. Schneider (1959) believed that these specific forms of delusions and hallucinations were distinct from the more general forms of hallucinations and delusions that could occur in a variety of other disorders. The work of Kraeplin, Bleuler, and Schneider strongly influenced efforts to develop systematized diagnostic criteria for schizophrenia that have a high degree of consensus and validity. The two most influential diagnostic systems in use are *DSM-IV* (*Diagnostic and Statistical Manual*, fourth edition), developed by the American Psychiatric Association (1994), and the *ICD-10* (*International Classification of Diseases*, tenth edition), which has been developed by the World Health Organization (1992). For a detailed review of the diagnosis and classification of schizophrenia, refer to Andreasen and Carpenter (1993).

Epidemiology

The lifetime prevalence for schizophrenia is 1%. The number of new cases of schizophrenia that appear in a year (incidence), although difficult to estimate precisely, has been approximated to between 0.11 to 0.7 per 1,000 population. There is little evidence to support differences in the prevalence of schizophrenia among various ethnic or racial groups. It appears that the incidence and prevalence of schizophrenia are uniform across the globe.

Although schizophrenia can first manifest anytime, the average age of onset of the first frank psychotic episode is 15 to 24 in males and 25 to 34 in females. This gender difference in the age of onset of psychosis and the observation that females have a milder illness is extremely significant and lends support to a biological nature of the illness. In addition, late-onset schizophrenia, regardless of gender, has a better outcome.

Schizophrenic patients tend to be born in winter and spring in the Western Hemisphere. This observation suggests that some seasonally varying environmental cause damages the developing fetus, resulting in an increased risk for schizophrenia. Of the many explanations offered to account for the seasonality of birth, prenatal infections, particularly viral infections during months 4 to 7 of gestation (second and third trimesters), have been most widely implicated with schizophrenia in adult life.

There is also consistent evidence that birth complications, such as prolonged labor or perinatal hypoxia, are a significant contributing factor in the etiology of schizophrenia.

The incidence and prevalence of schizophrenia is reported to be higher in lower social classes than in upper classes. This observation is most likely explained by the "downward drift" theory, according to which the concentration of schizophrenia in the lower socioeconomic stratum is a result rather than a cause of schizophrenia.

Phenomenology

Schizophrenia is a constellation of signs and symptoms typified by delusions and hallucinations occurring in the absence of a significant disturbance of mood or sensorium. No sign or symptom distinctively characterizes schizophrenia; the signs and symptoms can occur in a variety of other psychiatric or neurological illnesses and, even within individuals, symptoms change over time. Of profound importance is the heterogeneous clinical presentation of schizophrenia. Three models have been proposed to account for the heterogeneity of schizophrenia: (a) a single cause leading to different presentations similar to multiple sclerosis; (b) different causes leading to the same presentation similar to pneumonia, dementia, or mental retardation; and (c) specific clusters of symptoms that come together in different ways in different patients caused by different processes.

A significant proportion of individuals who eventually develop schizophrenia have premorbid characteristics that differentiate them from their peers who do not develop the illness. Adolescents who eventually develop schizophrenia have been described as introverted, shy, socially withdrawn, with few or no dates, aloof, suspicious, eccentric, or passive; they are described as preferring solitary activities that did not involve social interaction such as music, television, reading. As children, they are reported to have had few friends, odd behavior, and cognitive difficulties. As infants, they are described as having had delayed milestones. Of prognostic importance is that individuals with good premorbid functioning have a more favorable outcome of schizophrenia than do those with poor premorbid functioning.

The first period of acute schizophrenic psychosis is usually preceded by a stage of warning symptoms lasting from a month to a year. During this prodrome, an insidious change is noticed by people close to the patient, characterized by a gradual decline in the social, educational, personal, and work functioning of the affected individual. The affected individual becomes increasingly withdrawn, odd, or eccentric, and may manifest unusual speech, bizarre ideas or behavior, abnormal emotional states, and poor hygiene/grooming. As the illness progresses, affected individuals experience feelings of anxiety and depression, and often make valiant attempts to regain control of their lives.

No discussion of the phenomenology of schizophrenia would be complete without understanding the concept of positive and negative symptoms. *Positive symptoms* refers to the presence of hallucinations, delusions, thought disorder, agitation, and so on, and *negative symptoms* refers to social withdrawal, lack of motivation, lack of affect, and so on. In this section, a discussion of the phenomenology of schizophrenia will be presented using the positive and negative symptoms classification.

Positive Symptoms

These include delusions, hallucinations, thought disorder, and agitation. Delusions are false, unshakable beliefs of the patient that are not shared by the those from the sociocultural background of the patient. Delusions can be of the grandiose, persecutory, religious, bizarre, and somatic type. For example, the schizophrenic patient might believe that the government or its agency, such as the FBI, is monitoring his or her every move, or that machines have been planted in different parts of his or her body. These beliefs are held with extreme conviction even in the face of contrary evidence.

Accompanying delusions of persecution, patients sometimes may have ideas of reference, that is, that other people or the media are talking about the person, or that events occurring in their environment have a special relationship with them; for example, a patient might believe that the streetlights were switched on when he steps out of the house.

Sometimes patients believe that their thoughts are being broadcast to the public ("thought broadcasting"), or that thoughts not belonging to them are being inserted into their minds by other people ("thought insertion"), or that their minds are being "emptied" of thoughts by some force ("thought withdrawal").

Hallucinations are sensory perceptions in the absence of real sensory stimuli. These can involve every sensory modality: auditory, visual, olfactory, tactile, gustatory, and so on. Individuals with schizophrenia typically experience auditory hallucinations: voices that are perceived as arising from within or outside the body, providing a running commentary about the person, often ridiculing the person, and sometimes commanding/instructing the person to perform actions. On occasion, individuals with schizophrenia have committed suicide and homicide in response to the "instructions" from "the voices." To the schizophrenic person, the voices are very real and most often tormenting, preventing them from attending to even simple tasks that *normal* people would carry out with ease.

Other symptoms include disorder of thought, language, and communication. Patients with schizophrenia manifest disorder of the form and process of thought in addition to the previously described disorders of content of thought. This sign was believed by Bleuler to be a fundamental symptom of schizophrenia. Most often, patients are unaware that their communication is abnormal. The disorder can manifest as loosening of associations (association between words and their meaning is lost), tangentiality (communication shifts from one context to an entirely unrelated context or a tangent), circumstantiality (the train of thought diverges from the context but eventually returns to the original point), word salad (there is a complete breakdown of thought processes resulting in the production of a stream of thoughts composed of words lacking any syntactic or contextual continuity), flight of ideas (thoughts rapidly jump from idea to idea, though the context of thoughts is most often preserved), neologisms (new words that have meaning only to the patient), and echolalia (patients will echo exactly what is being said to them).

Negative Symptoms

These include flat affect, poverty of speech (alogia), poverty of content of speech, amotivation, apathy, anhedonia. One of the hallmarks of schizophrenia is flattening of affect, that is, the person's affect or emotional tone shows little of the normal fluctuation. Some experts consider this *the* cardinal symptom/sign of schizophrenia. It is experienced by the observer as an absence of an emotional tone.

Amotivation refers to the lack of desire to engage in any purposeful activity; often patients who were once involved in activities related to work, education, and social life become content lying in bed or sitting around. Patients lose all ambition or the desire to have goals. This results in significant loss of productivity.

Poverty of speech (the person rarely speaks spontaneously), poverty of content of speech (despite speaking, the speech is empty and does not convey much information), and thought blocking (the person stops in midsentence and, when asked, explains that the thought vanished) are considered to be negative disorders of thought, language, and communication.

The following is a list of typical symptoms of schizophrenia:

1. Marked social isolation or withdrawal
2. Marked impairment in role functioning as wage earner, student, or homemaker
3. Markedly peculiar behavior (collecting garbage, hoarding food, talking to self in public)
4. Marked impairment in personal hygiene and grooming
5. Blunted or inappropriate affect
6. Digressive, vague, overelaborate, or circumstantial speech, or poverty of speech, or poverty of content of speech
7. Odd beliefs or magical thinking, influencing behavior and inconsistent with cultural norms
8. Unusual perceptual experiences
9. Marked lack of interests, initiative, or energy

Diagnosis of Schizophrenia

A. *Characteristic symptoms:* Two (or more) of the following, each present for a significant portion of time during a 1-month period (or less if successfully treated):

(1) delusions

(2) hallucinations

(3) disorganized speech (e.g., frequent derailment or incoherence)

(4) grossly disorganized or catatonic behavior

(5) negative symptoms, i.e., affective flattening, alogia, or avolition

Note: Only one Criterion A symptom is required if delusions are bizarre or hallucinations consist of a voice keeping up a running commentary on the person's behavior or thoughts, or two or more voices conversing with each other.

B. *Social/occupational dysfunction:* For a significant portion of the time since the onset of the disturbance, one or more major areas of functioning such as work, interpersonal relations, or self-care are markedly below the level achieved prior to the onset (or when the onset is in childhood or adolescence, failure to achieve expected level of interpersonal, academic, or occupational achievement).

C. *Duration:* Continuous signs of the disturbance persist for at least 6 months. The 6-month period must include at least 1 month of symptoms (or less if successfully treated) that meet Criterion A (i.e., active-phase symptoms) and may include periods of prodromal or residual symptoms. During these prodromal or residual periods, the signs of the disturbance may be manifested by only negative symptoms or two or more symptoms listed in Criterion A present in an attenuated form (e.g., odd beliefs, unusual perceptual experiences).

D. *Schizoaffective and Mood Disorder exclusion:* Schizoaffective Disorder and Mood Disorder With Psychotic Features have been ruled out because either (1) no Major Depressive, Manic, or Mixed Episodes have occurred concurrently with active-phase symptoms; or (2) if mood episodes have occurred during active-phase symptoms, their total duration has been brief relative to the duration of the active and residual periods.

E. *Substance/general medical condition exclusion:* The disturbance is not due to direct physiological effects of a substance (e.g., a drug of abuse, a medication) or a general medical condition.

F. *Relationship to a Pervasive Developmental Disorder:* If there is a history of Autistic Disorder or another Pervasive Developmental Disorder, the additional diagnosis of Schizophrenia is made only if prominent delusions or hallucinations are also present for at least a month (or less if successfully treated). (American Psychiatric Association, 1994, pp. 285-286)

Course of Illness

The course of schizophrenia is characterized by onset in early adulthood heralded by a prodrome and followed by a period of acute psychotic symptoms. Resolution of the first period of acute psychosis (*first psychotic break*) is most typically, though not always, followed by a recurrence of acute psychotic symptoms over the years superimposed on chronic psychotic symptoms and a general deterioration in functioning. Therefore, the diagnosis of schizophrenia requires an examination of the longitudinal course of the illness, and, in fact, a period of at least 1 year of change is required for making a diagnosis as outlined in the preceding criteria of the *DSM-IV*. There is a wide range in the severity of the illness, with some patients having a deteriorating course and others having a relatively mild course. For most patients, schizophrenia begins in adulthood and persists, at some level, throughout life. Many patients fail to reach critical developmental milestones (e.g., living independently, marrying, earning money), whereas others lose these abilities after repeated hospitalizations and social failures. Many will end up as wards of the state or as wards of their families, with few overcoming the illness to lead "normal" lives.

Etiology

The cause of schizophrenia remains elusive. The search for the etiology of schizophrenia has followed several lines of investigation. Although the biological findings in schizophrenia are neither consistent nor conclusive, major progress has been made toward a neurobiological understanding of the illness. It is clear that schizophrenia is a neurobiological illness. In the following sections, we will review the genetic, neurochemical, and in vivo imaging data on schizophrenia.

Genetics of Schizophrenia

The earliest reference to the genetic contribution to the etiology of schizophrenia dates back to 1911 when Bleuler suggested that the relatives of schizophrenic patients were often "tainted by hereditary mental disease." Since then, several studies examining this

Table 10.1 Rates of Definite Schizophrenia Among Relatives of Schizo-
              phrenic Patients

Familial Relationship	Percentage Affected
Offspring of 2 schizophrenic patients	36.6
Siblings	12.1
Offspring of 1 schizophrenic patient	9.4
Half-siblings	2.9
Nieces or nephews	2.7
Grandchildren	2.8
First cousins	1.6
Spouses	1.0

SOURCE: Adapted from Gottesman and Shields (1982).

question have led to both some definitive answers and several
perplexing questions. Two lines of investigation have been applied
to characterize the genetics of schizophrenia—epidemiological and
linkage studies—and this section will expand on these studies
(Kendler, 1988; Kendler & Scott, 1993).

Epidemiological Studies

1. Familial Aggregation. Early studies (Kallman, 1938) showed that
the closer the genetic relationship between a person with schizophrenia and a relative, the greater that relative's risk of developing
schizophrenia. Familial aggregation studies have consistently demonstrated that first degree relatives of patients with schizophrenia
have a much higher risk for developing the illness than the general
population (Table 10.1).

Initial observations of familial aggregation led to the genetic
hypothesis of causality (Gottesman & Shields, 1982; Guze, Cloninger,
Martin, & Clayton, 1983). Researchers, however, questioned whether
the aggregation observed in families was due to familial environmental factors, such as rearing, learned behavior, and infectious
agents, or truly genetic factors.

Several study designs were employed to separate the environmental from genetic factors in the study of familial aggregation.
These include twin studies and adoption studies.

Table 10.2 Risk for Developing Schizophrenia

Population	Percentage
A. General population	0.9
B. First degree relatives of patients with schizophrenia	
1. parents	5.6
2. siblings	10.1
3. children	12.8
C. Twins	
1. dizygotic	20
2. monozygotic	60

2. Twin Studies. These studies (reviewed by Kendler, 1983) have shown that monozygotic twins (genetically identical) have higher concordance rates than dizygotic twins (sharing only about 50% of genetic material). Hence, in a pair of monozygotic twins, if one has schizophrenia, then there is a 60% likelihood of the other also having schizophrenia, whereas in a pair of dizygotic twins, the likelihood is 20% (Table 10.2).

Of the monozygotic twins, 40% are discordant for schizophrenia. This suggests either that (a) environmental factors may play a large role in the etiology of the illness either by combining with an underlying genetic diathesis or by inducing phenocopies of the disorder and/or (b) discordance may be due to phenotypic nonexpression of a genetic diathesis. Studies by Gottesman and Bertelsen (1989) suggest that discordance among monozygotic twins cannot be accounted for by the existence of nontransmissible forms of schizophrenia.

Even though the evidence seemed compelling, these twin studies were not completely able to eliminate environmental factors. This led to adoption studies, which were anticipated to further reduce environmental factors.

3. Adoption Studies. Adoption studies of different designs have been used to tease apart environmental from genetic factors (Rieder & Kaufmann, 1988).

Adoptee studies have clearly established, for offspring separated from their mothers soon after birth, that offspring of schizophrenic mothers have a higher risk for developing schizophrenia than do offspring of nonschizophrenic mothers.

In *adoptee's family studies* studies (Heston, 1970; Kety, Rosenthal, Wende, Schulsinger, & Jacobsen, 1975), schizophrenia and schizophrenia spectrum disorders were found to be more common in the biological relatives of schizophrenic adoptees than in the biological relatives of nonschizophrenic adoptees.

4. Cross Fostering. These studies (Wender, Rosenthal, & Kety, 1968) have shown similar rates of schizophrenia in adoptees whether their adoptive parents had schizophrenia or not. Twin adoptive studies have shown that monozygotic twins separated at birth and reared apart have shown high concordance rates for schizophrenia.

Summary

Family studies using differing methodologies and designs consistently indicate that the familial aggregation of schizophrenia is accounted for largely by genetic factors. The fact that 40% of dizygotic twins are discordant for schizophrenia suggests, however, that genetic factors do not completely account for the transmission of the illness. This suggests the role of nonfamilial environmental factors, such as prenatal, perinatal, and sociocultural factors, in the etiology of this illness. Despite the large body of evidence consistent with a significant heritable liability to schizophrenia, the mode or modes of inheritance, the gene or genes involved, and the phenotypic consequences of those genes remain elusive.

Linkage Studies

A powerful molecular genetic technique identified the gene contributing to Huntington's disease, Wilson's disease, and several other disorders. Linkage studies involve highly complicated methodological and technical issues that are out of the scope of this chapter (for a review, see Ott, 1991). In this section, only the basic aspects will be discussed.

The basis of linkage studies is the premise that two genes lying alongside each other on a chromosome tend to be inherited together. If a gene predisposes to a disease of interest and if the specific "marker" gene can be traced in a family through generations, then a linkage study can be done. If both the "marker" gene and the disease of interest are inherited together, then the gene contributing to the disease of interest probably lies close to the "marker" gene and is said to be *linked* to the "marker" gene. Statistical analyses confirm the significance of the linkage between the disease of interest and the "marker" gene.

Linkage Strategies

1. Favored Loci. This strategy has provided leads for genetic linkage of a number of diseases (e.g., Duchenne muscular dystrophy). A wide variety of chromosomal abnormalities have been associated with schizophrenia.

Regarding chromosome 5, in 1988, Bassett identified a pair consisting of a 20-year-old proband and his maternal uncle, both of whom had schizophrenia and dysmorphic facial features. This prompted cytogenetic analysis, which revealed extra chromosomal material on chromosome 11. Further analysis determined the extra chromosomal material to be from the long arm of chromosome 5. Bassett concluded that this partial trisomy of chromosome 5 was associated with the syndrome of schizophrenia and physical abnormalities.

Glucocorticoids are associated with steroid psychosis, which shares some features with schizophrenia. The gene coding for the glucocorticoid receptor resides on chromosome 5. This evidence and the report by Bassett, McGillivray, Langlois, Pantzar, and Wood (1990) spurred other investigators to focus on the region of chromosome 5.

In 1988, Sherrington et al. reported linkage between genetic markers on chromosome 5 and schizophrenia in a British and Icelandic pedigree. Since then, however, several studies (Kennedy et al., 1988) have shown evidence against linkage between chromosome 5 and schizophrenia. All these studies have methodological and statistical problems that make interpretation of the data difficult. Suffice to conclude that there is no compelling evidence for linkage between chromosome 5 and schizophrenia.

Sex chromosomes have also been implicated in schizophrenia. Evidence of the influence of the sex chromosomes on schizophrenia includes the following: (a) Individuals with extra X chromosomes (XXX females and XXY males: Klinefelter syndrome) show a higher frequency of psychoses; (b) siblings with psychoses are more likely to be of the same sex; (c) relatives of females with psychoses have a greater risk of psychoses than relatives of males; and (d) sex differences exist in the age of onset and course of psychoses.

2. Candidate Genes. In this strategy, a search is made for co-occurrence of schizophrenia with genes relevant to the disease. The genes to be studied are usually neurobiologically pertinent to schizophrenia, such as the gene coding for the dopamine receptor. Co-occurrence of the candidate gene with schizophrenia suggests the actual location of the disease gene on the chromosome or may be the disease gene itself.

The most favored pathogenetic theory of schizophrenia for the past three decades has been the dopamine hypothesis. Recently, genes for all the five dopamine receptors have been cloned. This prompted investigators to examine these five loci as candidate genes for establishing linkage to schizophrenia (Coon et al., 1993). The results have been disappointing, however, showing an absence of linkage. Hence, it is highly unlikely that an abnormality of the dopamine receptor is contributory to the etiology of schizophrenia, although there are other candidate genes.

3. Anonymous Markers. This strategy uses randomly drawn markers without regard to function. The non-DNA "markers" include blood and serum groups (Rh, ABO) and HLA. Studies using non-DNA markers excluded linkage between the "markers" and schizophrenia. There are a very small number of traceable non-DNA "marker" genes, which has resulted in the abandonment of non-DNA markers in linkage studies.

Regarding DNA markers, recombinant DNA techniques exploded in the 1980s, heralded by the first report of restriction fragment length polymorphism (RFLP) by Kan and Dozy in 1978. RFLPs loci are individual variations of DNA that are present on many areas of each chromosome. These variations can be identified by specific restriction enzymes that cut the DNA on recognizing a specific base pair sequence. Many of these variations are highly polymorphic and will segregate (be transmitted through a pedigree) in a Mendelian pattern because they reflect differences in the DNA molecules.

These variations in DNA provide a limitless supply of markers for studying linkage. Thus, far more than 3,000 RFLPs have been identified, and the numbers continue to rise.

Summary

The gene for schizophrenia has not been discovered as yet, but several modest gains have been made in the right direction. Currently, there is little doubt that schizophrenia, in its narrowest definition, aggregates in families. Several different molecular genetic techniques are being employed to establish linkage between schizophrenia and a gene or genes. The majority of reports of linkage have not been replicated. In short, linkage studies of schizophrenia have not lived up to their promise. The lack of confirmed findings has, however, spurred investigators to refine their methods of investigation. There is no doubt that, with sufficient time, linkage strategies could lead to unprecedented insights into the etiology of schizophrenia.

Methodological Problems

The following are issues of concern:

1. Transmission.

Whether transmission is dominant, recessive, or codominant
The parameters of transmission (i.e., penetrance)
Whether schizophrenia is polygenic or monogenic

2. *Phenotypic Heterogeneity.* Although schizophrenia represents a relatively stable syndrome, its boundaries are unclear. Most diagnostic systems have used phenomenological characteristics to define the disorder. The three diagnostic systems in existence—*DSM-IV* (American Psychiatric Association, 1994), *RDC* (*Research and Diagnostic Criteria*) (Feighner et al., 1972), and *ICD-10* (World Health Organization, 1992)—employ different criteria to make the diagnosis of schizophrenia. Hence, depending on the diagnostic criteria used, whether broad or narrow, the estimates of heritability of the disorder differ. The issue of defining a phenotype that corresponds to

the actual underlying genetic entity is a serious question that remains unanswered.

3. *Genetic Heterogeneity.* Just as mental retardation may be the end result of more than 300 genetic disorders, schizophrenia may also be genetically heterogeneous, making it difficult to test linkage.

Researchers are now beginning to use neurophysiological "markers" such as Event Related Potentials, Eye Tracking Abnormalities, and Continuous Performance Tasks to clarify the heterogeneity of schizophrenia. Other potential markers include response to standard antipsychotics.

Summary

In summary, genetic factors play an important role in the etiology of schizophrenia. No single gene seems likely to be the cause, and genetic factors do not completely account for the development of schizophrenia. Schizophrenia is more likely an illness produced by complex interactions between genetic and environmental factors.

Neurochemistry of Schizophrenia

Several neurotransmitter systems have been implicated in the neurobiology of schizophrenia. In addition to the dopamine hypothesis, there is burgeoning interest in glutamate, serotonin (5-HT), norepinephrine (NE), neuropeptides, NADPH, and so on. Some theories have been fleeting, whereas others, like the dopamine (DA) hypothesis, have prevailed despite intense criticism and scrutiny. It is out of the scope of this chapter to cover all the neurotransmitters implicated in the neurobiology of schizophrenia; however, the roles of dopamine, serotonin, gamma-amino-butyric acid (GABA), norepinephrine, and glutamate will be explored.

The Dopamine Hypothesis of Schizophrenia

The discovery of neuroleptic drugs in 1952 dawned a new era in the neurobiological exploration of schizophrenia. The advent of these drugs spawned the initial dopamine hypothesis of schizophrenia. The dopamine hypothesis, at its parsimonious best, postulated that overactivity of brain systems using the neurotransmitter dopamine was central to the neurobiology of schizophrenia. This theory has been the single most widely accepted neurobiological theory of schizophrenia for the past four decades. Since its inception, this hypothesis has been only partially supported and, therefore, has undergone several revisions. This section will review the dopamine hypothesis as it has evolved over the years into the various revisions that currently exist.

The dopamine (DA) hypothesis was based on early observations of the association between Parkinson's disease and deficits in brain dopamine. Chlorpromazine (Thorazine), which was effective in treating the psychosis of schizophrenia, also produced the signs of Parkinson's disease. It was inferred that deficits in brain dopaminergic systems produced by chlorpromazine were the mechanism of the antipsychotic effect and, therefore, psychosis was due to dopamine excess. The most compelling evidence was that antipsychotics, though varying in action on neurotransmitter systems, all had in common the ability to decrease dopamine activity in the brain. With the development of direct receptor assays, it was shown that antipsychotics were potent competitive antagonists of dopamine receptor binding, and, furthermore, the antipsychotic potency of a drug correlated well with the drug's potency at producing dopamine blockade. Antipsychotics were found to be able to block the behavioral effects produced by apomorphine and amphetamines, agents that were known to increase dopaminergic activity. Antipsychotics were also found to act synergistically with other agents that inhibited dopamine synthesis.

Early Findings Supporting the
Dopamine Hypothesis of Schizophrenia

1. Parkinsonian side effects of neuroleptics
2. Correlation between antipsychotic potency and ability to block dopamine receptors
3. Psychotomimetic effects of dopaminergic drugs
4. Accelerated turnover of dopamine metabolites by neuroleptics

From this early evidence supporting a DA hypothesis, several divergent lines of investigation were pursued in an attempt to consolidate the hypothesis. It is out of the scope of this section to provide a detailed review of the DA hypothesis; interested readers could refer to Carlsson (1988), Lieberman and Koreen (1993), Meltzer (1987, 1989; Meltzer & Stahl, 1976), Reynolds (1989), Seeman (1987), Snyder (1988; Snyder, Banerjee, & Yamamura, 1974), and Wyatt (1986).

The involvement of dopamine in the neurobiology of schizophrenia is based on direct and indirect evidence. Various factors, however, tend to refute a pure DA excess hypothesis of schizophrenia. It seems more likely that several neurotransmitter systems are involved. Despite these shortcomings, the strength of the dopamine hypothesis is that it provides a testable theory for a syndrome whose mechanisms remain elusive. As long as this and other theories are based on testable facts, rather than mere speculation, they are likely to provide a greater understanding of the neurobiology of schizophrenia and other neuropsychiatric disorders.

Revisions to the Dopamine Hypothesis

Several alternatives to the original DA hypothesis have been proposed (see Carlsson, 1988; Davis, Kahn, Ko, & Davidson, 1991; Reynolds, 1989; Weinberger, Wagner, & Wyatt, 1987).

Serotonin and Schizophrenia

The initial hypothesis implicating serotonin in the neurobiology of schizophrenia was based on similarities between the symptoms of schizophrenia and the perceptual distortions produced by LSD (lysergic acid diethylamide), a serotonin antagonist (i.e., a substance capable of combining with a receptor on a cell and initiating some activity). As more was learnt about the receptor pharmacology of LSD, this initial theory was abandoned and remained dormant for several years. Recently, with the advent of atypical antipsychotics such as clozapine, the characterization of serotonin receptors, and the use of probes specific to serotonin function, there is growing awareness of the important contributions of serotonin or 5-HT (5-Hyproxytryptophan) systems, particularly their relationship with DA systems, to the neurobiology of schizophrenia (for a review, see Iqbal, Asnis, Wetzler, Kay, & van Praag, 1991).

Although the available evidence does not support a single over-arching 5-HT hypothesis for schizophrenia, it is clear that 5-HT systems do play a role in the pathophysiology of schizophrenia. The future of this hypothesis lies in the complete characterization of interactions between dopaminergic and serotonergic systems and the development of newer, more effective, and less toxic antipsy-chotics based on this model (Meltzer, 1991).

Excitatory Amino Acids and Schizophrenia

The arylcyclohexamine phencyclidine (PCP), also known as "an-gel dust," was developed in the late 1950s as a dissociative anaes-thetic. PCP has been known to produce a psychosis resembling schizophrenia. At anesthetic doses, PCP also produces agitation, excitation, catatoniclike rigidity, hallucinations, paranoia, and thought disorder lasting beyond recovery from anesthesia (Luby, Cotman, Rosenbaum, Gottlieb, & Kelley, 1959). At subanesthetic doses, PCP and a related compound, ketamine, produced dissociative symp-toms as well as positive and negative symptoms strikingly similar to schizophrenia in healthy subjects (Domino, 1981; Krystal et al., 1994). Typically, the psychomimetic effects last 12 to 72 hours, but in rare instances, the psychosis induced by PCP has been reported to last weeks to months after the last use of the agent. When given to schizophrenic patients, PCP exacerbated the specific perceptual and cognitive abnormalities of schizophrenia. Several other agents, including amphetamines and LSD, have been used to produce a drug model of schizophrenia.

In contrast to amphetamines and LSD, PCP induces positive schizophrenic symptoms (thought disorder, hallucinations, delu-sions, paranoia, and even catatonia), negative schizophrenic symp-toms (apathy, emotional withdrawal), and dissociative symptoms. In the past, the preferred prototype in both human and animal models of schizophrenia was amphetamine, which induces some, though not all, of the positive symptoms of schizophrenia such as paranoia, delusions, agitation, and hostility. Other core symptoms of schizophrenia such as thought disorder, negative symptoms, and frontal lobe deficits are not induced by amphetamines (Angrist, Sathanathan, Wilk, & Gershon, 1974; Bell, 1965). Furthermore, amphetamines have inconsistent effects on positive symptoms

Table 10.3 Comparison of Drug-Induced Models of Schizophrenia

Effects	Ketamine	PCPDAT	LSD
Positive symptoms			
Paranoia	+	+	–
Hallucinations			
Auditory	+	+	–
Visual	+	–	+
Delusions	+	+	–
Thought disorder	+	+/–	–
Catatonia	+	–	–
Stereotypes	–	+	–
Negative symptoms			
Blunted affect	+	+	–
Emotional withdrawal	+	–	–
Incongruent affect	+	–	–
Neuropsychological			
Frontal lobe deficits	+	improves deficits	–
Depersonalization	+	–	+

(Lieberman, Kane, & Alvir, 1989) and may even improve the negative symptoms and frontal lobe deficits in schizophrenia. This suggests that dopamine may account for only some specific positive schizophrenic symptoms or that other neurotransmitter systems may be involved in reproducing the complete syndrome of schizophrenia. Serotonin receptor agonists like LSD produce visual hallucinations and euphoric mood in healthy subjects and patients with schizophrenia. In addition, unlike amphetamines and LSD, PCP and ketamine reproduce the frontal lobe deficits seen in schizophrenia as measured by the Wisconsin Card Sorting Test (Krystal et al., 1994). Thus, noncompetitive NMDA receptor antagonists mimic the symptoms of schizophrenia more authentically than amphetamines.

Receptors for *excitatory amino acids* such as glutamate and aspartate are widely distributed in the brain. Excitatory amino acids (EAAs) are important in mediating a wide range of functions including learning and memory, synaptic and developmental plasticity, sensory information processing, motor coordination, and, when overactivated, excitotoxicity and seizures (Cotman & Monaghan, 1987). The temporal lobe (hippocampus, parahippocampal gyrus, and amygdala) and basal ganglia regions, which are believed to be abnormal in schizophrenia, have a high density of EAA receptors.

The *NMDA receptor complex* regulates a cation channel that permits the influx of calcium. The amino acids glutamate and aspartate bind to a specific site on the complex, resulting in the opening of the channel. The neutral amino acid glycine is a positive modulator of the NMDA receptor, binding to a specific site on the receptor.

NMDA Interactions

There is growing evidence of a close interaction between glutamatergic, dopaminergic, and GABA-ergic pathways, particularly in the striatum. Dopamine receptors are located on the terminals of glutamatergic corticostriatal neurons and glutamatergic receptors on dopaminergic nigrostriatal neurons. Glutamate stimulates dopamine release from the striatum, and dopamine inhibits release of glutamate in the striatum. A corticostriato-thalamocortical negative feedback loop has been hypothesized, which serves as a filter to protect the cortex from being bombarded with information (Carlsson & Carlsson, 1990a, 1990b).

These findings suggest that the hyperdopaminergic state hypothesized to be the underlying cause of schizophrenia may actually be primarily due to a deficiency in glutamatergic transmission; conversely, Parkinson's disease may be a result of overactive glutamatergic transmission (Carlsson & Carlsson, 1990a, 1990b).

A Glutamatergic Hypothesis for Schizophrenia

The above-cited evidence supports the contribution of glutamatergic hypofunction to the pathophysiology of schizophrenia. A reciprocal control mechanism governing glutamatergic and dopaminergic neurotransmission in the striatum has been postulated as a substrate for the neurobiology of schizophrenia. According to this hypothesis, primary glutamatergic hypofunction is central to the neurobiology of schizophrenia.

Carlsson and Carlsson propose that hypofunction of the corticostriatal glutamatergic pathway could result in disinhibition of the dopamine-dependent thalamic filter, resulting in sensory overload to the frontal cortex.

Javitt and Zukin (1991) propose that primary NMDA hypofunction could account for (a) the cognitive deficit state associated with schizophrenia and (b) dopaminergic dysregulation with the consequent hyperdopaminergic state associated with positive symptoms (acute phase) of the illness.

Summary

Evidence supports a glutamatergic deficit hypothesis for schizophrenia. The hypothesis is based on the effects of PCP and postmortem observations of NMDA receptor function in schizophrenia. According to the hypothesis, deficits in NMDA receptor function contribute to the neurobiology of schizophrenia. Based on this model, treatment with glycine and glycine site agonists has been shown to be promising in the treatment of schizophrenia. Future studies need to fully characterize the interactions between dopamine, GABA, and glutamate.

GABA and Schizophrenia

The first hypothesis implicating GABA emerged in 1972 from observations on the reciprocal interactions of GABA and dopamine in the basal ganglia. According to this hypothesis, deficits in GABA contributed to the neurobiology of schizophrenia.

Another aspect of GABA function implicated in the neurobiology of schizophrenia is the interrelationship between GABA, glutamate, and dopamine in the striatum.

Clinical Implications

It is now common practice to add a benzodiazepine to the antipsychotic treatment of schizophrenia. This practice appears to reduce the dose requirement of neuroleptics and thus minimize side effects associated with neuroleptics. In fact, about 30% to 50% of schizophrenics receive some benefit from benzodiazepines (Wolkowitz et al., 1988), although it is clearly not antipsychotic. In combination, parenteral benzodiazepines and neuroleptics appear to be synergistic and have been extremely effective and safe in controlling acute agitation. GABA has also been implicated in the neurobiology of tardive dyskinesia. Several studies using GABA agonists in the treatment of tardive dyskinesia have been conducted, but the results have been disappointing.

Summary

There is evidence implicating a role for GABA-ergic systems in the neurobiology of schizophrenia (Benes, Vincent, Alsterberg, Bird, & SanGiovanni, 1992). The abnormalities have not yet been completely defined, however. Imaging studies are under way examining the benzodiazepine binding sites in schizophrenics using recently developed ligands. We hope these studies will further characterize the role of GABA-A receptors in schizophrenia. Further work needs to be done to fully characterize the interactions between GABA, glutamate, and DA systems in the basal ganglia, cortex, and thalamus.

Norepinephrine and Schizophrenia

In 1971, Stein and Wise proposed that norepinephrine (NE) played an important role in the neurobiology of schizophrenia. They proposed that schizophrenia may be related to a defect in the noradrenergic reward system or a selective norepinephrine degeneration producing the negative symptoms of schizophrenia.

Supporting Evidence

Major support for the presence of increased NE activity in schizophrenia was based on the successful, albeit limited, treatment of schizophrenia with the beta-blocker propranolol (Inderal). Propanolol, however, is an effective antipsychotic in only a very small minority of schizophrenics.

A number of-studies have examined central and peripheral indexes of noradrenergic function in schizophrenia. Some studies have reported higher concentrations of NE in the CSF of chronic schizophrenics, particularly paranoid schizophrenics, and increased NE concentrations in the limbic system of postmortem brain samples from schizophrenics. Van Kammen (1991) postulated that NE systems contributed to the neurobiology of acute psychosis and were dysregulated in a state-dependent manner during periods of exacerbations.

In addition, some antipsychotics are potent inhibitors of alpha-2 adrenergic receptors. Some researchers (Lieberman et al., 1991; Pickar et al., 1992) propose that clozapine's atypical clinical properties are due to its powerful alpha-2 adrenergic blocking effects. The pure alpha-2 receptor blocker prazosin, however, does not possess antipsychotic effects. Some data suggest that central adrenergic neurons may be suppressed by antipsychotic treatment and increased following discontinuation of the antipsychotics' drug and immediately before relapse. In general, the findings are neither robust nor reproducible and, therefore, are inconclusive.

Clinical Implications. The clinical applications of the involvement of NE in the neurobiology of schizophrenia have been limited. Some clinical trials with the beta-adrenergic blocker propranolol have been positive, particularly in schizophrenic patients with episodes of uncontrollable aggression. This application of propranolol is not specific to aggression related to the schizophrenic process, however, but to aggression in general. High-dose propranolol is recommended to all patients with episodic violence regardless of diagnosis. Of three controlled trials, two found propranolol equivalent to the placebo in the treatment of schizophrenia. Of greater relevance is the use of beta-blockers in the treatment of a relatively frequent and disabling side effect of antipsychotic treatment: motor restlessness termed *akathisia.*

Imaging Studies of Schizophrenia

One of the most exciting developments in psychiatry has been the application of imaging techniques to give a direct view of the structure and function of the living brain. The earliest in vivo imaging technique used in the study of schizophrenia was pneumoencephalography. This rather crude technique involved the injection of air into the subarachnoid space to provide sufficient contrast for the visualization of the CSF-brain interface by conventional X-ray imaging. As far back as 1927, Jacobi and Winkler reported enlarged ventricles and widening of the cortical sulci in schizophrenics. Other open studies in the 1930s confirmed this finding. These findings were correlated with negative symptoms of the illness. This invasive procedure, which was associated with significant morbidity, was soon abandoned, however, with the advent of computerized tomography in the 1970s. Initially, imaging studies were limited to structural examinations of the brain, but the development of functional imaging techniques has spawned a growing research effort into brain function in schizophrenia.

Structural Imaging

Structural imaging includes computerized axial tomography (CT or CAT scan) and magnetic resonance imaging (MRI). Both these techniques are useful in studying the anatomy of the brain but cannot be used to study brain function.

Computerized Axial Tomography

The earliest of modern imaging techniques applied to the study of schizophrenia was CT scanning. The first CT study of schizophrenic patients by Johnstone et al. (1979), which demonstrated ventricular enlargement in a group of chronic schizophrenics, spurred several other studies. Of the variety of findings reported, only a few are well replicated and without dispute. The most widely accepted findings are third and lateral ventricle enlargement and widening of cortical fissures and sulci. These findings, however, are

1. Not diagnostic of schizophrenia
2. Not exclusive to schizophrenia
3. Not seen in all schizophrenics

Lateral Ventricular Enlargement. The lateral ventricles are cerebrospinal fluid-filled spaces in each hemisphere. About 75% to 85% of studies of the lateral ventricles in schizophrenia have reported an increase in ventricular enlargement in schizophrenic patients as compared with nonpsychiatric controls. The ventricular enlargement in schizophrenia is extremely subtle, and hence special techniques have been employed to demonstrate differences between schizophrenics and controls. Linear measurement initially used to quantify ventricular size have given way to the ventricular-to-brain ratio (VBR) technique. The 15% to 25% of studies that did not demonstrate ventricular enlargement used measurement techniques, as well as patient and control selection criteria, that differed from the 75% to 85% that did demonstrate a positive finding. Ventricular enlargement is not exclusive to schizophrenia and has been reported in patients with depression, bipolar disorder, and schizoaffective disorder. The significance of ventricular enlargement remains unclear; however, these findings may reflect focal abnormalities in neighboring periventricular structures or a diffuse cerebral abnormality. The periventricular structures include the basal ganglia, thalamus, hypothalamus, hippocampus, amygdala, and so on, many of which have been implicated in the neurobiology of schizophrenia.

Third Ventricular Enlargement. The third ventricle is a midline, cerebrospinal, fluid-filled space that is connected to the lateral ventricles. Neighboring structures include the thalamus, hypothalamus, fornix, and habenula. More than 85% of all studies have shown a significant increase in mean third ventricular size in schizophrenics as compared with controls. The evidence suggests that the third ventricle, unlike the lateral ventricles, is not prone to enlargement from a variety of causes and, hence, is less likely to be subject to confounding variables. There is an absence of clinical correlates with third ventricular enlargement in schizophrenia.

Widening of Cortical Fissures and Sulci. This finding, a manifestation of cerebral atrophy, is more common in schizophrenia than in controls. The atrophy is diffuse, unlike the selective atrophy seen in Alzheimer's disease. Cerebral atrophy, though diffuse in schizophrenia, may be more pronounced in the frontal and temporal regions. The inference of cortical atrophy in schizophrenia seems to be supported by findings of ventricular enlargement and widening of cortical sulci. Although often associated with cognitive deficits and negative symptoms, this finding is present even in the absence of the above. Unlike ventricular enlargement, the presence of sulcal widening does not have any clinical correlation.

Other, less robust findings include cerebellar atrophy, changes in brain density, and reversed cerebral asymmetry.

Clinical Correlates. The CT findings in schizophrenia have been positively correlated to (a) poorer performance on neuropsychological tests, (b) poorer premorbid adjustment, (c) unemployment (associated with larger VBRs), (d) global monoamine disturbance and not dopaminergic overactivity, and (e) negative symptoms (brain atrophy) (Cazullo et al., 1989; Goetz & van Kammen, 1986). Positive symptoms are linked to overactivity of the dopaminergic system, and negative symptoms to deficits in dopaminergic systems. Hence, it is consistent that brain atrophy, which is correlated to dopaminergic deficits, has also been correlated to negative symptoms. Consistent with these findings is the poor response to neuroleptics seen in patients with brain atrophy; this is so because if dopaminergic deficits are present in patients with brain atrophy, neuroleptics that further decrease dopamine function would either produce no beneficial effect or worsen negative symptoms. It is clear that the abnormalities detected by CT are present even before the onset of clinical symptoms and are not an effect of antipsychotic medications. Furthermore, there is no correlation between ventricular size and duration of illness, and the changes remain static over the course of the illness. These two findings suggest that the brain atrophy seen in schizophrenia is not due to an ongoing degenerative process but to some early developmental neuropathological process such as abnormal neuronal migration. There is no association between age, age of onset of illness, or neuroleptic treatment and the CT findings. The clinical significance of CT findings includes an association with poor premorbid social adjustment, increased severity of illness, poorer response to antipsychotics, cognitive deficits, negative symptoms, and a worse outcome. It has been speculated that schizophrenic patients with brain atrophy represent a distinct subgroup.

Magnetic Resonance Imaging (MRI)

Compared with CT, the principles of MRI are more complex. Whereas in CT scanning, the image produced depends on the degree to which radiation is absorbed/attenuated as it passes through different tissues, magnetic resonance manipulates the electromagnetic properties of tissues and reconstructs images based on changes in these electromagnetic forces. MRI has a much higher tissue resolution and provides much greater information than CT. It is also clearly able to differentiate white matter from gray matter and can produce images in all three planes. MRI can visualize areas of the brain such as the posterior fossa, unlike CT.

Findings in Schizophrenia. The differences between schizophrenics and controls from both in vivo imaging and postmortem studies are slight, and a considerable degree of normal variation exists. Hence, the two groups overlap considerably. This has led to the argument that, whatever the neuropathological process underlying differences between schizophrenics and controls, the process affects only a small subgroup and is not characteristic of most patients. A method of reducing normal variation and increasing the power of structural brain differences is to compare monozygotic twins discordant for schizophrenia. Because monozygotic twins share the same genes and environmental factors influencing development, such comparisons reduce the influence of these factors on anatomical variations. In an influential study on monozygotic twins discordant for schizophrenia (Suddath et al., 1990), morphological changes were reported present in every twin with schizophrenia. The findings included ventricular enlargement and abnormalities in the temporal lobes (particularly the left lobe) and hippocampi. The findings were not present in any of the twins discordant for schizophrenia. The temporal lobe findings (Bogerts et al., 1990) have been localized in separate MRI studies to volume reductions in the neocortical superior temporal gyrus and to the limbic system (hippocampus, amygdala, and parahippocampal gyrus). Correlations between brain abnormalities and symptomatology have been consistent with the findings of CT studies. Enlarged ventricles and cerebral atrophy were correlated with a predominant negative symptom picture (Andreasen et al., 1989). Left temporal abnormalities were correlated with thought disorder.

Summary of Structural Abnormalities

1. Enlarged ventricles
2. Widening of cortical fissures and sulci (i.e., cerebral atrophy)
3. Temporal lobe abnormalities (volume reductions in the neocortical superior temporal gyrus and the limbic system, especially the left side)
4. Frontal and cerebellar structures found to be smaller
5. Corpus callosal abnormalities

Clinical Correlates of Structural Abnormalities

1. Poorer performance on neuropsychological tests

2. Poorer premorbid adjustment
3. Unemployment
4. Negative symptoms
5. Poorer response to medication

Functional Imaging

These techniques permit observation of the brain in action; cerebral metabolism, blood flow, and the state of neuroreceptors can be measured. The mainstays of functional imaging are positron-emission tomography (PET) and single photon emission computerized tomography (SPECT) (for a review, see Andreasen, 1987). Other techniques that have been recently applied to the study of brain function are magnetic resonance spectroscopy (MRS) and functional magnetic resonance imaging (fMRI).

Single Photon Emission Computerized Tomography (SPECT)

SPECT is based on the incorporation of a radioactive nuclide and a drug of interest into a radioligand, which is then injected into the brain. The subsequent radioactivity emitted by the radioligand from within the body is detected by external scintillation crystals and analyzed to provide information about the metabolism, blood flow, and neurochemistry of the brain. SPECT has two major strengths in clinical psychiatry: the capability of providing three-dimensional measurements and its availability. SPECT's main advantages over PET are its low cost and availability. Almost every medical center has a SPECT scanner, and the cost of scanning is a fraction of PET scanning. The disadvantage of SPECT scanning, however, is the poor resolution relative to PET scanning. With the development of newer radioligands for dopaminergic, serotonergic, cholinergic, and other neurotransmitters, the number of studies is rapidly increasing.

Positron Emission Tomography (PET)

Unlike SPECT, which involves the emission of only one photon, PET involves the emission of two photons. The principle of PET is not the production of an image per se but the measurement of physiological and biochemical processes. PET's advantage over SPECT is its higher resolution (< 6 mm in three dimensions). In general, PET studies of schizophrenia can be broadly divided into metabolic studies and receptor studies. The former refers to studies that measure either glucose metabolism and blood flow under conditions such as rest versus cognitive activation, unmedicated versus medicated, active versus remission, and so on. The latter refers to studies measuring the state/density of receptors such as dopamine, serotonin, and benzodiazepine receptors under different conditions. Several ligands have been developed to suit the type of measurement. For example, O 15 water is used to study the effects of cognitive activation on cerebral blood flow, and C11 raclopride is used to measure dopamine D2 receptors.

Functional Magnetic Resonance Imaging (fMRI)

Unlike SPECT and PET, fMRI is not based on the use of radiopharmaceuticals, and thus subjects are not exposed to radiation. Hence, it is ideally suited for measuring and accurately localizing the effects of repeated cognitive tasks on brain metabolism. Recently, this technique has been applied to the study of cognitive activation and drug effects on brain blood flow in schizophrenic subjects. These preliminary findings do not permit drawing any conclusions about their clinical significance in schizophrenia.

Magnetic Resonance Spectroscopy (MRS)

MRS is a technique based on nuclear magnetic resonance that permits the assessment of tissue metabolism and specific molecules on interest in vivo. A complete description of this technique is out of the scope of this chapter. Unlike fMRI, PET, or SPECT, MRS can provide a wide variety of information about high-energy phosphate bonds, lactate, amino acids, intracellular pH, and even ionic concentrations that reflect critical cellular processes in the brain. MRS does not involve radiation exposure to subjects and is cheaper than PET or SPECT as it does not require the supporting infrastructure required to operate PET and SPECT. Being a relatively new technique, few MRS studies in schizophrenia have been reported.

Neuropathology of Schizophrenia

Neuropathological investigation of schizophrenia probably preceded all other biological investigations of schizophrenia. In 1957, around the inception of the first antipsychotics, there were no fewer than 200 neuropathological studies of schizophrenia. The results of these studies were largely inconclusive, however, and for several decades, the neuropathological study of schizophrenia remained neglected. Today, there is renewed interest in the field with the development and application of quantitative-morphometric, histological, and statistical techniques.

Given the considerable variability of the human brain and the significant overlap in neuroanatomical findings between schizophrenic patients and controls, the subtle microscopic and macroscopic abnormalities presumed to underlie schizophrenia are extremely difficult to conclusively demonstrate. Several methodological problems in neuropathological studies have weakened the findings of previous neuropathological studies. These include (a) postmortem brain shrinkage and swelling, (b) too much time between death and fixation of brain tissue, and (c) brain changes secondary to drugs known to affect brain structure, concomitant neurological/vascular disease, and peripheral diseases with central effects. Given these shortcomings, there are some widely accepted neuropathological findings in schizophrenia.

Since the first report of reduced tissue volume of the temperolimbic structures of schizophrenia, there have been more than 30 studies that have examined these brain regions. The majority of studies have demonstrated *subtle* abnormalities in the limbic structures of schizophrenic subjects. The areas implicated include the hippocampus, parahippocampus, cingulate gyrus, entorhinal cortex, amygdala, and septum. The findings include (a) decreased volume of the hippocampus, parahippocampus, and amygdala; (b) enlargement of the left temporal horn, which is consistent with the previously mentioned finding; (c) white matter reductions in the hippocampus and parahippocampus; (d) abnormal architecture of then hippocampus, cingulate, and entorhinal cortices; and (e) decreased number and size of cells in the hippocampus, parahippocampus, and entorhinal cortex. Knowing the functional significance of the limbic system, the neuropathological findings "fit" many of the clinical symptoms of schizophrenia.

Several studies also reported minimal changes in the frontal cortex, basal ganglia, thalamus, and corpus callosum. These findings also correspond to the areas that have been implicated in structural neuroimaging studies of schizophrenia.

Of interest are the findings of abnormal cortical architecture (abnormal arrangements of cortical layers, cell clusters, and single neurons) (Benes, Davidson, & Bird, 1986), which strongly indicate that the neuropathological abnormalities in schizophrenia began during *early* brain development (Bogerts, 1993; Bogerts & Falkai, 1991). These findings support the notion that schizophrenia may be a *neurodevelopmental* illness in which the insult to the developing brain occurred early. Several clinical findings seem to support this view: Infants at risk for schizophrenia show signs of pandysmaturation and defective neurointegration, and patients with schizophrenia show an increased incidence of minor physical abnormalities. Though as yet unproven, this theory is gaining increasing support and may eventually change our approach to the treatment of schizophrenia to the preventative model used in other neurodevelopmental disorders.

Treatment of Schizophrenia

The complete treatment of schizophrenia involves a biopsychosocial approach, that is, a combination of medications, psychotherapy, and social interventions. Since the late 1960s, there has been a shift in health care policy from institutionalizing to rehabilitating/maintaining patients with schizophrenia in the community.

Pharmacotherapy

Antipsychotic medications, which were first introduced in the mid-1950s, revolutionized the treatment of schizophrenia and continue to be a critical component in the treatment of schizophrenia. After an initial flurry in the development of antipsychotics, however, there was a lull in the field of psychopharmacology for nearly 30 years. Antipsychotics have been convincingly shown to be superior than placebos in the treatment of acute psychosis and in reducing the recurrence of psychosis. No fewer than 17 conventional antipsychotics are available in the United States, and many more are available in Europe. Broadly speaking, conventional neuroleptics are classified according to the dopamine receptor blocking potency. Thorazine (chlorpromazine) is a low-potency antipsychotic and Haldol (haloperidol) is high potency. There is a close relationship between the potency of these agents and their side effects; hence, Haldol is associated with a greater incidence in

Parkinsonian-like symptoms, whereas Thorazine is associated with a greater incidence of sedation and dizziness. The atypical antipsychotic clozapine, which was discovered in the early 1960s, was reintroduced into the United States in the mid-1980s. Clozapine's reintroduction sparked a resurgence in the development of new antipsychotics. Today, there are several antipsychotics that are close to FDA approval that are purported to have significant advantages over the existing ones. Recent clinical research has focused on improving our ability to provide the most effective and least toxic pharmacotherapy.

The pharmacotherapy of schizophrenia can be broadly classified into two stages: *acute* and *maintenance* treatment. Currently, all the available research indicates that patients with schizophrenia need lifelong treatment and, furthermore, that the longer a psychotic episode is left untreated, the more difficult it is to treat.

The Acute Phase. The *acute phase* of the pharmacotherapy of schizophrenia is focused on alleviating the exacerbation of psychotic symptoms, most frequently the positive symptoms such as agitation, hallucinations, delusions, and thought disorder (see the section "Phenomenology"). During an acute episode of psychosis, pharmacotherapy takes a primary role. Among the conventional antipsychotics, no single drug or drug class is more effective than any other. Hence, the choice of medication is usually dictated by previous clinical response and history of side effects. In clinical practice, however, psychiatrists often begin treatment with haloperidol unless there exists some contraindication such as history of side effects to haloperidol in the past. The usual dose is between 10 and 15 milligrams of haloperidol or an equivalent dose of another antipsychotic. This represents a shift in prescribing practices following important research that showed that with doses higher than 15 milligrams of haloperidol, there were no significant advantages, and in fact the incidence of intolerable side effects significantly increased. In other words, the view that more is better is no longer held. There is, however, a small group of patients that does need doses higher than 15 milligrams of haloperidol equivalents. More often than not, side effects that require treatment will emerge during the course of treatment with antipsychotics. These side effects include drug-induced Parkinsonism (stiffness, motoric slowing, decreased spontaneous movements, shuffling gait, mask-like face, and so on), acute dystonias (spontaneous, involuntary, and painful spasmodic contraction of the jaw, neck, and tongue muscles), acute akathisia (a feeling of inner restlessness accompanied by an inability to sit/stand still), and sedation. The incidence of side effects can be minimized by prescribing smaller doses of medication, prescribing concomitant benzodiazepines (Valium or Ativan), and using specific antidotes. Sometimes a change of medications is warranted because of intolerable/untreatable side effects. Typically, with treatment, about a third of patients respond completely, a third respond partially, and a third do not respond. In those that do not respond or respond partially, a trial with an antipsychotic of a different class is warranted, or augmentation with lithium or an anticonvulsant such as Tegretol (carbamazepine) or Depakote (valproate) is often pursued. When all these measures fail, a trial with an atypical neuroleptic such as clozapine is warranted. Recently, however, several experts have suggested the use of clozapine as a first line drug. Unfortunately, the cost of clozapine curtails its availability to the majority of patients. With the advent of risperidone, an atypical neuroleptic, which, unlike clozapine, is not associated with life-threatening agranulocytosis (a precipitous drop in white blood cell count), and hence the preventive weekly blood monitoring, it is conceivable that in the near future, more patients will have access to the atypical antipsychotics, which are believed to have fewer side effects. The current view held is that typical or conventional antipsychotics are not as effective in treating negative symptoms as are the typical agents. This issue is promoting the wide use of atypical agents to treat the more enduring and more treatment-resistant negative symptoms.

The Maintenance Phase. The efficacy of long-term maintenance treatment of schizophrenia has been firmly established in numerous trials. The purpose of maintenance treatment is to minimize the risk of relapse. Because long-term pharmacological treatment is associated with significant side effects, in recent years, maintenance treatment studies have focused on improving the risk:benefit ratio of long-term treatment. From the available data, there is a strong consensus that for most patients, continuous long-term maintenance treatment is the best approach to preventing relapse. There may be a small group of patients that might benefit from intermittent treatment, but this approach is not without considerable risk. Continuous long-term maintenance treatment usually involves lowering the dose of the antipsychotic below that used to treat an acute episode. This approach significantly reduces the risk of side effects, both early and late onset, and thereby increases the chances of compliance with treatment. Of importance, however, is that pharmacotherapy alone does not avert every relapse. A combination of pharmacotherapy and psychosocial interventions is probably the most effective treatment in schizophrenia.

Psychosocial Interventions

Despite the widely held view that schizophrenia is a biological illness and that pharmacotherapy is the mainstay of treatment, there is compelling data demonstrating that the course of schizophrenia is profoundly influenced by environmental factors, which can in turn be manipulated to the patients' advantage; that is, psychosocial interventions can be effective. It is beyond the scope of this chapter to provide a comprehensive account of psychosocial interventions in the treatment of schizophrenia; hence, a synopsis will be provided.

Psychotherapy. There has been a shift in the type of psychotherapy offered to patients with schizophrenia. Whereas once an analytically oriented therapy was practiced, nowadays a more supportive psychotherapy with limited insight-oriented work is practiced. A flexible approach is adopted with adjustments in the therapy to accommodate the different stages of the illness. Hence, during the acute psychotic episode, the patient may not be able to tolerate a session of more than 10 minutes, and hence the treatment during an acute episode might consist of several brief sessions focused on reality testing and providing support.

Family Interventions. Multicenter World Health Organization studies have shown that the outcome for schizophrenia is often better in agrarian societies, possibly because of preservation of the family unit. It has long been recognized that the difference between good outcome and bad outcome, even in the industrial world, is often the involvement of the family in the patient's life. This represents a radical shift from the previously held view that the family caused the illness; terms such as the *schizophrenogenic mother* are considered a bad reminder of the past. With the deinstitutionalization of patients with schizophrenia, family members are being viewed as important factors in the management and social rehabilitation of patients. With few exceptions, research on family treatment for schizophrenia has suggested positive results for both the patient and other family members, especially when therapy was extended over years. The focus of family treatment is (a) to educate family members about the illness, thereby dispelling harmful myths, and (b) to improve the family unit's ability to manage difficult behaviors.

In combination with pharmacotherapy, it is likely that the role of psychological and family interventions in enhancing social functioning and reintegrating patients into the community will assume greater importance in the future.

References

American Psychiatric Association. (1994). *Diagnosis and statistical manual of mental disorders* (4th ed.). Washington, DC: Author.

Andreasen, N. C. (1987). *Brain imaging: Applications in psychiatry.* Washington, DC: American Psychiatric Association.

Andreasen, N. C., & Carpenter, W. T. (1993). Diagnosis and classification of schizophrenia. *Schizophrenia Bulletin, 19*(2), 199-214.

Andreasen, N. C., et al. (1989). Magnetic resonance imaging of the brain in schizophrenia. *Archives of General Psychiatry, 47*, 35-44.

Angrist, B., Sathanathan, G., Wilk, S., & Gershon, S. (1974). Amphetamine psychosis: Behavioral and biochemical aspects. *Journal of Psychiatry Research, 11*, 13-23.

Bassett, A. S., McGillivray, B. C., Langlois, S., Pantzar, T., & Wood, S. (1990). Familial 5q11. 2-q13: 3 segmental duplication cosegregating with multiple anomalies, including schizophrenia. *American Journal of Molecular Genetics, 35*, 10-13.

Bell, D. S. (1965). Comparison of amphetamine induced psychosis and schizophrenia. *British Journal of Psychiatry, 4*, 701-707.

Benes, F. M., Davidson, B., & Bird, E. D. (1986). Quantitative cyto-architectural studies of the cerebral cortex in schizophrenics. *Archives of General Psychiatry, 43*, 31-35.

Benes, F. M., Vincent, S. L., Alsterberg, G., Bird, E., & SanGiovanni, J. P. (1992). Increased GABA-A receptor binding in superficial layers of cingulate cortex in schizophrenics. *Journal of Neuroscience, 12*, 924-929.

Bleuler, E. (1950). *Dementia praecox or the group of schizophrenias* (J. Zinkin, Trans.). New York: International Universities Press. (Original work published 1911)

Bogerts, B. (1993). Recent advances in the neuropathology of schizophrenia. *Schizophrenia Bulletin, 19*(2), 431-446.

Bogerts, B., & Falkai, P. (1991). Clinical and neurodevelopmental aspects of brain pathology in schizophrenia. In S. A. Mednick, T. D. Cannon, C. E. Barr, & J. E.

LaFosse (Eds.), *Developmental neuropathology in schizophrenia* (pp. 93-120). New York: Plenum.

Bogerts, B., et al. (1990). Reduced temporal limbic structure volumes on magnetic resonance imaging in first episode schizophrenia. *Psychiatric Research, 35,* 1-13.

Carlsson, A. (1988). The current status of the dopamine hypothesis of schizophrenia. *Neuropsychopharmacology, 1,* 179-186.

Carlsson, M., & Carlsson, A. (1990a). Interactions between glutamatergic and monoaminergic systems within the basal ganglia: Implications for schizophrenia and Parkinson's disease. *Trends in Neurosciences, 13*(3), 272-276.

Carlsson, M., & Carlsson, A. (1990b). Schizophrenia: A subcortical neurotransmitter imbalance syndrome? *Schizophrenia Bulletin, 16,* 425-432.

Cazullo, C. L., et al. (1989). Cerebral ventricular enlargement in schizophrenia: Prevalence and correlates. In S. C. Schulz & C. A. Tamminga (Eds.), *Schizophrenia scientific progress* (pp. 163-166). New York: Oxford University Press.

Coon, H., Byerley, W., et al. (1993). Linkage analysis of schizophrenia with five dopamine receptor genes in nine pedigrees. *American Journal of Human Genetics, 52,* 327-334.

Cooper, J. E., Kendell, R. E., Gurland, B. J., Sharp, L., Copeland, J. R. M., & Simon, R. (1972). *Psychiatric diagnosis in New York and London* (Institute of Psychiatry, Maudsley Monograph Series No. 20). London: Oxford University Press.

Cotman, C. W., & Monaghan, D. T. (1987). Chemistry and anatomy of excitatory amino acid systems. In H. Y. Meltzer (Ed.), *Psychopharmacology: The third generation of progress* (pp. 197-210). New York: Raven.

Davis, K., Kahn, R. S., Ko, G., & Davidson, M. (1991). Dopamine in schizophrenia: A review and reconceptualization. *American Journal of Psychiatry, 148,* 1474-1486.

Domino, E. F. (Ed.). (1981). *PCP (Phencyclidine): Historical and current perspectives.* Ann Arbor, MI: NPP Books.

Feighner, J. P., Robins, E., Guze, S. B., Woodruff, R. A., Winokur, G., & Munoz, R. (1972). Diagnostic criteria for use in psychiatric research. *Archives of General Psychiatry, 26,* 57-63.

Goetz, K. L., & van Kammen, D. P. (1986). Computerized axial tomography scans and subtypes of schizophrenia: A review of the literature. *Journal of Nervous and Mental Disease, 174,* 31-41.

Gottesman, I. I., & Bertelsen, A. (1989). Confirming unexpressed genotypes for schizophrenia: Risks in the offspring of Fischer's Danish identical and fraternal discordant twins. *Archives of General Psychiatry, 46,* 867-872.

Gottesman, I. I., & Shields, J. (1982). *Schizophrenia: The epigenetic puzzle.* Cambridge: Cambridge University Press.

Guze, S. B., Cloninger, C. R., Martin, R. L., & Clayton, P. J. (1983). A follow-up and family study of schizophrenia. *Archives of General Psychiatry, 40,* 1273-1276.

Heston, L. L. (1970). The genetics of schizophrenia and schizoid disease. *Science, 167,* 249-256.

Iqbal, N., Asnis, G. M., Wetzler, S., Kay, S. R., & van Praag, H. M. (1991). The role of serotonin in schizophrenia: New findings. *Schizophrenia Research, 5,* 181-182.

Jacobi, W., & Winkler, H. (1927). Encephalographische studien an chronisch schizophrenia. *Archives Psychiatry Nervenkrankh, 81,* 299-332.

Javitt, D. C., & Zukin, S. R. (1991). Recent advances in the PCP model of schizophrenia. *American Journal of Psychiatry, 48,* 1301-1308.

Johnstone, E. C., et al. (1979). Temporal lobe structures determined by nuclear magnetic resonance imaging in schizophrenia and bipolar affective disorder. *Journal of Neurology, Neurosurgery and Psychiatry, 52,* 736-741.

Kallman, F. J. (1938). *The genetics of schizophrenia.* New York: J. S. Augustin.

Kan, Y. W., & Dozy, A. M. (1978). Polymorphism of DNA sequence adjacent to human B-globin structural gene: Relationship to sickle mutation. *Proceedings of the National Academy of the United States of America, 75,* 5631-5635.

Kendell, R. E., Cooper, J. E., & Goulay, A. G. (1971). Diagnostic criteria of British and American psychiatrists. *Archives of General Psychiatry, 25,* 123-130.

Kendler, K. S. (1983). Overview: A current perspective on twin studies of schizophrenia. *American Journal of Psychiatry, 140,* 1413-1425.

Kendler, K. S. (1988). The genetics of schizophrenia and related disorders: A review. In D. L. Dunner, E. S. Gershon, & J. E. Barrett (Eds.), *Relatives at risk for mental disorder* (pp. 247-266). New York: Raven.

Kendler, K. S., & Scott, D. R. (1993). The genetics of schizophrenia: A current genetic-epidemiological perspective. *Schizophrenia Bulletin, 19*(2), 261-285.

Kennedy, J. L., Giuffra, L. A., Moises, H. W., et al. (1988). Evidence against linkage of schizophrenia to markers on chromosome 5 in a northern Swedish pedigree. *Nature, 336,* 167-170.

Kety, S. S., Rosenthal, D., Wende, P. H., Schulsinger, F., & Jacobsen, B. (1975). *Mental illness in the biological and adoptive families of adopted individuals who have become schizophrenic: A preliminary report based on psychiatric interviews* (Genetic Research in Psychiatry, pp. 147-165). Baltimore: Johns Hopkins University Press.

Kraeplin, E. (1971). *Dementia praecox and paraphrenia* (Facsimile of original). New York: Robert Krieger. (Original work published 1919)

Krystal, J. H., et al. (1994). Subanesthetic effects of the noncompetitive NMDA antagonist ketamine in humans: Psychomimetic, cognitive, and neuroendocrine responses. *Archives of General Psychiatry, 51,* 199-214.

Lieberman, J. A., Jody, D., Pollack, S., et al. (1991). Biochemical effects of clozapine in CSF of patients with schizophrenia. In S. C. Schulz & C. Tamminga (Eds.), *Schizophrenia research: Advances in neuropsychiatry and psychopharmacology* (pp. 341-349). New York: Raven.

Lieberman, J. A., Kane, J. M., & Alvir, J. (1989). Provocative tests with psychostimulant drugs in schizophrenia. *Psychopharmacology, 1,* 415-433.

Lieberman, J., & Koreen, A. (1993). Neurochemistry and neuroendocrinology of schizophrenia: A selective review. *Schizophrenia Bulletin, 19*(2), 371-429.

Luby, E. D., Cotman, B. D., Rosenbaum, G., Gottlieb, J. S., & Kelley, R. (1959). Study of a new schizophrenomimetic drug sernyl. *Archives Neurology Psychiatry, 81,* 363-369.

Meltzer, H. Y. (1987). Biological studies in schizophrenia. *Schizophrenia Bulletin, 13,* 77-111.

Meltzer, H. Y. (1989). Clinical studies on the mechanism of action of clozapine: The dopamine-serotonin hypothesis of schizophrenia. *Psychopharmacology, 99,* S18-S27.

Meltzer, H. Y. (1991). The mechanism of action of novel antipsychotic drugs. *Schizophrenia Bulletin, 17,* 263-287.

Meltzer, H. Y., & Stahl, S. M. (1976). The dopamine hypothesis of schizophrenia: A review. *Schizophrenia Bulletin, 2,* 19-76.

Ott, J. (1991). *Analysis of human genetic linkage* (rev. ed.). Baltimore, MD: Johns Hopkins University Press.

Pickar, D., Owen, R. R., Litman, R. E., Konicki, E., Guiterrez, R., & Rappaport, M. H. (1992). Clinical and biological response to clozapine in patients with schizophrenia. *Archives of General Psychiatry, 49,* 345-353.

Reynolds, G. P. (1989). Beyond the dopamine hypothesis: The neurochemical pathology of schizophrenia. *British Journal of Psychiatry, 155,* 305-316.

Rieder, R. O., & Kaufmann, C. A. (1988). Genetics. In J. A. Talbott, R. E. Hales, & S. C. Yudofsky (Eds.), *The American Psychiatric Press textbook of psychiatry* (pp. 33-65). Washington, DC: American Psychiatric Press.

Schneider, K. (1959). *Clinical psychopathology* (M. W. Hamilton, Trans.). New York: Grune & Stratton.

Seeman, P. (1987). Dopamine receptors and the dopamine hypothesis of schizophrenia. *Synapse, 1,* 133-152.

Sherrington, R., Brynjolfsson, J., Petursson, H., et al. (1988). Localization of a susceptibility locus for schizophrenia on chromosome 5. *Nature, 339,* 305-309.

Snyder, S. (1988). Psychotogenic drugs as models for schizophrenia. *Neuropsychopharmacology, 1,* 197-199.

Snyder, S., Banerjee, S., & Yamamura, H. (1974). Drugs, neurotransmitters and schizophrenia. *Science, 184,* 1243-1253.

Stein, L., & Wise, C. D. (1971). Possible etiology of schizophrenia: Progressive damage to the normal noradrenergic reward system by 5-Hydroxydopamine. *Science, 171,* 1032-1036.

Suddath, R. L., et al. (1990). Anatomical abnormalities in the brains of monozygotic twins discordant for schizophrenia. *New England Journal of Medicine, 322,* 789-794.

Van Kammen, D. P. (1991). The biochemical basis of relapse and drug response in schizophrenia: Review and hypothesis. *Psychological Medicine, 21,* 881-895.

Weinberger, D. R., Wagner, R. L., & Wyatt, R. J. (1987). Neuropathological studies of schizophrenia: A selective review. *Schizophrenia Bulletin, 9,* 193-212.

Wender, P. H., Rosenthal, D., & Kety, S. S. (1968). A psychiatric assessment of the adoptive parents of schizophrenics. In D. Rosenthal & S. S. Kety (Eds.), *The transmission of schizophrenia* (pp. 235-250). Oxford: Pergamon.

Wolkowitz, O. M., Breier, A., Dolan, A. R., Kelsoe, J., Lucas, P., Paul, S. M., & Pickar, D. (1988). Alprazolam augmentation of the antipsychotic effects of fluphenazine in schizophrenic patients. *Archives of General Psychiatry, 45,* 664-671.

World Health Organization. (1973). *International pilot study of schizophrenia* (Vol. 1). Geneva, Switzerland: Author.

World Health Organization. (1992). *The international classification of mental and behavioral disorders* (10th ed.). Geneva, Switzerland: Author.

Wyatt, R. J. (1986). The dopamine hypothesis of schizophrenia: Variations on a theme (II). *Psychopharmacology Bulletin, 22,* 923-927.

PART III

Directions for Future Practice

New Directions for Service Delivery: Home-Based Services

WILLIAM EYBERSE

JAMES MAFFUID

GARY M. BLAU

Home-based services have existed in professional fields for more than a century. Doctors, social workers, and teachers all have historical roots in home visiting (Wasik, Bryant, & Lyons, 1990). Several decades ago, it was common to see the community doctor carrying his black bag to visit those patients who were unable to get to his office. More recently, however, home visiting has become less common as medical and social services have become concentrated in large, centralized complexes. As an example, from 1960 to 1975, Cauthen (1981) identified a 75% drop in physician home visits in the United States. Unfortunately, the most vulnerable and at-risk populations are less likely to seek out or have transportation to these services, resulting in reduced ability to access appropriate assistance. This problem is made worse by the already existing barriers to health care services for high-risk populations. As Blau, Whewell, Gullotta, and Bloom (1994) write:

> It is woefully ineffective to expect high-risk populations to simply walk into a center, admit to a problem, submit to questioning by a person who may or may not be sensitive to their needs and background, and come to scheduled appointments that may be in different parts of a city. (p. 93)

As health care services withdrew into "clinical" settings, such as institutions and large health complexes, there has been a concurrent increase in the treatment of disorder in out-of-home settings. Indeed, during the past two decades, there has been an increasing emphasis on out-of-home care for the purposes of child protection and child treatment. This trend has extended into many social service arenas (e.g., child welfare, mental health, substance abuse, juvenile justice), and the United States has witnessed the growth of center-based services including outpatient clinics, residential treatment, substance abuse facilities, and foster placements.

Although there has been an increase in the use of substitute care for the protection and treatment of children and adolescents, this has not necessarily meant better service or improved outcomes. Stroul (1988) calls the idea that treatment and protection occur in out-of-home settings a "myth" (p. 12). She states that the problems associated with out-of-home care have become increasingly apparent and often contraindicate out-of-home placements. These concerns include the overuse and reliance on out-of-home placement as a treatment tool, the lack of empirical evidence to substantiate efficacy, the high cost of substitute care, and the social and psychological risks to children and families when they are separated (Stroul, 1988).

As a mechanism to reduce out-of-home placements, and provide alternatives to center-based services, many professionals have suggested the increased use of home-based service options (Apone, Zarski, Bixenstine, & Cibik, 1991; Morton & Eyberse, 1993; Wells & Biegel, 1991; Woods, 1988). Perhaps the largest example of home visiting in the United States comes from the Head Start initiative, in which home visitors help parents by providing information about health, education, and social services (Love, Nauta, Coelen, Hewett, & Ruopp, 1976; Zigler & Black, 1989). Social workers have also continued to work in people's homes, providing assistance on such practical matters as housing, food stamps, and the use of community resources. Initially, such "concrete" services became synonymous with home-based interventions, and the provision of more traditional "therapeutic" services (e.g., therapy) was left to the office setting. Therapeutic strategies now have been added to the home-based service repertoire, however, and many of these are labeled under the rubric "family preservation."

Background

Family preservation is the term used to describe home-based interventions designed to help families remain together despite having a child (or children) at imminent risk of placement outside the home. Imminent risk can occur as a result of abuse or neglect, or the psychiatric needs of either adults or children. The overall premise is simple. Children have a basic right to grow up in safe and nurturing families because of the social and biological importance of the attachments between family members (Maluccio, 1991). Thus, unless contraindicated by factors such as repeated abuse or neglect, child welfare agencies and service providers should avoid the potential trauma of removing children from their homes. In lieu of placement, social service agencies must emphasize the protection and treatment of children within the context of their families. This means that, prior to the removal of a child from his or her family, or, conversely, to improve the probability of successfully reunifying a family, significant attempts should be made to improve family functioning (Precora, Fraser, Haapala, & Bartlome, 1987). Family preservation is based on the tenet that the family is the most important and powerful influence on a child or adolescent, and, consequently, the family should be supported and maintained whenever possible.

During the past decade, family preservation has evolved from an innovative way of working with families in crisis to an accepted and rapidly growing service model. Since the 1970s, protective service agencies across the United States have become inundated with abuse and neglect referrals (National Center on Child Abuse and Neglect, 1988). Increased reporting and public awareness have been cited as contributing factors. As a result, there has been a concomitant increase in the numbers of children and adolescents who have been placed in foster care, residential treatment centers, and other out-of-home settings. Unfortunately, many of these youngsters often remain in out-of-home care well beyond expectations. In fact, not only have out-of-home placements increased, so too have the length of placements and the average number of placements a youngster experiences (Roberts, Wasik, Castro, & Ramey, 1991). This phenomenon, originally referred to as "foster care drift," received national attention in the late 1970s, and, in 1980, after much discussion and debate, the Adoption Assistance and Child Welfare

Act (Public Law 96-272) was passed. The law provided incentives for states to develop and implement programs and services to reduce the reliance on out-of-home care as an intervention for distressed families. The idea was to provide intensive services prior to placement, such as home-based intervention, so that out-of-home removal could be avoided (Nelson, 1991). The law also provided the impetus for states to develop services that would assist in children's return to their families from out-of-home placements. Thus, beginning in the late 1970s and continuing into the 1990s, a new outlook emerged—one that viewed the family as the service unit (not just the child), one that sought to maintain the attachments of family members, and one that tried to reduce the barriers to service by providing assistance in a family's home. Service systems have also begun to shift their philosophies (from adversarial to facilitative) as a strategy to empower families, improve their functioning, and keep them together (Stroul, 1993). This new approach identified families, despite being dysfunctional, as preferable to placement outside of the home as long as basic safety and nurturing needs are met. In other words, as long as a family is perceived as "good enough," all attempts are made to allow parents to raise their own children, or at least to allow children the opportunity to be raised in a familylike setting (Rivera & Kutash, 1994).

The following chapter will focus on home-based family preservation services, considered to be the most promising treatment modality for families in crisis who have one or more children at imminent risk of placement. As an illustration, this chapter will focus on home-based services provided in the state of Connecticut. In response to the federal mandates of Public Law 96-272, Connecticut is one of the first states to offer intensive family preservation services to all its citizens, and detailed information has been collected and evaluated (Wheeler, Bogdan, & Ying-Ying, 1992).

Home-based intervention models have been developed that span the gamut from paraprofessional intervention to brief crisis intervention services to longer term, more traditionally therapeutic programs. Nelson (1991) has divided family preservation programs into three categories: crisis intervention programs, home-based services, and family treatment services. Paraprofessional services (i.e., parent aides) are included in this chapter to illustrate an additional service model. Whereas the paraprofessional model uses support and training as the intervention strategy, the crisis intervention model makes use of social learning theory, and the home-based model focuses on family-systems theory. The family treatment model also incorporates family-systems theory but is brief and less intensive than the other approaches.

Paraprofessional Model

The most widespread example of the paraprofessional model is provided by Parent Aide programs. In fact, the U.S. Department of Health, Education, and Welfare has produced a manual on the subject (Gifford, Kaplan, & Salus, 1979). Parent aide services are typically administered by paraprofessionals or volunteers. Parent aides may visit a home for 2 to 4 hours per week and are trained to provide emotional support, teach parenting skills, and assist in securing concrete resources such as medical care, food stamps, or Aid to Families With Dependent Children (AFDC). Parent aides may also help with concrete tasks such as home cleanliness and improving nutritional habits (Lines, 1987).

In a 5-year study of the effectiveness of Parent Aide programs, Lines (1987) compared a group of abusive mothers that received parent aide services with a group that did not: 36 clients received the services, and the average rate of monthly contact was 22 hours. Lines (1987) reports that the Parent Aide program was highly successful. Reabuse rates were less than 3% for program participants (1 in 36) compared with an average of 8% in the comparison group. Positive effects were also found in that the abusive mothers viewed their child or children more favorably, were able to identify appropriate resources, and felt more confident in their ability to cope with future crises. Parent Aide programs have also been found to be cost-effective (Daro, 1988; Miller, Fein, Howe, Gaudio, & Bishop, 1985). In contrast, however, Halpern (1984) and Haynes, Cutler, Gray, and Kempe (1984) reported no differences in outcome when clients of a Parent Aide program were compared with a control group. In addition, Barth (1991), in his experimental evaluation of in-home child abuse prevention services, reported that the efficacy of paraprofessional services continues to be suspect. This supports the recommendation that parent aides not be used in isolation but, instead, as part of a more comprehensive and therapeutic treatment approach (Barth, 1991; Hornick & Clark, 1986; Nelson, Landsman, & Deutelbaum, 1990).

Recent attempts to provide home-based services have expanded to include a wider array of services. With the evidence that clients receiving home-based programming needed more than supportive or concrete services, many professionals called for home-based service delivery to become more therapeutic, particularly for dysfunctional families that may be at risk for abuse and neglect (Barth, 1990; Woods, 1988). As a result, a trend began in several states to combine concrete services with clinical mental health services. For example, Homebuilders in Tacoma, Washington, began a concrete behavioral program that has enjoyed considerable support. In addition, Families First in Iowa used a systems-oriented family therapy approach to work with families in crisis and achieved considerable success.

Crisis Intervention

According to Pittman (1987), a crisis is a perceived traumatic event that represents a turning point. That is, a crisis presents both danger and opportunity. A crisis can also produce "teachable moments" when the family can best accept and use an outside force to guide them down different, more productive paths. Typical crisis intervention programs usually last between 4 to 6 weeks with each family being seen for up to 10 hours per week in their homes. Therapists are on call 24 hours a day, 7 days a week, and consider families to be their colleagues in crisis resolution plans. Workers try to respond to families within 24 hours of the referral and engage them in a spectrum of service planning and coordination. Referrals are typically made by state protective service workers, and the focus of the intervention is to intervene at the moment of crisis, help alleviate the crisis, and teach families the skills necessary to avert further crises (Kinney, Haapala, & Gast, 1981; Selig, Goldman-Hall, & Jerrel, 1992). The methods used are both concrete and behavioral. Homebuilders is an example of this model, and workers within this program may help families fix their homes, obtain transportation and public assistance, as well as implement behavioral charts. The crisis intervention model is based on social learning theory, and service providers emphasize a psychoeducational approach that incorporates techniques such as tracking behaviors, reinforcement, environmental controls, parent-effectiveness training, and anger management techniques (Kinney, 1978). Data on the effectiveness of this strategy have demonstrated impressive results (Rivera & Kutash, 1994). Precora, Fraser, and Haapala (1992) report more than a 93% success rate as defined by those cases that did not experience the removal of a child prior to case termination. Haapala and Kinney (1988) report that 66% of the families involved with Homebuilders remained intact after 1 year.

Home-Based Services

Home-based services is a term used to broadly define several approaches to family preservation that use family therapy as the basis for their model. Begun primarily in Iowa, where the National Association of Family Based Services is headquartered, programs of this type are operating all around the country, notably in Maryland, Iowa, and Wisconsin.

Home-based programs are characterized by the use of family therapy in their interventions, and are generally longer in term and less intensive than crisis intervention models (Clark, Zalis, & Sacco, 1982). For example, these services may continue for between 8 and 12 weeks, and the average service activity is 4 hours per week. Because these programs are primarily based on family-systems theory, structural techniques to reorganize the family, use of genograms to explore intergenerational patterns, reframing, paradox, and communication skills training are often employed. Again, data on these services have indicated much success (Berry, 1992; Henggeler, Melton, & Smith, 1992).

Family Treatment

The family treatment model uses a more "traditional" treatment philosophy, and services may be provided in both an office setting and the client's home. An example of this service model is provided by the Oregon Children's Services Division. Based on family-systems theory, this program uses the same techniques as the home-based model but is less likely to make use of concrete and supportive services compared with the home-based and crisis intervention approaches (Tavantzis, Tavantzis, Brown, & Rohrbaugh, 1986). The worker in this model is viewed as a therapist and is likely to favor the use of more clinical interventions, unlike the other models, which favor either concrete services or a balance between concrete and clinical services.

Despite the differences in treatment philosophy, a set of characteristics has been defined that describes the major features of all programs (Stroul, 1988). First, the intervention is to be delivered in the family's home. This reduces barriers to service, is often perceived as less threatening or intimidating, allows the entire family the opportunity to participate, and is less stigmatizing than an office setting. The second characteristic is that family preservation services are family focused, and the family unit is viewed as the client. In a traditional model, parents and families are often overlooked because the primary concern has been the child and his or her needs (Stroul, 1988). Third, services should have an ecological perspective. This means that providers must recognize the importance of the family's relationship with the community, and build on services and resources that are available from the community in which they live. Fourth, family preservation, by definition, is committed to maintaining or reunifying a family unless there is clear evidence that this is not in a child's best interest. This indicates that the emphasis is on support and assistance to families, but that the safety and well-being of a child must be constantly considered. Fifth, services must be flexible and responsive. Service delivery should occur at times that are convenient (e.g., evenings, weekends), and there must be 24-hour availability to respond to crises. Sixth, family preservation services are multimodal. Staff who work in these programs must wear many hats, including counselor, trainer, and service coordinator. Seventh, service intensity and duration are based on the program goals and the unique needs of each family. Most service programs have some flexibility, within certain boundaries, to create tailor-made interventions. Eighth, staff should have small caseloads to allow them to work intensively with each family. This is crucial given the multiple needs of the target population. Ninth, the relationship between the family and service provider is important if there is to be success. Stroul (1988) writes that providers and families must overcome the "professional distance barrier" (p. 19), and by doing so, families increase their trust and motivation. Finally, family preservation services are designed to empower families to help themselves. For a family to have long-term success, they must develop confidence in their own abilities and be able to maintain healthier levels of functioning without family preservation involvement. One strategy to accomplish this goal is to encourage family participation at all levels of service including goal setting and treatment planning.

Connecticut's Service Model

Beginning in 1988, the state of Connecticut began implementing Intensive Family Preservation Programs (IFPPs). At that time, two pilot projects were initiated, one in New Haven at the Yale Child Study Center and the other in New Britain at the Klingberg Family Center. Since then, 9 additional programs have been funded for a total of 11. These 11 programs are scattered throughout Connecticut's six regions, and thus access to family preservation services is available to any child and family living in Connecticut. The agencies providing these services were selected through a competitive bid process, and all are private, not-for-profit entities. An important component in the overall funding of family preservation initiatives has been the ongoing evaluation provided by Walter R. McDonald and Associates (Wheeler et al., 1992). The obtained data have been instructive and serve to guide program modifications and refinements. The authors of this chapter have been involved with Connecticut's family preservation initiatives since 1990. Bill Eyberse and Jim Maffuid have both served as coordinators for the Intensive Family Preservation Program at Child and Family Agency in New London. Gary Blau was the Director of Clinical Services at Child and Family Agency and now serves as Director of Mental Health for the State Department of Children and Families, which continues to fund these programs.

Service Model

Connecticut's original IFPPs were modeled after the Homebuilders concepts of service delivery. The key components are as follows:

- Families with youth at imminent risk of placement are eligible.
- The intervention is crisis oriented, and response to referral occurs within 24 hours.
- Service is family focused, flexible, and available 24 hours a day, 365 days a year.
- Structured referral, intake, and assessment procedures are used to ensure that no child is left in danger.
- Small caseloads allow for frequent interactions between workers and families.
- Psychoeducational approaches are used.

- Intervention is goal oriented and time limited.

From the inception of IFPP to the end of June 1992, 1,257 families were referred for services. Of these, 933 families received services. Completed data were collected on a total of 662 families, which yielded information on 1,000 adults and 1,775 children and youth. The following demographic information is taken from Wheeler et al. (1992):

59% of families were headed by a single parent

69% of the adult clients were female

63% of families reported income less than $10,000

89% of families reported income less than $20,000

65% of families received public assistance

65% of the adult clients were unemployed

43% of adult clients were Caucasian, 34% African American, and 21% Hispanic

The average age for adult clients was 32

7% of clients were teenage parents

76% of the adults had at least some high school education

94% of the children were living with a biological parent at the time of the referral

39% of the children were African American, 33% Caucasian, and 25% Hispanic

The average age of a child was 7.2 years

67% of the children had not had a prior placement at the time of the referral

Service Delivery

Intensive family preservation services have been described as involving a four-stage process that includes referral and intake, assessment and case planning, service delivery, and termination (Stroul, 1988). Services are intensive (averaging 70 hours of services to each family, which include direct face-to-face contact, collateral service, and travel) and time limited (averaging 6 weeks). All service delivery is voluntary, and although there may be consequences for refusing to participate, family preservation services are not court ordered or mandated in any way.

More than 60 different types of services were provided to participating families. The most commonly provided direct services were family therapy, individual counseling, assessment, parent skills training, case planning, crisis intervention, accompanying the family to other services, and transportation. The most frequent collateral services included case record keeping, service coordination, and case consultation. Importantly and logically, the intensity of services varied depending on the week of service. Service involvement was highest during the second week (average of 11.3 hours), gradually decreasing to 8.4 hours by the fifth week and to 2.1 hours by the eighth week. The initial activity begins quickly; however, before a family becomes overly dependent on the worker, the process of service coordination and termination occurs.

Collateral Services

A key component to any successful family preservation intervention is the incorporation of additional service delivery. Because family preservation is typically time limited, it is crucial to engage families in longer term services or to work in concert with other treatment providers. Often, family preservation workers must identify, coordinate, or access an array of services that include outpatient therapy, brief hospitalization, residential care, partial hospitalization, day treatment, and less traditional services such as self-help groups or linking families to needed assistance programs.

Cost and Success

Wheeler et al. (1992) used conservative estimates to identify the costs associated with family preservation. For example, in FY 1991-1992, using a total of 71,644 person days and a total expenditure of $2,197,061, the average daily cost for service to a family was $31. Not only does this compare favorably with the higher costs of placement, the savings in emotional costs to children and families is immeasurable. In addition, even bean counters would be pleased with the estimated statewide savings of public money. Using the conservative assumption that only 40% of family preservation clients would actually need placement were it not for the service provided, Wheeler et al. (1992) estimated that the state could anticipate a savings of $1.25 million over and above the cost for the service.

As one of the primary goals of family preservation is to reduce out-of-home placements, families were followed for 1 year after service delivery to evaluate their current placement status. Overall, 69% of the sample had no children placed out of the home after 1 year. More important, of the families identified as being at high risk by the referral worker, 82% did not experience a placement during the subsequent year. These data indicate the success of this service in reaching the goal of reduced placements. Scores on the Child Well-Being Scale (Magura, Moses, & Jones, 1987) also revealed improvements (Wheeler et al., 1992). Based on these types of data, family preservation is now identified as a successful, cost-efficient, family-focused approach that reflects the national trend toward service delivery within the least restrictive environment (Cole & Duva, 1990; Haapala & Kinney, 1988; Rivera & Kutash, 1994).

Family Preservation and Support Services

A clear indication of the national trend regarding children and families can be evidenced by the passing of Public Law 103-66. This legislation, titled Family Preservation and Support Services, is part of the Omnibus Budget Reconciliation Act of 1993. It is the new subpart 2 of Title IV-B—the Child and Family Service program of the Social Security Act. Under this act, new federal funds have been provided to state child welfare agencies for preventive services (family support services) and services to families at risk or in crisis (family preservation services). The amount of funding for the first year is $60 million, which is slated to increase to $255 million dollars in federal FY 1998. Unfortunately, as Congress develops plans to "block grant" these monies to states, it is unclear if the budget amounts will be supported.

Family support services are broadly defined as community-based prevention activities designed to alleviate stress and promote parental competencies. Examples of this include respite care for parents and other caregivers, early developmental screening of children, mentoring, tutoring, health education, home visiting, and parent support groups. Family preservation services are defined more specifically as the above services when they are used to help families alleviate crises that may lead to the out-of-home placement of children. Significantly, because the multiple needs of children and families cannot be addressed adequately through categorical programs and fragmented service delivery systems, the federal initiative has incentives to use portions of the funding as a catalyst for establishing a continuum of coordinated and integrated, culturally relevant, family-focused services for children and families.

Critical Issues

Although the statistics, anecdotal information, and trends indicate that family preservation programs are effective in reducing out-of-home placements, there are important questions that must be addressed. These issues include the imminent risk criteria, expanding the concept of family preservation, the rights of children, training, and prevention.

The Imminent Risk Criteria

Perhaps the most significant criticism of current methodology is that families referred for service are not truly at imminent risk of having a child or children placed. Wheeler et al. (1992), using a conservative approach, estimate that 40% of the referrals are "on target." This estimate, albeit conservative, suggests that 60% do not actually meet the criteria set forth in the guidelines. Some authors have stated that this diminishes the integrity of the research methodology because the admission criteria are not standardized and applied consistently. In addition, the use of out-of-home placements as a dependent variable has been questioned. For example, if 60% of the families do not meet the criteria, why then would a 1-year figure of 69% of children remaining in the home be remarkable? Furthermore, family preservation workers report that there are times when they must take action to remove a child. Early in treatment, or despite attempts to improve family functioning, a dangerous situation may develop to precipitate the removal of a child. In such a case, removal may be considered a positive outcome from a clinical standpoint as this alternative may be less emotionally traumatic than remaining in the home. This, however, is not factored into the outcome data and is rarely a part of evaluation studies.

One response to these issues has been a call for stricter adherence to referral criteria. The development of standardized protocols to evaluate referral reasons could create objectivity in the referral process. Many referral workers and their supervisors, however, believe that reducing their ability to make clinical judgments could result in serious harm to families. Another possible response could be to reexamine the philosophical framework used to describe family preservation. Obviously, given the language used to name the Omnibus Family Preservation and Family Support Act, changing the nomenclature is not likely at this time. Altering the eligibility requirements for program participation and modifying the research methodology, however, could be accomplished. For example, if standardized, quantifiable referral data are generated, families could receive different levels of service based on their individualized needs. Essentially, this creates a continuum of "family preservation type" services, and comparative data could be generated. Woven into this concept is the idea that the crisis-oriented, time-limited models may be effective at generating long-term gains for some participants, but not for others. Thus, differing home-based models may be needed to meet the unique needs of each child and family.

Expanding the Concept of Family Preservation

In the past few years, several authors have argued that home-based interventions should be expanded to serve different populations and for different lengths of time. For example, in 1991, Child and Family Agency of Southeastern Connecticut received a grant under the rubric of "family stabilization" that extended the treatment length from 6 weeks to 12 weeks. This program was designed to serve families referred for neglect, and because it was deemed clinically appropriate, workers provided a less intensive intervention in order to provide longer term involvement. Anecdotally, family preservation staff, in response to family complaints, occasionally referred to their program as "intrusive" family preservation rather than "intensive" family preservation, and often wondered why they had to discontinue service arbitrarily at 6 weeks. It may be that longer involvement, or more sporadic involvement over a much greater period of time, could be more beneficial to families with certain presenting difficulties compared with the more traditional approach. Such an approach would need to be supported by more flexible service models and close relationships between service providers, protective service workers, and families. But such an approach may be more responsive and family friendly than current approaches.

Another proposal has been that family preservation programs expand their focus to serve a broader range of family difficulties. One example of this comes from the juvenile justice field. Youngsters who have committed status offenses (e.g., truancy, unmanageability) could be diverted to home-based services as a way of providing an alternative to incarceration or residential care (Henggeler, Melton, Smith, Schoenwald, & Hanley, 1993). Similarly, adolescents with addictive disorders could be served in this type of modality. Finally, the increased use of home-based services for adolescents has also been discussed. In fact, according to Wheeler et al. (1992), although adolescents constituted only 5.4% of the service group, the results of family preservation services with this population are highly encouraging. This is also evidenced in the Henggeler et al. (1993) study with serious juvenile offenders.

Enhancing current techniques has also been discussed. Blau, Butteweg, and Anderson (1993) and Blau et al. (1994) suggest the need to enhance service options by the inclusion of medical staff in home-based services. When describing their agency's federally funded family preservation program, Blau et al. (1994) write that "without the nursing component, many referred families would remain without primary health care, and many undiagnosed medical conditions would go untreated" (p. 92).

The Rights of Children

Although in conflict with national family organizations such as the National Alliance for the Mentally Ill—Child and Adolescent Network (NAMI-CAN) and the Federation for Families, another significant criticism of family preservation initiatives has come from children's rights organizations. These children's rights groups posit that family preservation does not protect a child's right to safety, particularly when used with abusive families. Often, family preservation referrals are made for highly dysfunctional families, and children's rights groups suggest that these children should not remain with their parents; in fact, it represents a violation of their civil rights. Family preservation advocates retort that children have a right to grow up in their own family if at all possible, and that safety and protection *is* the first priority. Clearly, there are risks whether a child is removed from the home or not, and this debate is likely to continue, particularly if family preservation services receive additional dollars and expand into new arenas.

Training and Education

Another critical issue regarding family preservation, or home-based service delivery, involves professional education. Although initially reserved for social workers, the field of home-based services is expanding to include many disciplines. Unfortunately, some workers are not adequately prepared for the tasks and emotions they confront. In addition, mental health and child welfare professionals, who are often in positions of authority, must learn to accept parents as partners and must use a wide range of services including advocacy and treatment. The only method to improve the readiness and skill of family preservation workers is to continue to incorporate home-based training into curricula and workshops. As seasoned workers receive training, and new workers complete their schooling, the expertise and ability of workers will improve and the state of the art of the service will be pushed into the 21st century.

Prevention

A final comment on issues related to family preservation is the idea that such services could be used as a prevention tool. At best, current family preservation programs become involved only after serious dysfunction has occurred. The services remain crisis oriented and reactive. More recently, however, the boundaries of family preservation have been expanded to include alternative populations such as those who have less family dysfunction and are not at imminent risk of having a child removed from home. A further extension of this trend would be toward the use of home-based service models for primary prevention activities—that is, the development of home-based models that serve families before difficulties become evident. An example of this type of service is provided by Child and Family Agency's Mother's Friend program. In this program, local hospital social workers identify women with newborns who are believed to be at risk. With permission, a friendly visitor then goes to the hospital and offers a basket of gifts, a photo of mother and child, and information about available resources. It is hoped that young mothers will learn important information and experience a positive connection to supportive services (Blau et al., 1994).

Concluding Comment

Family preservation currently enjoys the national spotlight and promises to be a beneficial and effective service model. As the field continues to evolve, thoughtful consideration must be given to program refinements and modifications. Gone are the days when mental health was synonymous with a 50-minute hour, when placement was the only answer for children and adolescents, and when health care professionals alone were "the experts." As a result, it is likely that home-based service options will flourish. Family preservation must not be considered a panacea, however. Rather, it is one of many service options that must be considered in the context of treatment and permanency planning. In an ideal world, this would not be necessary. In an ideal world, all children and adolescents would be nurtured and cared for so they could grow to their full potential. As this is not so, maybe home-based services can make a difference.

References

Apone, H. J., Zarski, J. J., Bixenstine, C., & Cibik, P. (1991). Home/community-based services: A two-tier approach. *American Orthopsychiatric Association, 61*(3).

Barth, R. P. (1990). Theories guiding home-based family preservation services. In J. K. Whittaker, J. Kinney, E. M. Tracy, & C. Booth (Eds.), *Reaching high risk families: Intensive family preservation in human services.* Hawthorne, NY: Aldine de Gruyter.

Barth, R. P. (1991). An experimental evaluation of in-home child abuse prevention services. *Child Abuse & Neglect, 15,* 363-375.

Blau, G. M., Dall, M. B., & Anderson, L. M. (1993). The assessment and treatment of violent families. In R. L. Hampton, T. P. Gullotta, G. R. Adams, E. H. Potter, & R. P. Weissberg (Eds.), *Family violence: Prevention and treatment* (pp. 198-229). Newbury Park, CA: Sage.

Blau, G. M., Whewell, M., Gullotta, T. P., & Bloom, M. (1994). The prevention and treatment of child abuse in households of substance abusers: A demonstration progress report. *Child Welfare, 73,* 83-94.

Berry, M. (1992). An evaluation of family preservation services: Fitting agency services to family needs. *Social Work, 37, 314-321.*

Cauthen, D. B. (1981). The house call in current medical practice. *Journal of Family Practice, 13.*

Clark, T., Zalis, T., & Sacco, F. (1982). *Outreach family therapy.* New York: Jason Aronson.

Cole, E., & Duva, J. (1990). *Family preservation: An orientation for administrators and practitioners.* Washington, DC: Child Welfare League of America.

Daro, D. (1988). *Confronting child abuse: Research for effective program design.* New York: Free Press.

Gifford, C. D., Kaplan, F. B., & Salus, M. K. (1979). *Parent aides in child abuse and neglect programs* (#79-30200). Washington, DC: U.S. Department of Health, Education and Welfare, National Center on Child Abuse and Neglect.

Haapala, D. A., & Kinney, J. M. (1988). Avoiding out-of-home placement of high risk status offenders through the use of intensive home-based family preservation services. *Criminal Justice and Behavior, 15, 334-348.*

Halpern, R. (1984). Lack of effects for home-based early intervention? Some possible explanations. *American Journal of Orthopsychiatry, 54, 33-42.*

Haynes, C. F., Cutler, C., Gray, J., & Kempe, R. S. (1984). Hospitalized cases of nonorganic failure to thrive: The scope of the problem of short-term lay health visitor intervention. *Child Abuse & Neglect, 8, 229-242.*

Henggeler, S. W., Melton, G. M., & Smith, L. A. (1992). Family preservation using multisystemic therapy: An effective alternative to incarcerating serious juvenile offenders. *Journal of Consulting and Clinical Psychology, 60, 953-961.*

Henggeler, S. W., Melton, G. M., Smith, L. A., Schoenwald, S. K., & Hanley, J. H. (1993). Family preservation using multisystemic treatment: Long-term follow-up to a clinical trial with serious juvenile offenders. *Journal of Child and Family Studies, 2, 283-293.*

Hornick, J. P., & Clark, M. E. (1986). A cost/effectiveness evaluation of lay therapy treatment for child abusing and high risk parents. *Child Abuse & Neglect, 10, 309-318.*

Kinney, J. (1978). Homebuilders: An in-home crisis intervention program. *Children Today, 7*(1), 15-17.

Kinney, J., Haapala, D., & Gast, J. (1981). Assessment of families in crisis. In M. Bryce & J. C. Lloyd (Eds.), *Treating families in the home: An alternative to placement.* Springfield, IL: Charles C Thomas.

Lines, D. R. (1987). The effectiveness of parent aides in the tertiary prevention of child abuse in South Australia. *Child Abuse & Neglect, 11, 507-512.*

Love, J. M., Nauta, M. J., Coelen, C. G., Hewett, K., & Ruopp, R. R. (1976). *Home start evaluation: Final report, findings and implications.* Ypsilanti, MI: High Scope Educational Research Foundation.

Magura, S., Moses, B. S., & Jones, M. A. (1987). Assessing risk and measuring change in families: The Family Risk Scales. In S. Magura & B. S. Moses (Eds.), *Outcome measures for child welfare services: Theory and applications.* Washington, DC: Child Welfare League of America.

Maluccio, A. N. (1991). Family preservation: An overview. In A. L. Sallee & J. C. Lloyd (Eds.), *Family preservation.* Riverdale, IL: National Association for Family Based Services.

Miller, K., Fein, E., Howe, G. W., Gaudio, C. P., & Bishop, G. V. (1985). A Parent Aide program: Record keeping, outcomes, and costs. *Child Welfare, 44,* 407-419.

Morton, E. S., & Eyberse, W. (1993). Epilogue: Family preservation and social change: The need for future dialogue. In E. S. Morton & R. K. Grigsby (Eds.), *Advancing family preservation practice* (pp. 150-152). Newbury Park, CA: Sage.

National Center on Child Abuse and Neglect. (1988). *Study of national incidence and prevalence of child abuse and neglect: 1988* (Contract 105-85-1702). Washington, DC: U.S. Department of Health and Human Services.

Nelson, K. E. (1991). Populations and outcomes in five family preservation programs. In K. Wells & D. E. Biegel (Eds.), *Family preservation services: Research and evaluation* (pp. 72-91). Newbury Park, CA: Sage.

Nelson, K., Landsman, M. J., & Deutelbaum, W. (1990). Three models of family centered placement prevention services. *Child Welfare, 69,* 3-21.

Pittman, F. S. (1987). *Turning points: Treating families in crisis.* New York: Norton.

Precora, P. J., Fraser, M. W., & Haapala, J. D. (1992). Intensive home-based family preservation services: An update from the FIT project. *Child Welfare, 71,* 177-188.

Precora, P. J., Fraser, M. W., Haapala, J. D., & Bartlome, J. A. (1987). *Defining family preservation services: Three intensive home-based treatment programs.* Salt Lake City: University of Utah, School of Social Work, Social Research Institute.

Rivera, V. R., & Kutash, K. (1994). Family preservation services. In V. R. Rivera & K. Kutash, *Components of a system of care: What does the research say?* Tampa: University of South Florida, Florida Mental Health Institute, Research and Training Center for Children's Mental Health.

Roberts, R. N., Wasik, B. H., Castro, G., & Ramey, C. T. (1991). Family support in the home: Programs, policy, and social change. *American Psychologist, 46*(2), 121-137.

Selig, W. R., Goldman-Hall, B. J., & Jerrel, J. M. (1992). In home treatment of families with seriously disturbed adolescents in crisis. *Family Process, 31,* 135-149.

Stroul, B. A. (1988). *Series on community-based services for children and adolescents who are severely emotionally disturbed: Vol. 1. Home-based services.* Washington, DC: Georgetown University Child Development Center, CASSP Technical Assistance Center.

Stroul, B. A. (1993). *Systems of care for children and adolescents with severe emotional disturbance: What are the results?* Washington, DC: Georgetown University Child Development Center, CASSP Technical Assistance Center.

Tavantzis, T., Tavantzis, R., Brown, L., & Rohrbaugh, M. (1986). Home-based structural family therapy for delinquents at risk of placement. In M. P. Mirkin & S. Koman (Eds.), *Handbook of adolescent and family therapy.* New York: Gardner.

Wasik, H., Bryant, D. M., & Lyons, C. M. (1990). *Home visiting: Procedures for helping families.* Newbury Park, CA: Sage.

Wells, K., & Biegel, D. E. (Eds.). (1991). *Family preservation services: Research and evaluation.* Newbury Park, CA: Sage.

Wheeler, C. E., Bogdan, G., & Ying-Ying, Y. T. (1992). *Evaluation of the State of Connecticut's intensive family preservation initiative: Phase VI report.* Sacramento, CA: Walter R. McDonald & Associates.

Woods, L. J. (1988, May-June). Home-based family therapy. *Social Work*, pp. 211-214.

Zigler, E., & Black, K. B. (1989). America's family support movement: Strengths and limitations. *American Journal of Orthopsychiatry, 59*, 6-19.

• CHAPTER 12 •

School-Based Health and Social Service Centers

THOMAS P. GULLOTTA

LYNN NOYES

GARY M. BLAU

Consider the statement, "If something makes sense then it will happen." On the blustery winter evening these words are being penned, this truism has all the strength, warmth, and wisdom old New Englanders can muster against a driving evening sleet pelting already iced windows. And yet we are also confronted with another old New England saying, "Your sense is nonsense." For some, this chapter will resound of the first adage. For others, resistive to school systems extending themselves to meet the needs of the whole child, the second may hold greater meaning. In this chapter, we examine the factors that are increasingly moving school systems to become physical centers for health and social services. This is a trend that we believe will accelerate in the coming years (Morrill, 1992). We also examine a model in which services may be most effectively delivered—the school-based health center.

Schools as Social Service Centers

If evolution were applied to the history of education, then little more would need to be said about the movement of school systems into areas not immediately involved with academic study (Larson,

Gomby, Shiono, Lewit, & Behrman, 1992; Tyack, 1992). The expansion of school systems into athletics, the provision of hot school lunch meals, school nursing, and school guidance services are some examples of the gradual movement of school systems into social services since World War II. In the past decade, these now generally accepted services have been joined by the expansion of breakfast meal programs and after-school "latchkey" programs aimed at keeping youth occupied and under adult supervision while parents work. These new expansions have not come without criticism. Each new step has been greeted with concern about education losing sense of its purpose. Each new step brings reminders that the purpose of educational tax dollars is to teach young people the essentials necessary to govern with a representative government. Those time-honored essentials are the ability to communicate, to read, and to calculate.

To understand our belief that school facilities will become the center of health and social service activity in the coming years, it is important to venture into the realm of demography. Dramatic population changes are under way in the United States. Assuming there is not a large immigrant influx of young, well-educated European males in the next 20 years, shifts in the ethnic, racial, and gender makeup of the United States will have a lasting and profound influence on the labor force of the next century. The United States is in transition from a predominantly white, European ancestry, male labor force to a labor force that will be female, black, Asian, and Hispanic in makeup. To illustrate, it is projected that between 1985 and 2000, only 15% of new workers will be white males born in the United States: 42% of this new labor force will be white U.S.-born women; 13% will be nonwhite U.S.-born women; 7% will be nonwhite U.S.-born men; and immigrant women and men will make up 13% and 10% of the new labor force, respectively (Nothdurft, 1989). Concerns have been expressed about the quality of the educational and family life experience of this future labor force (Hodgkinson, 1989; Nothdurft, 1989; Popenoe, 1993):

> This emerging workforce approaches the world of work with significant handicaps. A disproportionate number . . . come from families that are poor or headed by a single parent who are themselves poorly educated and largely unskilled. These young people are three times more likely than others to drop out of school. Indeed, an estimated

700,000 young people—most of them minorities—drop out of school each year. . . . Another approximately 700,000 young people complete high school but remain functionally illiterate. The working-age immigrants entering the country not only lack language skills but are generally poorly educated as well. (Nothdurft, 1989, pp. 2-3)

The first pressure on the educational system is to improve their services to better educate the upcoming labor force of the next century. To do this will require different interventions than previously used if women are to be encouraged to pursue mathematics and science careers and black and Hispanic males are to complete their educations (Adams, Gullotta, & Markstrom-Adams, 1994).

Additional profound changes will occur in the age distribution of the U.S. population. One area in which this clearly can be seen is in the estimated percentage of youth in the total population from 1995 to 2050. From a historical perspective, it is worth noting that at the time of the American Revolution in 1776, the average age of a colonist was 18 (Adams & Gullotta, 1983). As a percentage, it has slipped over the past 200+ years so that in 1995, an estimated 26.1% of the population of the United States was 18 or less compared with 14.2% of the population over the age of 65. In the year 2020, the U.S. Bureau of the Census estimates that the percentage of the population 18 and younger will drop to 23.6%, whereas those 65 and older will grow to 18.7%. By the middle of the next century, the percentage of individuals over the age of 65 (25.5%) will be greater than those less than 18 (23.2%). At that same time, the very elderly—that is, those over the age of 85—will make up 4.9% of the population, whereas youth in middle adolescence (ages 14 to 17) will constitute an estimated 5.2% of the population. This is an astonishing difference of only three tenths of 1% (U.S. Bureau of the Census, 1993).

The graying of the United States raises questions about the future allocation of limited financial resources to serve and care for the general population. Assuming the elderly of the United States do not embrace euthanasia, disagreements are likely to occur over the needs of the elderly and the needs of youth. One of the first battlegrounds for these disagreements will be over the commitment of funds for education. There are already signs of a weakening interest and willingness of taxpayers to support public education (Goetting, 1994).

To counter that trend, two budding movements appear to be under way. The first is the transformation of the school into a community center used by all age groups for educational, cultural, recreational, and senior service purposes. The second is the broadening of the mission but not the financial responsibility of school systems to include social services for children and their families.

We contend that these last observations identify movements that will continue to gather force and will merge in the coming years. The rationale for this belief is found in the fact that an enormous capital investment has been made already for education buildings and attached athletic facilities. Second, these facilities are not fully used during weekdays (evenings, in particular) and are used still less on weekends and during summers. Next, no single other social institution can gather youth in the same numbers to be at one place at one time. Finally, infrastructure capabilities like transportation (school buses), existing building maintenance capacity (custodial staff), and building flexibility ranging from food preparation areas, classrooms, performance halls, to libraries support a prediction that school facilities will evolve into community centers early in the next century.

It should be observed that we have drawn an important distinction between the facilities of school systems and their operating budgets. Although it is hypothetically possible that school systems may be called on in future years to operate and administer the social service programs that will occur in school facilities, there is also reason to believe this will not happen. We believe the model that will evolve will rely on other institutions to deliver needed social services. Several common examples of this arrangement currently exist. For instance, it was noted earlier in this chapter that breakfast and hot lunch meals are increasingly found in public schools. It should be mentioned that many of these programs are subcontracted to private vendors. Latchkey services are often operated by nonprofit groups like the YMCA and YWCA. After-school recreational services are funded, operated, and administered by municipal park and recreation departments or by nonprofit agencies. We believe that it is this service model that will continue in operation for the following reasons.

The first is concern over the concentration of power and authority in the hands of a few educators. Our representative form of government is built on a system of checks and balances, and our other social institutions mirror that system. Choice and the right to privacy are fundamental rights Americans expect. We do not believe the political support exists currently or will develop in the future to add social services to the work agenda of school systems.

Next, the constituency groups that are forcing school systems to respond to the noneducational needs of students and others are unlikely to relegate their authority to educators. It has been because of their advocacy that these special needs are being discussed and in some cases addressed. Many of these needs, such as recreational programs for the elderly or health care services for family members of school-based health center-enrolled youth, are outside the mandate of school systems.

Finally, in comparison with other social service operations, school-administered programs are costly. Currently, most services are offered only during the school year, or approximately 180 days per year. Continuing a trend that began in the late 1980s, it is reasonable to expect that privatization of many government services will continue. For these reasons, we believe that collaboration between school systems and social service agencies is the most likely model to emerge.

Schools and Social Service Agencies as Collaborators

From 1970, when the first school-based health center was established in Dallas, to 1984, when 31 centers were in existence, the number of school-based health centers has grown to approximately 500 sites across the United States and Puerto Rico (Levy & Shepardson, 1992; Riessman, 1991). Over the next several years, the number of centers may grow dramatically as the result of two factors. The first is need. Growing numbers of youth are not being served for reasons that will be discussed in the next section. The second factor potentially influencing the growth of centers is national health care reform. Centers offer the possibility of extending comprehensive, integrated preventive care to youth that can increase the probability of promoting their health and reducing the incidence of their dysfunctional behavior.

Why Are Youth Medically Underserved?

Unlike many other developed nations, the United States does not provide its citizens with universal health care coverage. This is estimated to affect 34 million individuals in the United States. Of this number, 9.8 million youth under the age of 18 were uninsured in 1990. Income and access to health care are related. Nearly 68% of the youth living in the United States reside in families able to afford private insurance or whose employers provide medical insurance. Nearly 21% of young people live in families who, because of poverty, qualify for Medicaid or other public insurance. The remainder (11%) live in families unable to afford medical insurance and whose employers either do not offer medical insurance or offer it with copayments the employees cannot afford (U.S. Department of Health and Human Services [DHHS], 1993a).

Even if universal health care were to be developed in the United States, there are reasons to believe that adolescents would continue underusing medical services (Gans, Blyth, Elster, & Gaveras, 1990). The first reason is the conflict that exists between medical office hours and schooling. In a society in which the ability to walk to services has been lost to development's sprawl, transportation from home to medical care and then to school is complicated by the reality that parents and guardians may find it extremely difficult to receive work release time. Next, the most friendly medical office is an unfriendly environment for adolescents. Either decorated for young children with pastel dinosaurs that painfully remind youth of their only recently lost interest in make-believe or playing innocuous background music that parents insist be tuned to on the car radio, adolescents fidget with an "I want out of here now" behavior. Furthermore, continuing a practice begun with the first visit to the pediatrician, parents intrude on the possibility that a confidential relationship can develop between doctor and adolescent. Parents' inquiries (e.g., "How's my daughter doing?" or "I want you to be sure to tell my son not to use drugs!") can have a deadening effect on the development of a trusting relationship. Adolescents have no assurance that if they confide information, the medical provider would or even could comply with their request for confidentiality.

To illustrate, consider a 14-year-old boy who expresses the need for help in handling sexual feelings toward another male. What assistance can a physician offer in a visit lasting minutes that would not trigger a waiting parent's suspiciousness? With patient scheduling averaging 10 to 12 minutes per visit (Panel on High-Risk Youth, 1993; Perrin, Guyer, & Lawrence, 1992), the most well-intentioned physician would be hard-pressed to spend more than 20 minutes with this youth. After that visit, what action on the physician's part should next be taken that ensures the privacy of the adolescent and extends to him the emotional support and guidance he seeks? To schedule a return visit is certain to raise questions on the parent's part, if not directed to the physician then to the son. To protect the youth's right to privacy but refer the adolescent to another provider would likewise raise the parent's suspicions, especially a provider of mental health services.

From the adolescent's perspective, we suspect that although the interest in receiving help from the pediatrician may exist, the risks of conflict and emotional pain at home would keep these sexual feelings hidden from the pediatrician. And even if these formidable hurdles could be successfully negotiated while protecting the adolescent's right to confidentiality, the practices of third-party payers expose the youth to being revealed.

Health Risk Factors in Adolescence

The second decade of life is remarkably free of life-threatening illness for most youth. Even so, an estimated 2 million have chronic conditions that impede activity. These conditions include chronic respiratory illnesses such as asthma and bronchitis that afflict approximately 406,000 youth (or 21%). Muscle and skeletal disorders such as arthritis affect 295,000 adolescents (15%). Illnesses of the nervous system such as multiple sclerosis, epilepsy, and cerebral palsy strike 115,000 young people (6%), and hearing impairments affect an estimated 80,000 adolescents (4%). But by far the single greatest cause for disability in adolescence is emotional illness: 32% (approximately 634,000) of the 2,000,000 youth estimated to be disabled suffer from mental disorders (Starfield, 1992).

Nearly all of these emotional disorders can be prevented (Albee & Gullotta, 1986; National Commission on Children, 1991). As the National Commission on Children (1991) has noted:

Malnourishment, obesity, and the incidence of many illnesses are related to nutritional intake. Sexually transmitted diseases, accidents and injuries, and physical and mental impairments are directly attributable to early, unprotected sexual activity, drug and alcohol use, and

delinquent behavior. . . . In fact, better control of a limited number
of risk factors . . . could prevent at least 40 percent of all premature
deaths, one-third of all short-term disability cases, and two-thirds of
all chronic disability cases. Changes in health behaviors can also
reduce medical costs and limit losses in productivity. Illnesses attributable to smoking cost individuals and society more than $65 billion
a year. The total cost of alcohol and drug abuse exceeds $110 billion
each year. (pp. 126-127)

Poor decision making leading to the development of dysfunctional habits or destructive impulsive behaviors, lack of access to
positive role models, and the absence of opportunities for success
can have lifelong negative consequences (Adams et al., 1994; Gullotta, Adams, & Montemayor, 1990). For example, it has been
estimated that 5% of adolescents are obese—that is, 20% over their
recommended weight for their height (Gans et al., 1990). Another
3% of the female adolescent population and an unknown number
of male youths are estimated to suffer from problems of anorexia
and bulimia (Adams et al., 1994). Many more youth are concerned
about their weight and are at risk for unhealthy practices to control
their weight. Nearly 18% of the 1990 senior class have reported
using nonprescription diet pills in their lifetime. Females were three
times more likely than males to have used nonprescription diet pills
(28.3% versus 7.8%) (Johnston, O'Malley, & Bachman, 1991).

The pathway to alcohol, cigarette, and other substance misuse
begins in early adolescence. Although longitudinal data are encouraging in the smaller number of youth who have ever experimented
with any illicit drug, use of alcohol and cigarettes remains relatively
unchanged. From a peak in the late 1970s to early 1980s, wherein
65% of the senior class reported the lifetime use of an illicit drug, 1990
data continue a decade-long trend downward to 47.9% (Johnston et al.,
1991). This encouraging trend is less evident with cigarettes and
alcohol. Despite the well-advertised health hazards of tobacco
products, 64.4% of the 1990 senior class reported lifetime use of
cigarettes. This is a decline of slightly more than 6% since 1980.
Even so, a disturbing 5.9% of those surveyed acknowledged the
consumption of one-half pack per day. The decline in alcohol use
is smaller still. The 1990 data indicate 89.5% of the senior class
reported lifetime use as compared with 93.2% for the senior class
of 1980. Nearly 9% of the sample admitted to drinking five or more

alcohol beverages in a row three to five times in the 2 weeks prior to the survey (Johnston et al., 1991).

For several drugs, substance use in early adolescence is pronounced. For example, Johnston and his associates (1991) report that nearly 13% of adolescents used marijuana prior to the ninth grade. Inhalants were used by 9.1% of the class of 1990 prior to the ninth grade. Almost 38% of students in the middle school years (grades 6-8) used alcohol, with 21% "getting drunk." Nearly 41% used cigarettes, with 7.5% smoking daily.

Youth are also at risk of running afoul of legal authorities during adolescence. In 1992, criminal misconduct for the following offenses was highest during the years from childhood to age 18: Youth committed 42% of car thefts, 34% of burglaries, 49% of arson crimes, and 45% of vandalism offenses. Equally disturbing are data indicating that 14.5% of murders, 16% of forcible rapes, and 15% of aggravated assaults were committed by young people in 1992 (U.S. Bureau of the Census, 1994).

Sexual experimentation for most individuals also begins during this life stage. For example, in 1990, by age 17, 41% of adolescent females had experienced intercourse, with the percentage growing to 74.4% by age 19. As many adolescent and early adult sexual encounters are without the benefit of contraceptive devices, up to two thirds of sexually active youth are exposed to unplanned parenthood and a host of sexually transmitted diseases, some of which (e.g., AIDS) are fatal (Jorgensen, 1993; U.S. DHHS, 1993a).

To illustrate, published studies over the past decade reported adolescents using contraceptives more than occasionally—33% (Zelnick & Kanter, 1980) to 79% (Sonenstein, Pleck, & Ku, 1989) of the time. Contraceptive use increased as the relationship extended over time. Whether intended or unintended, there were 1,033,730 adolescent pregnancies in 1988, with 488,941 resulting live births; 28,000 of these were to females under the age of 15 (U.S. DHHS, 1993a). As young women giving birth are currently less likely to place their infants for adoption and more likely to be unmarried without financial support from the child's father than previous cohort groups, they experience poverty and a host of other difficulties (such as school failure, dropping out, higher career dissatisfaction, poorer health in greater numbers than nonpregnant youth), as do their infants (Jorgensen, 1993).

Unprotected sexual intercourse may also expose youth to sexually transmitted diseases. In 1990, 689,854 cases of gonorrhea were reported to the Centers for Disease Control; 32% (208,799 cases) of infected youth were 10 to 19 years of age (Leukefeld & Haverkos, 1993). For the same year, 50,224 cases of syphilis were reported; 11% (5,507 cases) involved young people 10 to 19 years of age (Leukefeld & Haverkos, 1993). For young people between the ages of 13 and 19, 872 suffered with AIDS as of June 30, 1992. Although 60% of white youth were infected by HIV-tainted blood products, more than 60% of black and Hispanic youth were infected as a result of sexual activity (U.S. DHHS, 1993a). For that same period of time, there were 8,911 cases of AIDS-infected young adults between the ages of 20 and 24. In contrast to adolescents, 91% of AIDS cases in this age group could be traced to homosexual activity (63%), heterosexual activity (11%), and injecting drug use (17%) (U.S. DHHS, 1993a). Understanding that a several-year delay exists between exposure to the HIV retrovirus and the onset of AIDS, it is very likely that these young adults were infected with HIV during adolescence (Adams et al., 1994).

For the year 1990, the leading causes of death among adolescents 15 to 19 years of age were unintentional injuries, homicide, and suicide. The category of unintentional injuries comprises motor vehicle accidents, followed by drownings, burns, firearms, and falls. Although white adolescents had a death rate twice that of blacks for motor vehicle accidents and suicide, black adolescents died violently from homicides at a rate eight times greater than that of white youth (Gans et al., 1990; Perrin et al., 1992; U.S. DHHS, 1993a).

School-Based Health Centers

Given these preventable threats to the emotional and physical health of young people, considerable interest has been expressed by private groups such as the Robert Wood Johnson Foundation (Garfinkel, 1993), the states, and the federal government (Office of Technology Assessment, 1991) in the development of school-based services to reduce the incidence of these harmful behaviors and improve the health of youth. School-based or linked health centers represent a model of providing integrated social, mental, and physical health care services to youth in as barrier-free a manner as possible. In an evolving health care system that may or may not have federal involvement, the school-based health care center offers the possibility of providing initial care or entry point services to youth with referrals to providers of specialty care.

Although at the present moment national health care reform appears to be stalled, it is nevertheless useful to examine how school-based health centers would have been treated in the Clinton health care plan. In that proposal, school-based health centers would have received $100 million in FY 1996 for expansion grants, which would have increased to $400 million by FY 1999. These grants would have been used to establish nearly 3,500 new school-based or school-linked health centers nationally and would have better enabled school-based health centers to actively participate in emerging national health and managed care movements (Koppleman, 1994).

To illustrate the linkage between managed health care and school-based health centers, the federal Department of Health and Human Services (1993b) reported on the status of the coordination between school-based health centers and managed care. Not surprising, the level of coordination between managed care providers and school-based health centers varied widely across the country. In some instances, school-based health centers acted as a provider, needing prior authorization from the managed care plan before providing a very limited number of services; in other instances, school-based health centers were reimbursed for all services they delivered to children and adolescents in the plan.

The U.S. DHHS (1993b) identified seven examples of how states promoted the coordination and integration of school-based health centers into managed care arrangements. Table 12.1 summarizes the findings of that U.S. DHHS (1993b) report.

Clearly, as the data suggest, the relationship between school-based health centers and managed care is evolving. Many health care reformers believe that school-based and school-linked health care services have proven themselves to be an effective alternative to reach high-risk populations that would otherwise go unserved. It is not unreasonable to believe that if health care reform continues its current movement toward increased managed care, school-based health centers will emerge as a gatekeeping system for children and adolescents. In "Cambridge"-like school-based health centers in which parents are

Table 12.1 States' Promotion of Health Centers Into Managed Care

City, State	Mechanism for Coordination
Multnomah County, Oregon	State law requires Medicaid managed care providers to coordinate with school-based health centers
St. Paul, Minnesota	Legal contract between managed care provider and school-based health center
Baltimore, Maryland	Protocol for referral and treatment between managed care provider and school-based health center
Minneapolis, Minnesota	Including managed care providers in coalitions that fund and develop school-based health centers
Brooklyn, New York	Public entities that administer both school-based health centers and managed care plans
Hillsborough County, Florida	Managed care providers authorize school-based health centers to provide care and bill Medicaid directly for service
San Francisco, California	Managed care gives expedited patient care on school-based health center referrals
State of Connecticut	School-based health centers are mandated as an essential provider of service by the state Medicaid agency

also eligible for services, the school-based health center may also become the central entry point for most family health care.

Currently, 75% of school-based health centers and 60% of school-linked services are operated by organizations whose principal identity involves physical health care (i.e., community health centers, public health departments, hospitals, and medical schools). Fewer than 10% are administered by school systems (Riessman, 1991). In light of the literature reviewed, other providers of services, such as child and family organizations, private medical practices, and community action programs, may also be ideal program agencies for operating school-based health centers.

For several years, the state of Connecticut has encouraged a variety of program administration models. We will illustrate this by examining the state's funding of a children's organization to provide this service. The only member agency of the Child Welfare League of America currently providing school-based health center services, Child and Family Agency is a comprehensive family service organization that defines itself as focusing on the whole needs of youth in the context of their families and community.

The agency began offering school-based health center services 8 years ago after a school assessment established the service need and no physical health care organization stepped forward to meet that gap in services. As the agency offers early childhood programs; social competency and social skills programs; a school-based young parents program; outpatient, home-based, and family reunification counseling services; and extensive diagnostic, assessment, and education services, the extension into the delivery of physical health care services was a logical but nevertheless challenging step.

The practice model chosen to meet that challenge established a partnership between area private pediatricians and the agency. Child and Family Agency employs a master's in social work director for its health and social services division. This decision to employ a nontraditional director (i.e., not a physician or nurse) reflects the reality that the vast majority of delivered school-based health center services are mental health/social service in nature. An additional four full-time nurse-practitioners and eight master's-level clinicians provide health and social services to 10 preschool through high school sites in two communities. Medical supervision for this staff comes from three area physicians who provide from 1 to 4 hours of consultative and direct service care weekly. Supervision for mental health services is provided by the director. Young people requiring medical care beyond the scope of Child and Family Agency's capacity are referred for service to local physicians, area community health centers, or community hospitals.

As an example of the service delivery provided by the school-based and school-linked centers operated by Child and Family Agency, the following list presents selected statistical information obtained between July 1, 1993, and June 30, 1994. These data were taken from MIS reports prepared for the funding body:

- High school students enrolled in the program: 1,234 of a possible 1,721 students, or 72%

Table 12.2 Demographic Characteristics of Students Using Services

---

Gender
  male: 47%
  female: 53%
Ages
   6-12: 31%
  13-16: 46%
  17+: 23%
Race/ethnicity
  white (not Hispanic): 42%
  black: 28%
  Hispanic: 25%
  Asian/Pacific Islander: < 1%
  Native American: < 1%
  other: 4%

- Middle school students enrolled in the program: 557 of a possible 696 students, or 80%
- Elementary school students enrolled in the program: 670 of a possible 1,563 students, or 43%
- Total number of students served (unduplicated): 1,631, or 66% of enrolled youth
- Total number of visits: 7,483 for an average of 4.6 visits per youth using the service

Readers may wonder why elementary school enrollment was significantly less than for middle or high school students. The answer can be found in the length of time these elementary school-based health centers had been open. The elementary schools' centers have been open for less than 2 years. Even in those cases where centers have been open for several years, however, enrollment has not exceeded 80%. The two principal reasons for this are parents choosing not to enroll youth for personal reasons and students' school transfers. It should also be noted that not all enrolled youth use the service in a year.

The gender data in Table 12.2 are in keeping with national findings. Females are somewhat more likely to use services than are males. The racial/ethnic data are reflective of the area served. This suggests that the service is not viewed as existing for any special racial or ethnic group.

Table 12.3 Medical Procedures Provided

Histories: 1,751	Medical follow-up: 204
Partial physical exam: 696	STD education: 26
Physical exam: 925	Pelvic exam: 10
Immunizations: 62	Pap smear: 1
TB test: 401	STD screen: 15
Health education: 1,079	Pregnancy counseling: 147
Vision screen: 164	Nutrition education: 42
Scoliosis screen: 438	Weight management: 17
HIV/AIDS test: 0	HIV/AIDS counseling: 7
Well child care: 76	Prescriptions issued: 372

NOTE: Number of visits will exceed 7,483 as more than one procedure was done during a visit.

Table 12.4 Mental Health Procedures Provided

Crisis counseling: 233	Family problems: 2,838
Psychosocial evaluation: 75	Violence counseling: 229
Depression counseling: 373	Abuse/neglect: 433
Substance abuse counseling: 62	Loss/grief counseling: 884
Peer problem counseling: 3,558	Stress management: 1,199

NOTE: Number of visits will exceed 7,483 as more than one procedure was done during a visit.

Like the majority of school-based health centers in the country, these centers do not have permission from the local board of education either to prescribe or to dispense contraceptives. HIV and AIDS tests are referred out.

It is important to note that the majority of services provided to enrolled youth involve education, the offering of advice, or guidance. Not surprising, training in living peacefully with one's peers represents the single largest category of service offered.

From this basic model of school-based health service delivery, more elaborate systems can be designed. Where funding permits, dental services are often provided from school sites. Vision and nutritional services are other services also offered with increased levels of financial support. In growing numbers of communities that are using their schools for community centers, the school-based health center is extending its operating hours into the evening and to the parents and siblings of enrolled children—the so-called Cambridge model of care.

Summary

This chapter has reviewed the demographic, health, and social issues that lead us to conclude that school-based health centers will continue to grow and develop in the United States over the next decade. Although the defeat of national health care reform in 1994 will slow the development of school-based health centers, demographic, health, and social pressures coupled with the growth of managed care will encourage school-based health center growth.

References

Adams, G. R., & Gullotta, T. P. (1983). *Adolescent life experiences.* Monterey, CA: Brooks/Cole.

Adams, G. R., Gullotta, T. P., & Markstrom-Adams, C. (1994). *Adolescent life experiences* (3rd ed.). Pacific Grove, CA: Brooks/Cole.

Albee, G. W., & Gullotta, T. P. (1986). Facts and fallacies about primary prevention. *Journal of Primary Prevention, 6,* 207-218.

Gans, J. E., Blyth, D. A., Elster, A. B., & Gaveras, L. L. (1990). *AMA profiles of adolescent health: Vol. 1. How healthy are they?* Chicago: American Medical Association.

Garfinkel, S. (1993). *The answer is at school: Bringing health care to our students.* Washington, DC: School-Based Health Center Program.

Goetting, A. (1994). Do Americans really like children? *Journal of Primary Prevention, 15,* 81-92.

Gullotta, T. P., Adams, G. R., & Montemayor, R. (Eds.). (1990). *Developing social competency in adolescence.* Newbury Park, CA: Sage.

Hodgkinson, H. L. (1989). *The same client: The demographics of education and service delivery systems.* Washington, DC: Institute for Educational Leadership.

Johnston, L. D., O'Malley, P. M., & Bachman, J. G. (1991). *Drug use among American high school seniors, college students, and young adults, 1975-1990.* Washington, DC: Government Printing Office.

Jorgensen, S. R. (1993). Adolescent pregnancy and parenting. In T. P. Gullotta, G. R. Adams, & R. Montemayor (Eds.), *Adolescent sexuality* (pp. 103-140). Newbury Park, CA: Sage.

Koppleman, J. (1994). *Delivering health and social services at school: A look at the full service school movement* (Issue Brief: National Health Policy Forum, No. 645). Washington, DC: George Washington University.

Larson, C. S., Gomby, D. S., Shiono, P. H., Lewit, E. M., & Behrman, R. E. (1992). Analysis. *The Future of Children: School-Linked Services, 2*(1), 6-18.

Leukefeld, C. G., & Haverkos, H. W. (1993). Sexually transmitted diseases. In T. P. Gullotta, G. R. Adams, & R. Montemayor (Eds.), *Adolescent sexuality* (pp. 161-180). Newbury Park, CA: Sage.

Levy, J. E., & Shepardson, W. (1992). A look at current school-linked efforts. *The Future of Children: U.S. Health Care for Children*, 2(1), 44-55.

Morrill, W. A. (1992). Overview of service delivery to children. *The Future of Children: U.S. Health Care for Children*, 2(1), 32-43.

National Commission on Children. (1991). *Beyond rhetoric: A new American agenda for children and families*. Washington, DC: Government Printing Office.

Nothdurft, W. E. (1989). *School works: Reinventing public schools to create the workforce of the future*. Washington, DC: German Marshall Fund of the United States.

Office of Technology Assessment. (1991). *Adolescent health* (Vol. 1, [OTA] H-468). Washington, DC: Government Printing Office.

Panel on High-Risk Youth. (1993). *Losing generations: Adolescents in high-risk settings*. Washington, DC: National Academy Press.

Perrin, J., Guyer, B., & Lawrence, J. M. (1992). Health care services for children and adolescents. *The Future of Children: U.S. Health Care for Children*, 2(2), 58-77.

Popenoe, D. (1993). American family decline, 1960-1990: A review and appraisal. *Journal of Marriage and the Family*, 55, 527-555.

Riessman, J. (1991). *School-based and school-linked clinics: The facts*. Washington, DC: Center for Population Options.

Sonenstein, F. L., Pleck, J. H., & Ku, L. C. (1989). Sexual activity, condom use and AIDS awareness among adolescent males. *Family Planning Perspectives*, 21, 152-158.

Starfield, B. (1992). Child and adolescent health status measures. *The Future of Children: U.S. Health Care for Children*, 2(2), 25-39.

Tyack, D. (1992). Health and social services in public schools: Historical perspectives. *The Future of Children: School Linked Services*, 2(1), 19-31.

U.S. Bureau of the Census. (1993). Nation's population projected to grow by 50 percent over next 50 years. In *Census and you* (Vol. 28, p. 1). Washington, DC: Government Printing Office.

U.S. Bureau of the Census. (1994). *Statistical abstract of the United States* (114th ed.). Washington, DC: Government Printing Office.

U.S. Department of Health and Human Services. (1993a). *Child health USA '92* ([HRSA] MCH-92-6). Washington, DC: Government Printing Office.

U.S. Department of Health and Human Services. (1993b). *School-based health centers and managed care: Examples of coordination*. Washington, DC: Government Printing Office.

Zelnick, M., & Kanter, J. F. (1980). Sexual activity, contraceptive use and pregnancy among metropolitan-area teenagers: 1971-1979. *Family Planning Perspectives*, 12, 230-237.

CHAPTER 13

Comments on Adolescent Behavior Problems: Developing Coordinated Systems of Care

GARY M. BLAU

DAVID A. BRUMER

What have we learned about the treatment of adolescent disorders? What can be done to improve adolescent functioning? According to national estimates, between 14% and 20% of all children and adolescents have some type of emotional or behavioral disturbance (Brandenburg, Friedman, & Silver, 1990). Although each of the preceding chapters has provided insight into many of these complex problems, taking a disorder-by-disorder approach unavoidably creates the compartmentalization of adolescent behavior and creates the impression that adolescent behavior is addressed only in discrete units. In reality, of course, this is not the case. Adolescent behavior comprises a holistic set of circumstances that include a physical/biological context, a cognitive/intellectual context, an emotional/affective context, and a social/interpersonal context.

Specific disorders and their treatment, as discussed in this volume, focus on the individual and individual factors related to adolescent problems. Broad systems are required, however, to ensure that care and treatment are available to meet the needs of all teenagers who have behavior problems. In other words, the treatment of emotional and behavioral disorders must be accomplished as part of an organized system of care.

The need to identify an array of services, and to integrate these services into broader systems of care, began to receive national attention with Knitzer's 1982 book *Unclaimed Children*. Knitzer (1982) documented the failure of service systems to adequately meet the needs of emotionally disturbed youth and called for a fundamental change in service delivery. This change included the development of a community-based approach to systems of care. The idea for community-based systems of care for children and adolescents is not new. In 1969, for example, the Joint Commission on the Mental Health of Children recommended that coordinated networks be developed to serve youth and their families. These recommendations have also been echoed by other task forces and commissions such as the President's Commission on Mental Health (1978).

Despite such recommendations, few systems of care were implemented before the mid-1980s. In 1984, the U.S. Congress funded an initiative through the National Institute of Mental Health called the Child and Adolescent Service System Program (CASSP). The CASSP initiative was created to promote systems change, assist states and communities in the development of comprehensive community-based systems of care, and encourage collaboration among service providers, parents, advocates, and policymakers. During the first several years of CASSP, 24 states received grant money to promote these concepts and strategies. Based on the experiences of those states, Stroul and Friedman (1986) developed a comprehensive guide that focused on system development. These authors found that a system of care must include a coordinated array of services (ranging from residential to nonresidential care) to meet the individualized needs of youth and families requiring services. As defined by Stroul and Friedman (1986): "A system of care is a comprehensive spectrum of mental health and other necessary services which are organized into a coordinated network to meet the multiple and changing needs of severely emotionally disturbed children and adolescents" (p. iv).

What evolved during the 1980s was the establishment of a philosophical framework for systems of care consisting of two core values and 10 guiding principles. These guiding principles were developed by CASSP participants in collaboration with numerous advisory groups and interested parties. The first core value was that systems of care be child centered and family focused, with the needs of each child and family dictating the provision of services. This is significant because it is not the availability of services that is important but what the child and family need—even if that means creating services or providing nontraditional services. The 50-minute therapy hour may not be what a family needs or wants to get better. In fact, the family may prefer respite care or mentoring, and a respectful system of care engages families in the treatment planning and decision-making process. A child-centered, family-focused treatment philosophy means that service providers, in partnership with children and families, find the way to provide "whatever it takes" to improve functioning and health outcomes.

The second core value is that the system of care be community based, with the locus of services and decision-making authority housed at the community level. Children and adolescents are part of families; families are part of communities; and by empowering communities, families are empowered. The inclusion of families in the service planning process is viewed as a hallmark of any successful system of care, and systems must develop family-friendly terminology and a "customer-driven" service philosophy. The following 10 guiding principles for the system of care were described by Stroul and Friedman (1986):

1. Emotionally disturbed children should have access to a comprehensive array of services that address the child's physical, emotional, social and educational needs.
2. Emotionally disturbed children should receive individualized services in accordance with the unique needs and potentials of each child, and guided by an individualized service plan.
3. Emotionally disturbed children should receive services within the least restrictive, most normative environment that is clinically appropriate.
4. The families and surrogate families of emotionally disturbed children should be full participants in all aspects of the planning and delivery of services.
5. Emotionally disturbed children should receive services that are integrated, with linkages between child-caring agencies and programs and mechanisms for planning, developing and coordinating services.

6. Emotionally disturbed children should be provided with case management or similar mechanisms to ensure that multiple services are delivered in a coordinated and therapeutic manner, and that they can move through the system of services in accordance with their changing needs.

7. Early identification and intervention for children with emotional problems should be promoted by the system of care in order to enhance the likelihood of positive outcomes.

8. Emotionally disturbed children should be ensured smooth transitions to the adult service system as they reach maturity.

9. The rights of emotionally disturbed children should be protected, and effective advocacy efforts for emotionally disturbed children and youth should be promoted.

10. Emotionally disturbed children should receive services without regard to race, religion, national origin, sex, physical disability or other characteristics, and services should be sensitive and responsive to cultural differences and special needs. (p. vii)

In the context of these guiding principles, Stroul (1993) provides five major goals when developing service systems. The first goal is to develop and provide a full array of community-based services. One failure of service systems is that they do not allow for a range of service capacities, and to be successful, available service options must go beyond traditional outpatient or inpatient treatment. In Connecticut, for example, the Children's Mental Health Plan outlines a continuum of services that include prevention, early intervention, and family support as well as the more traditional therapeutic services. The second goal for a comprehensive service system is to reduce reliance on restrictive forms of treatment and out-of-home placement. The rationale for this is simple. Restrictive settings and out-of-home placements have been overused, do not necessarily improve a youngster's functioning, and represent the most expensive form of service. In addition, at some point, youngsters are discharged from such settings, return to their communities, and remain in need of community-based treatment. Therefore, except in cases of dangerousness or psychotic behavior, the family and community are the preferred location for service delivery.

A third goal, as written by Stroul (1993), is to increase interagency coordination and collaboration in the planning, development, and delivery of services. The idea is again simple. When people share responsibility and decision making, their commitment is increased and better service plans are created and implemented. This also means that more people must participate in the process. No one group has all the answers, and to develop comprehensive service plans, decision makers must include families, family advocates, and professionals from the fields of mental health, substance abuse, child welfare, juvenile justice, education, and others (e.g., housing and Medicaid). This ensures that all the needs of a child and family are taken into account, and that children and families are viewed holistically.

A fourth goal is to provide individualized services that are tailored to the unique needs of each child and family. This concept, often referred to as "wraparound" services, identifies the need for service systems to develop individual service plans and to create funding strategies that are flexible and noncategorical. Too often, youth receive services that already exist because they meet the required category, and little thought is given to other service options. This should not be the case in a flexible system of care.

The final goal for a system of care is to demonstrate cost-effectiveness. Most of the dollars spent on mental health service delivery are for services at the most restrictive end of the continuum. Residential and hospital-based treatment are by far the most costly— often costing between $50,000 and $200,000 per child per year. In a community-based service system, the goal is to divert money from the "back end" of the system to the "front end," allowing more dollars to be spent on services that are alternatives to more restrictive care.

To accomplish these goals, Stroul and Friedman (1986) and Stroul (1993) indicate that multiple service components must be available in a comprehensive and coordinated system of care. These authors divide local systems of care into seven major service components:

- *Mental health services* include a range of activities from prevention and early identification to outpatient and home-based treatment to therapeutic out-of-home services.
- *Social services* include child welfare activities (i.e., protective services), financial aid, and home aid and respite care.
- *Educational services* range from resource room assistance to self-contained classes to home-bound and residential school instruction.

- *Health services* include primary medical care, health education and prevention, and long-term care.
- *Vocational services*, which are particularly germane to adolescents, include career education, skills training, job finding, and supported employment.
- *Recreational services* include after-school programs, camps, and special recreational projects.
- *Operational services* include activities such as transportation, legal services, service coordination, and advocacy.

Many local communities across the country have implemented the system of care model described above. Most communities accomplish this through local programs that reflect their commitment to this type of service philosophy (Cole & Poe, 1993). Examples include Kentucky's Impact program, the Ventura, California, project, the Alaska Youth Initiative, and the Fort Bragg, North Carolina, initiative. Although preliminary, the data obtained from these projects identify significant accomplishments from which several preliminary conclusions have been drawn (Rivera & Kutash, 1994). One trend in the data is that children receiving services in an organized system of care are less likely to be placed in restrictive environments such as a hospital or residential facility (Rosenblatt & Attkisson, 1992). In addition, if the youngster is placed, the length of stay is reduced as compared with youngsters not receiving services as part of an organized system of care. Another finding is that children receiving services within a system of care have fewer contacts with the juvenile justice system, and they demonstrate improvements on dependent variables such as school attendance and school performance (Illback, 1993). Parents of these youth also report more satisfaction with the services and support they receive, and initial cost data suggest that services provided within a system of care are cost-effective. Behar (1992) reports a 51% reduction in per client expenditures as a result of the Fort Bragg, North Carolina, initiative. These data and initial findings reflect a growing body of evidence that systems of care, based on the guiding principles outlined in this chapter, allow for better outcomes from both the clinical and the administrative viewpoints.

As evidenced in this chapter, and in the preceding chapters, developing integrated and collaborative service systems for children and adolescents is of paramount importance to meet the needs of all children and adolescents. As the cost of health care continues to rise, and the needs of vulnerable populations continue to increase, local communities will need to develop an array of service options as part of their systems of care. Such options include treatment services (e.g., outpatient, home-based, residential) but must also include prevention and early-intervention activities. When you consider that one child placed in a residential treatment center for long-term care costs upward of $1 million, service systems to enhance or expand preventive activities (that reach hundreds or thousands of youth) are clearly warranted.

Primary Prevention

An appropriate system of care places significant emphasis on prevention and early-intervention activities, and an important component of this discussion is how primary prevention might reduce the incidence of adolescent dysfunctional behavior. Historically, evaluating the effectiveness of treatment and promoting individual service have long been the tradition of human services. Reducing the incidence of dysfunctional behavior, however, must be accomplished given existing service capacity and cost. It is estimated, for example, that more than 38 million people need mental health services, but that the service system cannot adequately meet this need. The reality is that none of the ills of society will be solved through treatment alone. The issues of poor education, poor employment and economic opportunities, and poor housing conditions cannot be addressed via a treatment-oriented approach, and quite often these conditions are concomitant to the development of dysfunctional behavior. The real need is for prevention activities that promote individual and societal change.

By definition, primary prevention occurs prior to the onset of dysfunctional behavior. Immunizations, such as those available to prevent polio and measles, are excellent examples. Preventive activities most naturally occur in several arenas: schools, religious and other social institutions, and families. Gullotta (1987, 1994; see Chapter 2, this volume) identifies four "tools" that can be used in each of these venues to encourage functional behaviors in adolescents. The first tool is education. Although this is the tool most often used to prevent such problems as drug and alcohol abuse and teen pregnancy, it is often considered the weakest approach. The second tool is competency promotion. The idea is to increase a person's competence (e.g., self-esteem, behavioral skills) to promote resiliency and adaptive functioning in society. As an example, for drug and alcohol abuse, the competency promotion approach would identify the need to improve self-esteem and assertiveness (i.e., the ability to say "no" to drugs). As Gullotta (1994) writes: "The distinction between education and competency promotion involves outcomes. In the first case, the outcome is increased knowledge leading to attitudinal and behavioral change. In the second instance, the outcome is connectedness leading to an investment in society" (p. 11).

The third tool of prevention is community organization/systems intervention (CO/SI). Preventive interventions using this methodology are interested in modifying or removing system barriers, increasing community resources, and developing community action strategies. Examples of this approach are seat belt and helmet laws that promote safety when operating an automobile or motorcycle. Gullotta (1994) states that CO/SI is often the most powerful of prevention's tools, but is the least discussed by service professionals. CO/SI approaches, however, often enable people to work toward societal change. Gullotta (1987, 1994) identifies prevention's fourth tool as natural caregiving. The idea is that supporting and caring for others is an effective strategy to reduce the potential for maladaptive behavior.

Many studies have documented that the use of prevention's four tools has helped reduce dysfunctional behavior in adolescents. Reilly, Leukefeld, Gao, and Allen (1994) identify the positive impact of drug and alcohol abuse prevention programs. Dryfoos (1990) and Blau and Gullotta (1993) identify successful teen pregnancy prevention strategies. Significantly, however, one prevention model or tool cannot, by itself, create long-lasting change. Multiple strategies must be employed. As treatment and prevention are integrated into comprehensive systems of care, the service infrastructure will become more responsive. As Schinke (1994) writes, researchers, practitioners, and policymakers are developing more complex models as they attempt to prevent and treat dysfunctional behavior, and the increased sophistication will no doubt help address the many issues facing young people today.

References

Behar, L. (1992). *Fort Bragg Child and Adolescent Mental Health Demonstration Project.* Raleigh: North Carolina Division on Mental Health, Developmental Disabilities, and Substance Abuse Services, Child and Family Branch.

Blau, G. M., & Gullotta, T. P. (1993). Promoting sexual responsibility in adolescence. In T. P. Gullotta (Ed.), *Adolescent sexuality* (pp. 181-203). Newbury Park, CA: Sage.

Brandenburg, N., Friedman, R., & Silver, S. (1990). The epidemiology of childhood psychiatric disorders: Prevalence findings from recent studies. *Journal of the American Academy of Child and Adolescent Psychiatry, 29,* 76-83.

Cole, R. F., & Poe, S. L. (1993). *Partnerships for care: Systems of care for children with serious emotional disturbances and their families.* Washington, DC: Washington Business Group on Health.

Dryfoos, J. G. (1990). *Adolescents at risk: Prevalence and prevention.* New York: Oxford University Press.

Gullotta, T. P. (1987). Prevention's technology. *Journal of Primary Prevention, 8*(1-2), 4-24.

Gullotta, T. P. (1994). The what, who, why, where, when, and how of primary prevention. *Journal of Primary Prevention, 15*(1), 5-14.

Illback, R. (1993). *Evaluation of the Kentucky Impact program for children and youth with severe emotional disabilities, year two.* Frankfort, KY: Division of Mental Health, Children and Youth Services Branch.

Knitzer, J. (1982). *Unclaimed children.* Washington, DC: Children's Defense Fund.

President's Commission on Mental Health. (1978). *Report of the sub-task panel on infants, children and adolescents.* Washington, DC: Government Printing Office.

Reilly, F. E., Leukefeld, C. G., Gao, J., & Allen, S. (1994). Substance misuse among rural adolescents. In T. P. Gullotta, G. R. Adams, & R. Montemayor (Eds.), *Substance misuse in adolescents* (pp. 123-146). Thousand Oaks, CA: Sage.

Rivera, V. R., & Kutash, K. (1994). *Components of a system of care: What does the research say?* Tampa: University of South Florida, Florida Mental Health Institute, Research and Training Center for Children's Mental Health.

Rosenblatt, A., & Attkisson, C. (1992). Integrating systems of care in California for youth with severe emotional disturbance. III. Answers that lead to questions about out-of-home placements and the California AB377 evaluation project. *Journal of Child and Family Studies, 2,* 119-141.

Schinke, S. P. (1994). Prevention science and practice: An agenda for action. *Journal of Primary Prevention, 15*(1), 45-58.

Stroul, B. (1993). *Systems of care for children and adolescents with severe emotional disturbance: What are the results?* Washington, DC: Georgetown University Child Development Center, CASSP Technical Assistance Center.

Stroul, B., & Friedman, R. (1986). *A system of care for severely emotionally disturbed children and youth.* Washington, DC: Georgetown University Child Development Center, CASSP Technical Assistance Center.

Index

ABCX model, 25-27
Adaptation to stress, 27
Adolescent drug abuse, 114-132
  consequences, 115, 116
  etiology, 118-123, 127-129
  prevalence, 115
  risk and protective factors, 117, 118
Adoption Assistance and Child
    Welfare Act, 249, 250
Adventures of Huckleberry Finn, The, 4-10
Aggressiveness, 77, 127, 229
AIDS, 147-148
Aid to Families With Dependent
    Children (AFDC), 156, 251
Alcoholics Anonymous, 182
Amenorrhea, 168
American Civil Liberties Union
    (ACLU), 30
An Act Concerning Outpatient Mental
    Health Treatment for Minors
    and Defining Community Health
    Centers, 202
An Act Concerning the Prevention of
    Youth Suicide, 202
Anorexia, defined, 167-169
Antidepressants, 101, 200
Anxiety disorders, 83-105
  contributing factors, 87-89
  DSM-III, 83
  DSM-III-R, 85-87
  DSM-IV, 83, 85
  incidence, prevalence, and
    comorbidity, 86-105
Anxiolytics, 101

Assessment, 195-198
Attachment, 88, 89, 119, 121
Attachment theory, 66
Attention Deficit Hyperactivity
    Disorder (ADHD), 37-57, 62
  core symptoms, 40-43
    hyperactivity, 41, 42
    impulsivity, 42, 43, 62
    inattention, 40, 41
  DSM-IV, 37
  history of ADHD, 39, 40
  related problems, 43-47
    academic failure, 43
    comorbid disorders, 45, 46
    family problems, 44, 45
    peer rejection, 43, 44
  treatment, 48-55
    family intervention, 51, 52
    medication, 46-51
    peer relationship intervention, 53, 54
    problem solving, 54
    school-based intervention, 52, 53
    therapy, 55, 55
Autonomy, 67

Behavioral genetics, 22, 23
Behavioral treatment, 176, 178, 179
Benzodiazepines, 177, 239
Bingeing, 169, 170, 172, 177
Bulimia, defined, 169, 170

Cambridge model, 277, 281

Caring About Kids, 29
Child and Adolescent Service System
    Program (CASSP), 285
Child and Family Agency, 255, 279
Child Behavior Checklist, 83
Child Welfare League of America, 279
Child Well-Being Scale, 258
Children of Divorce Intervention
    Project, 104
Children's Support Group (CSG), 104
Chlorpromazine (Thorazine), 222,
    237, 238
Clinton health care plan, 277
Clozapine, 239
Cognitive behaviorism, 14, 73, 93,
    98-100, 102, 104, 176, 200
Cognitive distortions, 76
Cognitive restructuring, 75, 76
Computerized axial tomography (CT),
    230
Concordance, 173
Conditioning, 72, 91
Conduct disorder, 46, 62
Conjoint structural-strategic family
    therapy (CFT), 123
Constituent validity, 11
Contingency management, 74, 93, 97, 98
Continuum of services, 284-291
Contraception, 154-156
Counterconditioning, 94
Crisis intervention, 199, 200, 252

Delinquency, 63, 65, 78, 120, 126,
    191
Dementia Praecox and Paraphrenia,
    207
Depakote, 239
Depression, 71
Desensitization, 94, 95
Developmental theory, 21, 22
Developmental Understanding of Self
    and Others (DUSO), 104
Deviance, 4, 63
Divorce, 71
Divorce Adjustment Project, 104
Dizygotic twins, 173
DNA, 22, 24, 219, 220

Dopamine hypothesis, 221-223
Drug abuse, 114-132, 144
DSM-III, 39, 83
DSM-III-R, 85, 87
DSM-IV, 37, 61-65, 83, 85, 207, 214,
    220
Dysfunctional behavior:
    cautionary note, 4-10, 27
    defined, 4

Eating Disorder, Not Otherwise
    Specified (ED-NOS), 167
Eating disorders, 167-183
    clinical interventions, 175-182
    contributing factors, 171-175
    definitions, 167
    DSM-III-R, 167-171
    DSM-IV, 167-171
    incidence and prevalence, 171
    overview and history, 167
    prevention, 182, 183
EKG, 180
Emotive imagery, 95, 99
Excitatory amino acids, 224-226
Exposure therapies, 93

Familial aggregation, 215
Families First, 252
Family interaction, 66-72, 148, 149,
    155, 173
Family intervention, 51, 52, 178, 179,
    240, 241
Family preservation, 249, 255-257
    Connecticut's model, 255
    cost data, 257
    model expansion, 260
    prevention, 262
    statistics, 256, 257
    training and education, 262
Family Preservation and Support
    Services, 258
Family-systems theory, 121, 122, 131
Family therapy, 74, 93, 123-126, 220
Fear, 87-89, 91, 99
Federation of Families for Children's
    Mental Health, 261

Flooding, 95
Foster care drift, 249

GABA, 226, 227, 228
Generalized anxiety disorder, 85
Genetics, 90, 214-221
Glutamatergic hypothesis, 226-227

Haloperidol (Haldol), 237
Health risks in adolescence, 273, 274
  alcohol, 274
  criminal misconduct, 275
  drug use, 274
  obesity, 274
  sexual experimentation, 275
HIV, 146, 147, 153
Home-based services, 74, 247-263
  characteristics, 254
Homebuilders, 252, 253
Human Development Program, 104

Imaging, 229-235
Imminent risk, 249, 259
Impulsivity, 42, 43, 62, 118
Inpatient, 77, 179, 181, 200

Klingberg Family Center, 255

Latchkey, 268, 270
Learning theory, 91
Lithium, 239
LSD, 223, 224, 225

Magnetic resonance imaging (MRI),
  232, 233
Magnetic resonance spectroscopy
  (MRS), 235
Marker genes, 218, 219
Medically underserved youth, 271
Medication, 46-51, 101, 177, 200,
  222, 237-239
Minimal brain damage, 39

Miss America Pageant, 174
Modeling, 14, 73, 91, 93, 96, 97,
  118, 119, 112
Monozygotic twins, 173, 216, 233
Mothers Against Drunk Drivers, 30
Mothers of Murdered Sons, 30
Multidimensional Family Therapy
  (MDFT), 125

National Alliance for the Mentally
  Ill—Child and Adolescent
  Network (NAMI-CAN), 261
National Association for the
  Advancement of Colored People,
  30
National Institute of Mental Health
  (NIMH), 29
Negative attributions, 76
Negative reinforcement, 14
Neuropathology, 235-237
Never Too Late, 21
Norepinephrine (NE), 221, 228

Obesity, 173
Obsessive-compulsive disorder (OCD),
  85, 87, 92, 101, 102
Omnibus Budget Reconciliation Act of
  1993, 258
One-person family therapy (OPFT),
  123
Operant learning, 72, 73
Oppositional defiant disorder (ODD),
  46, 61-80
  clinical interventions, 72-78
  contributing factors, 65-72
  DSM-IV, 61-65
Oregon Social Learning Center
  (OSLC), 124
Overanxious disorder, 85

Panic disorder, 224, 225
Paraprofessional service, 251
Parent Aide, 251, 252
Parent training, 77
Parkinson's disease, 222

Partial hospital programs (PHP), 180, 181
Partnership for a Drug Free America, 8, 9
Paxil, 177
PCP, 224, 225
People, 174
Pharmacotherapy, 93, 100, 101, 237, 238
Playboy, 174
Positive reinforcement, 14
Positron emission tomography (PET), 234, 235
Posttraumatic stress disorder (PTSD), 86
Prevention, 78, 79, 103, 104, 145, 152, 153, 156, 157, 182, 183, 200-203, 262
Prevention equation, 24
Prevention's technology, 28, 290, 291
  community organization/systems intervention (CO/SI), 29, 30, 291
  competency promotion, 30, 31, 291
  education, 28, 290, 291
  natural caregiving, 31, 291
Primary prevention, 23, 24, 290
Problem solving, 69, 75, 104, 116, 120, 156, 157
Prozac, 177
Psychoanalytic theory, 13
Psychodynamic theory, 67, 171-173, 175, 176
Psychological theories, 12-14
Punishment, 14
Purdue Brief Family Therapy model (PBFT), 125
Purging, 169, 170, 172, 177

Rational-emotive therapy (RET), 98
Reinforcement, 14, 74, 197, 19, 142-145
Relaxation training, 94, 104
Response prevention, 94, 95
Restricting, 169

Safe sex, 145

Schizophrenia, 206-241
  DSM-IV, 207, 214, 220
  epidemiology, 208-209
  history, 206-208
  ICD-10, 208-212
  phenomenology, 209-210
  symptoms, 210-212
  treatment, 237-241
School-based health centers, 156, 276
  statistics, 279-281
School-based health centers and managed care, 277-278
School-based intervention, 52, 53
School-based prevention, 79
Schools and social service agencies as collaborators, 271
Secondary prevention, 79, 103
Self-esteem, 15, 44, 64, 104, 163, 172, 193
Serotonin, 223, 224
Service system components, 288, 289
Service system goals, 287, 288
Sex crime, 142
Sex offenders, 143, 145
Sexual abuse, 140-145, 150, 172
  biological factors, 150
  effects, 143-145
  family risk factors, 150
Sexual activity, 120
  and STDs, 147
  social influences, 149, 151
Sexual aggression, 142, 143
Sexual assault, 141, 142, 144
Sexual behavior problems, 139-157
Sexual initiation, 146, 154, 155, 157
Sexually transmitted diseases (STDs), 145-153
  contributing factors, 147
  high-risk behaviors, 145
  individual differences, 149
  intervention, 151, 152
  prevalence, 146
  prevention, 152, 153
Sexual victimization, 139-145
  prevalence, 140
Shaping, 97
Single photon emission computerized tomography (SPECT), 234-235

Social development model, 128, 129
Social exchange theory, 16, 17
Social learning theory, 14, 119, 120, 153
Social phobia, 85
Social psychological theory, 15-17
Social support, 31, 291
Sociocultural theory, 17-21
Stress theory, 24-28, 121
Structural-functional theory, 17, 19
Substance use, 71
Suicidal Ideation Questionnaire (SIQ),
    197
*Suicidal Behavior History Form
    (SBHF)*, 197
Suicide, 187-203
  early warning signs, 193, 194
  myths, 189
  prevention, 200-203
  risk factors, 190-195
  statistics, 187, 188
  treatment, 199, 200
Suicide attempts, 198, 199
Symbolic interaction theory, 15, 16
Systematic desensitization, 73
Systems of care, 284-291

Systems theory, 19-21

Tegretol, 239
Tertiary prevention, 79, 103
Theoretical frameworks, 11-32
Theory, defined, 11
Token economy, 74
Triangulation, 70
Twin studies, 173, 216, 233

Unclaimed children, 285
Unplanned pregnancy, 153-157
  contributing factors, 154-156
  prevalence, 153, 154
U.S. Bureau of the Census, 62, 269

Yale Child Study Center, 255
YMCA, 270
YWCA, 270

Zoloft, 177

About the Editors

Gary M. Blau (Ph.D., Clinical Psychology) is currently the Director of Mental Health for the Connecticut Department of Children and Families. He also holds a clinical faculty appointment at the Yale Child Study Center. In his capacity as Director of Mental Health, he provides leadership and oversight to Connecticut's mental health service delivery system for children and adolescents. He is an active member of the national organization SMHRCY (State Mental Health Representatives for Children and Youth), and he serves on the SMHRCY Executive Committee. He has been appointed to several statewide advisory boards, including one involving the development of a Medicaid-managed care program that highlights the needs of children. Prior to work in state government, he was the Director of Clinical Services at Child and Family Agency, where he supervised all outpatient, school-based, and home-based services. Since receiving his Ph.D. from Auburn University, Auburn, Alabama, in 1988, he has worked in children's mental health with a primary emphasis on issues of victimization, child custody, permanency planning, and innovative service models. He serves on the editorial board of the *Journal of Primary Prevention* and has numerous publications and presentations in the areas of child custody, primary prevention, and clinical service delivery.

Thomas P. Gullotta is CEO of the Child and Family Agency in Connecticut. He currently is the editor of *Journal of Primary Prevention*. He is a book editor for the **Advances in Adolescent Development** series and is the senior book series editor for **Issues in Children's and Families' Lives.** In addition, he serves on the editorial boards of the *Journal of Educational and Psychological Consultation,* the *Journal of Early Adolescence,* and *Adolescence* and is an adjunct faculty member in the psychology and education departments of Eastern Connecticut State University. His published works focus on primary prevention and youth.

About the Contributors

Burton I. Blau has been on the faculty at the University of Central Florida, Orlando, since 1972, and he currently serves as Coordinator of the Graduate Clinical Program. He teaches a variety of undergraduate and graduate courses (e.g., psychopathology, psychopharmacology, developmental psychology, interviewing and counseling, and sleep and dreams). In addition, he has been a provider of direct psychological services to individuals and families since 1968. His research interests have been broad, focusing on personality variables in relation to behavioral functioning, ethical issues, and sports psychology. He received his Ph.D. in clinical psychology from Southern Illinois University, Carbondale, in 1966.

H. Ann Brochin is a licensed psychologist in private practice in Madison, Connecticut. Her interests include the evaluation and treatment of childhood depression, oppositional defiant disorder, and ADHD. She earned her Ph.D. in school psychology from the University of North Carolina, Chapel Hill.

David A. Brumer is Coordinator of Community Mental Health Services for Connecticut's Department of Children and Families. Following his undergraduate training at the University of Louisville, he attained an M.A. in Community Psychology from the University of New Haven and a 6th-year postmaster's Professional Diploma in Human Relations from the University of Bridgeport. He also holds certificates in family therapy from the Graduate Center for Family Clinical Studies and in adolescent outreach from Yale University's Drug Dependency Institute. In his role as Coordinator of Community Mental Health Services for Connecticut, he has led the state in planning, development, and implementation of the state's Children's Mental Health Plan and System of Care Development initiative for children and adolescents. He is also Associate Director of the Sterling Center for Counseling and Family Relations, a community-based counseling and treatment center. He has extensive training and experience in system development, adolescent treatment, Ericsonian approaches to treatment and hypnosis, and sexual offender treatment.

Barry R. Burkhart is Professor of Psychology at Auburn University. He received his Ph.D. in Clinical Psychology from Florida State University and completed his internship in Clinical Psychology at the University of Southern California/Los Angeles County Medical Center in 1974. He is a Fellow of the Academy of Clinical Psychology, having received his Diplomate in Clinical Psychology from the American Board of Professional Psychology in 1984. He is also a Fellow of Divisions 12 (Clinical) and 29 (Psychotherapy) of the American Psychological Association. His primary research interests include violence and victimization, trauma and recovery, and the dynamics and development of sexual aggression in men. In clinical practice since 1975, he has specialized in the assessment and treatment of adolescents and the prevention and treatment of sexual victimization.

Deepak Cyril D'Souza (M.D.) is Assistant Professor of Psychiatry at Yale University School of Medicine. After completing his residency at SUNY Downstate, Brooklyn, he joined Yale as a fellow in psychopharmacology. He is currently Director of the Outpatient Schizophrenia Research Clinic and the Movement Disorders Clinic at the West Haven Veterans Affairs Medical Center, Yale University School of Medicine. He is a recipient of the Veterans Affairs Neuroscience Research Fellowship (1993), the National Alliance for Research on Schizophrenia and Depression (NARSAD) Young Investigator Award (1993), the Scottish Rite Schizophrenia Fellowship Program (1994), and the International Congress for Schizophrenia Research Young Investigator (1995).

William Eyberse, M.F.T., is a Certified Marriage and Family Therapist and a clinical member of the American Association of Marriage and Family Therapy. He is currently Clinical Services Coordinator at Quinebaug Valley Youth and Family Services, a multiservice agency serving Northeastern Connecticut. He is also in private practice with Coastal Counseling Services, in East Lynne, Connecticut, specializing in blended and divorcing families and couples issues. He was previously Coordinator of Home-Based Services at the Child and Family Agency of Southeastern Connecticut in New London, Connecticut, where he was responsible for several home-based programs, including Family Preservation, Family Stabilization, and home-based addiction services.

Joseph A. Horvath is Associate Research Scientist in the Department of Psychology at Yale University, where he conducts research on practical intelligence, workplace learning, and leadership. He holds a doctorate in cognitive science from Brown University.

John Harrison Krystal (M.D.) is Associate Professor of Psychiatry, Yale University School of Medicine, Deputy Chief for Research and Academic Affairs, and Director of the Clinical Division of the Schizophrenia Biological Research Center at the West Haven VA Medical Center. He graduated from the University of Chicago and Yale University School of Medicine and completed his residency in psychiatry at Yale.

Howard A. Liddle is Professor of Counseling Psychology and Director of the Center for Research on Adolescent Drug Abuse at Temple University. He is a licensed psychologist (California, Pennsylvania) and a Diplomate of the American Board of Professional Psychology in Family Psychology. He has taught family psychology and therapy since 1974 at many universities and institutions. He has lectured on his family therapy model for adolescents in the United States and internationally. He is Fellow in two divisions (43 and 29) of the American Psychological Association and the American Association for Marriage and Family Therapy. He is founding editor of APA's *Journal of Family Psychology*; his own publications include two edited books and more than 75 papers. He was the recipient of the 1991 APA Division 43 Psychologist of the Year award.

James Maffuid, M.F.T., is a Connecticut-certified marriage and family therapist as well as a clinical member of the American Association for Marriage and Family Therapy. As Coordinator of

Home-Based Services at the Child and Family Agency of Southeastern Connecticut, he has worked closely with children and adolescents who are at risk due to abuse and neglect. He is active in the Connecticut Association for Marriage and Family Therapy, and he also works with children, adolescents, and their families in a private practice setting in Colchester, Connecticut.

Harry L. Mills, Ph.D., has over 20 years experience as a psychotherapist, health care executive, consultant, and educator. Graduate training was obtained at Tulane, University of Mississippi Medical School and the University of Southern Mississippi where he obtained his doctorate in Clinical Psychology completing an internship specializing in behavioral medicine. He is licensed in Florida and Tennessee and had faculty affiliations with Ole Miss Medical School, Southern Mississippi, and Vanderbilt University. He has extensive experience in treatment of anxiety, stress, and traumatically induced disorders and programs for those with chronic illness such as multiple sclerosis. He was cofounder and Director of Training for the Cumberland Consortium where he trained doctoral level students from Vanderbilt and other universities in cognitive-behavior therapy and behavioral health. He is the author of numerous chapters and articles on topics ranging from anxiety disorders to preventive health programs.

Lynn Noyes, M.S.W., A.C.S.W., received her master's degree from Boston College School of Social Work in 1977. Since that time, she has worked in a variety of clinical and administrative positions. For the past 10 years, she has been employed by the Connecticut Department of Public Health supervising school and adolescent health programs as well as maintaining a private clinical and consulting practice. She is the Director of the Robert Wood Johnson Foundation funded project, "Making the Grade in Connecticut." She holds appointments at the Yale University School of Nursing and University of Connecticut School of Medicine Department of Pediatrics and is a field instructor at both the University of Connecticut and Southern Connecticut University Schools of Social Work. She holds membership in the National Association of Social Work, State Adolescent Health Coordinators Network, and the Association of Maternal and Child Health Programs and is on the board of the Colchester Connecticut Youth Service Bureau. She is a consulting editor for the *Journal of Primary Prevention*.

Ruth Baugher Palmer, Ph.D., is an adjunct faculty member at the Philadelphia Theological Seminary in Roxborough, Pennsylvania, where she teaches courses in pastoral psychology pertaining to adolescence and the family. She is also in private practice in Jenkintown, Pennsylvania, focusing on family therapy for adolescent behavior problems. Throughout her doctoral training, she served as a graduate research assistant for the Center for Research on Adolescent Drug Abuse and the Center for Education in Inner Cities. Within those settings, she contributed to ongoing research projects, conducted her own research, and coauthored several publications pertaining to the treatment of various adolescent problems in the context of the family.

Lisa Terre, Ph.D., is Associate Professor of Psychology at the University of Missouri at Kansas City. Her research interests focus on clinical health psychology, especially in the areas of health promotion and disease prevention.

Robert J. Weinstein is Manager of the Eating Disorders Programs at the Institute of Living in Hartford, Connecticut. He received his Ph.D. in child and family clinical psychology at Michigan State University. Over the past 5 years, he has worked on the development and refinement of comprehensive eating disorder programs to provide various levels of treatment and respond to the demands of the changing health care situation.